D1462097

EXPERIMENT IN LIBERTY

The First Five Hundred Years of Freedom in America

EXPERIMENT IN LIBERTY

The First Five Hundred Years of Freedom in America

by
William Moore Gray III

Sunflower University Press®
1531 Yuma • P. O. Box 1009 • Manhattan, Kansas 66505-1009 USA

Cover: by Dave La Fleur.

Dave La Fleur is an illustrator, designer, and painter who serves clients throughout the U.S. from his Atchison, Kansas, studio.

His U.S. Postal Service stamp designs have included four commemorative stamps featuring American folk heroes. His most recent stamp, "Stars and Stripes Forever," was released in August 1997.

La Fleur has received numerous awards from Communication Arts, Print, Graphics, Key Art Awards, and The Society of Illustrators of New York and Los Angeles. His original paintings are in the collections of the University of Iowa, Pizza Hut, Van Kampen American Capital, and the U.S. Postal Service, as well as in collections of sports figures Tom Watson, Lee Trevino, and others.

Layout by Lori L. Daniel

ISBN 0-89745-219-4 pb
ISBN 0-89745-220-8 hb

Sunflower University Press is a wholly-owned subsidiary
of the non-profit 501(c)3 Journal of the West, Inc.

For all those entrepreneurs like
Bill Ellis
whose intellectual curiosity and generous spirit
have kept us going.

Experiment in Liberty is published
with the support of the
Kathryn Ellis Foundation,
Chicago, Illinois

Contents

Acknowledgments

I F IT HAD NOT BEEN FOR Bill Ellis, who built Farley Candy from a small ailing company to a part of the Favorite Brands International conglomerate, you would not be reading this book. He kept us going through research and rewrites.

Bill Ellis has been benefactor to many — organ-sharing groups, battered women's movements, tort reform, education. A Kansan and a graduate of the University of Kansas at Lawrence, his story is one that moves from dishwasher to compassionate philanthropist . . . a great American saga.

Appreciation is also due Michael H. Blechner and Michael J. Hightower of Tulsa, Oklahoma, and Mike Kautsch of the University of Kansas at Lawrence for constructive critical comments.

For editorial work and advice on scholarly content, my gratitude to Professor J. Rufus Fears, G. T. and Libby Blankenship Chair in the History of Liberty, University of Oklahoma at Norman.

For moral support and encouragement, and for their unwavering belief in the merits of the message contained in this book, my thanks to my sister Lael G. Dixon and Dean Sims of Tulsa.

For his generous service as liaison among us all, my thanks to Dean Foster of Chanute, Kansas.

Foreword

*T*HIS IS A CHALLENGING AND provocative book, one that will arouse controversy of the best sort, discussions that force us to reevaluate comfortable assumptions and current fads in historical writing. *Experiment in Liberty* traces the course of freedom in America from the time of Columbus until our own day. However, in no sense is it a conventional survey of American history. It is an interpretative study written from a clearly defined philosophical framework.

As Gray states in his Introduction, his study of American history is intended as an essay in "the understanding of man's present condition under the government of the United States of America." Gray strongly believes that "it is of no gain to know what happened [in those 500 years] unless we thereby gain understanding about the state of affairs in the world today. Conditions in the present are the products of the past. If we know only the recent past, we know nothing about what is soon to happen or is actually taking place already."

This book is a testament to Gray's belief that we study the past in order to understand the present. As such, *Experiment in Liberty* takes its place squarely in the most fundamental tradition of historical writing — that of Herodotus, Thucydides, Tacitus, and Edward Gibbon. Each sought to make his factual account of history as accurate as possible. However, each also understood that a factual account of the past achieves meaning only if put into a broader philosophical perspective and only if it provides the reader with the knowledge to make judgments about the present. The founders of the United States shared this view that the purpose of history is to provide guidance to our actions in the present and future; and for that reason they considered history to be the most useful of disciplines. For that same reason, statesmen like Theodore Roosevelt and Winston Churchill have written history.

Gray's book also shares with these great authors the conviction that liberty is the grand story of history. Gray defines freedom as "that condition of man wherein the individual's liberty to act is not restricted beyond the limits set by natural laws of cooperative action."

Like Gibbon, Roosevelt, and Churchill, Gray is not an academic historian. He is a student of history, whose work has evolved from years of experience in the business world. Economics and economic history are fundamental to much of his analysis of American history. As Gray states early on, his book employs the theoretical constructs of Ludwig von Mises and other representatives of the Austrian school of economic thought to interpret American history. I dislike labels, as being a sign of intellectual sloth; but others will certainly label Gray's book a "libertarian" history of the United States.

Although Gray uses von Mises' ideas of "praxeology" — the science of human action — to give an interpretative structure to his view of American history, the book itself is an American original. To say that Gray writes out of the same concern with liberty and with the same idea of the purpose of history as did Tacitus or Gibbon is not, obviously, to rank him with those historians. Nor is it to say that they or the founders of our country would have agreed with Gray. There is certainly much in the work with which I disagree. However, what Tacitus, Gibbon, or Jefferson would say is that Gray's ideas deserve to be heard.

William Gray's *Experiment in Liberty* represents a pronounced voice in American society today. It is a voice that played a significant role in the national elections of 1994 and in the growing alienation from American politics by those who believe that the promises of that election have not been kept. In those terms, it merits a serious readership and serious consideration.

> *J. Rufus Fears*
> G. T. and Libby Blankenship Chair
> in the History of Liberty
> University of Oklahoma, Norman

The world has never had a good definition of the word liberty, and the American people, just now, are much in need of one. We all declare for liberty; but in using the same word, we do not all mean the same thing. With some the word liberty may mean for each man to do as he pleases with himself and the product of his labor, while with others the same word may mean for some men to do as they please with other men, and the product of other men's labor. Here are two, not only different but incompatible things called by the same name, liberty. And it follows that each of the things is, by the respective parties, called by two different and incompatible names — liberty and tyranny.

—Abraham Lincoln, from a speech delivered in Baltimore at the Sanitary Commission Fair, April 18, 1864

... The favorable evolution of human affairs depends ultimately on the ability of the human race to beget not only authors but also heralds and disseminators of beneficial ideas. — Ludwig von Mises

Note from the Author

*M*ANY YEARS AGO, as a young man in high school, I became skeptical of the validity of the material being presented to me about society and social behavior. The answers our school system gave me about *why* this and *why* that did not seem to jibe with logic. At that time, I decided to determine for myself the real reasons social behavior and society evolved as they did, and to determine the truthful answers to the questions I had then in mind about why Americans lived so well and the rest of the world seemed to be in such destitute circumstances. I wanted to write, for my offspring, the truth as I should determine it.

The first product of this commitment is *Experiment in Liberty*. I began my research in the late 1970s, and devoted full time to it when I liquidated my business in 1982. When I began writing, I realized that I had inadequate understanding of the principles of economics, and thus it required that I study the subject until I believed I had sufficient grasp to proceed. Understanding the events of history can evolve only if the individual has a proper comprehension of how society and the individual in society act in response to the circumstances encountered. This is the substance of economic theory.

I read the works of John M. Keynes, Ludwig von Mises, Murray Rothbard, John Kenneth Galbraith, and others. I concluded that the Austrian scholars presented the more logical explanations. And thus, at that time, I prepared a condensation of von Mises' *Human Action*, which enabled me to clarify my understanding of economics so that I could proceed with my interpretation and understanding of history.

The original thesis for *Experiment in Liberty* was no more than *"Why?"*. Why do so many of our citizens discriminate against the black American? Why are the people of most other countries so poor while we in the United States live quite well? Why do our laws treat the American Indians differently than most inhabitants of the United States? Why is our Constitution being so ignored by our judicial system?

As I read what was available to me, I became convinced that *liberty* was involved in all these questions. And to my dismay, I found that our personal liberty was being restricted more and more by actions of our government. I did not concur with the majority that this was a necessary development for the strength of society in the United States.

And, thus, *why* do I write? . . . Because I feel compelled to put my thoughts on paper for those who could be interested in my way of thinking. *Experiment in Liberty* reviews the first 500 years of man's quest for individual freedom in America. It views the impact of that experience on a civilization entering the 21st century. I intend this work to be one tool among many to aid concerned citizens in making intelligent choices, for though American Presidents and its Congress in the 20th century have at times made a mockery of the Statue of Liberty, citizens of the United States remain free to choose — either liberty or tyranny by majority vote.

William Moore Gray III
March 1998

Present knowledge has demonstrated that, for social cooperation, socialism is not a viable alternative to free-enterprise capitalism. . . . **Experiment in Liberty** *presents an understanding of the history of this nation based on the philosophy of freedom.*

Preface

WHENEVER MAN ALTERS THE theories of one of his sciences, a new history needs to be written from this altered viewpoint. No history merely relates what happened in the past. The historian approaches his subject with a knowledge of the other sciences of human action — praxeology, economics, sociology, psychology. On the basis of this knowledge, he selects events that illustrate the viewpoint he has in mind. He then interprets them to emphasize their significance at that time and their relationship to the present. This present study takes into account the late 20th-century changes in the "sciences of human action."

For nearly eight decades many historians have approached the narrative of American society from the viewpoint of social cooperation with common ownership, or at least control, of the productive resources — socialism. Naturally, their selection of events and interpretations have been colored by beliefs about the economic and sociological theorems in the socialist philosophy of government.

Present knowledge has demonstrated that, for social cooperation, socialism is not a viable alternative to free-enterprise capitalism. In the latter half of the 20th century, Dr. Ludwig von Mises, his students, and his followers in the Austrian school of economics have elaborated an understanding of the theorems of human action that demonstrates the futility of socialism. Their interpretation of the laws of social cooperation presents the case for freedom — private ownership and control of the productive resources. On the basis of this new knowledge, the history of man needs to be revisited. *Experiment in Liberty* presents an understanding of the history of this nation based on the philosophy of freedom.

While preparing these comments on history, I became aware that few present-day Americans fully understand the minorities in America, especially its blacks and native Indians. We cannot understand present social conditions without knowing these minorities that so many texts slight. The experiences of both groups not only reveal a great deal about the meaning of liberty, but also influence the condition of life in the United States in the late 20th century. Consequently, Negro slavery and the American Indian have been given a broader treatment here than one might expect to find in a work this size.

About Semantics

When referring to the race that many writers would now call *Afro-American* or *African-American,* I have often used the words *Negro* and *blacks* depending on the era involved. Some writers use *American blacks.* For many decades Americans referred to the black race of Africa as "Negro." This word never confused writers or readers as to the specific peoples included in that designation. It had never carried a demeaning slur on those who suffered slavery at the hands of American colonists. Webster's Ninth New Collegiate Dictionary defines *Negro* as

> *a member of the black race of mankind distinguished from members of other races by usu. inherited physical and physio-*

logical characteristics without regard to language or culture; esp: a member of a people belonging to the African branch of the black race.

Because not all black-skinned peoples are Negroid — such as the Indians of South Asia — the word *black* is not precise in referring to American Negroes alone. Because not all people living in Africa are Negroes (there are Arabs, Anglo-Saxons, Caucasians, and Egyptians as well), it is even less precise to call Negroes "Afro-Americans." For these reasons, when dealing with the period of slavery in America, I believe that precision demands that *Negro* be used to designate the race that Americans exclusively enslaved in the early days of the nation. For more current times, *blacks* is used.

Additionally, the word *man* and its plural form *men* along with the pronouns *he, him,* and *his*, are used throughout this work in their most general meaning, a life form distinct from other mammals. (Webster: *"man, n. pl. men. (1) a member of the human race; a human being."*) These are not terms of gender. They include everyone — male or female. It is unfortunate that the words do have other meanings — man, the male of the species as distinct from the female — and that there are no singular forms of the common-gender pronouns *they, them,* and *theirs*.

Although some writers distinguish between *freedom* and *liberty,* I have used them interchangeably. Similarly, England historically is not synonymous with Great Britain (or Britain), English with British, Englishman with Briton. Common usage for many years, however, has more or less abandoned the difference. Consequently, the terms are used synonymously. Britain, Great Britain, and England refer to the presently united nation of peoples occupying the British Isles. References specifically to the Scots, the Irish, and the Welsh have a particular significance. English and Englishmen, however, refer to the Britons, the collective whole of all citizens in Great Britain.

Various terms have been applied to the racial groups who inhabited the Americas before Europeans settled on the North and South American continents. Columbus first called them *Indians.* To distinguish them from the inhabitants of India, some writers have used *Amerindians, American Indians,* or *Native Americans.* The presently living descendants of these American people generally refer to themselves as Indians. Because this book has no need to refer to inhabitants of India, I believe there is no confusion created by accepting their choice, *Indian,* to apply to these early natives of the Americas. Of the alternates, *Amerindian* might cause more confusion than clarity; *American Indian* and *Native American* seem clumsy.

William Moore Gray III
Chanute, Kansas
March 1998

. . . We may define liberty as **the condition of man wherein the individual's freedom to act is not restricted by government beyond the limits set by natural laws of cooperative action**. *. . . Economic freedom is the product of competition, not a largesse extended by government.*

Introduction

About Liberty

ℰACH LIFE FORM enters the world with restrictions on its liberty. Only within limits can each experience liberty in providing its own food, its own shelter, its own mate for procreation, and its own safeguard against the endless process of eating or being eaten. Absolute freedom does not exist on this earth. Liberty is relative freedom, not absolute freedom.

Freedom for man means freedom of an individual within society. Without society, a primitive, self-sufficient person is free only as long as he does not interfere with the desires of someone stronger. Under conditions of biological competition, the world belongs to the strong. Might makes right. The weaker individuals can choose nothing but subservience. Even the strongest person knows limitations; he is regularly obliged to subdue challenges from aspiring subordinates. Primitive man is not free.

The laws of social cooperation restrict man as surely as do the laws of nature. A person can choose to act in any manner he likes, but he must be prepared to suffer the consequences. The use of heroin may appear to please, but it damages health after continued use. Physical laws are conspicuously self-policing. Likewise the laws of social relations are self-enforcing, but the connection between cause and effect is less apparent. A businessman may be rude to his customers, but that rudeness will cause a loss of sales. Consumers may boycott a seller, but they may lose their only source of supply. Unrestrained robbery will cause a complete collapse of industry because confiscating the produce of labor will cause people to quit laboring. Men cannot have the advantages of the division of labor under social cooperation and at the same time be at liberty to do things that destroy society. People must choose between obeying rules and living in otherwise ambiguous perpetual biological competition. These laws that limit freedom are no less rigid than the laws of nature.

Well before recorded history, men recognized the advantages of cooperation to maximize the benefits of the division of labor. They organized government as a cooperative means to relieve each person from having to assert his freedom by constant physical combat. They empowered government to enforce and protect personal and property rights. In order for government to function, men established rules of conduct for all citizens — laws of society — and granted to government a monopoly on the use of coercion to enforce these laws.

In the modern world, freedom means something only in reference to the way government operates. As long as the government uses coercion simply to prevent antisocial action, citizens enjoy what can be called liberty. The action restrained is conduct that would destroy social cooperation. When government, however, goes beyond protecting society against disruptive persons, it restricts freedom beyond what is necessary for peaceful cooperation.

Consequently, we may define liberty as *the condition of man wherein the individual's freedom to act is not restricted by government beyond the limits set by natural laws of cooperative action.* Free men deny to individuals only such conduct as disregards the existence of other members of their species.

Men live under conditions of freedom when members of society cooperate by contract. Cooperation under a system of free choice means the citizens are not bound to serve a master. As far as one serves another person, he does so of his own accord in exchange for something he values. Free men freely exchange services and goods. If the individual chooses to live self-sufficiently, there is nothing stopping him. The benefits of the division of labor, however, require exchange and cooperation. The individual's desires for items he does not produce compel him to integrate himself into cooperative society. He exchanges the things he can make for the items he does not produce.

Free men are by no means independent. All the members of society depend on each other — buyers on sellers and sellers on buyers, workers on employers, and vice versa. True, the employer can discharge an employee; but if he does so to indulge some personal bias, he damages his own interests when there is no qualified replacement. Not government coercion, but self-interest drives free men to serve fellowmen and curbs arbitrariness. Within society citizens cooperating by contract are free because in serving others they serve themselves.

No freedom exists other than that provided by limited government. In a hegemonic society, the only freedom for the individual is the freedom to die. Government with unlimited power denies freedom of choice to all citizens. To prevent this, men have to curb the power of government. American colonists fought the War of Independence to preserve liberty and to limit the power of the British Parliament and King George III. Americans adopted their Constitution, Bill of Rights, courts, and laws in order to restrict government power. In the realm of social cooperation, liberty means restraint on the exercise of power by the government.

Neither can freedom be maintained when government completely controls the "economic" sphere of people's lives. Government does not guarantee liberty unless its authority is restricted to the preservation of economic freedom. Without economic freedom, constitutions and laws become meaningless.

Economic freedom is the product of competition, not a largesse extended by government. Neither workers nor buyers depend on any particular business firm. If a laborer loses his job, he finds other employment. The consumer can patronize any business he likes. Neither buyers nor sellers bestow a favor to the other; both make the exchange because of self-interest. A consumer decides for himself what he deems less important to him and chooses how to spend his money accordingly. A free society has no way to force workers to change where they work or what they do; it can simply pay more to those who please the consumers. Many people consider this kind of pressure the major evil of capitalism, the evil they seek to abolish. They do not realize that eliminating control by consumers necessarily requires government officials to determine where each person works and what he does.

Economic planning by government removes freedom and leaves to individuals the mere "right" to obey. The director of economic affairs determines what consumers consume and what workers do. It does not matter to the authority that consumers want more of this and less of that, or that individuals want to work more or to enjoy more leisure. The will of the director is what matters. Precisely this condition characterized the way of life in communist USSR. Under communism, citizens had no freedom to select their occupations, and consumers found empty shelves for products they desired. Under the pretext of economic expediency, the Politburo sent citizens it disliked to Siberia and assigned them to "hard labor" for life.

When government denies economic freedom to its citizens, all political liberties disappear. Freedom of the press means nothing when government controls all the printing presses and paper plants. Without the right to choose a career or select products to buy, all the other rights become meaningless. Freedom exists only for individuals who are at liberty to make their own plans. They may enjoy freedom from want and possibly even freedom from fear, but so did many Negro slaves in the South before the War Between the States.

History and Knowledge

Studies about what men do, why they do them, and the consequences of their actions can be grouped under three headings: praxeology, psychology, and history.

Praxeology evaluates the appropriateness of the ways people choose for achieving their purposes, and elaborates the consequences of using those means. Praxeology studies human action in the social setting. It describes how individuals interact. Economic theory is the best-developed aspect of this discipline. *Psychology* examines why people behave as they do and why they choose the goals they seek. *History* is the science of understanding the past. It does more than recite events; by using the theorems of praxeology and psychology, it tries to understand the significance of those events. In brief, history is concerned with the past, praxeology with the future, and psychology with the why of human action.

This treatise deals with history, employing the theorems of praxeology as elaborated by Ludwig von Mises in his book *Human Action* and further clarified by Murray Rothbard in *Man, Economy, and State.* It is limited to the five centuries after the voyage of Christopher Columbus in 1492, and is further limited to understanding man's present condition under the government of the United States. It is of no gain to know what happened in those 500 years unless we thereby gain understanding about the state of affairs in the world today. Conditions in the present are products of the past. If we know only the recent past, we understand nothing about what is soon to happen or is actually taking place already.

The experiences of man — his history — are the products of innate forces and of the individual's knowledge of his world. The interacting forces of his nature determine his choice of ends and the means of achieving them. They may be described as the *Laws of Human Nature.* Individuals do not respond uniformly to their influence. Their impact on society derives from the extent of their influence on the great majority of people. A list of man's driving inner forces is given below. Although not necessarily complete, this list is sufficient for our purposes.

The course of history is determined by the value judgments of individuals and by the effects of their behavior. We interpret these actions relative to the sciences of human action. History interprets man's behavior by using the other sciences of human action (praxeology, sociology, psychology) to determine significance, but there always remains a great body of events that no science can clarify.

What cannot be explained by the theorems of the known sciences must be studied by use of understanding. A historian tries to appreciate the effects of an action; he tries to assign its relevance and its bearing on subsequent events. His explanations, however, must never contradict the theorems of other branches of learning. An Aztec historian could report that the sun god Quetzalcoatl, displeased with his human wards, caused the moon to conceal the sun, and that the sun reappeared only after the immediate sacrifice of ten strong warriors. No contemporary historian would consider such a report. Present knowledge of astronomy explains a solar eclipse in different terms.

In order to understand the present, one must necessarily draw upon the past. Man is born into a real world; he does not live in the abstract. Each is a member of a family, a nation, a cultural environment, and holds a position in place and time. Each begins with a mind free of ideas and concepts and adopts ideas from his associations, including the past. He learns, assesses, discards, and accepts. He is heir to everything that preceded him. This is the substance of history. Knowing history helps a person confront the conditions of contemporary life. As Dr. Ludwig von Mises stated:

> *We have tried to demonstrate the service that history renders to acting man in making him understand the situation in which he has to act. . . . But there is more than this in the study of history. It not only provides knowledge indispensable to preparing political decisions. It opens the mind toward an understanding of human nature and destiny. It increases wisdom. It is the very essence of that much misinterpreted concept, a liberal education. It is the foremost approach to humanism, the lore of the specifically human concerns that distinguish man from other living beings.* (Mises [1957] 1985. 293)

The objective of this book is to help the reader (1) identify the forces that influence the historical drama, (2) understand how these forces have affected the human condition today, and (3) foresee the direction they are carrying man's future. This study should raise questions about the future of society and prepare people to confront these questions.

The method used is to examine events and analyze their significance. It is hoped that from this the reader will be able to answer the "why" question. Why is it important to know about Columbus's 1492 voyage? Why is it significant that General Jackson stood firm against the British at New Orleans? What difference does it make anyway?

For example, if Colonel Travis's command had not made that heroic stand at the Alamo in 1836, Americans might not be able to buy in the supermarket some of the finest citrus in the world. More importantly, the stand at the Alamo furnished the people of the United States with low-cost energy for over 50 years. Possibly the mass use of automobiles in America would have been delayed a half-century or more had Colonel Travis surrendered the fort to General Santa Anna seven days earlier than it fell by siege. The emotional reaction to the massacre at the Alamo was the key to successfully concluding the Texans' struggle for independence from Mexico.

This text supplements the study of American history. It examines events of the period that exerted material influence on conditions today. The degree of that influence and its effect on freedom have determined the events chosen for comment. This treatise is not a recitation of facts; it is commentary about facts.

Where my concepts differ from those in other texts, the reason is most likely that I disagree with those authors about the science of human action – praxeology. A historian proceeds with previously formed ideas about the theorems of other sciences. He then interprets historical processes in light of these theorems. Interpretation and understanding are impossible without them. Perhaps the primary disagreement exists over the validity of deductive (*a priori*) knowledge. Some historians deny the validity of knowledge gained without experience; they approach history as an assemblage of facts, and infer causal relationships from a study of such facts.

I reject the underlying premise of that methodology. Because human actions issue from so many interacting forces, an empirical approach can yield misleading conclusions. Correct analysis of historical process has to rely on correct theorems of praxeology, which are developed *a priori*.

A Fundamental Law of Might

When discussing the fate of the American Indian and his lands, a United States senator quipped, "We stole it fair and square." That gentleman intended to be clever, to bring smiles, to be quoted. He succeeded. What he intended as a facetious quip, however, was a statement of harsh reality that has been covered over by all the moralizing about how European immigrants betrayed the Indians and took their land. Did the immigrants take their land? Yes, but betray? This is where moralizing enters in and clouds an intelligent approach to the lessons of history.

What is involved here is a fundamental law of life: who gets what, how, and why. An anonymous quotation says, "Possession is nine points of the law." Of course, under the laws of organized society, possession is only one factor; it is of little consequence in the face of clear evidence of title. In pure reality, however, possession is the law, and nothing else is of any consequence. Ownership of anything comes from the ability to take and hold it against all others. The Indians lost the land because they could not hold it against all comers. Disapproving of this action does not change the reality that the world belongs to the strong. Might makes right! If not right, then certainly real. Or as Mises says, when discussing fatalism among Moslems:

> *The leaders of the Moslem armies which . . . conquered a great part of the Mediterranean area did not put a fatalistic confidence in Allah. Rather they believed that their God was for the big, well-equipped, and skillfully led battalions.* (Mises [1957] 1985. 79)

At no point in life should we overlook this primary law of might.

Civilization and Government

As man became civilized and joined his fellows to form government, he sought some system whereby person and property could be protected by cooperation rather than by individual force. Even so, outsiders could intrude. Unless he and his fellows defended successfully, intruders could take their women, their children, and their crops; destroy their homes, and put the defenders to death. History records such events in ancient Greece, in medieval Europe, in America before the end of the 19th century, in 20th-century Germany under the Nazis, and today in less-developed countries. To prevent this from happening, civilized man formed government as a cooperative means to protect his societal organization from forceful intrusion by those who would not respect the laws of his organization. The primary task of government is to defend the social system against domestic criminals and external foes. If free people want to preserve their freedom, they must be prepared to defend it. Government has been additionally charged with other responsibilities; but first and foremost the responsibility of government has always been to defend against invasion from without and to enforce a system of law within. This dual objective can be achieved only if it is supported by citizens who give of themselves.

Morality has little to do with the "goodness" of war. If all peoples of the world accepted the principles of liberty, there would be no reason for war. Today, however, aggression by peoples living under hegemony threaten free nations. Time and time again history has demonstrated that to remain free, either men fight or they die. A time may come when this will not be so; but until then, reality forces man to accept this state of societal relations.

Maintaining government — with its prisons, police, courts, and armed forces — requires money. Levying taxes to finance these functions is consistent with freedom. Men and women must pay taxes to support government, and must give their time and possibly their lives when needed. The person who will neither fight nor pay taxes to support the military is simply aiding those who would enslave him. Those unwilling to pay taxes for defense or to fight to protect what is theirs will eventually lose everything — their property, their families, their freedom, their lives. The corollary is clear: freedom and safety can be assured solely through fighting or a willingness to fight. If the government of a free nation requires every citizen to cooperate to repel aggressors, it does not go beyond the limits of freedom as defined above.

In the real world of today, unconditional pacifism is the same as unconditional surrender to the enslaver. The man who wants to remain free must fight unto death those who would deprive him of his freedom. Because an isolated action is of no avail in a struggle between the free and the autocrats, only cooperative resistance organized through government can hope to succeed.

To acknowledge this, however, is not to approve use of conscripts in wars that do not threaten the freedom of the citizens, such as America's war activities in Vietnam and Korea. Neither can one justify today's confiscatory and discriminatory taxes for such efforts. In the existing atmosphere of interventionism, governments also employ taxation as a way to influence individual conduct. Such acts of government go beyond protecting smooth social cooperation and so restrict freedom unduly.

The world is the way it is because of man's actions in the past, and these actions were the product of his nature. If the world is ever to be different, man must, through knowledge of the past, learn to control the impact of his basic nature on social conduct. Until then, man's actions based on his inner nature will continue to create conditions of life that repeat familiar patterns. Studying history enables a person to understand the present, and from that understanding to see better the direction social cooperation is moving. Man rose above the level of primitive culture by using his intellect. He has not, however, achieved perfection. Further advancement will arise from continued mental efforts stimulated by greater knowledge — particularly a better understanding of himself, his nature, and his conduct. Within the time frame of recorded history, man's nature has not changed. Because it does not change, the past has a great deal to teach him.

Knowing history becomes the key to correctly understanding man in society. It becomes the key to liberty.

The Laws of Human Nature

The internal forces that make man what he is and drive his actions I have described below as the *Laws of Human Nature*. The first of these laws is the *Law of Self*. Each being strives to preserve itself and stay alive. In the case of humans, self includes the direct offspring. The two corollaries are (1) the *Law of Self-Interest,* which drives each individual to place his self-interest foremost in decisions, and (2) the *Law of Boredom,* which recognizes that life is experience. A mind at rest is tantamount to death; so a person directs his actions to stimulate his mind into some activity.

Second is the *Law of Love*. Loving an individual, a cause, or an object can override the law of self. There are instances where an individual has sacrificed his life to save someone else; and in extreme cases, a person has given his life for a cause in which he strongly believed.

The third law of human nature, the *Law of Preference*, states that in a choice between alternatives, man always selects the one that he prefers. This law has four corollaries: (1) the *Law of Inertia*, man tends to delay as long as possible adjusting to change, especially if such adjustment requires effort; (2) the *Law of Least Resistance*, man seeks the most efficient means to gain a desired end; (3) the *Law of the Disutility of Labor*, man prefers leisure to work; and (4) the *Law of Sensual Self-Gratification*, man is basically a pleasure-seeking being; he seeks foods that please the palate, clothes that please the senses, and sexual relations with a pleasing partner.

The *Law of Fear*, that man's only fear is of the unknown, is the fourth law of human nature. He fears and resents change, death, uncertainty — anything beyond his ready comprehension. This is man's only true fear (fear of the known is embodied in the law of preference). The law of fear has three corollaries. The first, the *Law of Security*, says that because freedom involves risk of the unknown, man will forego freedom and exchange many other conditions to achieve security. Most people never realize that security is a pot at the end of the rainbow. The *Law of Ignorance* states that being aware of a condition beyond a person's understanding confronts him with an unknown that creates fear. To avoid that condition, he prefers ignorance; if he does not know about the circumstance, it does not exist. The third corollary is the *Law of Responsibility*. Man avoids responsibility. The few who accept its burdens demand great reward.

Fifth is the *Law of Pride*. Having once taken a position publicly, a person will frequently defy logic and deny facts in order to maintain his commitment. "A man convinced against his will, holds the same opinion still." The first corollary of the law of pride is the *Law of Face*. Man will go to extremes to preserve appearances before his peers, long after he knows his case is lost. The *Law of Blame Avoidance*, the second corollary, declares that man has a need to avoid accepting blame for his own conduct. As the sense of guilt grows, the need to avoid blame grows with it.

The *Law of Greed*, the sixth law of human nature, indicates that, no matter how much someone acquires, he wants more — wealth, leisure, knowledge, and so forth. This trait, along with its four corollaries — the laws of *Envy, Jealousy, Vengeance*, and *Power* — creates much havoc in society. According to the *Law of Envy*, man envies another person who has more or better of anything; he tries to acquire a like amount or kind or — failing in this — tries to destroy what the other has. Within the individual who has acquired something, the *Law of Jealousy* creates anxiety lest it be taken from him. Influenced by the *Law of Vengeance*, a jealous or envious person will attempt to harm the responsible party. Because of the *Law of Power*, a person revels in his ability to command an action that requires little effort on his own part. He will support a means to this end even when he knows it may harm his fellowmen.

The seventh law of human nature is the *Law of Intolerance*. Man will use government coercion to deny freedom to others that he denies to himself because of some self-imposed morality.

Eighth is the *Law of the Present*. Man prefers immediate satisfaction to delayed satisfaction. Often he will fulfill his present wants with little regard for future consequences.

The ninth law, the *Law of Inquisitiveness*, causes man to eagerly seek the facts about matters that are not readily apparent.

Influenced by the tenth law, the *Law of Immorality*, under the right circumstances a person will cheat, lie, or commit almost any act regardless of the mores of his society; individuals differ only as to the circumstances. Said with less euphemism, "Every man has his price."

Eleventh is the *Law of Recognition*. Because man is a thinking being, each member of society seeks to have his individuality recognized by his peers. Its corollary, the *Law of Conspicuous Display*, says that an individual will consciously try to show his fellowmen the extent of his achievements. Under the influence of this drive, he will succumb to peer pressure and become a sheep if he cannot be a goat.

Man seeks a hero figure on whom to focus his reliance for leadership and guidance. This observation constitutes the twelfth law, the *Law of Idolatry*.

Thirteenth is the *Law of Disagreement*. Because each person sees life from the viewpoint of his own genetic makeup and lifetime experiences, disagreement between persons is common.

The fourteenth is the *Law of Impatience*. Because of man's eagerness to reach the achievable now, he strives to achieve beyond even his own acknowledged capability.

The fifteenth law of human nature might appear to contradict ones stated earlier. The *Law of Freedom* recognizes that no one voluntarily submits himself to slavery under another. Slavery, the complete absence of self-determination, has always been a condition imposed by some power the individual cannot resist. Many people, however, so withdraw from responsibility for their own actions (the Law of Responsibility), seeking security (the Law of Security), that they relinquish a great degree of liberty. They often fail to realize that their action virtually assures their subjugation into slavery.

The sixteenth and last law, the *Law of Eternity*, indicates that man seeks immortality almost as eagerly as he seeks to preserve life. Because eternity exists only in the minds of the living, man does what he hopes will cause his successors to remember him.

The Industrial Revolution, of which the conquest of the oceans was only a part, required an atmosphere of freedom. Involved here is an inescapable reality of human nature: men restricted by bureaucratic rules rarely undertake what has not first been proven to be safe.

Chapter 1

Fall of the Ocean Barrier

The Great Turning Point in Modern History

ON OCTOBER 12, 1492, men from a sea expedition under the command of the Genoese navigator Christopher Columbus landed on an island in the Caribbean. The natives put out from shore in canoes to greet them. This marked the first significant meeting between Western civilization and primitive Indians of the Americas. The meeting set into motion forces that have greatly altered the lifestyles of both the Indians and the people of Europe. The Indians were displaced, enslaved, or eliminated. They lost control of lands they had occupied for 50,000 years or more. They became the Vanishing Americans.

From the Indians, Europeans acquired plants that today furnish over half of the world's food supply. The opening of a vast new frontier provided European people with a safety release for conflicting social forces ready to burst forth. The American continents were a place for the dissidents and excess numbers in Europe. They offered a large territory where men could be free from rigid social classes and free from despotism. The most conspicuous and immediate result in Europe was the great enrichment of the Catholic monarchs in Spain. American gold and silver perpetuated Spain's position as the great world power for the next 100 years.

Columbus thought he had landed among islands along the eastern shores of India. The Indians did not know the identity or origin of these people with white skin; some thought they were gods whom their priests had been expecting for centuries. Both groups sought to get acquainted, and there was much celebration.

Why Columbus?

Conditions then present virtually decreed that an expedition from a Mediterranean civilization, rather than one from Asia, would first sail to the Americas. Had Columbus not made his voyage in 1492, another member of Western civilization would have done it at a later date. Most likely, Asians would not have led the West to the Americas in that age.

China had an advanced civilization for centuries before the birth of Christ. Much scientific knowledge and many inventions known to Western civilization in 1492 originated with the Asians. Yet they lacked the one ingredient that might generate sea exploration: political freedom. Asians had no property rights or established rules of acceptable conduct. They did not know what rules their emperor might apply when they were charged with a violation of his wishes. Citizens of China, like those of ancient Egypt, had no protection of individual rights and no understanding of what liberty might mean. Their languages did not even contain a word for *liberty.*

Although freedom as men know it today in the United States did not exist anywhere, peoples of the Mediterranean area had known a degree of liberty from the early days of the Athenian democracy. The long-standing tradition of freedom among the Europeans can be traced back to the introduction of rule by law in Athens, Greece, during the reign of Draco in the 7th century B.C. "Rule by law" means protection of both individual and property rights. Committed to writing under Draco, the law was understood and predictable. Christianity fortified recognition of the dignity of the individual, and in medieval times people began restricting the power exercised by royalty — a process that culminated in England with the writing of the Magna Carta in the 13th century. In writing about Europe of the 15th century, Fernand Braudel remarks about freedom among the peoples of the Mediterranean:

> *What were Europe's differences and original features? Its towns were marked by an unparalleled freedom. They had developed as autonomous worlds and according to their own propensities . . . . Urban freedom in Europe is a classic and fairly well documented subject.* (Braudel [1979] 1981. 509-510)

Asian rulers tolerated no such condition. Men remained free there only as long as they behaved in a manner approved by their rulers. In China and the other areas of Asia, the people were ruled by an autocratic government.

Every Asiatic ruler was continuously harassed by ambitious chieftains. Any emperor who became weak in his control of armies would soon be overthrown. Perhaps the most well-publicized of these warlords was Genghis Khan, the Mongolian. Genghis organized the Mongol tribes into a great army that swept over all of China as far south as the Yellow River, west into Middle East Asia and Europe, north to the end of the steppes of outer Mongolia, and all of Manchuria. Soon after he died, his grandson Kublai consolidated the empire and ruled China until his death. The dynasty of the great Khans lasted for over 80 years till the establishment of the Ming dynasty in 1368.

Although each great Asiatic ruler tried to create a living government that would survive him, continuity of policies could not last. The ideas of the next warlord would govern. The only condition common to all rulers in the East for centuries and centuries was a strong bureaucracy to control the people. The ideas and nature of the sitting emperor determined every aspect of life for the citizens. Because rule by military force required material resources, each emperor naturally sought to control all wealth. He needed to fear only those would-be usurpers who had accumulated wealth.

As in all ages, the reigning authority used the religious leaders to supplement his bureaucracy and control the masses. The religious leaders considered it improper for the masses to do anything but menial labor;

they discouraged education and free thinking among them. Islam had an equally stifling caste system. Consequently, outside of Europe the greatest resources of the country, the minds of men, were kept sterile and wasted. Only in Europe could people become wealthy and educated and enter into ventures of their own choosing.

Chinese rulers in particular restricted their subjects. And what had caused China's bureaucratic rigidity? At the beginning of the second millennium of the Christian era, China had the most advanced civilization in the world. Merchants and tradesmen prospered. Private capital increased. An industrial revolution appeared to be on the horizon. China provided technology and scientific discoveries that benefited the entire world. All civilizations looked to Asia for leadership in knowledge. Yet, by the 15th century, only the rulers were eligible for an education. Rulers limited written material to scholarly works, and denied to the masses what contemporary society calls practical knowledge. China's leaders had succumbed to the forces of the Laws of Envy and of Power. The bureaucracy of China had thoroughly strangled individual initiative.

A religious leader of the middle ages in China supplied the following observation:

> *"The question of the utility of machines and working animals is not so easy to decide, at least for a country where the land is barely sufficient to feed its inhabitants. What use would machines and working animals be there? — to turn part of the inhabitants into philosophats* [sic], *that is to say into men doing absolutely nothing for society and making it bear the burden of their needs, their well-being, and what is even worse, their comical and ridiculous ideas . . . ."* (Quoted by Braudel [1979] 1981. 339.)

How could the masses better their position materially under the control of such repression? Progress in either wealth accumulation or education was stopped before it could begin. This attitude arrested societal and economic development in China before the Christian era, perhaps as early as the second millennium B.C. Since that time it has continued to stifle innovation. It prevented advancement in China in the 15th century, and it remains a major deterrent in their current attempts to develop industry. Only free men — free to take advantage of their own knowledge, daring, courage, and desire for wealth or recognition — will adventure into the unknown. A social order that so completely discourages independent thought among its people will never produce an explorer like Columbus. By controlling the wealth, religion, and education of their subjects, societies that preceded Western civilization kept the masses completely subservient.

It was natural that, out of the thousands of free and educated people of the Mediterranean, one would soon emerge who had daring, desire for fame and riches, and imagination, and who could convince one of the monarchs that sea exploration could yield great wealth and its attendant power. The availability of knowledge, created by the printing press, was the ingredient that developed a Columbus. If it had not been Columbus, it would have been someone else with his Mediterranean heritage.

In the 15th century, the wealthy lords of Europe obtained from Asia many treasured items. These goods came over land controlled by the Turks, or by water to the Isthmus of Suez and then overland to the ships on the Mediterranean, an alternate trade route soon to be controlled also by the Turks. Oriental goods cost the Europeans dearly. The Spanish and lesser European powers believed that whoever opened a free water route to the Indies could reap riches in this commerce through lower costs of transport. No longer would Europe be captive to the Turks for silks and spices from the Orient.

In the Mediterranean of Columbus's time there existed two competing empires, the Turks and the Spanish. The Turks were people of the land, not men of the sea. The Spanish was composed almost entirely of coastal cities and cities along the southern European rivers. They were seafaring merchants. The Turks, who profited at that time from the Indies trade, had little to gain from change; whereas the Spanish, with their backs on the Atlantic Ocean, had reason and opportunity to benefit from sea exploration. Only the Catholic monarchs had (1) motive, (2) opportunity, and (3) the capability to venture on that uncharted voyage of 1492. As a result, it would be men of the Mediterranean and the Catholic monarchs in particular who would send forth a fleet to explore the sea and ultimately discover the Americas. The Spanish Crown provided the financing, and the likes of Christopher Columbus provided the knowledge and daring.

Columbus had taken his plans first to Portugal's monarch with no success. At that time, Portugal and Spain were competing in sea exploration. Portugal's king took the plans submitted by Columbus and sent out his own crew to sail west to the Indies. They returned empty-handed. Only Columbus was left, and fear of the unknown proved to be his greatest opponent. Until he convinced others of his ability and demonstrated a proven means of open-ocean navigation, sailors of merit were reluctant to trust their lives to such an endeavor.

Only Europe Exploited the New Freedom

Breaking free from the ocean barrier was simply the logical development of educating the masses of seafaring men. Conquering the high seas gave Europe a world supremacy that lasted for centuries. Why then was ocean navigation not shared by all the maritime peoples of the world once its feasibility had been demonstrated? Islam, India, China, and Japan had ships capable of open-sea travel; they had navigators, and were the first to use the compass (in the 11th century). Although all could have entered the competition opened by sea travel, only Europe made use of the capability.

The explanation for why Europeans moved onto the high seas and Asians and Orientals did not, lies in one word: *freedom.* The Laws of Boredom and of Inquisitiveness function to the advantage of man only among free people. Only in Europe were individuals free to engage in ventures of their own design. All major undertakings among Asians originated with the rulers and had to be approved by a committee. And the Asians had permitted education only to a few. If, perchance, a merchant accumulated wealth in China, the monarch confiscated it. This practice effectively denied to those outside of government the ability to undertake any independent endeavor. At the end of the 11th century A.D., China's emperor Yung Lo had sent expeditions to Java and Ceylon. Thereafter, merchants from China traded as far west as the coastal regions of Africa. Yet the Confucian bureaucracy of China in 1436 issued an imperial edict banning construction of ships capable of open-sea travel.

The Industrial Revolution, of which the conquest of the oceans was only a part, required an atmosphere of freedom. Involved here is an inescapable reality of human nature: men restricted by bureaucratic rules rarely undertake what has not first been proven to be safe. The Laws of Blame Avoidance and Inertia override everything else. Novelty, invention, and progress in the application of innovations cannot develop except among free men. The mere fact that a person has unrestricted power over the resources of his country does not alter this reality. Napoleon underestimated the value of the steamship as a tool for the invasion of England. In the United States prior to World War I, General Billy Mitchell met considerable resistance from the military bureaucracy in his attempts to make military use of the airplane.

For thousands of years the bureaucracies of China were filled with scholars. Each emperor in his turn would gather around him a staff of the brightest individuals in his organization. These would be educated for the task of ruling. This form of rule accounts for the bureaucratic inertia that has for centuries prevented development within China, and it will happen in any nation so governed. It can happen also under freedom. It is happening in America.

With economic advancement, men become able to meet their basic needs with less and less labor. Spared the need of spending all their energies on producing food and shelter, they specialize. Some devote their time to scholarly pursuits, and a new class of men evolves — the thinkers. As these scholars learn more and more about man and society, they discover a startling truth: a free society rewards doers more than thinkers. Doers, even some who lack the refinements of a formal education, gain riches that society withholds from scholars. As Allan Bloom points out:

> *Although the opposition between the vita activa and the vita contemplativa is as old as philosophy, if not older, Goethe's moment is the first where the side of action is taken by theory itself. . . . The theoretical life is groundless because the first thing is not the intelligible order but the chaos open to creativity. There can be no contemplation where there is nothing to see. . . . The modern objection to scholarship is that it lacks the urgency of commitment to action. Most simply, the historian — the very model of the modern scholar — chronicles deeds. But if deeds are the most important thing, then the scholar is by definition inferior to the doer. Moreover, such a reasoner is incapable of the leap into darkness that the deed demands. . . . The hidden premise of the realm of freedom is that action has primacy over thought.* (Bloom 1987. 303)

Because freedom does not grant the greatest rewards to scholars, demagoguery appeals to them. Catering to the mass envy of riches, they passionately advocate "reform," and who besides themselves are most qualified to conduct the reform and lead the people? With all their knowledge, are they not the ones best prepared to plan and manage society? Intellectuals denounce wealth accumulated by private interests. The only fair way is ownership by the whole society — *socialism.* And the scholars, being the most all-knowing, are the logical choice as overseers. Bureaucratic strangulation follows. By the 15th century, China's scholarly leaders had turned away from the world.

Socialism, with its autocratic leadership, is as old as government. But until the masses learn that their interests are best served under freedom, the siren's song of the scholarly despot is ever the fatal attraction. The world has seen this happen in all earlier civilizations. They have declined; it is happening in the West in the 20th century. In this century the Rhodes scholarship was created by such a despot. Cecil John Rhodes believed that the common man was incapable of handling his own affairs. He committed his wealth to training the brightest and most promising students to take charge of matters through the only institution that possessed the required coercive power over the citizens: government. He designed his scholarships to create scholarly despots.

The record of history presents the hazard of granting all control of government to the intellectuals. *Freedom demands that the influence of intellectuals be countered by practical men educated through experience and deeds.*

Difficulties of Sea Exploration
Columbus encountered a great deal of this bureaucratic inertia when he sought financing for his voyage. In addition, he met with resistance from sailors when he was looking for a crew. The art of open-sea navigation was quite crude; until then no navigator had sufficient confidence in his skill to venture onto the open sea. In the 15th century sailors stayed within sight of land and put into port at night. Not only did this practice benefit the crew, who had no beds on board ship; but navigators needed to be on land to get reasonably accurate results with the instruments then available for determining latitude. Accurate readings could not be made on shipboard because of the continuous motion of the ship. Columbus did have a compass to determine direction, but an instrument for determining longitude did not exist. On his 1492 voyage Columbus determined longitude by estimating his speed and keeping an accurate log of time. In this sense, he sailed across the Atlantic by "dead reckoning," which means plotting a course and position on a chart by figuring direction, speed, and time. Some

historians have declared Columbus one of the three truly great navigators of recorded history. The other two, Sir Francis Drake and Ferdinand Magellan, appeared on the historical scene after the 1492 Atlantic crossing.

Sailors with sufficient experience to be considered for a long open-sea voyage would have known about these difficulties. Every day at sea out of sight of land would increase their anxiety. Fear of the unknown delayed open-sea exploration until a navigator of great courage and remarkable skill would appear and show the way.

Some writers have suggested that sailors of 1492 believed that any ship venturing too far from the mainland would be enveloped in a huge mass of seaweed, stalling it forever; that out of the weeds would come great monsters to eat the sailors as their ship lay immobilized; that if by some freakish bit of good luck the ship escaped entrapment in that seaweed, it would soon fall off the edge of the earth into a bottomless void, lost forever. These may have been real beliefs among some sailors of the 15th century, but quality sailors of experience surely must have known from observation that the earth was not flat.

In defense of the seaweed-monster belief, there is the Sargasso Sea, a great area in the Atlantic Ocean west of the mouth of the Mediterranean that is composed of deep, calm, clear, warm water in which float large masses of the seaweed *sargassum*. Because of the sargassum and the typically calm air currents of this area, small sailing vessels might become stalled there, which would give some credence to the legend. The part about the sea monsters was, of course, pure fable; the largest life form in the Sargasso Sea is the seal. Columbus did sail through the southern edges of the Sargasso, but found the presence of the seaweed no obstacle. (Morison 1974. 58)

Columbus's westward voyage ended at an island in the Caribbean that he believed was near the shores of India; so he named this area the West Indies. Later explorations revealed the existence of two large continents not previously known to Europeans, continents that cartographers subsequently named the Americas, North and South.

The Significance of Columbus's Voyage

The great significance of Columbus's voyage was not the discovery of the Americas, though certainly that would unfold to be of great moment in the history of the world. Strictly speaking, he did not discover the Americas. Columbus himself was never certain about his discovery. In the journal of his third voyage to the Americas, he expressed his suspicion that he had discovered in fact a large continent previously unknown to Europeans.

Columbus's great achievement was dispelling the fear of the unknown in open-sea navigation. He demolished the open-ocean barrier to sea travel, and removed the shackles that had kept men tied to the land masses. Columbus opened the door to sea exploration. Men of less courage could then venture forth and determine the facts about the seas and continents of the world. As Fernand Braudel recognized:

> *Europe's own achievement was to discover the Atlantic and to master its difficult stretches, currents, and winds. This late success opened up the doors and routes of the seven seas. From then on the maritime organization of the world was at the service of white men.* (Braudel [1979] 1981. 62)

Soon after Columbus crossed the Atlantic Ocean, another Mediterranean navigator, Ferdinand Magellan, led an expedition that sailed around the world, proving the continuity of the open seas. Sea exploration was released from ignorance, superstition, and fear of the unknown; and Spanish ships filled every part of the oceans.

Following Columbus's lead, other explorers from Spain came to the Americas during the 16th century. Their direct influence was limited to Central America, South America, and Mexico. In the area now comprising the United States, visible Spanish influence remains only in the architecture of churches and established missions — St. Augustine, Florida; Santa Fe, New Mexico; southern Texas; and southern California. The Spanish were interested in gold and silver, and the then-existing mines were in South and Central America and in Mexico. Spain's conquest of the three major Indian cultures in Central and South America does not make pretty reading, but it is a fact of life.

The story of the spread of Western civilization provides much detail about the period when Spain was the dominant power in Europe and on the seas. By the last half of the 16th century, however, under the rule of Philip II, the power of Spain was diminishing. The 1588 sea battle in which English sailors destroyed the "invincible" Spanish Armada more or less marks the turning point when Britain overtook Spain in dominating the high seas. In his *Eminent Domain* (1973), John Keats presents an interesting account of this struggle between Spain and England during the expansion of sea exploration in the 15th and 16th centuries.

Until the English established their first successful colony in the New World, the Spanish, in their search for gold and silver, exercised the predominant influence on natives in the area of the United States. English influence on this region began to appear at the beginning of the 17th century.

The Miracle of Freedom

Cooperation among men requires a fairly advanced degree of understanding, with knowledge of the benefits that accrue from the division of labor. Developing knowledge and understanding is a slow process. Man cannot move beyond simple tribal cooperation without the knowledge discovered by other tribes and other generations. The spoken word can never reach large numbers of individuals, which severely limits the scope of information it can convey. A written record of the ideas and discoveries of his predecessors can provide such a foundation. Each advancement in cooperation among men developed from a more efficient means of transmitting information among individuals and between ages — first the spoken word and then the written record. It seems evident that progress in communication skills must precede progress in civilization. This remains true today. The great strides in communication during the past five decades have opened up opportunities for free men to make discoveries as yet unimagined. This will happen in the United States if the government permits the citizens enough liberty to develop and promote their own ideas.

Several instruments were available to Western civilization that set its peoples apart from more primitive societies. They had written languages with alphabets comprised of a small number of characters; they also had the printing press and freedom to use the new technology. *The Encyclopaedia Britannica* makes this interesting observation about the history of printing:

> *Although printing as it is known today began in Germany during the mid-15th century, the Chinese, Japanese, and Koreans used printing much earlier. Printing was invented independently in the West and developed along dissimilar lines. The major reason for the separate development is the difference between*

Asian and European scripts. Mass production of movable letters for the 15th-century European alphabet of 23 letters was a simple affair; for a language demanding thousands of complicated ideographs, it was impossible. (*Encyclopaedia Britannica,* Vol. 18, 1970 ed., Encyclopaedia Britannica, Inc., William Benton, Publisher. 541)

Printing with movable characters originated among the Koreans and was soon used in China, but the technology was not fully developed in Asia until recent years. A technology means little until it is put into general use. The Koreans are known to have cast type in bronze by the late 14th century. This technology was soon carried to both Japan and China. Yet not until the 20th century did the use of metal type supersede the use of wood blocks as the principal printing method among Orientals.

Bureaucratic strangulation no doubt exerted a stifling influence, delaying the adaptation of the new technology. Chinese rulers limited the numbers of copies and the variety of texts that could be produced by their printers. They generally restricted subject matter to the wisdom of their great rulers. No true freedom existed that enabled individuals to print and distribute the words of liberty. Only in Western civilization did the common man receive printed material dealing with a great variety of topics.

Each printing of a book in the Asiatic culture took countless hours for a sculpture to carve the required blocks. To produce numerous titles would have required monumental labor on the part of their printers. Each title was relatively costly, and therefore beyond the reach of the common man. The existing bureaucracy could easily restrict distribution of knowledge that would disturb the ruling elite.

Some emperors in China did encourage education among their supporters; but because the bureaucracy controlled virtually all capital resources, few titles opposing the ruling elite ever saw the light of day. Consequently, none of those Asiatic cultures could use the printing press to convey revolutionary thought to the general populace.

This circumstance denied to all peoples other than Western civilization the imaginative ability of individuals. But people in Western civilization were free to use the printed word. Consequently, the knowledge of Western peoples was not only recorded, but could be distributed economically to thousands and thousands of the common people.

Before the printing press made knowledge available in a form that was not able to be controlled by rulers, there could be no meaningful development of freedom. Knowledge frees people from domination by the ruling classes; it is the liberating force to destroy slavery; it is the key to liberty. Before the printing press and books by the thousands, rulers could keep the masses ignorant by controlling the written word. If a ruler chose to do so, he could virtually destroy all knowledge available to his wards by destroying the books that existed — and this was attempted from time to time with varying degrees of success. When an invading army conquered a city, they first plundered the area of all movable wealth, executed all the surviving individuals, and then burned and destroyed the buildings and contents. This was a regular occurrence in China and the Middle East from before the Christian era until the 20th century. It also occurred in Europe during the Middle Ages. When the Spanish invaded Central America, the conquistadors were ordered to destroy all written records of the Mayan civilization, and they executed the order with great success.

Until man invented (1) language, (2) the written word, (3) an alphabet for that language, and (4) a means to mass-produce the written word, he was condemned to be ruled by whichever warlord organized the strongest army. It took Western civilization thousands of years to acquire the first three of these, but once the printing press had been devised, civilized man blossomed in the West. Since that time, his civilization has produced a virtually unstoppable flood of discoveries.

Spread of the printed word caused a flood of knowledge that rulers could no longer control. Human freedom was the inescapable result. The creations of the past 500 years attest to the amazing achievements that imaginative, free men will attain.

The marvelous power of freedom stems from the unrestrained capability of human minds. At liberty to act in any manner that does not interfere with the freedom of others, man can put in place whatever he can imagine. Living under freedom, Henry Ford needed no bureaucratic approval to employ the technologies of assembly-line production and standardized interchangeable parts. Later, he could defy the considered best judgment of his contemporaries and increase the wages of his workers above industry standards. The Wright Brothers needed no committee approval to demonstrate how to fly a heavier-than-air craft.

Changes during the 20th century were the predictable results of unleashing the creative power of human minds. In the United States, people were free from government restrictions on property rights; so the financial resources of the Western world flowed to America, where people sought profitable employment building railroads, automobiles, airplanes, cotton gins, corn pickers, farm tractors, and combines. American and foreign capital introduced the radio and motion pictures in the 1920s, air conditioning in the 1930s, television in the 1940s, and — after World War II — recorded music on magnetic tape and then on compact discs. At the turn of the century, gas lights began to give way to electric lights. By mid-century, nearly every home in the nation had electricity. Every electrical appliance common today has come into use during the 20th century.

First appearing in mid-century, computers made space navigation a reality by the 1960s, and man walked on the moon in the next decade. In 1492 Christopher Columbus took a month to cross the ocean from Africa to the West Indies; supersonic airplanes cross the Atlantic today in a few hours. In 1849 men spent three months traveling from New York to the gold fields of California. Traveling on regular air transport today, a New Yorker can fly to California after breakfast, conduct business over lunch, and return home in time for dinner.

The knowledge now used daily by doctors was discovered in the last 100 years. The wonder drugs penicillin and sulfa came on the scene after World War I. The killer diseases whooping cough, measles, scarlet fever, tuberculosis, tetanus, typhoid fever, yellow fever, poliomyelitis, diphtheria, smallpox, influenza, typhus, rabies, anthrax, cholera, and plague have disappeared only in the last 100 years — most during the last five decades. An epidemic of influenza in 1918 infected nearly a quarter of the world's population and killed over 20 million worldwide. The threat of a similar epidemic in 1976 never materialized because medical science had developed a vaccine to prevent the infection. Savings in the hands of men free to employ them produced these contemporary miracles.

These are the products of men free to earn, free to save, free to invent, free to change. Without freedom, innovations will not appear. In 1904, one man, on seeing the marvels displayed at the St. Louis World Fair, remarked that he truly believed man had reached the millennium, that no further inventions remained. Yet man has replaced nearly all the then-existing technologies. He uses countless products not even imagined at that time. Late 20th-century Americans accept these conditions with little wonder. They are so commonplace that young men and women cannot imagine a world without them.

Quite naturally, no individual living now can imagine the inventions men will devise in the next century, but none will become commonplace without freedom and protection for private property rights. The innovative pioneer appears only when there is freedom to initiate and develop his concepts without approval from the establishment. If required first to secure approval from the existing authorities, the innovator is defeated before he begins, because he is trying to overthrow the ideas earlier approved by that same authority. His activities challenge the accepted way of doing things. Innovation disappears with loss of liberty, and erosion of liberty for Americans increases daily.

The freedom man enjoys today in the United States, however, will be difficult to destroy completely — except by government confiscation and destruction of libraries, and control of paper factories and printing presses. This, however, is becoming more possible because of inventions for destruction that man has devised for other purposes. Consequently, continued freedom is not necessarily assured just because the U.S. now produces so many books, magazines, and newspapers.

The concepts of freedom that guided the colonists in framing the Constitution . . . had been advocated earlier by philosophers and accepted in ancient Greek civilization.

Chapter 2

The Colonial Period, 1592-1764

Ideas Are More Powerful Than Guns

HEN PEOPLE MOVE, they take with them more than their families and possessions; they take with them their way of life — their ideas, prejudices, language, habits, and political and religious beliefs. To understand these immigrants, we need to examine their ways and beliefs before they came to the new frontier. If we know the ordinary Englishmen of the 17th century, we know the majority of American immigrants.

Perhaps the broad use of the printing press exerted the greatest influence on the thinking of 17th-century Englishmen. For the first time, ideas could be distributed economically. Much as people today receive unsolicited materials in the mail or on their doorstep, 17th-century Englishmen received pamphlets expounding ideas of reformers and revolutionaries. These thinkers wrote in the language of the common man rather than in Latin or Greek, the international languages of intellectuals. Printed material was read to others wherever people gathered. People discussed freedom, politics, and interpretations of the Bible.

The king and the church fully disapproved of such conduct. The law required church attendance. The king used the church to control the common man's thoughts as well as his actions. He allowed no free thinking among the masses. Only the clergy could interpret and disseminate ideas. Distribution of printed matter, however, could not be controlled as easily as the writing of manuscripts.

The printing press brought to men ideas that had been previously confined to secluded halls where select men of education gathered. It destroyed the king's control over the minds of his subjects. Newly formed religious groups opened church meetings to general discussion after the sermon. Church congregations challenged old concepts. Women at quilting sessions and men at the pub talked about ideas that reached them through printed material. The printed word brought freedom to the masses. The revolution in England — which ultimately resulted in civil war with the execution of the first minister Laud, the archbishop of Canterbury, and King Charles I — grew out of this new invention.

Following are some of the ideas then being disseminated:

1. In courts, replace trial by a judge or a clergyman with trial before a jury of one's peers.
2. Write laws and conduct trials in the language of the people, not in Latin or Law-French.
3. Let the common man interpret the Bible for himself. No longer should the king and his clergy dictate the form of religion (separation of church and state).
4. Let God, not church courts, punish sin. Let the unruly man be controlled by the civil magistrate. Morality is a spiritual concern of the individual, not a concern of the law.
5. Remove the power of government from the operation of the church. Abolish the mandatory, government-enforced tithe to the church.

6. Eliminate class distinctions between men before the law and in government. Require the law to treat all men as equals.
7. Decentralize administration of church and government (the current Federal system in America). Let people have local churches with their own appointed clergy. Keep land records in local (county) agencies of record.
8. Legislation about taxing and spending must originate in the lower house, the House of Commons, the unit of government most nearly representative of the people.
9. Education should no longer remain a monopoly of the privileged professions — divinity, law, and medicine. Make schools, conducted in the vernacular, available to all. (Hill 1972. 58, 79, 129, 210-217, 239, 288; Trevor-Roper 1956. 240-241, 349-350)

Pamphlets that circulated among the people advocated these ideas of freedom, ideas that further inspired the revolutionary movement in England. The power of the king, destroyed with the execution of Charles I in 1649, could never again hide such ideas from the populace. These ideas in England came with immigrants to the Colonies as fundamental to their culture. The Constitution clearly shows the influence of such principles on the organization of government in the United States.

Americans today consider freedom of speech one of their most vital safeguards of individual liberty. Equally vital are separation of church and state, protection against unlawful search and seizure, trial by jury, mobility of labor, equal protection under the law.

The concepts of freedom that guided the colonists in framing the Constitution did not simply pop out of the air. Many had been advocated earlier by philosophers and accepted in ancient Greek civilization. Many of these same ideas, supplemented by concepts from Germanic tradition and feudalism, became fundamental to the English constitutional tradition, as evidenced by the Magna Carta and common law. They were kept alive by free-thinking men and printed in books and pamphlets for distribution to the general public.

The printing press helped man escape political oppression. It released the power of ideas, always a force greater than the guns of kings. "The pen is more powerful than the sword."

The English revolutions of the 17th century carried their influence into the English Colonies, leading to the War of Independence, which separated the Colonies from English rule. Christopher Hill's *The World Turned Upside Down* presents an excellent treatment of this period in English history. His work examines in detail the thinking of Englishmen outside the seats of authority, the lower classes. This mentality must be kept in mind when we study the political history of America and in particular the development of revolt against England in 1776.

Englishmen who supported the traditional ways of government did not migrate. English emigrants to America came from those most imbued with revolutionary beliefs — the poor, the disenfranchised, the disadvantaged. But, when English leaders reestablished the monarchy under James II in 1660, emigration received an additional boost. Men of position and wealth, educated men who had supported the Commonwealth under Cromwell, found it expedient to investigate conditions in America.

Early emigrants to America were men of like mind. Conditions in England caused the departure of those most convinced of the dignity and freedom of individuals, those firm in their belief in the benefits of representative government. Swiss, German, and French Protestants came to the new country also seeking freedom for expressing their beliefs. The search for personal liberty brought to the English Colonies men of a common ideology.

The French and Indian Wars

From the Norman conquest of England in the 11th century until the English defeated the French under Napoleon at Waterloo in 1815, periods of war and peace between these two powers alternated about equally. When both monarchs set up colonies in North America, these ongoing wars affected life there as well. Furthermore, the colonists had their own reasons to scrap. English and French valued the fur trade. In New York and New England, English colonists pressed north and west toward the Great Lakes, establishing a trading outlet on Lake Ontario at Oswego. The English crossed the Appalachians into the Ohio watershed in pursuing this trade. The French traded along the St. Lawrence River, the Great Lakes, and the Ohio River. By trying to do business with the same Indians, French and English colonists eventually came into conflict.

In order to keep these wars properly identified, the following table lists them as named in European and American histories.

Wars		
In Europe		**In America**
War of the League of Augsburg	1689-1697	King William's War
War of the Spanish Succession	1702-1713	Queen Anne's War
War of the Austrian Succession	1740-1748	King George's War 1744-1748*
The Seven Years' War	1756-1763	French and Indian War 1754-1760*

* Because the Colonies made no separate treaties, these dates are not related to any official acts of governments.

Additionally, English and French kings claimed the same land. By reason of John Cabot's explorations along the Atlantic seaboard, the English claimed all land west from the Atlantic to the Pacific. By virtue of their explorations down the Ohio and Mississippi Rivers to the Gulf of Mexico, the French claimed all the land in these watersheds. As was customary in disputes between kings, the best title belonged to the victor in war. This was the conflict involved in the long-running French and Indian Wars in the American Colonies (1689-1763), so called because both sides enlisted the aid of Indians. The Iroquois supported the English; the Algonquin, bitter enemies of the Iroquois, allied with the French.

Studying the continued conflict between the English and French colonies (1689-1760) is important for three reasons. The most obvious is that it shows why Canada, with its large French-speaking population, remains to this day English instead of French. In the end, the English won the decision, and France ceded the Canadian colony to them.

Secondly, such a study makes evident the strong feeling of independence among the English colonists. Even when fighting a common enemy, their cooperation developed slowly. Individual merchants failed to support their own colonial government because they believed they could live peacefully and prosperously under French or English control. To them this conflict represented a quarrel between kings; it was not their concern. This spirit of independence, so intense in the Colonies, would later influence the cause of revolution in 1776. It preserved the rights of free men when Colonial leaders wrote the Constitution of the United States.

Thirdly, of great significance for military and industrial leaders, a study of the French and Indian conflicts illustrates the importance of leadership in any enterprise involving great numbers of individuals. War and big business unite the efforts of many people toward one objective. Success goes to those with the most able leadership. From 1690 until 1759 the English and the colonists launched campaign after campaign to force the French from Canada. In many of these ventures the French were poorly prepared. Yet the English and the colonists failed by virtually stumbling over their own feet. In particular, the English General Edward Braddock lost nearly two-thirds of his force without taking Fort Duquesne on the Ohio River, a fort that the French commander believed he could not successfully defend. Preparing for an orderly withdrawal, the French commander dispatched a small force to delay General Braddock's army. This group of Frenchmen completely routed the English. General Braddock was killed and his army decimated in a skirmish along the approach road, in a battle that the French should never have been able to join much less win. Nearly every detail of that campaign displays poor leadership by Braddock and his junior officers. The Colonial militia was the one exception. Led by a young Virginian, George Washington, the militia prevented the rout from becoming a massacre.

This conflict with the French dragged on for 70 years because of poor leadership and the colonists' lack of unity. Most unsuccessful efforts against the French were not so devastating as General Braddock's, but English failures can be attributed principally to weakness in the leaders.

The English Colonies would no doubt have ultimately prevailed in the long-running conflict with the French, even without military support from England. The English colonists greatly outnumbered the French, and they were fighting for their homes. Frenchmen had come to Canada not as colonists but as mercenaries, either to work in the fur trade or to fight the English. History has shown that mercenaries seldom succeed in war against free men fighting for their homes. English colonists would have united against the French, much as they did later in a common cause against Parliament and King George III. The British expedition against Quebec, ordered by William Pitt under the command of General James Wolfe, merely settled the issue decisively in 1759.

In place of the incompetent Duke of Newcastle, in 1756 William Pitt succeeded to the power, if not the title, of English prime minister. France and England were again at war, the Seven Years' War, known in America as the French and Indian War. Pitt recognized the importance of settling this ongoing conflict. Early in 1759 he dispatched to America a sizable force under the command of General Wolfe. Quebec fell to the English by September, and Montreal fell the next spring. In the treaty that ended the Seven Years' War, France ceded to England all claims in Canada and in the Ohio River watershed. France retained her claims west of the Mississippi. Peace came to the Colonies.

In light of Pitt's decisive leadership in handling this cause against the French, the question naturally arises: What could prompt ungrateful colonists to rebel against their mother country in less than 16 years? The answer is that a change of leadership took place in England. King George II died shortly after the fall of Canada, which resulted in a power shift in Parliament. Under the new king, George III, Pitt lost his position of influence. The war had left the English government deeply in debt. George III and the new leaders in Parliament took action aimed at making the Colonies pay a major portion of the costs for the campaign in America. This may have been appropriate, but bungling by King George III alienated the colonists in 16 short years. Discontent with English authority on relatively minor matters turned into frustration that could be resolved only through rebellion and complete political separation.

Seeds of Revolt

Self-government in the English Colonies developed more from necessity than intention. In the early years, organized groups of immigrants expected to be governed by their proprietors or by their king in England. In reality, colonists were neglected more than governed by their principals. The need to establish political power in Europe occupied the minds, treasure, and manpower of English monarchs. During those early years Englishmen in power considered support to the Colonies a waste of resources. This became especially true when English ships returned from America with no gold or silver. Neglected, even ignored by their directors, the colonists did what they had to do. When a Governor died or proved inadequate, they replaced him from among their own ranks. They changed the laws forbidding private ownership of produce from farming. They constructed their own forms of self-government. With the passing of years they became accustomed to taking care of themselves. As a consequence, having survived neglect from their lawful leaders, they naturally resented later attempts to restrict their liberty to govern themselves. English citizens in the Colonies rebelled in 1776, not to gain freedom, but to retain the freedom they feared they were losing.

English revolutionaries of the 17th century established the principle that all legislation dealing with money would originate in the house representing the people, the House of Commons. By extension of this principle, English colonists expected this practice to be observed in America. As each colony developed its own house of representatives, the people believed English law recognized that tax measures had to originate in their colonial government.

Ordinarily men outside the government take little interest in details of its operation. English colonists, however, considered one matter quite important even to the man on the street: the origin of tax legislation and the dispensing of tax funds. Belief in this tradition stirred strong feelings that ultimately led to the War of Independence. Its influence carried over into the structure of the new nation's government. This understanding helps explain to the 20th-century people why the United States became an independent nation. Knowing the legal relationship between the Colonies, their king, and Parliament helps a person understand the force of this tradition.

American colonies were of two types, royal (Crown) and proprietary. Both forms of organization had in common one vital feature: they derived their legal standing by grant of the English monarch. In a royal colony the king appointed the governor, designated the geographical limits of his jurisdiction, and outlined the laws that governed settlement. In a proprietary colony the king granted to a proprietor the power to determine rights of settlement and to govern the defined area. In both cases the king had the final say on all items of legislation. In all colonies the king delegated to the proprietors or the Governor the right to originate legislation. By practices that developed over the 150 years of the Colonial period, the people had assumed this power to originate legislation through their local representative assemblies — the town meeting, the legislature of the colony, the house of burgesses, by whatever name the council might be called. Although colonists had acquired a considerable degree of self-government, the Governor or the proprietor retained the right of veto as agent for the king. The people became accustomed to having control over legislation subject only to the king's veto. In none of the Colonies did the people vote for representatives in Parliament. They did not consider it necessary, because they had their own parliaments that functioned for them as the London Parliament did for Englishmen in the British Isles.

Because the colonists elected no members to Parliament, they accepted none of its actions as binding on them. The line of authority ran from the colonists through their representatives directly to the king. They especially wanted to preserve this arrangement in matters of taxation and spending. When dealing with the pocketbook, the colonists would accept only the authority of their own assemblies.

The king and those whom he controlled in the London Parliament did not agree with this thinking. Therein lay the conflict that would eventually end in war. Members of the King's Parliament considered the Colonies part of their dominion. In their eyes Parliament was the supreme government of the whole British Empire. English colonists in America rebelled because they believed strongly that Parliament was usurping the authority of their own colonial governments. The colonists not only considered British tax measures offensive and burdensome, but they believed Parliament had no right to levy them.

This does not mean that the colonists should not have been taxed. They might have agreed to a tax levy had they been allowed to devise the specific measures. At least in the beginning, they surely recognized that the taxes were for paying off the debt incurred in sending ships, supplies, and troops to drive the French from the Ohio River, the Great Lakes region, and Canada. The situation demanded that the king and his Parliament recognize the English tradition in devising tax measures, but the situation needed capable leadership and diplomacy. The unfortunate event of historical significance was the death of George II so soon after the defeat of the French in the Colonies. George III became King of England, William Pitt lost his influence in Parliament, and the new leadership handled the entire matter poorly.

In human history, major events have often been controlled by simpletons, with results that affected generations that followed. It happened in the 1770s between the English and their American colonies. With hindsight one can understand the viewpoint of Parliament and that of the colonists. Each group had justification for its contentions. The circumstance called for capable leadership from both sides. One would think that among eight million Englishmen and two million colonists there would have been at least a dozen men who could lead their governments to an amicable solution. Most colonists did not want independence. As late as

1775, even after shots had been fired at Lexington and Concord, Benjamin Franklin remained in England to negotiate a peaceful settlement. The colonists considered revolt and independence a resolution of last resort, and not a satisfactory one at that.

In England it was quite another story. Even though many Englishmen and some members of Parliament did understand the true nature of the conflict, George III controlled those in leadership and ineptly handled the affairs of State, casting good judgment aside. A war followed that could have been avoided.

Early Settlement in North America

The Spanish limited their interest in the Americas to enriching the treasury of the monarchs. Because only the natives of Central and South America had gold and silver in quantity, the Spaniards soon lost interest in regions north of Mexico. Their monarch sent missionaries to liberate the Indians from their heathen ways and soldiers to liberate them from their silver and gold. They founded only one colony on the Atlantic seaboard in what is now the United States — St. Augustine, Florida. Established first by the French as a base for naval operations, it was later expanded by the Spanish to house soldiers for defending the region against attack by other European interests. Spanish Catholic missionaries also entered southern California and New Mexico to convert the Indians to Christianity. Some of these missionaries survived; many died at the hands of those they sought to educate.

France sent first Jacques Cartier and then Samuel de Champlain to explore America in search of a northern water passage to the Pacific Ocean and the Orient. Failing in this endeavor, the French tried to colonize in the region of their explorations, the St. Lawrence waterway and the Great Lakes. Their efforts in the 16th century failed; but concurrently with English settlement in the Massachusetts Bay region, they developed self-sustaining colonies at Quebec, Louisbourg, Montreal, and a few other settlements of less importance.

The Dutch founded colonies in the 1620s along the Hudson River in New York. During the next decade, Swedes colonized south of the Dutch, along the Delaware River.

Mass migration, however, came from England. With colonies founded first by the Virginia Company at Jamestown in 1607 and by the Plymouth Company in Massachusetts in 1620, English immigrants spread all along the Atlantic seaboard. By 1700 they had established colonies from Maine to Carolina, and through armed force had taken over the Swedish and Dutch colonies along the Delaware and the Hudson Rivers.

Most immigration came more from a desire to escape existing conditions than to settle in America. In England and on the continent, being born poor meant being poor for life. There existed no freedom to improve one's place in the society of the Old World. Opportunity in the New World meant both freedom and escape from poverty.

Excess numbers in England burdened the crown; hence, the government encouraged colonization either in Ireland or in the Americas. By contrast, perhaps a major reason the Dutch and Swedes failed to hold their lands in the New World was that the stable populations in Sweden and Holland did not prompt people to leave. There were exceptions, of course. Scots who had settled earlier in Ireland left to escape the state-enforced Anglican religion. Protestants left France, Germany, and Switzerland to escape state-enforced Catholicism. Quakers and Puritans left England looking for freedom of religion. For most emigrants, however, freedom from poverty provided the greatest impetus to leave. All new arrivals on the frontier could acquire land, the principal source of wealth at that time.

Early immigrants to the Colonies faced a difficult adjustment. Sickness, poor food, exposure to a climate foreign to their homeland, and Indian attacks took their toll. In most colonies, over half the immigrants died within three years. For this reason, we should look at conditions in early 17th-century Europe in order to understand why men would by choice come to the harsh circumstance of life in America.

In Europe, whenever famine and disease caused large decreases in population — which recurred several times each century — forests and wild animals took over the uncultivated fields. In 1420, wolves invaded the streets of Paris. In 1500, they occupied the forests all over Europe from the Urals to the Straits of Gibralter, and bears roamed in all the mountains. In 1640, wolves entered Bescancon and ate children along the roads.

Then in Europe — as now in China, India, Mexico, Africa, South and Central America — increasing populations put stress on the social institutions. Hundreds of thousands could find no employment on the farms or in the towns. Society considered it a solution to place the poor in a position where they could do no harm. In Paris they put the sick and invalid in hospitals. The fit, chained together in pairs, were employed at cleaning sewers of town. The Poor Laws of England, appearing at the end of

Elizabeth's reign, established houses for the poor and undesirable, condemning them to forced labor in workhouses. In Dijon, France, the municipal authorities prohibited citizens from exercising private charity. In the 17th century, beggars were whipped and treated as convicts. In 1483 in Crepy, a third of the town went begging about the countryside, and old people died in squalor every day. Paradoxically, country peasants depended on towns, merchants, and nobles. They had few reserves of their own; so they had no option during famines except to go to town, begging in the streets and often dying in public squares, as in Amiens, France, and Venice, Italy, in the 16th century. (Braudel 1981. 72-76)

The more venturesome of these individuals shared the forests with the wild animals. Representative of these — the unruled, the thieves, the predatory bands of opportunists — were Robin Hood and his band of Merry Men, popularized in legends of 12th-century Sherwood Forest, England. No band of thieves, however, was ever as merry or as gallant toward their fellowmen.

Maurice Ashley gives us a brief look into the home atmosphere of the 17th-century English farm worker:

> *. . . he lived . . . in a small house in the village street with a singular absence of comfort: a few pots and pans, a trestle table, a few stools, no chairs, and boards to lie on.* (Ashley 1961. 281-282)

These workers lived a step above the poor. Imagine how the poor must have lived. An 18th-century author wrote about conditions in Ireland:

> *It is a melancholy object to those who walk through this great town or travel in the country, when they see the streets, the roads, and cabin-doors crowded with beggars of the female sex, followed by three, four, or six children, all in rags, and importuning every passenger for an alms. These mothers, instead of being able to work for their honest livelihood, are forced to employ all their time in strolling to beg sustenance for their helpless infants.* (Jonathan Swift. "A Modest Proposal." 1729)

Christopher Hill described conditions in England of the 17th century:

Beneath the surface stability of rural England, then, the vast placid open fields which catch the eye, was the seething mobility of forest squatters, itinerant craftsmen and building labourers, unemployed men and women seeking work, strolling players and jugglers, pedlars [sic] and quack doctors, vagabonds, tramps: congregated especially in London and the big cities, but also with footholds wherever newly-squatted areas escaped from the machinery of the parish or in old-squatted areas where labour was in demand. It was from this underworld that armies and ships' crews were recruited, that a proportion at least of the settlers of Ireland and the New World were found, men prepared to run desperate risks in the hope of obtaining the secure freehold land (and with it status) to which they could never aspire in overcrowded England. (Hill 1972. 39)

Restrictions imposed on selling their produce aggravated the sorry plight of the peasants. Denied access to free markets, peasant farmers could not command a price for their crops that properly compensated them for their effort. Even until the 1789 revolution, the French peasant was obliged to sell his grain at the market of the nearby town. Obstacles to free trade and private initiative existed until the teachings of 18th-century economists promulgated the principles of political and economic freedom that ushered in the Industrial Revolution. To these supernumeraries in England and on the Continent, freedom for their person and opportunity to acquire wealth offered by migration to the New World overpowered the risks involved. Even so, the weak and the timid stayed behind.

Self-Government Requires Knowledgeable Citizens
The Colonial period involved a 150-year development before the colonists established a successful system of united government that was representative of the people. Events during the subsequent 200 years, however, have challenged that system of government. It remains to be seen whether such an experiment can succeed through time.

Today, Americans accept without thought the right of all adults to vote. Only by universal suffrage does a country earn the designation *democracy*. But does the vote assure representative government? In the recently dissolved Soviet Union, although all adults could vote, did their government represent the will of the voters? Were the elected officials answerable to the people? Could voters turn the "ins" out with the next election? The Communist Party in Russia included about ten percent of the voters. Only party members were then eligible to hold office, and the party elite selected all candidates. Consequently, the right to vote in the USSR was merely the right to choose between alternatives selected by the Politburo. The system gave the masses no voice in government. The right to vote was meaningless. Events in late 1989 began a political revolution in the Soviet Union, but the final outcome of these events has not yet become clear. Again, only the future will disclose what that government will become as a result of these events. Some Russian citizens, speaking in the United States, claim they do not expect any significant change.

In the United States the vote has always been meaningful, but self-government in the English Colonies did not exist as Americans now know it. In Colonial times most adults could not participate in government. Only free, male members of the colony could vote, and these men had to own land of qualifying acreage. Women, indentured servants, and slaves were excluded. In some colonies only members of the recognized church could vote and hold office. The only similarity between self-government then and now exists in principle, *i.e.*, a government organized and managed by citizens as opposed to government by a monarch. It remained for later generations to extend the franchise to all adult citizens of the nation.

Representative government developed in England over a period of nearly 600 years. Each step was small, and the people had ample time to adjust before taking the next. When the step was too large, as in 1649 — when the revolutionaries beheaded King Charles and full responsibility of government rested in the hands of Parliament — the process took a step backwards. Parliament selected another king and installed him in office. In the process of development from absolute monarchy to representative government, England experienced two civil wars — in the 1640s and the 1770s.

The Colonies benefited from this heritage. They also benefited from the experiences of 13 independent Colonial governments. Involvement in these governments enabled the citizens to learn firsthand how to handle the voting privilege. Each government started small with limited power. As their experience grew, the colonists assumed more power in government, and a workable system of representation evolved.

The history of democracy underlines the necessity for gradual change. Englishmen and the colonists did not set up their representative governments overnight; they evolved over hundreds of years. The errors and conflicts that arose should be known. Many resulted in loss of life. Some conflicts, such as the American Civil War in the 1860s, were frightfully bloody.

Knowing how long it took Englishmen and the American colonists to establish some workable form of representative government, enables us to consider this question: On what basis can people today expect India, Ethiopia, Zimbabwe, the Philippine Islands, and the South and Central American nations to establish successful democracies immediately? What arrogance do Americans show when they insist that all countries must function under some form of self-government. All such instantaneous democracies are doomed to failure. Representative government can operate successfully only among people who have shared in the learning process, among people experienced in exercising the responsibilities of liberty, among literate and knowledgeable masses. Even then, self-government remains a fragile institution that is easily destroyed. After more than 200 years, the people of the United States have not yet demonstrated that they can continue to operate successfully under such a system. No representative government in England or America has yet endured the test of time through many centuries. Prior to the Roman Empire, the Roman Republic lasted 450 years before the Romans granted all power to a dictator.

History declares that the United States has based its foreign policy toward Third World nations on wishful thinking. The basic premise is at odds with the lessons of experience. Representative government must start small, as from a seed, and grow. The people themselves must want it with sufficient earnestness to pursue a course of learning. They must desire unity and cooperation. In 1861-1865, Americans fought a costly war to learn this truth. The people must agree to subordinate their tribal, religious, and regional jealousies to the greater cause of unity. Proof of this truth can be observed in the republics of the former USSR and all the Third World nations that have gained independence in the past 50 years. The failure of representative government in all these countries was foreseeable. American efforts to save democratic government in these areas are hopeless. The only significant help is to give them knowledge. People can use their influence to see that leaders who take control seriously commit their government to informing the masses and ultimately developing individual freedom. Experience shows that rushing the unfolding of history jeopardizes the interests of the individual. Successful self-government requires experience gained over years.

It remains to be seen whether the United States itself will succeed for another 200 years as a nation of free people. Unless public opinion reverses itself and demands that governmental policies conform to the science of praxeology, the next 200 years could easily witness an end to this great experiment in government of, by, and for the people. In turn, until citizens and leaders understand better the laws of human relations, American influence on other countries will be negative.

The Colonies Try Socialism

Even such a comprehensive work as *The American Heritage History of the Thirteen Colonies* (edited by Ralph K. Andrist, 1967) neglects some important aspects of early Colonial experiences. For present generations perhaps the most important of these experiences involved the Jamestown Colony in Virginia and the Plymouth Colony in Massachusetts. Each colony nearly failed because of famine and for a common reason: they adopted a socialistic form of organization.

In the spring of 1610, the colonists of Jamestown who had survived the preceding winter — perhaps 60 of more than 500 — abandoned their colony. Aboard ship bound for England but still in the harbor, they met three other ships bringing new colonists and supplies. This chance meeting saved the young colony. Among members of the Virginia colony, that previous winter was known for generations as "the starving time."

Why would men starve in a land filled with wild game and other food available for the harvesting, on a soil exceedingly rich for cultivation, and bordered by waters filled with fish? Historians frequently declare that they starved because the male members of the colony at Jamestown were gentlemen, sons of English lords and gentry, who were not accustomed to work. Perhaps this is true, but under the military rule of Captain John Smith they had survived. Furthermore, even a gentleman who has never used an ax or a hoe, left alone in a land of plenty, will exert considerable resource when he realizes that his survival depends entirely on his own efforts.

A more reasonable explanation lies in the nature of the colony's laws, which forbade colonists to produce for their own use. The Virginia Company required colonists to place all produce in common store. From this stock the Governor issued supplies to each colonist as needed. This is the core characteristic of socialism and communism: every member works according to his ability and receives according to his needs. The director, not the individual, determines both the citizen's ability and his needs.

Experiences before leaving England suggested socialism to the colonists. Men transmit their ideas, customs, and prejudices more by daily contact than through formal education. People play together; they meet at the market and discuss the events of the moment; youngsters ask questions of their elders and discuss the answers among themselves. Person-to-person contact implanted concepts in the minds of the individuals who migrated to America. They imported a preference for communism even though they had never tried it. They chose communal ownership as a means of avoiding the evils they wanted to leave behind. The masses perceived the rigid class structure in England, with its private property rights, to be their greatest barrier to freedom and wealth.

In the early 17th century, English society separated its citizens into distinct classes, forming a rigid socioeconomic structure, enforced not only by ideology but by the State. The king, members of his court, and all great landowners — archbishops and bishops of the church, earls, dukes, and princes — were at the top. The church owned wealth in land that rivaled that of the king and his noblemen. These landowners had acquired their holdings through force of arms. Even the church had obtained much of its land by what would today be considered confiscation.

The rules of the governing institutions supported this condition. Officials of the ecclesiastical courts, as accuser, judge, and jury, levied fines on the citizens for acts of sin. The tithe, ten percent of the produce on the land, went to the church by law, enforced by the government. At death, the church took possession of the deceased person's property and took its ten percent before releasing the property to the heirs. Noblemen and the king, as landowners, received a share of all produce from their holdings, either a third or a half. The king assessed taxes on everyone: commoners, gentry, craftsmen, merchants, noblemen, and the church. Owning land meant access to income.

The parish priests, the merchants, the craftsmen, and the gentry constituted a small middle class below these lords. Although not of the nobility, the gentry owned tracts of land, usually quite small. Few in number, the merchants and craftsmen managed a decent living; some saved enough to buy land and become gentry.

Below the gentry and parish priests, below the merchants and craftsmen, at the base of the socioeconomic structure were the commoners, the great mass of people. They owned no land but held a right of "commons" — the right to grow vegetables and grain on the cultivable acreage held in common; to tend sheep, swine, and cattle on the common pastures; and to hunt small game and cut wood for their fires in the common forests. These peasants tilled the lands of their lord and tended his livestock.

Beyond the jurisdiction of law lived the outcast — the beggar, the thief, the highwayman. This group included many second-born males who had lost their inheritance. The first-born male alone inherited the right of commons among the commoners, the land of the gentry, the title and the land of the nobleman.

The economies of England and Europe were based on agriculture. Wealth came from the land. Industry, as we know it, did not exist. For the vast majority, the mere ability to exist depended on access to the use of land. The story of the Colonies in America is the story of the struggles of the gentry, the commoners, and the outcasts to break out of this rigid class structure and achieve respectability, freedom, and a better life, both material and ideal.

Remembering that land ownership had for the most part been accomplished by confiscation, the commoners opposed private ownership of land. To them, private property meant thievery and usurpation by the lords and the church. So commoners wanted to prohibit private property and produce in any society of their making. They turned from oppression by landowners to the only alternate institution they knew, the "commons," the land they all shared. Communism is the institution they brought with them to Jamestown, Virginia, in 1607 and to Plymouth, Massachusetts, in 1620.

Fortunately for later generations, in that region of fertile soil, these colonies of good and virtuous men tried socialism. The result is instructive.

Under the leadership of Captain John Smith, the colonists at Jamestown marched to the fields in step to the beat of a drum. There they labored under his close supervision. In 1607 and 1608 the colony survived by reason of this military discipline. In the spring of 1609, Captain Smith returned to England, leaving the colonists to their own devices. Neglected fields produced that year a harvest insufficient to carry the colony through the winter. Over four-fifths of the people perished during the winter, some from disease but most from starvation. Some authorities report that one man killed his wife and ate her. Of course, the other colonists viewed this action with disfavor, and promptly saw to his execution.

The Pilgrims at Plymouth were organized as a commune identical to that at Jamestown. During the winters of 1621 and 1622, they suffered from insufficient food, but death by starvation never reached the extent experienced in Jamestown in 1610.

Both colonies embraced the same solution to famine. The Governor assigned to each colonist a portion of land to cultivate for his own use. The colonists recognized the right of private property, with favorable results in both colonies. Never again did they starve.

The experiences of the Plymouth colonists are documented in the words of their Governor, William Bradford:

[In the spring of 1623, after two years of insufficient food production while organized as a commune,] *they began to consider how to raise more corn, and obtain a better crop than they had done, so that they might not continue to endure the misery of want. At length after much debate, the Governor . . . allowed each man to plant corn for his own household, and to trust to themselves for that; in all other things to go on in the general way as before. So every family was assigned a parcel of land, according to the proportion of their number with that in view, — for present purposes only, and making no division for inheritance, — all boys and children being included under some family. This was very successful. It made all hands very industrious, so that much more corn was planted than otherwise would have been . . . and gave far better satisfaction. The women now went willingly into the field, and took their little ones with them to plant corn, while before they would allege weakness and inability; and to have compelled them would have been thought great tyranny and oppression.*

The failure of this experiment of communal service, which was tried . . . by good and honest men proves the emptiness of the theory of Plato and other ancients, applauded by some of later times, — that the taking away of private property, and the possession of it in community, by a commonwealth, would make a state happy and flourishing. . . . For in this instance, community of property (so far as it went) was found to breed much confusion and discontent, and retard much employment which would have been to the general benefit and comfort. For the young men who were most able and fit for service objected to being forced to spend their time and strength in working for other men's wives and children, without any recompense. The strong man or the resourceful man had no more share of food, clothes, etc., than the weak man who was not able to do a quarter the other could. This was thought injustice. The aged and graver men, who were ranked and equalized in labour, food, clothes, etc., with the humbler and younger ones, thought it some indignity and disrespect to them. As for men's wives who were obliged to do service for other men, such as cooking, washing their clothes, etc., they considered it a kind of slavery, and many husbands would not brook it. This feature of it would have been worse still, if they had been men of an inferior class. . . .

Let none argue that this is due to human failing, rather than to this communistic plan of life in itself. I answer, seeing that all men have this failing in them, that God in His wisdom saw that another plan of life was fitter for them. (Bradford [1909] 1920. 115-116)

. . . The effect of their particular planting was well seen, for all had, one way or another, pretty well to bring the year about, and some of the abler sort and more industrious had to spare, and sell to others, — in fact, no general want or famine has been amongst them since. (Ibid. 125)

Pertaining to the year 1624, Bradford wrote:

I must say a word about their planting this year. They felt the benefit of their last year's harvest; for by planting corn on their own account they managed . . . to overcome famine. This reminds me of a saying of Seneca's . . . that an important part of liberty is a well-governed belly. . . .

The settlers now began to consider corn more precious than silver; and those that had some to spare began to trade with the others for small things . . . for they had no money, and if they had, corn was preferred to it. In order that they might raise their crops to better advantage, they made suit to the Governor to have some land apportioned for permanent holdings, and not

> *by yearly lot, whereby the plots which the more industrious had*
> *brought under good culture one year, would change hands the*
> *next, and other would reap the advantage; with the result that*
> *the manuring and culture of the land were neglected. It was well*
> *considered, and their request was granted. Every person was*
> *given one acre of land, for them and theirs. (Ibid.* 141-142)

This failure of a society organized according to the principles of social-ism demonstrates perhaps the most important historical lesson to come from the Colonial period. Under socialism each individual realizes small gain from his own efforts, yet he bears the whole cost through the loss of his leisure. Also, if he does no work, he gains completely through the benefits of his leisure and suffers but a small loss by reason of the portion that he fails to produce. As demonstrated both in Jamestown and in Ply-mouth, however, socialism results in disaster. In a socialist environment the forces of the Law of the Present and the Law of Disutility of Labor cause most men to perform little work and produce next to nothing. Even the threat of starvation provides insufficient incentive to work when the individual does not receive the fruits of his own labor.

As the touching story of the First Thanksgiving is read — with feasting and games for three days the colonists at Plymouth entertained the Indian chief Massasoit and 90 of his braves, it is well to keep in mind that this celebration took place in the fall of 1623. William Bradford, Governor of the colony, in his history of Plymouth Colony makes no mention of this celebration. He does fix 1623 as the year when land was assigned to indi-vidual colonists for cultivation with full ownership rights to the produce. *The American Heritage History of the Thirteen Colonies* (page 41) quotes from a letter the colonist Edward Winslow wrote to a friend in England; the celebration is described much as it appears in most history texts. Winslow speaks of the event as having just occurred, and his letter is dated 1623. This First Thanksgiving is more likely to have occurred in 1623 than in either of the preceding two years. The settlers at Plymouth had reason to celebrate that year and not before. By changing to a system of private property and free enterprise, the colony had concluded a bountiful harvest, their first since arriving.

Thanksgiving should be an annual reminder that Americans twice tried socialism and failed, that free enterprise succeeded and saved the colonists from starvation, and that the surest way to destroy the bounty in America is to abandon free enterprise and the protection of private property. Whenever the suggestion arises that government should operate some enterprise under the system of ownership in common, the experiences of the colonists at Jamestown and at Plymouth should be remembered.

Conflict with the Indians Did Not End

Peace with France in Europe did not end the Indian phase of the French and Indian Wars. No longer opposed by the French, the colonists felt no restriction against settling west of the Appalachians. Immigrants, arriving by the thousands, sought land. They cleared the forest and built villages. They hunted the wild game wherever they settled. Many negotiated no agreement with Indians accustomed to hunting that same land, and the natives considered those frontier settlers to be squatters.

The Indian tribes being squeezed out of their traditional hunting grounds quite naturally resented this invasion. They handled the matter as they had always handled encroachment by other tribes; color of skin made no difference. Indian war parties attacked frontier settlements to drive the intruders from their hunting grounds. They killed women and children as well as men. This was their way, but to Europeans such behavior was outrageous. In Europe, soldiers never disturbed noncombatants and their homes. That was the way of war in civilized countries. Wars were fights between kings; they did not concern the people. Consequently, Europeans in America considered Indians to be uncivilized savages. But due to the Law of Disagreement, the squatting settlers never once thought of themselves as thieves.

Some historians indicate that the English king and his Parliament understood the situation better than the settlers did. In October 1763 King George issued a proclamation forbidding settlement west of the Appalachians. Only men involved in the fur trade with the natives could cross these hills. But one British cabinet minister revealed the king's true thinking. He stated that colonists would be more useful to the mother country if kept close to the seaboard, instead of located in the heart of America out of the reach of government. The difficulty of procuring European commodities might compel them to commerce and manufacture "to the infinite prejudice of Britain." (Morison 1965. 183)

This attempt to control met with the same lack of success as had all earlier measures that were intended to restrict the settlers. To many immigrants on the frontier, especially to those not English citizens by birth,

English law meant little unless the enforcer wore a red coat, was supported by better arms, and came in greater numbers. Colonial governments had little desire to enforce this ban on Westward migration. Most colonists felt that the Westward advance of the frontier removed them ever farther from possible confrontation with the savages. Frontier settlers wanted land, and the established colonists happily encouraged them to take it from the natives.

The fundamental Law of Might prevailed. The white-man's tribe proved stronger than the tribes of Indians. Conflict between them did not end until the white man reduced the number of Indians to insignificance.

When it served the interests of the English monarch and the colonists, they treated Indian tribes as English citizens. When it was otherwise convenient, the Indians became "those savages." English law protected the Iroquois as English subjects. Throughout their wars with the French, the English and the colonists encouraged Iroquois leaders to participate in decision making with regard to operations within the region of their tribal lands. Later, during the conflict between colonists and Parliament, colonists never consulted the Iroquois. At least no record remains of such cooperation at the level of command.

As pioneers moved West, some settlers and Indians negotiated terms of peaceful coexistence. But settlers made no offers to make peace on the basis of unity of government with equality of rights. Development followed the lines of negotiations between independent nations in conflict over possession of the same land. The new nation to be called The United States of America was not organized with the Iroquois or any other Indian group as equal, participating members. The nation became a union exclusively of 13 English Colonies. Only once did the invaders consider accepting Indians in their government as equals. A proposal surfaced to make a state of an area then inhabited solely by Indians. The Americans, however, gave such talk no serious consideration.

In the United States today, pockets of free Indians still remain. They are free within the confines of the area that the U.S. government has reserved. Those few Western tribes that showed the least resistance to encroachment by the white man have larger areas set aside for their use, in particular the Shoshone tribe of central Wyoming. But what has happened to the friendliest of the Indians, the Iroquois Alliance of the Six Nations? The immigrant white men own their tribal lands. Their people have gone. Most of their descendants live in Canada.

Generations now living and those to follow need to address this situation. People familiar with the facts agree on only one thing, that present conditions among the Indians are deplorable. Disagreement exists over what to do about it. The cause of the Indian differs little from that of the blacks, the Hispanics, and the Orientals in America. The Indian may one day become again an American, and share with all the privileges and responsibilities attendant with citizenship in a great country. Whatever men decide, may they let the free individual choose.

The Original 13 Colonies	Date Established
Virginia	1607
Massachusetts*	1620
(Includes both Plymouth Colony and Maine)	
New Hampshire	1623
Maryland	1634
Connecticut	1635
Rhode Island	1636
North Carolina**	1653
New York (Dutch 1613-1664)	1664
New Jersey	1664
South Carolina**	1670
Pennsylvania	1681
Delaware (Swedish 1638-1682)	1682
Georgia	1733

*Plymouth Colony was formed under a charter separate from the colony of Massachusetts and later absorbed.

**The Carolinas were formed under one charter. They were informally separated in 1661.

The American Revolution presents a good view of contrasts arising from different philosophies of government. Quality of leadership in Great Britain deteriorated because of the absence of opportunity among its people. At the same time, the Colonies grew strong through the positive force flowing from individual liberty.

Chapter 3

The Colonies Rebel, 1764-1783

Conditions Leading to Rebellion

AT THE CONCLUSION OF THE French and Indian Wars, the Colonies experienced the business slump that generally follows war, the economic adjustment forced on governments by their method of financing war. Prices fell; competition in trade returned. The business boom, induced by credit expansion based on fiat money (see page 91), became a business bust as Great Britain turned to retiring debt. As with all booms created by credit expansion, the end of that expansion brings on an adjustment known as "recession." Consumer demand created by credit expansion cannot last. Eventually banks can no longer expand credit and maintain their liquidity. Often they cannot maintain even the then-existing level of credit. The period of adjustment is necessary in order to prevent destruction of the monetary system. In the experiences of the United States, this boom-bust cycle has happened again and again.

Into this atmosphere of hard times, King George III and his Parliament, heavily in debt, assessed taxes on the Colonies to raise funds for debt retirement. Although the Molasses Act of 1764 reduced the levy under the existing Sugar Tax, George III made it clear the tax would be collected. By wholesale smuggling, colonists had previously avoided this tax, which if enforced disrupted profits from their trade in rum made out of molasses from the West Indies. The Stamp Tax, enacted in 1765, required all legal documents — some 50 items in all, including newspapers, bills of lading, diplomas, playing cards, marriage licenses — to be executed on specially stamped and taxed paper. In 1767 the Townshend Acts imposed a levy on trade in glass, white lead, paper, and tea. Every tax imposed a heavy financial burden on some group of merchants. These merchants stirred up resistance on grounds of principle, that no tax could be just when imposed by foreign authority. Colonists delayed payments, and some even refused to obey. Parliament revoked each in turn only to replace it with another.

Every act of government creates change, and change always benefits some individuals more than others. Those directly affected by the change realize their position and become vocal for or against the measure. The great majority, who seldom see the benefits or the damage, remain unorganized and seldom heard. It was so in the 1770s. When an act of Parliament adversely affected some group of colonists, that group worked to arouse a constituency in opposition. In 1773 the British ministry tried to save the British East India Company from financial ruin by granting it a monopoly on tea. Colonial tea merchants, confronted with financial disaster because of this enactment, stirred up local opposition. In the South they stored the Company's tea in damp warehouses, where it spoiled. In New York, colonists did not permit ships carrying tea to dock and unload. In Boston, they dumped the tea casks overboard.

In the atmosphere of that decade after the French and Indian War, colonists gradually became suspicious of every act of Parliament that affected their affairs. It matters little whether King George III, his Cabinet, or Parliament initiated the efforts to tax and regulate the Colonies. Hindsight clearly shows the poor judgment in using Parliament as the instrument. It is difficult to imagine how the colonists could have been approached in a more offensive manner. They quarreled not so much with the monetary burden of the tax as with the principle of being taxed by an outside authority. In 1764 they might have accepted an order by their king requiring them to tax themselves to help retire the debt, but they rejected taxation by Parliament.

When the colonists openly resisted Parliament's actions, George III insisted that his government punish them. He designed acts of Parliament that would subdue the upstart colonists. The resolution accompanying the repeal of the Townshend Acts (1768) declared that Parliament did have the authority to tax the Colonies; and, to emphasize the declaration, the measure retained a tax on tea. The Quartering Act of 1774 essentially empowered British military commanders to seize such buildings as might be useful to troops present in the Colonies — troops not there to protect the colonists but to enforce Parliament's unpopular measures. The series of Intolerable Acts of 1774 dissolved the Massachusetts Assembly and closed Boston harbor.

George III, through his ministers in Parliament, dictated these actions. By the time the colonists adopted their Declaration of Independence on July 4, 1776, they no longer doubted who was responsible. That document identified King George III as the tyrant, as the source of all evil doings by the mother country. The Declaration lists in detail all their grievances, following this statement:

> *The history of the present King of Great Britain is a history of repeated injuries and usurpations, all having in direct object the establishment of an absolute tyranny over these states. To prove this, let facts be submitted to a candid world.*

As yet peaceful, this struggle forged a unity among the colonists. They had not united during the conflict with the French; they did not view the French as a threat to liberty. But when Parliament sent soldiers to America to enforce the new revenue and regulatory measures, the threat to the colonists' freedom and self-government became too real to be ignored. They resorted to war, not to gain their freedom but to preserve it.

King George III

Society always has those who tolerate no opinions that conflict with their own. When in positions of authority, such persons select subordinates who agree with them. In accordance with the Laws of Responsibility and of Blame Avoidance, only individuals with little leadership ability accept subordinate positions as "yes men." The success of activities undertaken by such leaders depends on the abilities of the one person at the top.

King George III was such a leader; he tolerated no independent thinking by his subordinates. He believed completely in his own abilities to govern. In his view, Parliament should neither think nor act independently but should implement only his ideas. When he became king in 1760, he took control of Parliament and installed ministers of his own choosing. His cabinet and the leaders in Parliament were "yes men." He effectively eliminated from his cabinet "every particle of independence, and of wisdom." (Trevelyan [1899] 1964. 89)

Because King George had thus separated himself from the counsel of wise and independently thinking subordinates, his reign suffered the limitations inherent in his abilities; and George III was not a particularly capable man. Surrounded by the incompetents of his own choosing, he led Great Britain into a period of floundering. Though it survived his rule, the Empire suffered major losses. Perhaps the greatest loss came with the revolt of the Colonies in America.

The root cause of the American War of Independence lay in the character of the British king. Even as late as 1776, representatives to the Continental Congress spoke of the evil doings by Parliament, while in the same breath reasserting their strong allegiance to their king. The acts of Parliament that the Colonies resisted, however, were measures dictated by George III. He not only initiated war, he wanted war with the Colonies. On receiving the resolutions adopted by the first Continental Congress, he openly declared that he considered the New England governments to be in a state of rebellion, that blows must decide whether they were to be subject to his rule or independent. When he learned that the quarrel could not be patched up, he made no attempt to conceal his satisfaction. As early as 1775, more than a year before delegates of the Colonies declared their independence, George had committed himself to war with his American Colonies. His actions have been interpreted as clearly forcing their rebellion.

At the execution of Britain's King Charles I in 1649, Parliament had taken control of government. After the period of the Commonwealth and return of the monarchy under Charles II in 1660, the monarchs from

Charles II to George II more or less acquiesced to this condition. When George III ascended the throne, however, tradition has it that his mother said, "George, be king," and "George did his best to obey." (Churchill 1957. 163) To his contemporaries in Europe and to many in Britain, King George's intent was poorly concealed. He had become king in a land where the people had greatly limited the king's power. He intended to restore the power to that office. In the opinion of Frederic the Great of Prussia:

> *If . . .* [British citizens] *allowed the Sovereign to act according to his good pleasure, and abandoned the Colonies to the lot which he destined for them, that lot would sooner or later be shared by England.* (Trevelyan [1899] 1964. 206)

Possibly for that very reason the war was unpopular with many Britons — army officers, merchants, and middle- and lower-class citizens. In the end, British public opinion, not Colonial military victories, ended the war. In 1782 the British people deliberately abandoned the attempt to reconquer America; to them it was both wrong and foolish. There remains little doubt that King George III brought on and lost the American War of Independence.

Freedom Develops Leaders

While George III was ridding his government of capable leaders, natural selection under freedom in the Colonies brought the most capable men to the fore. These leaders aroused Americans to the developing dangers. No royal coercion silenced Sam Adams in Boston, John Dickenson in Pennsylvania, and Patrick Henry in Virginia. When the Massachusetts Assembly in 1774 urged all colonies to send delegations to Philadelphia, men of ability responded. John Adams, Richard Henry Lee, Thomas Jefferson, John Jay, Benjamin Harrison, Thomas Lynch, and George Washington joined Dickenson, Henry, Sam Adams, and others. In all, 56 men met in Carpenters' Hall on that late summer day to deliberate the resolution:

> *A Congress should be appointed . . . from all the colonies to concert a general and uniform plan for the defense and preservation of our common rights and continuing the connection and*

> *dependence of said colonies upon Great Britain under a just,*
> *permanent and constitutional form of government.*

Talk of independence did not appear in the deliberations of that body until 1776.

Of course, any list of great leaders from this period should include the remarkable Benjamin Franklin, who as an agent for Pennsylvania had spent 14 of the last 17 years in London pleading the cause of the colonists. Along with John Adams and John Jay, he served also at the Paris conference in 1783 to negotiate the terms of peace.

It has been suggested that the Colonies were fortunate to have such a great body of capable leaders at the time of revolution, as if this were a mere happenstance. At that same time, Great Britain had an adequate number of leaders quite capable and experienced in the affairs of state, but the character of George III completely emasculated their effectiveness in the conduct of government. In his analysis of the American Revolution, George Trevelyan had this to say about Britain's leaders:

> *Second-rate and third-rate place-holders now trifled with the*
> *welfare and honor of the country; while their betters were inex-*
> *orably excluded from office because they were unacceptable to*
> *the King. Patriots and statesmen like Edmund Burke, Lord*
> *Camden, and Sir George Savile, were left unemployed; and*
> *England was governed by such sinister or paltry figures as*
> *Sandwich and Rigby, Lord Weymouth and Lord George Ger-*
> *main.* (Trevelyan [1899] 1964. 298)

No, luck played no part in placing the affairs of the Colonies in the hands of capable leaders while incompetents handled affairs for the mother country. This is the great strength of a nation ruled by government that supports individual freedom; the country's greatest resource is not stifled and wasted as happened in Britain under George III.

Not all the great leaders of a period serve as direct representatives of the people, as these 56 did. Many serve as businessmen, farmers, and professionals because the resources of the land must be properly utilized for the support of the nation. An individual may set himself before his fellowmen as a merchant, lawyer, grocer, farmer, or teacher; but he remains in this position only as long as his fellow citizens keep him there by seeking his services or buying his wares. In a society not shackled by government, those who by performance demonstrate their superior ability are the ones most often chosen to lead. When left free to choose, men select leaders from men who have distinguished themselves in some commercial or intellectual service.

This moment in history (1764-1783) is not unique in exemplifying the operation of this law of human relations. It merely illustrates the results more dramatically. The American Revolution presents a good view of contrasts arising from different philosophies of government. Quality of leadership in Great Britain deteriorated because of the absence of opportunity among its people. At the same time, the Colonies grew strong through the positive force flowing from individual liberty. This force brought capable men into leadership in the Colonies. It always works that way.

Militarily Speaking

The American War of Independence contributed little new to military science. In the early phases of the war, commanders on both sides lacked knowledge of military science or competence or both. Certainly the troops carrying the fight lacked training. Victory in battle often went to the side that made fewer mistakes. Seldom did the combined forces in any one battle number as many as 30,000 troops. This war represents six years of posturing, skirmishing, suffering from exposure and starvation, and missed British opportunities to deliver a decisive blow to the weak Colonial forces. As in most wars, however, the quality of leadership ultimately determined the outcome. The British were led by George III, a simpleminded, frustrated dictator, sided by his chosen Secretary of State for the Colonies, Lord George Germain. K. B. Smellie's observation about the king is revealing:

> At every level the tension between the deference owed to birth . . . and the challenge of natural ability was very great. . . . The simple-minded George III was driven to madness by the effort involved in accommodating himself to the problems presented by the genius of a Chatham and a Pitt and the pretensions of a Rockingham, a Bedford, and a North. (Smellie 1962. 86)

Germain was the leader who had showed himself militarily incompetent when in command against the French at Minden. As Bruce Lancaster points out:

> *It will be remembered that Germain had cost the British a crushing victory at Minden when, in a state of utter funk, he would not turn his cavalry loose on the beaten French.* (Lancaster 1955. 260)

This same Lord Germain sent General John Burgoyne on his mission out of Canada to execute a pincers movement in cooperation with General William Howe, but neglected to inform Howe of his part in the operation. Germain also left General Howe in charge of military operations in the Colonies long after Howe had wasted numerous opportunities to confront and possibly defeat the Colonial forces under General Washington.

The British naval commander Sir Peter Parker took the combined navy to Charleston, South Carolina, and stayed at anchor without action for weeks. During this delay, his troops became weakened by the heat, inadequate sanitation, and poor food and water aboard ship. The delay gave the colonists time to complete their fortifications and emplace their shore defense guns. When Parker did commit his troops, he landed them in an area where they could not operate to confront the enemy. He then sailed his fleet into the very face of the shore batteries, suffering heavy losses without inflicting any counter damage to the Colonial defenses. Poor military judgment and insufficient intelligence about the field of operations defeated Parker. Of even greater import, Parker's attack on Charleston alienated many loyal residents of that community. Until that attack, South Carolinians had strongly supported the king. The attack gained nothing militarily; yet it solidified unity among the Colonies.

When General Sir Henry Clinton relieved Howe in command of the British forces, he immediately withdrew from Philadelphia to New York and remained there, inactive, for the last three years of the war. Clinton's lack of aggressive action left General Washington free to employ his combined forces against the smaller British force under command of Lord Charles Cornwallis at Yorktown, Virginia.

A virtual void of positive direction from the top, from the king and his ministers, left the whole affair adrift. Of the five field commanders Great Britain employed in America — Gage, Burgoyne, Howe, Clinton, and

Cornwallis — only Cornwallis aggressively pursued the Colonials in that war.

About Colonial Leaders

At the outbreak of war, the colonists had two men with a fair amount of formal military training, Horatio Gates and Charles Lee. Both proved to be inadequate to high-level command. Convinced of the invincibility of the British, Lee at Monmouth Court House in June 1778 ordered a retreat from British troops who had already been defeated.

Even though General Washington objected, Congress sent Gates to command the New York operations against Burgoyne. By the time Gates arrived, the Colonial forces had already commenced their operation against the two British columns moving south through New York. Although Gates never took the field, he issued enough orders so that he could claim all honor and glory if Burgoyne was defeated, and he could separate himself completely from all responsibility if the Colonial forces failed. Burgoyne lost at Saratoga to a better-led army of colonists under the command of Benedict Arnold, and Gates received credit that he had not earned. It is interesting to ask: Had General Arnold then received the recognition he deserved, might he have been forestalled from his subsequent act of betrayal? Later, in 1780, when in command and on his own against Cornwallis at Camden, South Carolina, Gates failed.

When Congress permitted General Washington to remove from command these two senior military incompetents, he placed proven leaders in charge. Men who had learned the art of combat in action then led the Colonial army. Washington could count on such men as Nathaniel Greene, Anthony Wayne, Francis Marion, Daniel Morgan, John Sullivan, John Glover, Alexander Hamilton, Wade Hampton, William Washington, William Henderson, John Laurens, and Henry Knox. They had been with Washington through those frustrating years of learning. By the time Washington confronted Cornwallis, he had capable, experienced subordinates and an army trained to the standards ordered by the German officer Baron von Steuben.

The failure of British generals to move aggressively gave the colonists time to develop an army adequate to the task. Given the time and opportunity, free men always develop capable leaders whenever conditions demand.

Washington's inability to place a strong force in the field at an earlier moment can be attributed to (1) the restrictions imposed on his command by Congress, forcing on his service the two incompetents Gates and Lee; (2) the limited term of enlistment for his troops — one year, and (3) the lack of experienced subordinate officers. In the beginning, Washington himself, though a proven leader of men, had only limited military training and experience in war. He made mistakes in command. He devised plans of operation improper for the combat conditions of the moment. But because of his intelligence and his dedication to the cause, he did learn. When Congress finally gave him a free hand in the conduct of the war — to enlist men for service to the end of the war, to advance officers to such command and rank as he saw fit, to requisition supplies wherever they might be found — Washington was ready. He built a well-trained army, he had capable subordinates, and he used them wisely. This typifies the experiences of free men. It never happens that way under a dictatorial bureaucracy.

Britain's War Was a Loser from the Start

King George's handling of the war virtually assured success to the Colonies. Bungling caused by his incapable subordinates cost Great Britain in loss of troops and heavy expenditure of wealth. For example, King George's Secretary of State for the Colonies, Lord Germain, personally ordered the action from Quebec into New York that ended with the surrender of General Burgoyne and what remained of his army. Some historians classify this action as one of 15 decisive actions of the War of Independence. The details of Burgoyne's campaign demonstrate the impossibility of success from the outset because of the specifics of Germain's orders, or lack of orders, coupled with the low level of competence in the man selected by Germain to lead the campaign, General John Burgoyne. Bruce Lancaster makes an enlightening observation when he states that it was Burgoyne's "conviction that high command should have 'no damned nonsense about merit attached to it.'" (Lancaster 1955. 264)

In a military action, the commander-in-chief, his financial supporters, and the field commander should all thoroughly understand and strive to achieve common objectives. These common objectives should be reasonably achievable, and the military minds involved should understand what it takes to achieve them.

The objectives for Britain in the American War of Independence were virtually impossible to attain. For success, the British needed (1) to destroy entirely the effectiveness of the Colonial leaders and all military resistance, (2) to install a new Colonial government, and (3) to occupy the region with a policing force large enough to ensure the people's continued compliance with the laws enacted by Parliament. Considering the geography of America, the temperament of the colonists, and the economic costs and benefits to be attained, the affair would not have become cost effective for many years, if ever. If at the start George III had committed the full resources at his command, he no doubt could have achieved a military victory. The effort, however, would most likely have pauperized his government. Great Britain would have been left too weak to confront the forces of Holland, Spain, and France when they entered the fray. Great Britain would have been destroyed as a world power even if the forces of George III had succeeded in capturing General George Washington and all delegates to the Continental Congress, and in taking possession of all the major ports and cities of the British Colonies. Even in the affairs of government, the ability to pay must always be considered. Even with full control of the money supply, no government has as yet successfully overcome the need to consider costs when determining its actions.

British leaders never adequately assessed their objectives in the American War of Independence and what those objectives required. Consequently, British commanders in the field had no clearly defined goal. Gage, Howe, Clinton, and Cornwallis acted independently, each as he saw his task. When one of them did develop some concept of his military objective, his contemporaries failed to cooperate. Howe did not cooperate with Burgoyne; Clinton remained in New York while Cornwallis became trapped in Yorktown.

This lack of clear objectives virtually assured failure because it led to stalemate. Lincoln learned this military lesson while conducting the War Between the States, a lesson that evaded the High Command for the Confederacy in the same war. In that conflict, the Confederacy won most of the early battles but in the end lost the war. In the War of Independence, the forces of the Colonies lost nearly every battle but won victory for their cause. British commanders would repeatedly defeat the Colonial army, retire from the field, and celebrate. They never followed through to destroy the Colonial army and perhaps capture their field commander. Any hope for British success required that they destroy or capture military leadership in the Colonies, at least Generals Washington and Greene.

Similarly, lack of a clear, achievable objective led to stalemate in Korea in the 1950s and in Vietnam the next decade. General Douglas MacArthur understood this and tried to redirect the effort of his command in Korea. President Harry S. Truman removed him from command when MacArthur went to the people with their disagreement over this matter. For the British in the Colonies, for the Confederates in the War Between the States, for the Americans in Korea and Vietnam, stalemate was the same as defeat.

In the end, British forces gained a qualified commander, Cornwallis, but his military position was no better than that of his predecessors. His supply line lay over 3,000 miles of ocean. He operated among unfriendly civilians and on unfamiliar ground. The land occupied by his opposition stretched along 1,000 miles of seacoast. The interior was heavily forested and thinly settled. Even though at one time or another the British did occupy all the major population centers, these successes scarcely dented the strength of resistance among the colonists. Cornwallis operated under the no-win, lack-of-direction policies of George III. His field success could lead only to a stalemate. Success for the British had to involve a complete destruction of the colonists' will to continue the struggle. Because of the Britons' unawareness of this objective and what it would require, and because of the high cost for them to pursue military action against such odds, time favored the Colonies.

Men should have learned of the difficulty, nay, hopelessness, of waging war under such conditions. Some U.S. military men did learn, and they have repeatedly spoken out, for example, against U.S. military involvement in Asia. Yet, acting either in ignorance of historical lessons or under the influence of unwarranted arrogance, Presidents Truman, Kennedy, and Johnson sent American troops to Asian soil to fight wars in Korea and Vietnam that could not be won.

Mercantilism

At this point in the narrative of American history, many textbooks discuss *mercantilism*. It would be of little consequence to people today except that this set of false economic doctrines still influences foreign and monetary policies in the United States. Political circles engage in much public hand-wringing over such matters; so attention should be directed to these 17th-century government policies.

Before 18th-century economists began to teach the benefits of freedom, the economic doctrines of kings guided government policies. Monarchs believed that their fortunes prospered by the amount of trade they controlled. Accordingly, they enacted laws forbidding their subjects to do business directly with parties outside the kingdom. All shipping, especially what originated beyond the national boundaries, had to be carried on national ships. Even when the cargo was destined for another foreign port, it had to clear through a national port so the king could tax the goods. Preferably, raw materials had to be shipped to his kingdom, where the treasury could tax finished goods processed from these materials. The monarch strove to maximize the excess of exports over imports in order to cause a net inflow of gold and silver into the royal treasury. As a group, these policies have been labeled "mercantilism."

Even after economists demonstrated that these policies retarded economic development and that free trade maximized the wealth of a nation, kings persisted in mercantilist controls. The king rightly observed that even if free trade did enrich the kingdom as a whole, he lost control of the individuals who would benefit. Wealth in the hands of free people was not nearly so easily appropriated as wealth directly in the hands of his treasury.

Mercantilism suited kings, not the people. It worked to the benefit of heads of state, but to the detriment of individual subjects, especially those living in the Colonies. Mercantilism restricted colonists' freedom to manufacture at home and to trade freely in the most profitable markets. Because mercantilism drained gold from the Colonies, as did King George's requirement that colonists pay their taxes in gold, gold coin remained scarce in the Colonies. The physical difficulty colonists had in complying with the tax measures of George III merely added to their frustrations. Only as free men enlarged their control over government were mercantilist policies reduced.

Mercantilism infects present-day thinking. Governments in autocratic nations restrict emigration in order to prevent citizens from leaving with their wealth, which puts them beyond the reach of tax collectors. In free countries, it appears in a concern over the nation's balance of trade. Writers speak of a trade balance as favorable when exports exceed imports, and unfavorable when imports exceed exports. Monarchs warring with each other placed significance on this condition; no manufacturer of war matériel would sell to a monarch unless paid in gold or silver. When the British king fought with the French monarch, his war needs caused a drain on the royal treasury. War required an inflow of gold and silver from trade and conquest. No comparable justification for such concern remains today over the balance of trade in commodities.

The aspect of mercantilism most significant to 20th-century men lies in the economic impact of actions taken by government on the basis of trade deficit. Because people know so little about the facts and understand even less, politicians use the trade deficit as an excuse to grant special favors to constituents who give money to legislators' campaign funds and "non-profit charities." Governments seek not only to restrict imports that the citizens want to purchase, but also to manipulate interest rates, the money supply, and exchange rates of foreign currencies. Governments try to regulate foreign trade to a greater degree. Such "protectionist" laws only stifle trade and reduce the standard of living for those not subsidized by these laws. In time, business activity suffers to such an extent that everyone's living standard remains lower than it would otherwise be.

Such maneuvers would be more tolerable if a trade deficit truly harmed the people, but such is not the case. A trade deficit occurs because foreigners want dollars. They want dollars for their cash holdings in order to escape the inflation in their local money. They want dollars to invest in American enterprise. Herbert Stein, a former chairman of the President's Council of Economic Advisers, estimated that foreign investments had increased the stock of productive capital in the United States during the 1980s by over $700 billion. (Herbert Stein, "Don't Worry About the Trade Deficit," *The Wall Street Journal*, May 16, 1989.) This increase in capital has benefited American workers by increasing their efficiency, which translates into higher wages. Admittedly, American businesses pay more interest and dividends to foreigners because of this investment, but the additional capital provides the means for making this payment, while at the same time advancing U.S. labor's standard of living.

Foreigners want dollars also in order to service their debts to American creditors. They can get dollars only by selling for dollars more goods than they buy. If the United States government should succeed in balancing the dollar value of exports and imports, these debtor nations could not get the dollars they need to pay principal and interest on their dollar-denominated debts.

In the late 20th century, balance of trade has no significance. It is a statistical measure concerned with only one part of foreign exchange, the movement of physical goods. Statisticians exclude from the calculation movement of money and exchange involving services. The significant element in trade between nations is net payments in money. There will always be a balance in payments. When considering the historical significance of the balance of trade, whether favorable or unfavorable, we must recognize that governments in the 17th century were concerned about the movement of gold. When a country imported more goods than it exported, payment required that gold be shipped out of the country to offset the difference in trade. Obviously, an unfavorable balance of trade remained possible only as long as that country could continue to export gold. In the 20th century, South Africa and Russia as producers of gold can continuously conduct such a balance of trade. Russians and South Africans certainly do not consider this unfavorable. They must import more merchandise than they export in order to sell their gold.

Today the United States produces no gold for export. The ability of U.S. citizens to import more goods than they export depends on the acceptance of paper dollars by citizens in other countries. Currently an unfavorable balance of trade for the United States means only that people in other countries willingly accept paper dollars in exchange for their goods and services, for reasons set forth above.

Concern over the trade balance is founded in eagerness for, or fear of, war. In America no statistician computes a measure of trade balances for individual states. Because no war is likely between the states, whether or not Arkansas and Missouri ship in more commodities than they ship out has no significance to any citizen. The same would be true between sovereign nations if it were not for the disruptions in trade caused by wars. Differences in commodity movements between states and nations are offset and settled by transfers of money. By seeing to their own personal needs for money, individual citizens assure a region or a nation that it will never run out of money. As money becomes scarce in a particular region, consumers there reduce their purchases and increase their sales. An imbalance in payments never persists. During a given time interval, people of a country may purchase from foreigners more goods than they sell to foreigners. They cannot forever continue to do this unless the outflow of gold or domestic money (1) is offset by local production of gold, as in South Africa, or (2) returns to that country through transactions of another nature, as occurs in the United States with debt service to American creditors and with foreign investment. Payments of money restore a balance. Left alone, an imbalance in trade on commodities sets in motion forces that control the situation.

The Indian and the American Revolution

The Indians became the big losers in the quarrel between King George III and his American Colonies. The Six Nations of the Iroquois had consistently remained loyal to Great Britain throughout the long struggle with the French. When the colonists and the redcoats went to war, the Iroquois Confederation remained loyal to Great Britain. They tried to stay neutral, but many colonists, especially those along the frontier, had the attitude that "if you are not with me, you are against me." The war simply furnished an excuse for Indians and colonists alike to give vent to old grievances. Small war parties of Indians attacked and killed isolated farm families of colonists. Colonists attacked and killed peaceful Indian hunting parties.

On his campaign from Quebec down the Hudson River valley, General Burgoyne employed Indians, as the French had done in the earlier wars. This stirred resentment among the colonists against all Indians. Many colonists did not differentiate between one Indian tribe and another. All "savages" were alike to them. This narrow attitude among Americans still exists today toward all minorities.

In time, Indian raids on the colonists in New York, Pennsylvania, and along the Ohio River became such a threat to his rear guard that General Washington could ignore it no longer. He sent a strong force into the region of the Six Nations, with instructions to destroy their villages and their food, growing and in storage, and to take as many Indians hostage as possible. The Colonial forces captured few hostages, but they did destroy most of the houses and nearly all the growing crops and stored food throughout the territory of the Six Nations. They succeeded in so weakening the Indian's ability to survive the winter that many perished from hunger and exposure. Indian raids continued, but General Washington no longer feared a large, organized assault.

Warfare with the colonists coupled with starvation reduced the numbers in the Six Nations by more than half. They suffered even greater damage, however, from the changed official attitude of the colonists. No Indians participated with representatives of George III and the Colonies meeting in Paris in 1783 to work out the terms of peace. None had been invited to do so. In that Treaty of Paris, the British recognized the independence of the Colonies and ceded to them all the land south of the Great Lakes, east of the Mississippi River, and south to the southern boundary of Georgia. Great Britain retained in North America only the Quebec colony, later to become Canada. Florida was returned to Spain. The Paris Treaty of 1783 made no reference to the status of native Americans. It was a case of Tom and Dick dividing Harry's possessions without so much as an "if you please" to Harry. Colonists conveniently recognized the Indians as British subjects. Congress adopted the official position that the Indians, as British citizens, had relinquished all claims to the lands ceded by Britain. Such lands as the colonists thereafter permitted Indians to occupy they granted to them out of charity. Anthony F. C. Wallace concludes:

> *Treaties of peace . . . were still to be made with the Indian tribes, who had not been mentioned in the Treaty of Paris, but these treaties were to be considered as unilateral actions by which the United States "gave" peace to already conquered tribes and "gave" them such tracts of land as it, or its member states, might out of humanitarian motives wish to allot from the public lands. If the Indians were unwilling to surrender on these terms, the war would (theoretically) be continued until they were either annihilated or expelled.* (Wallace 1970. 151)

This position constituted one of the greatest land-grabs of modern times. Naturally, the Indians did not agree, and for generations could not even comprehend the immense proportions of such a claim. Most natives had never participated in these affairs between the Colonies and their king. When the insurgent Anglo-Europeans began moving onto the Indian's land, the natives resisted with armed might. And why not?

Although the federal government soon officially returned to treating Indians as rightful owners of their tribal lands, the people did not. Too often, individual citizens continued to act as if by the treaty that ended the War of Independence, Indians as British citizens had given up all claims to the land. They held this belief even though most tribes never took part in that war.

Some people believe the Fourteenth Amendment (1868) made Indians citizens, and that an act of Congress in 1924 guaranteed their rights under the law. Nonetheless, Indians even now remain second-class citizens. Many Americans do not understand this minority. Anthony Wallace presents the facts of the matter well in his narrative about the Senecas, and Annette Rosenstiel succinctly expresses the viewpoint of the Indian, a starting point for everyone that wants to understand native Americans. She writes:

> *In all these places* [United States and Canada] *the Indians were rendered undereducated for life, no longer proficient in their traditional tribal ways and ignorant of the ways of the white man's world. The process of Europeanization, or Americanization, was never completed, and most Indians remained in a cultural limbo, suspended halfway between the two worlds.* (Rosenstiel 1983. 8)

If Indians are ever to receive fair treatment in their relationship with the white man of America, the white man must understand the historical facts and the Indian's viewpoint. Both Wallace's and Rosenstiel's books make rewarding reading.

A study of this period should not overlook the colonists' interference with the religious and cultural life of the Indians. In the 1780s, American colonists judged their own culture to be superior to that of the Indians and attempted to change their culture. The Indians resented this interference as much as they resented confiscation of their land. At this early period appeared the signs of arrogance and intolerance that even now remains strong among many Anglo-Americans. The North American Anglo views other peoples of the earth with arrogance, an attitude completely at odds with the principles of human relations. Recall the admonition that says: "Judge not, lest you be judged." Similarly the Indian said never to judge a fellowman until you have walked two miles in his moccasins.

When addressing an audience in New York City in 1870, Chief Red Cloud of the Sioux Nation expressed the resentment the Indians felt against pressure exerted on them to change their culture. He made his plea for understanding:

> *My brothers and my friends who are before me today, God Almighty has made us all, and He is here to hear what I have to say to you today. The Great Spirit made us both. . . . When the Almighty made you, he made you all white and clothed you. When he made us, He made us with red skins and poor. . . . The Great Father* [President Ulysses S. Grant] *said we must go to farming, and some of our men went to farming near Fort Laramie, and we were treated very badly indeed. . . .*
>
> *. . . We do not want riches but we do want to train our children right. Riches would do us no good. We could not take them*

with us to the other world. We do not want riches. We want
peace and love. . . . (Ibid. 136-138)

Nearly 100 years earlier, Jefferson included this simple statement in the Declaration of Independence, though worded differently: "We hold these truths to be self-evident: That all men are created equal; that they are endowed by their Creator with certain unalienable rights; that among these are life, liberty, and the pursuit of happiness."

American Indians have made it very clear that they prefer a culture different from that of Anglo-Americans; that they want only the freedom to continue to live as their forefathers did, by standards of their own culture; that they worship the same Great Spirit as Christians do, but they use a different ritual; and that they want to be treated as free men, equal to all in the eyes of the law.

Is their claim so different from the claims of many ethnic minorities? Is what they seek so different from what most colonists sought when they migrated to the Americas? If we Americans can understand ourselves, certainly we should be able to understand other people. The American Revolution, with its War of Independence, was a movement to establish an atmosphere wherein tolerance of individual differences could endure in peaceful coexistence. Is it not time we Americans recognize that many people of the world do not want to be like the Anglo-Americans in the United States?

While the Declaration of Independence states that all men are created equal, nothing in that document says that all men must speak English; that all must be Christians in the Catholic, Baptist, Methodist, or Anglican faith; that all must be Whigs or Tories, Republicans or Democrats. That declaration stated the position as the founding fathers saw it. It humbly requested other peoples of the world to understand the colonists.

If we Americans can justify our request that others accept us in the world of differing peoples, we can behave no differently ourselves; we must tolerate differences among all peoples. If we are to honor our own heritage, we owe a debt to those who fought and secured for us an independent nation — a debt that burdens us to understand all our brothers, whether they are white, red, yellow, black, European, African, Asian, or American.

The future always remains hidden; but if the past gives any clue, assimilation will resolve the differences among racial and ethnic minorities.

Even so, such a future possibility does not release people from the need to understand those who are different. Americans can start by learning to understand those minorities present in the United States. It is in our self-interest to do so. In a world of 5.5 billion souls, Americans remain a very small minority. We can learn to understand others, or we had better learn to live as a misunderstood minority ourselves. Very likely the United States will not always be the top world power. American intolerance and arrogance may come home to roost.

Revolt Was a Minority Action?

Many historians have declared that, like all revolts, the American Revolution was a minority action. Such a declaration is misleading. Because less than 20 percent of the people could vote, every act of government was technically a minority action. In the sense that no majority expressed positive support for the movement, this is a correct statement. In a country of free men, a position taken by government will never be supported unanimously and often not even by a majority. To the very end, a large number of colonists undoubtedly opposed independence and the war.

We must consider these facts, however. When signing the Declaration of Independence — adopted by the Continental Congress meeting two years after that body first convened, the delegates did not act in haste. Neither did the signatories take their action lightly. Those men indicated not only their agreement with the statement contained therein; they committed their entire material resources, their sacred honor, and their lives. Of the 56 who signed that declaration, 49 sat as delegates to that congress at its adoption. Only three disapproved of the Declaration and refused to sign. In recognition of this, it seems difficult to accept a claim placing responsibility for the War of Independence on a minority.

Lest some think that the Continental Congress was some rump meeting of discontents, the process of its formation and the procedures those men adopted must be noted. In the summer of 1774, when the call went out for delegates from all the Colonies to meet and consider a set of resolutions, each colony routinely selected its governing body by vote. Again by democratic process — the vote — these legislative bodies selected delegates to represent their colonies in that Congress.

Colonists did not have their heads in the sand. They knew full well about events of the decade just past. To represent them they chose conservatives like John Dickenson and radicals like Patrick Henry. Those delegates shared a common and sincere concern for the interests of the Colonies. After selecting a president and a secretary to record the proceedings, the delegates turned their attention to the "how" for making decisions. Should each delegate have one vote? Should each delegation's vote be weighted on population or on geographical area? Should each delegation vote as a unit? The members of this assembly proceeded in an intelligent, orderly manner. They laid aside emotions of the moment until they had organized and everyone had agreed to a method of proceeding.

In the end, they decided that each colony would have one vote. On every question, each delegation in caucus would decide the position that best represented the beliefs of its members and their colony. From the very outset of deliberations they avoided a despotism of the majority. No proposal could be considered an action of the Congress unless approved unanimously. It took 13 yeas to approve any action; one nay could defeat it.

How can action stemming from such an assembly ever be labeled an action of a minority? Admittedly, the 56 men who signed the Declaration of Independence did not constitute a majority of a population of 2.5 million. Certainly, many colonists believed independence was the same as national suicide. But a unanimous vote by the delegations that had been selected by democratic process can scarcely be called a minority decision. It would be a credit to the current Congress if all important measures, especially declarations of war, would be so supported.

In Summation

Historians have asked why Britons permitted war to erupt out of the differences between King George III and the Colonies. The evidence that the colonists did not want war and independence is overwhelming. In the resolutions calling that first meeting of the Continental Congress, the colonists declared their desires to develop some means to preserve their freedom of self-government, which to them differed not one whit from what all Britons enjoyed. Only when King George III forced their hand did they declare their independence and adopt war.

George III forced war on the colonists as a first move to restoring the power of the king throughout his Empire. He considered the colonists the weakest of his opponents and the most easily subdued.

This conclusion presents an interesting commentary on the depth to which George III had studied the project he would undertake. The question that is most pertinent — with which George III should have confronted himself, and which men today should consider in similar undertakings — is this: What is to be required in order to accomplish our objective? George III did not give adequate thought to that question. President Truman, when ordering U.S. troops to Korea, and Presidents John F. Kennedy and Lyndon B. Johnson, when committing American lives to the conflict in Vietnam, likewise gave this question insufficient consideration. Just maybe the Politburo of the Soviet Union made the same error when entering Afghanistan in December 1979.

If any person should feel impelled to form an opinion on any of these decisions, he must consider the financial costs of the operation, the support that can be expected from the people, and all the military problems of logistics and leadership that are involved in such a commitment. Any opinion formed without a thorough consideration of these factors is based on ignorance.

This simply points up one more reason that, as voters and members of society, all citizens should study history, including the history of warfare. Because human nature does not change, man can learn from the past how to conduct his affairs more wisely. But, as a wise man once cautioned mankind, *those who remain ignorant of history are condemned to repeat man's errors of his past.*

Public opinion controls the conduct of government. Public opinion formed from accurate information can be a force working beneficially for a people. Public opinion formed in ignorance can precipitate disaster. Ask the prisoners of war who returned from Vietnam how they feel about their experience in the POW compounds, some for as many as ten years, while public opinion vacillated about ending that conflict. Public opinion and top-level decisions, both based on ignorance, can be charged with the responsibility for those long imprisonments of many Vietnam War veterans.

Should Americans again decide to enter a war, they have an obligation to those young men and women who will fight and die. The decision to fight should be made only after cool deliberation, and with intelligent understanding of the conditions of combat.

Britain — or rather George III, since the great masses of Britons did not support this enterprise — was destined to fail in the conflict with the American Colonies. By the time fighting began, the colonists had experienced too many years of self-government; their population had become too numerous to be subdued by an army the size Great Britain could commit; and Colonial society was too secure in its capacity for independent action. The colonists did not appreciate their own strength, but the 56 signatories to the Declaration of Independence had faith in their ultimate success.

The story of the War of Independence tells of suffering, internal dissension, incompetence, frustration, and individual valor as well as humiliation. It demonstrates again the vital need for competent leadership. The events of that period show how deeply the feeling of independence ran among the colonists. An awareness of the hardships they accepted, Tories and Whigs alike, promotes great respect for their desire to endure. Their dedication to freedom and to the dignity of the individual provided a moral force that sustained the survivors to make the experiment in liberty succeed. The experiment those revolutionary colonists began is now in our care. Americans today remain free to choose; it is not yet too late. We may choose servitude to a professional bureaucracy or freedom under law. Votes based on ignorance or on correct knowledge will make the difference. Again we say, "All men need do to lose freedom is for good men to do nothing."

*Immigrants to the Colonies brought with them these revo-
lutionary ideas: (1) separation of church and State, (2)
decentralization of power, (3) law that protects the individual from oppression by church or State, (4) education
of the masses, and (5) elimination of class distinctions.*

Chapter 4

A New Nation,
1783-1789

A Common Experience

COMMON EXPERIENCE IS ONE INGREDIENT that unites
people in a peaceful society. At the beginning of the War of
Independence, colonies on the continent numbered more than
13. Great Britain had colonies also in Canada and in the
Caribbean; Spain had settlements in Mexico, along the Mississippi
River, and in areas now part of New Mexico, Arizona, and California. But only the 13 British Colonies along the Atlantic seaboard
from Maine to Georgia shared the common experience of self-government. This fact determined participation in the Declaration of
Independence, the War of Independence, and the cooperative agree-

ment that established union in government after the War of Independence, namely, the Articles of Confederation. In each of these actions, other colonies in America had been invited to participate. Nonetheless, as the record shows, only the 13 that had shared in self-government chose to join in forming a nation.

Common experience operated in later years to influence the formation of new states to join the union. As people from the United States settled in Texas, the West, Alaska, and Hawaii, they formed governments that sought the status of statehood in the union of states. The shared experience of a common heritage determined the outcome. Possibly in time to come, people from other areas will seek statehood in the United States due to some common experience. Geography will be no obstacle. The people in Puerto Rico, Canada, Mexico, or the Virgin Islands could develop a mix of individuals whose heritage common with U.S. citizens could prompt them to request statehood.

The 13 English Colonies had participated in the American revolution by sending delegates to the Continental Congresses, by declaring their independence from England, by uniting in action under the Articles of Confederation. Only 12 states sent delegates to the Constitutional Convention, but all 13 ratified the document and joined the United States. (For details of that four-month period in 1787 when delegates wrote the Constitution, see Catherine Drinker Bowen's *Miracle at Philadelphia.* She presents the material in an interesting manner.)

Many differences in the social organization of these colonies existed at that time. The common unifying experiences, however, dwarfed these differences. After all, cooperation between tradesmen, farmers, fishermen, and merchants involves no major problem. The common benefit from cooperation overrides the differences. The force of "enlightened self-interest" among free people succeeds over parochial, territorial, and occupational interests. An uncooperative spirit generally results from one group attempting to coerce others into action that conflicts with their interests. The Southern states in 1860 seceded to escape coercion they perceived to be coming from a federal government beyond their control. One way or another men will resist coercion. Free men use the vote; others use violent rebellion.

In the world today, the unifying force of common experiences still creates cooperation between people of independent States. Despite differences in geographical location and historical background, peaceful cooperation prevails among all nations of free people. The common experience of self-government has not, as yet, created cooperation between all free men under one political entity, but neither has the story of man been written to its conclusion.

The Great American Experiment

Self-government had been tried earlier, with just partial success. At the height of their civilization Athens and Rome functioned under democratic governments. They each contributed greatly to developing the concepts of liberty. Those concepts provided the necessary foundation for the development of liberty in the 18th century. Both, however, failed to secure a permanently democratic government, ultimately ending in civil strife. The Athenian democratic government ended with the Peloponnesian wars late in the 5th century B.C. The Roman Republic lasted nearly 450 years and ended in civil war about the time of the birth of Christ. By popular vote, the Roman people made Julius Caesar their Emperor. Writing at the end of the 18th century, Alexander Fraser Tytler, in *The Decline and Fall of the Athenian Republic*, remarked:

> *A democracy cannot exist as a permanent form of government. It can only exist until the voters discover that they can vote themselves money from the Public Treasury. From that moment on the majority always vote for the candidates promising the most benefits from the Public Treasury with a result that a democracy always collapses over loose fiscal policy always followed by dictatorship.* (Tytler)

At that remarkable meeting in Philadelphia, the founding fathers knew about these past experiences. They were suspect of the success of any government that gave all citizens the right to participate in government, so they did not then grant voting rights to the masses. They tried to give the greatest possible freedom to the people to control their government by reserving to each colony the right to determine who could vote.

Delegates to that Constitutional Convention also broke new ground by organizing with a written constitution. Some of the Colonies had written constitutions when adjusting to their status under the Declaration of Independence. Before 1787, however, no people had ever designedly formed a democratic government under a written document that detailed the construction and powers of that institution. Previously governments had evolved. They had simply grown like Topsy. Consequently, the United States has been labeled "The Great American Experiment," an experiment in liberty.

English Civil War and Concepts in the Constitution

The seedbed for some important ideas in the American Constitution was laid by 17th-century British revolutionaries, who were educated middle class commoners. Those at the bottom of the social structure — the outcasts, the very poor — remained uneducated. One step above these outcasts, the commoners comprised the great mass of people who had legal rights and held a place in the society. They were farmers of the common land, laymen in the church, soldiers in the common army. They read the Bible and the revolutionary literature of the Calvinists and Lutherans, of the French and British. Law-abiding, God-loving men and women, they wanted to live with enough freedom to feed and clothe their children, and to see them grow and reproduce without interference from government or church. Drawing on traditions imbedded in the English Common Law and the Magna Carta, and influenced by Protestantism, revolutionary thinkers sought to restore the dignity of the individual. Their ideas became most effective among the majority of people who were being squeezed by the institutions of the times.

After the death of Queen Elizabeth, these people's lot became steadily worse. They suffered oppression from noblemen of the royal court and from the courts of the church. Their illiteracy in Latin and Law-French, the languages used exclusively in civil and church courts, forced them to employ lawyers. At every turn of their lives, commoners met demands for payment from one of these three. So they perceived lawyers, clergy, and noblemen to be the villains.

These commoners rebelled, and in 1649 executed the heads of these sources of oppression: Charles I, the king; Laud, the archbishop of Canterbury; and the Earl of Strafford, the king's chief minister. The people became free from dictation by the church; Oliver Cromwell became the head of State; Great Britain was without a royal court; the period of the Commonwealth followed.

During this time, educated commoners and freedom-loving philosophers discussed issues of religion, liberty, and government. Immigrants to the Colonies brought with them these revolutionary ideas: (1) separation of church and State, (2) decentralization of power, (3) law that protects the individual from oppression by church or State, (4) education of the masses, and (5) elimination of class distinctions. By the time England restored the monarchy with Charles II, the spirit of individual freedom had been installed in the Colonies. It became a force that would not be denied.

More spontaneous than willful, the movement for freedom issued from the most fundamental of forces. It was a revolt against tyranny. The people saw no difference between the princes of the church and the indolent noblemen of the king's court. To the people both appeared to be oppressive, unjust, extravagant, and corrupt. And the masses felt the full burden of feeding, clothing, and supplying sustenance to these members of the "classes." Gerrard Winstanley, a contemporary of that period, wrote:

> *The laws of kings have been always made against such actions as the common people were most inclinable to, on purpose to ensnare them into their sessions and courts; that the lawyers and clergy, who were the Kings' supporters, might get money thereby and live in fullness by other men's labours. . . . The law is the fox, poor men are the geese; he pulls off their feathers and feeds upon them.* (Quoted by Hill 1972. 216)

These ideas greatly influenced delegates at Philadelphia when they wrote the rules for the new government.

Revolution Creates a Void

Whether peaceful or by force of arms, successful revolution creates a void at the top. Revolt casts aside the old system and leaves chaos in its place. History offers only one instance — that of the English Colonies in America — when the rebelling group had an organized government ready to install in the void.

Frenchmen rebelled in 1789. They beheaded their king in 1792; yet by 1798 a monarch, Napoleon Bonaparte, again ruled France. By a plebiscite in 1806, the people approved Bonaparte to be emperor for life with the right of succession to his heirs. Because the revolutionaries of 1789 had no organization to replace the monarchy they destroyed, the strongest leader filled the vacuum. Had Bonaparte's ambitions been more limited, he might have remained in power, but he pushed his subjects for conquest and an enlarged empire. In 1815 he fell to his overreaching ambitions. The organized opposition of other powers in Europe toppled him completely at Waterloo in June of that year. France reinstated the monarchy with Louis XVII, and Frenchmen had to wait many more years for government responsible to the people.

For 150 years before they broke with the mother country, British colonists in America had been fashioning their own governments. With this experience of 13 state governments behind them, the Colonies became the exception to history. Upon declaring their independence, they formed a new, united government under the Articles of Confederation. With a government in place, the Colonies moved to independence. Then, recognizing the imperfections of that union, they peaceably improved its reorganization with a new constitution in 1788.

The history of independent sovereign nations throughout the world provides numerous examples of revolt, of destroying a link with an organized government, and of void filled with chaos, all ending in rule by a tyrant. It requires a knowledgeable constituency to organize representative government. Among ignorant multitudes, the strong claim the power of government for themselves. The successful Russian revolt in 1917 merely overturned rule by the Tsar. It did not place government in the hands of the people. The elite of the organized Socialist (Communist) Party took over by filling the void. The Russians merely substituted a different dictatorial leader for the Tsar. At this writing, the disintegration of communist control in the old USSR reveals no government in place fully answerable to the people. Time will first bring chaos to the Russians and then a new dictatorial government. Similarly, Cuba substituted Fidel Castro for Batista y Zaldivar. Many African states, on gaining independence from their European protector, have had their attempt at democracy end in rule by a dictator who surfaced from their most populous tribe. Mexico broke free from Spain in 1821 only to experience more than a century of bloody wars between men seeking control of government. Even now, Mexico is struggling to establish a government answerable to the people.

In South Africa the white ruling class has stepped aside to grant control of government to the masses. If the white leaders withdraw completely from positions of authority, a black dictator will take control. But the people, black or white, will have no voice in the new government. Nature abhors a vacuum; and no alternate, wholly black organization exists in South Africa to replace the present government. Without a well-organized government, the native tribes, who are the majority, will compete for control. Until one tribe takes charge, anarchy will prevail. On becoming the controlling authority, the strong man of that winning tribe will use government to persecute, if not destroy, all other tribes. The change of government will not occur by peaceful process through elections. It will happen through bloody violence when members of the white population lose control. This happened in Ethiopia and Somalia. And where else?

History teaches that, in managing any activity of social cooperation, men should never throw out an institution until they have a replacement. Truly, it is unwise for a man to dig a hole until he has something to put into it. When men violate this dictum, they generally live to regret it.

The Constitutional Convention

At the end of the War of Independence each of the 13 English Colonies operated as a sovereign State. During the war, through their representatives in the Continental Congress, they had adopted the Articles of Confederation. These articles created a relationship no stronger than that created by treaty; they did not create a political entity of united states. Congress could enact no laws binding on the citizens or the governments of the states. It had no power to tax. Like the League of Nations created in the Treaty of Versailles (1919), the Continental Congress was little more than a debating society composed of representatives from the 13 Colonies and powerless to enforce its decisions. The small colony of Rhode Island had one vote in this confederation, equal in influence to that of Virginia, Massachusetts, or Pennsylvania. Yet the population and geographical area represented by each of these states varied considerably.

The same condition exists today in the United Nations. That body has no taxing authority and no enforcing powers. The United States, which finances a quarter of the budget, has a vote no greater than that of Zambia, Cuba, Iran, or Nicaragua. The majority power in the UN is exercised by a group of nations that together represents only a fraction of the world population and contributes an insignificant portion of the funds that finance the operation of that body.

The deficiencies of such a cooperative confederation soon became apparent to Colonial leaders. Led by the delegation from Virginia, the Congress took action to correct this weakness. It called on the Colonies to send representatives to a special convention for the purpose of suggesting amendments to the Articles of Confederation. By May 1787, 12 colonies had a delegation in Philadelphia; Rhode Island, however, declined and never participated.

No one at that time considered this special meeting a Constitutional Convention, although history has given it that label. Its early deliberations showed that merely revising the Articles would not address the real need. The delegates soon realized the need for a new principle of union. The Articles of Confederation called for the formation of a "Perpetual Union." The recommendations for the new Constitution called for a "more perfect union." This seemingly small distinction would later be a crack through which the Southern states would crawl out of the Union. Meaningful cooperation could exist only if the states would relinquish their independent sovereignty and grant certain powers to a central government.

It took four months of deliberation for these 55 delegates to agree on the specific powers to be allocated to the central government and to outline its organizational structure. The resulting document defined the limited powers that the states would relinquish to the union of states. Those delegates intended to grant to the central government only the powers specifically set forth in the agreement. They reserved all other powers to be exercised by the states or the people.

The Constitution granted these powers to the central government: to make treaties, to declare war, to authorize privateers, to maintain a standing army and a navy, to coin money, to issue paper money, to pass legal tender laws, to regulate and levy duties on foreign and interstate commerce, to establish a postal service, to establish a court system for interpreting and enforcing the federal statutes, to issue patents and copyrights, to punish crimes on the high seas, to call out the state militias, to make laws for the District of Columbia and other federal areas, to pass naturalization laws, and to enact such laws as were necessary to administer these powers. These powers were exclusive to the central government; they were denied to the several states. In addition, the central government was granted powers it would share with the states: to levy taxes on the people, to borrow money, to pass bankruptcy laws.

With virtual unanimity the delegates agreed that the Constitution granted to the central government only such powers as were specified in that document. For this reason they believed there existed no need to specify the powers denied to the central government, except for those also denied to the states. The Constitution forbids all governments to grant titles of nobility, to enact bills of attainder and *ex post facto* laws, to interfere with the slave trade before 1808, to levy taxes on exports. All powers not mentioned were reserved to the people, to be executed through local governments. This limitation on powers, they believed, made a bill of rights superfluous. Why was it necessary to deny to the federal government specific powers not granted to that government in the first place? Would not such an inclusion create the assumption that the federal government possessed all powers not so denied to it? (Because the people did later adopt a Bill of Rights — the first ten Amendments — 20th-century autocrats successfully defend usurpation of power by arguing that the Constitution, being silent on the matter, does not forbid Congress to do so.)

Among the delegates to the Constitutional Convention, only Alexander Hamilton believed in a strong central government. His suggestions, presented in an eloquent speech lasting nearly two days, received a favorable vote of only one, his own. The delegates feared despotism. They reluctantly granted powers to the new office of President, to the Congress, to the newly created federal courts. The small states feared domination by the large states; the Southern states feared oppression by the Northern states; and nearly all delegates feared the great majority. They could see the threat of despotism by the majority, and they sought to protect the individual, his rights, and his property. The proceedings of that Convention make it clear that this document granted no power to government not specifically recited therein.

The delegates rightly feared despotism by the majority. Before the War Between the States, the Northern states used their majority power to enact laws detrimental to the interests of the South. In the 20th century, with the approval of the federal Supreme Court, Congress has assumed virtually unlimited power in spite of the Constitution, and now threatens the protection of individual rights, even some rights guaranteed by the first ten Amendments. The news media write questioningly about where the courts are finding such individual rights as "the right of privacy." They ask, "Where does the Constitution grant individuals such protection?"

The first ten Amendments guarantee these rights: freedom of religion, speech, the press, assembly; the right to petition the government for a redress of grievances; the right to keep and bear arms; freedom from the requirement to quarter troops in their homes; freedom from unreasonable search and seizure; right to certain protection when on trial, and not to be deprived of life, liberty, or property without due process of law; the right to a speedy and impartial trial by jury; common law and jury trials under same is guaranteed; excessive fines and unusual punishment forbidden; powers not delegated to the United States nor prohibited to the states are reserved to the states or to the people.

It is too early in this study to deal with recent developments, but the reader should know the intentions of those men who wrote the Constitution and worked for its ratification by the states. In their attempts to limit the power of government by means of a written constitution, the delegates probably succeeded as well as any group ever could. Because of the nature of man, however, no constitution can survive public opinion. Public opinion in the 20th century has discarded the principles of this Constitution to such a degree that the U.S. government no longer functions under its terms as adopted by the states in 1788-1789. Succeeding chapters will reveal how this has come about.

This Constitution did work, and for nearly 150 years it controlled and restricted the power of government. Under it men lived free, and free men thrived. Those 150 years can honestly be called the golden age of freedom. But, as free Romans voted to make Caesar their emperor and as free Frenchmen voted to make Napoleon Bonaparte Emperor of France, free Americans voted in the 20th century to enslave the citizenry to a despotism of the majority, and again the power of government has been elevated above the rights of individuals. Under the influence of the Law of Security, Americans panicked in the 1930s and permitted government to usurp powers never considered by the framers who convened in 1787. (See Chapter 14.)

After 1819, no doubt remained about the broad powers of Congress, and the events of history have demonstrated just how far Congress has been willing to go. . . . Congress has stepped into the lives of individuals and done what would have delighted the most ambitious monarch of earlier Europe, especially George III.

Chapter 5

Consolidation, 1789-1815

Washington Fulfills His Destiny

A RIOTING MOB STORMED AND destroyed the Bastille in Paris on July 14, 1789. Just six weeks earlier George Washington had become the first President of the United States. While the French destroyed their government, the people of the Colonies strengthened their union of states with a new Constitution. Much remained to be done. The United States had then no money of its own, no financial credit with foreign interests, and no recognized strength in world affairs. Britain still treated the Colonies as part of its Empire. In violation of provisions of the 1783 Treaty of Paris, the British continued to occupy their forts and trading posts west of the Appalachians. Unless American ship captains observed the terms of the old Navigation Acts, the Britons seized their ships, confiscated the cargo, and forced the sailors to serve on British ships. Mediterranean pirates openly preyed on American ships, and did so with virtually no fear of interference.

Many leaders in both Europe and America considered it likely, perhaps even desirable, that the Colonies would rejoin the British Empire. With Frenchmen in violent rebellion, no one feared acts of conquest from that quarter. Uprisings in South and Central America occupied the Spanish monarch. Consequently, the British simply sat on their hands waiting for the expected call for help from their former American Colonies.

Conditions virtually demanded that a hero of major stature take charge. The people looked to George Washington, and once again he answered the call to serve. The Law of Idolatry dictated the selection of Washington to lead his nation through that insecure period of its infancy. He was the popular commander in a successful war. Throughout history, kings and princes have led their armies in war for the express purpose of strengthening their popularity at home. In this way Julius Caesar became Emperor of Rome and Bonaparte became Emperor of France. Human nature loves a hero. World War I excepted, every successful war has produced an American President; and the hero of World War I, General John J. Pershing, could have become President in 1920 had he accepted the nomination from either major political party.

George Washington rightfully deserved this position of esteem. Of sound judgment and good character, though not a man of great brilliance, he would accept responsibility. Although he did avail himself of the opportunity to profit financially from his position, his motivation for service flowed from dedication to his country. Washington understood the need for a heroic leader and accepted the position even though he would have preferred that another serve. He has been the only man elected to the presidency of the United States without actively seeking it. Two thousand years earlier another great leader of his people had prayed to his God to "lift this burden from my shoulders." George Washington's private papers reveal that he would have gladly relinquished this task to another, but his countrymen would accept no other; and fortunately for the nation, Washington accepted the mantle of leadership and served well the needs of the time. He earned his position in history as "the father of his country."

Washington's Cabinet

When Washington took office, he sought the support of those he had most trusted as commander of the armed forces. Thomas Jefferson, for many years ambassador to France, became Secretary of State. It is well to recognize that the great statesman and popular foreign diplomat Benjamin Franklin was at this date too old and feeble to serve his country in any official capacity. Henry Knox, the onetime bookseller of Boston, the self-made artillery general, the man who had so ably supported General Washington throughout all the trying years of the War of Independence, became the Secretary of War. Washington entrusted financial matters to Alexander Hamilton as Secretary of the Treasury.

Henry Knox proved to be a man whose time had come and gone. He never failed his duties, but he contributed little to the advancement of his country. He can rightfully be assigned to the history of the past after 1789. The time for Jefferson had not yet come. In spite of his contributions in 1776 in writing the Declaration of Independence, Jefferson was at odds with the majority of Congress. Though popular with the public, his views opposed those held by businessmen of the Northeast and the men in government. He would rise to a position of major influence in the destiny of his country after Washington's death in 1799.

Alexander Hamilton, a 32-year-old lawyer from New York, held center stage. This is the same Hamilton whose ideas for a strong central government had been supported only by his own vote at the Constitutional Convention; this is the Hamilton who cared not one whit for President Washington as an individual, but who served him in order to exercise the power of government by virtue of the President's great love and admiration for him. In a private letter to his father-in-law, Hamilton wrote:

> *"I believe you know the place I had in . . .* [Washington's] *confidence and counsels, which will make it the more extraordinary to you to learn that for three years past I have felt no friendship for him."* (Passos 1957. 12)

Washington appointed Hamilton to be Secretary of the Treasury, and by consistent support made him in effect his second in command, his first minister.

About Alexander Hamilton

"Give all power to the many and they will oppress the few. Give all power to the few and they will oppress the many." So declared Alexander Hamilton when addressing the Constitutional Convention in 1787. As those men in convention well understood, the problem of democratic government is to organize government in a way that protects the many from tyranny by the few and protects the few from despotism by the majority.

Oddly enough, the man who stated the problem so succinctly before the Constitutional Convention, became the very one who exercised his later position in government to weaken constitutional safeguards against such tyranny. Hamilton could not sway the delegates at the Convention, but he succeeded completely in influencing the new President. Because of Washington's continued support, a majority of Congress accepted Hamilton's recommendations.

Throughout the Constitutional Convention, the delegates resisted every suggestion to eliminate the power of the states. Vote after vote went against measures to create a strong central government that would supplant state governments. Because Alexander Hamilton could secure no support in that Convention for his plan of an all-powerful national government, he left the Convention at that time and took no further part in its deliberations. He returned to the Convention, probably on a call from Washington, to serve on the committee on style, which phrased the wording of the Constitution. This committee left no record of its proceedings, only the completed document; but even though the records of the Convention contain no reference to *general welfare* in resolutions pertaining to the powers granted to Congress, the completed document includes that expression in two places — in the preamble and in Article I, Sec. 8, Par. 1. Hamilton undoubtedly inserted this reference to be available later for his use in expanding the powers of the central government.

Hamilton wrote most of the material in the *Federalist Papers,* a series of published articles supporting ratification. He must have concluded that he should first devote his efforts to getting the Constitution in force, and then work within its framework to expand the power of the central government.

Consider his actions as the most influential member of Washington's cabinet. In 1789, as Secretary of the Treasury, Hamilton proposed that the United States redeem and refinance at par — full face value — all obligations of the former Confederation. Article VI, Par. 1 of the Constitution required the new government to honor these obligations. Nonetheless, the new government could have purchased a substantial amount of this paper on the open market at figures below face value. This alternate action would have supported the credit of the nation equally well at a lower cost. Similarly, Hamilton proposed that the central government assume all debts of the various states, and pay these at full value by exchanging new federal debt instruments for them. Congressmen had not anticipated such action; no delegate at the Convention had even suggested it. By this measure Hamilton sought to reduce the importance of the states and enhance the power of the central government. It was a power play, pure and simple.

To put these recommendations in proper perspective, keep in mind that soldiers of the War of Independence had been paid with paper promises. These promises, as well as the other debt instruments of the Continental Congress, had for years been trading on the open market at or below ten cents on the dollar. In 1789, bonds and notes of some state governments had become worthless. Hamilton suggested that the new government put its power of taxation behind all these obligations on the basis of 100 cents on the dollar; he would redeem all at full value. What a bomb to drop into the financial markets.

This suggestion caused a near dissolution of Congress; many congressmen left to buy up all the Continental paper they could while the price remained so low, and Congress often found it difficult to convene a quorum. Men sent agents by fast horse, by ship, by whatever means possible into the farthest reaches of the nation to purchase this "worthless" paper. Talk about insider trading; there was no Securities and Exchange Commission (SEC) then nor were there any outraged congressional inquiries into such conduct. The only outraged congressmen were those who failed to purchase enough old Continental paper before Congress could approve these proposals.

In all fairness to Alexander Hamilton, we must acknowledge that no evidence has yet surfaced to indicate that he speculated to profit personally from this action. We may dispute the wisdom of his program, but it appears that he acted in good faith.

Senator Albert Gallatin, a conservative member from Pennsylvania, advocated a different approach. He maintained that the new government should control finances in such a manner as to develop a revenue surplus.

This surplus should be applied toward redemption of the debts of the Continental Congress as might from time to time be determined just. He maintained that through such sound financial management, the new country would develop a credit worthiness within world financial markets that would meet all reasonable needs of the new government.

Gallatin's proposal would have retired the debt, but was not consistent with Hamilton's overall scheme. Hamilton wanted a perpetual debt. He wanted bankers and wealthy individuals to support the central government. If these financial interests were creditors of the government, he reasoned, their own self-interest would dictate that they support union.

Refinancing the debts of the Confederation passed easily. The Constitution contained a directive to do so. Assuming the debts of the states presented quite another matter. Some states had paid their obligations. Their representatives asked why they should now, through the new United States government, pay debts of other states. This good question so influenced enough members of Congress that the measure would not have passed had Hamilton not made a deal with Jefferson. Hamilton pledged the support of New Yorkers for locating the new capital city on the Potomac River if Virginians would support Assumption. Jefferson delivered the votes of the Virginia representatives; Hamilton delivered those of the New Yorkers. Congress located the capital city, Washington, D.C., on the Potomac River between Virginia and Maryland, and Assumption passed.

If President Washington had vetoed the measure, no doubt Gallatin's position would have prevailed. Hamilton could not have marshaled enough votes to override a presidential veto, but there was no veto. As in nearly all matters where Washington could with honor support Hamilton, he supported him. He signed the bill for Assumption.

Hamilton had far less trouble with his banking proposal. Using the banking practices of England for a model, he advocated that the United States establish a central bank with branches throughout the country. He reasoned that this banking system would facilitate collection of taxes, that its bank notes would circulate as money, and that the central bank would act as an agency to make it easier for the new government to borrow money. The national government would own 20 percent, and the other 80 percent would be sold to private investors.

Congress was then considering the other laws needed for creating the structure of government envisioned in the Constitution. The federal judiciary was one such institution yet to be formed and have its scope defined.

When Congress considered Hamilton's proposals, no judiciary existed; judicial review of congressional actions had not emerged. It took years before the federal Supreme Court established its power to review acts of Congress to determine their constitutionality. Consequently, when opponents argued in 1789 that the Constitution did not grant Congress the power to create a central bank, the final decision rested with President Washington.

Hamilton argued for a central bank as being well within the powers of Congress under Article I, Sec. 8, Par. 18, which authorized Congress to enact "all laws which shall be necessary and proper for carrying into execution" the powers so granted to it. Hamilton reasoned that because the bank was essential for collecting taxes, Congress could create it as a means to execute its power to levy taxes. Many considered such an argument so unreasonable as to present a frightening hazard to freedom. Jefferson wrote to President Washington:

> *To take a single step beyond the boundaries thus especially drawn around the powers of Congress, is to take possession of a boundless field of power, no longer susceptible of any definition.*

President Washington was a planter, not a lawyer. He sought the counsel of his cabinet — Jefferson, Knox, and Hamilton — and asked for an opinion from his Attorney General, Edmund Randolph. When the four men divided evenly, Washington had to decide. Always consistent during his two terms in office, he supported the position advocated by Alexander Hamilton. He signed the bill establishing a central bank. When Washington accepted the argument for a flexible interpretation of Article I, Sec. 8, Par. 18 of the Constitution, he established a precedent to this day. Writers frequently refer to this paragraph in the Constitution as the "elastic clause."

In *Federalist Paper 84,* written in support of the ratification of the Constitution, Hamilton defended the absence of a bill of rights, "For why declare that things shall not be done which there is no power to do?" This was the same Hamilton who later, as a member of Washington's cabinet, argued that Article I, Sec. 8, Par. 1 of the Constitution empowered Congress to do anything that Congress deemed proper in order to promote the general welfare of the nation. This paragraph states, "The Congress shall have the power to lay and collect taxes . . . to . . . provide for the . . . general welfare of the United States." Hamilton then coupled this power with that elastic clause that grants to Congress the power "to make all laws which shall be necessary and proper for carrying into execution the foregoing [enumerated] powers." By broadly interpreting these two paragraphs, Hamilton argued that the federal government could constitutionally perform any act not specifically denied to it or reserved to the several states.

Hamilton had been dead only 15 years when the Supreme Court adopted much of his reasoning on interpreting the Constitution. In *McCulloch v Maryland*, 4 Wheaton 316, 4 L. Ed. 579 (1819), Chief Justice Marshall wrote:

> *A government, entrusted with . . . powers . . . must also be entrusted with . . . means for their execution. . . . We think the sound construction of the constitution must allow to the national legislature that discretion, with respect to the means by which the powers . . . are to be carried into execution. . . .*
>
> *Let the end be legitimate, let it be within the scope of the constitution, and all means which are . . . plainly adapted to that end, which are not prohibited . . . are constitutional. . . . To undertake here to inquire into the degree of its necessity, would be to pass the line which circumscribes the judicial department.*

In effect, the Court stated that when the framers of the Constitution granted powers to Congress, they naturally meant for Congress to be able to adopt the appropriate means to exercise these powers. The "elastic clause" merely affirms this intent. Consequently, the Court's first duty was to see whether the Constitution did so grant the power that Congress was exercising. If so, then the Court believed whatever means Congress selected in order to exercise this power lay within the framework of the Constitution unless specifically forbidden therein. The Marshall Court in 1819 distinguished between powers and means. By 1941 the Court had abandoned this distinction and granted to Congress all power not specifically forbidden, as so succinctly stated by Robert H. Jackson, Attorney General under President Franklin D. Roosevelt and later a Supreme Court justice:

> *The Supreme Court has drawn out of the big top hat of due process some rabbits even more astounding. . . . Until very recently, it has held that prices of other commodities and of labor cannot be regulated at all.* **There is nothing in the Constitution which provides that there shall be no power to regulate prices or wages.** [Emphasis added] (Jackson 1941. 53)

After 1819, no doubt remained about the broad powers of Congress, and the events of history have demonstrated just how far Congress has been willing to go. With a broad interpretation of the "general welfare" clause and of the power to "regulate interstate commerce," Congress has stepped into the lives of individuals and done what would have delighted the most ambitious monarch of earlier Europe, especially George III. Almost before Congress could fully form the national government under the provisions of the Constitution, the concept of limitations on the powers of Congress had begun to erode. Today, the Court restricts the power of Congress to act only wherein the Constitution specifically forbids. Under General Washington's powerful cloak, Hamilton succeeded at accomplishing what the convention in Philadelphia two years earlier had unanimously rejected. John Dos Passos quotes a senator in Congress at that time:

> [His contemporary] *William Maclay . . . senator from Pennsylvania . . . made the entry in his diary: "Congress may go home. Mr. Hamilton is all-powerful and fails in nothing he attempts. . . . If there is treason in the wish, I retract it; but would to God this same General Washington were in heaven. . . . We would not then have him brought forward as the constant cover to every unconstitutional and irrepublican act."* (Passos 1957. 224)

Perhaps Americans are fortunate that the people adopted the first ten Amendments before the Supreme Court began broadly interpreting the Constitution. These Amendments, the Bill of Rights, specifically deny certain powers to the federal government. Otherwise, relying on the premise that the people did not need this protection — "For why declare that things shall not be done which there is no power to do?"— would have been relying on a mirage. Hamilton's victories in the early days of

Congress began reversing the basic presumption relating to the limitation of powers in the federal government.

Hamilton's measures for handling the debt established another precedent that remains with influence in the 20th century. He contended that government was stronger when fully supported by the moneyed interests, and the existence of a perpetual debt would best secure this backing. He supported this claim by pointing out that creditors seldom advocate destroying their debtors. Since the inception of the United States under the Constitution, the federal government has seldom been debt free. Some have questioned the wisdom of a perpetual debt, but politicians always support it. It gives them the means to spend on projects for which the citizens are not willing to be taxed.

Hamilton additionally proposed a tax on whiskey. He did not present this excise tax as a revenue measure, but as a means to assert federal power in the West. Frontier farmers had two ways of marketing their grain: (1) float it down the Ohio and Mississippi Rivers to New Orleans, or (2) make whiskey out of it and haul it over the Appalachians by muleback to city markets along the Atlantic seaboard. Until roads, railroads, and canals connected the Ohio River watershed with the Atlantic plains, Midwest farmers had to use pack trains of mules and horses for overland transport. As a result, a tax on whiskey in 1789 was in reality a discriminatory tax on farm produce in the Ohio River valley.

This whiskey tax naturally aroused strong resentment on the frontier, exactly as Hamilton had anticipated. The farmers along the Ohio River became overly enthusiastic in making their resentment felt. They tarred and feathered one tax collector and destroyed the possessions of others. Hamilton had his rebellion, and he convinced President Washington that as head of the Treasury Department he should take a military force into the frontier area and put down this rebellion. By this maneuver, Hamilton achieved one of his lifelong ambitions; he became a general.

Commonsense arguments advanced by their own frontier leaders quieted this so-called Whiskey Rebellion. With a force of 16,000 militia, Hamilton met no armed resistance, but he could honestly announce the rebellion had ended. He could return home a hero and be thereafter called General Hamilton. Hamilton's personal affair in order to attain military glory cost the new government more than twice the annual revenue generated by the tax levy. Hamilton released the leaders of this "rebellion" after he had questioned them. Of the 20 or so men arrested and taken to court, only two were tried and convicted of wrongdoing. The President pardoned these.

After Washington's death in 1799, Alexander Hamilton never again served in national public office. Had he not been martyrized by falling to Aaron Burr's bullet in a duel five years later — July 11, 1804, he would likely have disappeared quietly from the pages of history. The circumstances of his death, however, erased all memory of his misdeeds and made him a national hero. American currency commemorates him along with George Washington, Thomas Jefferson, Abraham Lincoln, Andrew Jackson, Ulysses S. Grant, and Benjamin Franklin. His likeness appears on the $10 bill.

About Despotism and Rule by Law

Enacting these measures proposed by Hamilton demonstrated that the government of the United States was the only government of consequence among the Colonies. The new arrangement of powers reduced state governments to handling local affairs. All four of Hamilton's recommendations became the law of the land. Almost instantly the U.S. government had credit worldwide. Some acclaimed Hamilton a genius, that he "touched the dead corpse of Public Credit, and it sprung upon its feet." (Daniel Webster 1831)

We should not overlook the possibility that the cause of revived credit might have been the terms of the new Constitution, which gave Congress the power to tax and thereby raise funds for its financial needs. We should also consider many possible causes for revived prosperity, which had returned under the Confederation. These matters need a book of their own. Today's student should recognize that Hamilton did broaden the powers of the federal government. Since that time, the several states have had little power over affairs in which the federal government has chosen to become involved.

Has anyone been deceived by these machinations of government to subvert the intents of the men who wrote the Constitution? Yes. Textbooks are full of the palliative that Supreme Court justices use as a lead-in to their decisions. Typical are the following: In *McCulloch v Maryland,* "This government is . . . one of enumerated powers. . . . It can exercise only the powers granted to it." In *United States v Butler,* 297 U.S. 1 (1936), the Court said: "The United States is a government of delegated powers

. . . that those not expressly granted . . . are reserved to the states or the people." Robert Cushman summarizes:

> *Perhaps the most difficult problem faced by the government of a large nation is the reconciliation of local and national interests. . . . The American Revolution stemmed from the failure of George III to allow his American colonies sufficient local autonomy, and the framers of the new Constitution knew that they must find a wiser adjustment of these competing interests and loyalties if the country was to endure as a political unit.*
>
> *The solution they worked out was to delegate in Article I, Sec. 8, certain enumerated powers to the national government. The Tenth Amendment declared that those powers not so delegated were left to the states, or to the people, to be later assigned by constitutional amendments.* (Cushman 1982. 59)

Nevertheless, that line in a Supreme Court decision generally precedes an opinion that approves further expansion of federal powers that restrict individual freedom. Justice Stone, writing for the Court in *United States v Darby,* 312 U.S. 100 (1941), stated:

> *The power of Congress over interstate commerce is not confined to the regulation of commerce among the states. It extends to those activities intrastate which so affect interstate commerce . . . as to make regulation of them appropriate means to the attainment of a legitimate end. . . . Congress . . . may choose the means . . . even though they involve control of intrastate activities.*

In *Youngstown Sheet and Tube Co. v Sawyer,* 343 U.S. 579 (1952), Justice Black applied this principle to labor relations:

> *The power of Congress to adopt such public policies . . . is beyond question. It can authorize the taking of private property for public use. It can make laws regulating the relationships between employers and employees, prescribing rules designed to settle labor disputes, and fixing wages and working conditions in certain fields of our economy.*

Some authorities have advanced the view that the clause to "provide for the . . . general welfare" is more than a mere grant of power to tax and spend for the general welfare; it authorizes Congress to legislate generally for that purpose. This view, however, which would expand the power of government beyond limit, has not (through 1998) been directly recognized by the Court. If the Court ever does adopt this concept of the General Welfare clause, Congress could use any means to attain any objective it might believe was for the general welfare of the nation. The only limitation on the power of government would then rest with a five-justice Court majority. Similarly, the Court would have unlimited discretion in adjudicating cases before it.

How far has this trend developed? Congress now delegates to a bureaucrat the power to tell a farmer how many acres of grain he may plant for feeding his cattle. (*Wickard v Filburn,* [1942] 317 U.S. 111). The Racketeer Influenced and Corrupt Organization Act (RICO) empowers the Justice Department to attach a defendant's entire property in order to deny him the ability to employ counsel of his choosing for his own defense. The Supreme Court now considers demands by public opinion that can mean the final destruction of personal protections guaranteed by the Bill of Rights. In the interrogation of witnesses before Congress, both the media and members of Congress have deplored the right of an individual to remain silent, as expressed in the Fifth Amendment. Many citizens today believe that *after all, the public has a right to know. No individual is above the rights of the majority.* Yet those who insisted on constitutional amendments spelling out a Bill of Rights wanted them in order to protect the individual citizen against precisely such despotism, whether exercised by a majority or by a tyrant.

The framers of the Constitution intended to accomplish three things: (1) to create a united government capable of defending the country from external interference and internal dissension; (2) to create a central government sufficiently powerful to prevent the separate states from destroying each other; and (3) to protect individuals from the tyranny of government. Current trends in Congress and the courts now endanger this third objective. (See Chapter 16.) Protecting the individual rests in the hands of a five-member Court majority, a majority that vacillates in its legal views. Many people believe the individual no longer has rights that lie beyond the reach of the majority. After all, "fair is fair and the majority rules." If the Court follows public opinion, protections guaranteed to the individual by the Constitution will disappear. The Court has already sanctioned restrictions on the freedom of commercial speech. Congress has given bureaucrats power to define legal advertising and to dictate how and where it may appear.

Throughout most of history, men have lived under government by man versus government by law. The heads of government arbitrarily made the rules that control the operation of government and the conduct of its citizens. They functioned as legislator, accuser, jury, and judge. Some rulers followed local customs, but others changed the rules at their whim. Under such a system there existed no set of rules to guide a person in his daily conduct, nor to guide and restrict a judge hearing a dispute in a legal suit. A citizen did not know the terms of the law that a judge might use or the prejudices that might influence his decision. People cannot know freedom under such conditions.

In the 7th century B.C., Draco, a ruler of Athens, changed this unjust system. He published written rules of government, a code of law. Under Draco, Athenians began living under government by laws. The great Greek teacher Socrates taught that only through observance of the law could civilized man live in harmony. At the last, unfairly condemned to death by the law, offered by his friends a chance to escape, Socrates chose to die rather than make a mockery of his teachings. Socrates gave his life to advance the cause of government by law, as did those who died in the English and American revolutions. Rule by law is one of the chief objectives of popular revolt. Only under government by law can man know freedom. Government by man is despotism.

During the supremacy of Rome, men perfected the system of codified law. Greece gave Western civilization the philosophy, and Rome gave it organization. As the power of Rome declined, men of Western civilization lost the benefit of government by law. The English Revolution, customarily dated from the signing of the Magna Carta in the 13th century, was the struggle of Englishmen to regain it. In the 18th century, George III tried to go against the tide of this movement only to be destroyed by his failure to stop it as it spread to America.

When the leaders of the 13 Colonies met in Congress, they placed foremost the need to put in writing a set of rules that would guide the operation of their government. They sought to protect the individual from despotism. By 1789 the United States of America had a new life, organized and operating under a system of written laws, the Constitution. Not a rigid structure, but containing its own means of adjusting to changing times, this contract among the people includes a section that defines the mechanics for amendment. Since its ratification, the people have amended the Constitution 26 times. The first ten amendments, the Bill of Rights, were adopted virtually as part of ratification.

Operating under this written constitution, a citizen knows the rules. It protects him against unfair action by officers of his government. When taken to court, he knows the rules that will be applied by the judges in deciding the issue. He knows that the rules will not be hastily or frequently altered. He lives under a system of government by laws, not government by man subject to the whims of any one man or small group of men in high office.

Or so it seems.

Operating under rules, men need umpires to settle disputes when the parties cannot agree on the interpretation of the rules. In the American constitutional system, the Supreme Court acts as that body. These judges decide what the Constitution means when litigants cannot agree. Any action of Congress or the executive can be challenged as being in conflict with the established rules. The Supreme Court interprets the Constitution and decides whether the disputed action coincides with powers granted by that document. This is as it should be; some final authority must exist to settle disputes.

Once a Supreme Court makes an interpretation and renders a decision, all courts decide later litigation on the basis of this interpretation. This is called observing legal precedent, the doctrine of *stare decisis*. Should the public disagree with the Court's interpretation, the Constitution provides a mechanism to set things right; the people can amend it to express their wishes. Following legal precedent is entirely consistent with government by law. The rules are clear and predictable. But in 1937 this all began to change. The greatest danger today exists in the Court's abandonment of the doctrine of *stare decisis*. As observed by Edward Corwin:

> *Judicial Review as exercised by the Supreme Court takes on today increasingly the character of a species of arbitration between competing social interests rather than of adjudication in the strict sense of the term, namely, the determination of the rights of adverse parties under a settled, statable rule of law. . . .*

> *In short, Judicial Review as exercised by the Supreme Court today is often a political power in the broad sense of a power, and duty, to advance the best interests of the American community, and its exercise involves the use of political judgment in the same broad sense. . . . one proof being the Court's own recognition of the weakness of the principle of* stare decisis *in the field of Constitutional Law.* (Corwin 1958. vii-viii)

What happens when the Supreme Court decides a dispute contrary to previous decisions of the Court, upsetting precedent? The Court is said to reverse itself. Such a decision changes the law after the fact. When the disputed action occurred, the parties involved understood the law as declared by prior court decisions. By ignoring precedent, the Court destroys vital characteristics of all law: clarity and predictability. This action changes the rules of government in a manner that violates the Constitution. By this seemingly innocent act — which members of the Court justify as setting right a long-standing wrong — the Court substitutes government by man for government by law. Thereafter, no one knows the rules. By such action, the Court in effect abolishes all rules. A rule of law has meaning only when the people are aware of it, and its application to human conduct is predictable. Knowledge of the law and predictability of consequences are vital. Without reasonable expectations in human relations, there can be no society. Judicial decisions that reverse long-established expectations under a law leave people to act under legal relations they cannot apply to their own conduct. This is not only unjust to the parties involved in the action before the Court, it destroys further observance of existing law. Frederick A. Hayek makes this pertinent observation:

> *It is not only difficult but also undesirable for judicial decisions to reverse a development, which has already taken place and is then seen to have undesirable consequences or to be downright wrong. The judge is not performing his function if he disappoints reasonable expectations created by earlier decisions. . . . [A]lthough he may clearly recognize that another rule would be better, or more just, it would . . . be unjust to apply it to transactions which had taken place when a different rule was regarded as valid. In such situations it is desirable that the new rule should become known before it is enforced; and this can be*

effected only by promulgating a new rule which is to be applied only in the future. Where a real change in the law is required, the new law can properly fulfill the proper function of all law, namely that of guiding expectations, only if it becomes known before it is applied. (Hayek 1973. 88-89)

Article III, Sec. 9 of the Constitution forbids all units of government to enact *ex post facto* laws. An *ex post facto* law alters the law after the fact. It criminalizes an act that was legal at the time of action. It alters the legal circumstances between litigants after the disputed action occurred. At no time have men suggested repealing this part of the Constitution. Yet, when the Supreme Court reverses legal precedent in adjudicating a case, it does precisely that; it changes the law that applies to the action involved in that case "after the fact," *ex post facto.* If the people allow their judges to do this once, nothing prevents judges from deciding future cases based on their personal views. The written law, as interpreted by courts in earlier decisions, becomes meaningless. Citizens live under government by man in place of government by law.

No one claims that all laws are just, or that the people consider all legal precedent to be correct and fair. Amendment as set forth in the Constitution, however, provides the only process for changing the Constitution (and Court interpretations that the people consider improper) that is consistent with government by law. Similarly, revision by elected legislative bodies remains the only means, consistent with government by law, to change court interpretations of statutes. Such change does not affect the legal circumstances of past action. It does not destroy clarity and predictability. The new rule is known before it is enforced. But changes by the Court that upset legal precedent alter the legal status of the action under adjudication after the fact.

How can such action by judges be other than unconstitutional? No public officer, whether the president, a member of Congress, or a Supreme Court justice, holds office beyond the power of the people. Either the citizens exercise their power peaceably through Constitutional law, or they resort to armed revolt when such tyranny becomes so abusive that they will no longer tolerate it.

History shows that tyranny must run to excess before the people resort to rebellion. Consequently, reason favors a peaceful solution timely taken. This is the heritage Americans have in their Constitution. Government by law can be preserved without violent action. Acting through their representatives, the people can preserve government by law if they act in time.

Justice Davis, writing for the Court in *Ex Parte Milligan*, 4 Wallace 2; 18 L. Ed. 781 (1866), says of the importance of the law:

> *No graver question was ever considered by this court, nor one which more nearly concerns the rights of the whole people; for it is the birthright of every American citizen when charged with crime, to be tried and punished according to law. . . . By the protection of the law human rights are secured; withdraw that protection, and they are at the mercy of wicked rulers, or the clamor of an excited people.*

Public opinion has demanded that courts interpret the Constitution as a living document, flexing with changes in the sentiment of the people — in other words, abandoning rule by law in favor of rule by man. The Supreme Court has followed this lead, as demonstrated in later chapters. The rigid Constitution of 1789, supported by a Supreme Court that follows the written law as previously interpreted, can provide individuals their only safeguard against despotism.

When the Supreme Court ignores legal precedent, it ignores the Constitution and all established law. Men then live under rule by tyranny, not rule by law. Americans have strayed from the ideas of freedom that prompted men to die fighting for independence and liberty. By permitting judges to continue ignoring legal precedent, the citizens are in fact saying to Socrates, to those who gave their lives in the English and American revolutions, to those who gave their time to write the Constitution, "We think you were fools!" They are saying to later generations, "If you want freedom, you will need to fight for your own escape from tyranny; we chose to abandon liberty without a struggle."

The Legacy of Alexander Hamilton

Alexander Hamilton's Federalists designed their policies to keep the country's men of industry and finance fully interested in the government and under its control. Toward this end, Hamilton advocated a central bank and a permanent public debt. The citizens never fully supported a permanent national debt, and in 1835 the U.S. government became debt free. President Washington and Congress did approve the central bank, and its operations brought on the financial panic of 1819. Few ever really contested the philosophy of central banking until President Jackson in 1833 vetoed the bill to extend the charter of the second United States Bank.

This philosophy of government-sponsored monopolies and aristocratic control caused two major movements in the period now being considered: (1) labor unrest, leading to unionism, and (2) the Bank Wars between hard-money advocates and supporters of easy-money and inflation. Consider first the beginnings of unionism, a product of special-interest government.

A panic, brought on by the central bank in 1819, caught a great many small businessmen unprepared. When the bank ordered its branches to cease renewing loans, the existing boom came to a sudden end, causing problems for sound and unsound businesses alike. Credit expansion based on fiat money — credit and paper currency exceeding bank reserves — had fed the preceding boom. As always, the credit expansion had to end, either in runaway inflation or in a deflationary money panic. Officers of the Bank of the United States chose to end credit expansion before inflation destroyed the monetary system. The ensuing slump in business activity caused substantial unemployment along with the usual suffering among wage earners, who had nothing to do with causing their predicament.

During the panic of 1819, many innocent people suffered. The workers who became unemployed blamed the bank as the monster. To them the bank symbolized all government-created monopolies and grants of privilege to special interests. Since incorporation was a privilege granted by government but not to everyone, all corporations became suspect. The later panics of 1831 and 1837, resulting from too much fiat money, also caught the workingman in a bind and created even more animosity toward monopolies and corporations. Some unscrupulous businessmen bought paper money on the market at a discount and used it at par to pay employees. Small wonder that sooner or later the evils of special-interest legislation would antagonize wage earners, who received no favors from government. Labor reacted by organizing. It sought to develop a power base from which to counter the power in government wielded by the financial and business interests. This power struggle did not occur in a free market; it occurred within government to determine who would receive the indulgences dispensed by Congress.

In the early years of the Republic, only male citizens with sufficient property could vote. Hamiltonianism fully intended that only men of wealth would manage government. Even though representatives at the Constitutional Convention unanimously rejected Hamilton's concepts, the first six years of President Washington's administration witnessed his concepts established in government, and the Marshall Supreme Court supported them. Moneyed interests ran the government, and they sponsored legislation favoring their own interests. By establishing the Bank of the United States, Congress sponsored monopoly in banking. It set the precedent. Citizens, singly or as a group, could not engage in banking without a charter from the government. Later, President Martin van Buren advocated free banking, but his voice was but a whisper in the wind. His suggestion received no support from those in control of legislation.

Since its inception, the central government not only made banking a monopoly privilege, but it enforced monopoly control on all major business activity. Any operation that wanted corporate status had to get a charter from some governmental unit. People had no universal liberty to enter corporate business. Control of bank-note issue and financial loans, operation of a factory, the very right to be an employer constituted special privilege granted by government. Today, any business may incorporate by filing the intent with the state government. For most types of businesses this application has become a mere formality; but banking remains a monopoly privilege granted and protected by government, and — more to the point — allowed only to a few.

Political freedom and economic freedom cannot be separated. How can a person be free if the government controls where he works and what he does? There can be no free labor market when the power of government favors employers against the worker. If government will not grant freedom for all citizens to engage in any economic enterprise of their choice, those on the outside are forced to organize and seek government grants of favor for themselves. This force operated to create present-day unionism. The new class of workingmen — working for wages in contrast to farmers and craftsmen who sell their own product — began to organize in the 1820s in order to influence government. Over the last 150 years, that conduct has destroyed the free market and created the most devastating economic disruption of modern times — the depression of the 1930s. It was the predictable result of special-interest government.

Unfortunately, this political struggle between management and labor has resulted in the view that the interests of business, labor, and consumers are opposed to each other. Hamiltonian Federalism and the methods employed by those working to counter that influence gave it birth. In truth, wage earners, entrepreneurs, owners, and consumers all depend on a successful enterprise. When an enterprise efficiently serves consumers, all interests benefit. When government interferes by granting privilege to some, the respective interests of labor, business, and consumers become opposed. Each group then depends on actions within government. This *harmony of rightly understood interests* is elaborated by Ludwig von Mises and Murray Rothbard. When government protects all freedom, no conflict of interest exists between owners and workers, producers and consumers.

The movement to organize labor resulted in two political interest groups: the Workingman's Party and Locofocoism. Because neither group became large enough to elect candidates, most members soon joined the party that supported Andrew Jackson, that champion of the common man. Jacksonian Democrats included all those people who opposed the Hamiltonian philosophy of government control by moneyed interests. Under Thomas Jefferson the democrats had grown to be the majority party by supporting the common man against Hamiltonianism. A one-party situation evolved as Jeffersonian democrats adopted Hamiltonian ideas. It remained for a new leader to appear, Andrew Jackson, to champion the common man and build a new power base in opposition to government controlled by business and financial interests.

Jay's Treaty of 1794

History demonstrates that periods of peace between nations are mere interludes of rest in preparation for the next war. Certainly the 500-year period under discussion here is no exception. So it was with England, the United States, Spain, and France when they signed the Treaty of Paris in 1783. France and England returned to war in 1793 and again in 1803, 1812, and 1815. Spain joined in some of these matters as did the United States. After a period of fighting, the citizens tire of war, the national treasury runs low, and the combatants find an excuse to cease hostilities. They draw up a treaty, an instrument describing the state of affairs at the moment. The treaty then becomes the jumping off point for the next war.

Most participants in the treaty understand that it describes peace terms only at that moment. Sometimes, the naiveté of individual leaders make them think that war has ended for all years to come. Some principals may even believe the other signatories to the treaty will abide by its terms.

Because naive men sometimes lead their country, treaties become useful instruments by which others gain an advantage until the next war.

Many times nations have signed and broken treaties. England and the United States signed a treaty in 1783; yet neither side honored all its terms. The British refused to vacate their forts and trading posts along the Ohio River; from these bases they supplied guns and whiskey to the Indians. On the high seas, they harassed American merchant ships, impounded cargoes, and impressed American sailors into the Royal Navy. England had to defeat Napoleon twice to end his escapades in Europe. Bonaparte escaped from his first imprisonment in exile and returned to raise another army. In 1919, Germany made treaties with all of Europe. In 1935, German armies again took the offensive. Other treaties followed; yet Germany invaded Poland in 1939, bringing on World War II. Japan had emissaries in Washington in December 1941, negotiating a treaty with the United States to ensure peace in the Pacific. The Japanese ordered the attack on Pearl Harbor even as the negotiators conferred.

Opposing powers in combat employ treaties to achieve advantage. Only the uninformed consider a treaty a binding agreement that all parties will observe in its entirety. Treaties are made to be broken. This does not say that treaties serve no purpose; they do become useful in the hands of astute negotiators. During the interval between wars, the terms of the latest treaty furnish the basis for peaceful pressure and persuasion. The whole affair concerns bluff and posturing. A treaty holds war at bay as long as both sides feel uncertain about the prospects for success in war. The terms of the past treaty are the cards each nation holds in hand in this bluff and posturing.

John Jay went to England in 1794 to negotiate a peaceful resolution to the grievances the United States held against Britain because of that nation's conduct west of the Appalachians and on the high seas in violation of the treaty of 1783. At that time, the British knew about France's popularity with Americans. In every city he visited on his arrival in 1793, Americans enthusiastically received the French envoy Edmond Charles Edouard Genet. Some contributed money to outfit privateers in the French cause against England. The hero of Ohio River valley operations during the War of Independence, George Rogers Clark accepted command of a military force organized by Genet to move against the Spanish and English along the shores of the Gulf of Mexico. The British foreign minister Baron Grenville knew about this enthusiastic American support for

France. The British wanted assurance that the United States would not take part in their scrap with Bonaparte. Jay held a strong bargaining position to arrange a treaty favorable to American interests. Grenville eagerly anticipated seeing him.

Jay's mission failed, scuttled by Alexander Hamilton's ignorant conceit. Hamilton would not leave negotiation in the hands of the State Department where it belonged. Hamilton believed that, no matter what the task, no one could do it as well as he. His success in directing President Washington and in influencing Congress had no doubt so inflated his ego that he believed himself to be virtually omniscient. The Secretary of State, Thomas Jefferson, and the special emissary John Jay were much better positioned to see to U.S. interests. Foreign relations lay entirely outside the scope of Hamilton's responsibilities as Treasury secretary. Nevertheless, Hamilton did interfere. He informed the English ambassador in America that the United States had no intention of becoming actively involved in the European conflict. He made it clear that his nation would follow the Declaration of Neutrality issued the previous year by President Washington.

This news reached England before Jay could secure a commitment from the British. From that moment on Jay could scarcely get an interview with Grenville or any other member of the English cabinet. In the end he had to accept a treaty that many Americans considered a high-handed insult to the interests of the nation.

Hamilton had played the naive dunce; not only had he played out his cards first, he had acted without authority from his government. Hamilton appears to have lacked familiarity with the art of intrigue. He had no experience in dealing with foreign courts; he had never served as a foreign diplomat; as an adult he had seldom been outside the continental United States. By contrast, both John Jay and Thomas Jefferson had spent years in Europe as government representatives. Their experience in foreign diplomacy far surpassed that of Hamilton.

Hamilton's arrogance in the end became his downfall. He lost the support of many friends when in 1800 he attacked the character of President John Adams. His duel with Aaron Burr arose from his attacks on Burr's character. Martyrdom alone saved his image, but what a heavy price to pay.

The Treaty of Paris in 1783 formally ended the War of Independence. That George III and his Parliament had accepted defeat was pure fiction.

England pressed the new nation in every way it peaceably could to restore the colonies to the British Empire. As noted earlier, the English ignored the terms of the treaty of 1783 that required them to withdraw from their forts and trading posts west of the Appalachians. Perhaps more distressing to the new nation, British Men-of-War ignored the sovereignty of U.S. ships carrying the Atlantic trade. The United States at that time had no navy, and the War Department supervised a standing army of a mere 600 men. The new government possessed virtually no financial resources. Plainly put, the United States could not deal with a war with any country. Necessity dictated that President Washington accept, for the moment, all the insults being worked on his nation by England. But this was only a matter of buying time while the nation prepared for another war with England to complete the unfinished task begun in 1776. When in 1794 he sent John Jay to negotiate with the ministers of King George III, President Washington knew that the best interest of his country demanded a longer period of peace before it could countenance renewed fighting. Had Jay's negotiations not been undercut by Hamilton's interference, the later War of 1812 might have been averted. Negotiations might have brought the leaders of the U.S. and Britain to realize that the best interests of both nations lay in peaceful trade between them. The United States provided the largest market for English goods as well as England's best source for raw materials for their manufacturing industry. Leaders of both nations did finally realize this, but not until 20 years of bickering and a brief war had bankrupted the government of the new nation and caused severe economic stress in England.

In spite of strong opposition, the Senate approved and Washington signed the treaty. At that time they had in truth no alternative. No American liked the terms of Jay's Treaty, but conditions forced the President to accept it, causing his public image to fall to a new low. An aging and tired man, he had twice left his beloved Mount Vernon for an eight-year service to his country. At the last, as thanks he received open criticism by his countrymen and a public hanging in effigy.

With the benefit of hindsight, we can see the misunderstanding that lay at the root of this trouble between the United States and England. Hamilton's arrogance had carried him far out of touch with public sentiment. Consequently, he misled the British ambassador who in turn misled his principals. Incorrectly sensing the mood of the American public, the British government did not adjust their conduct toward their former

Colonies. The rank and file in the United States in time realized that the Colonies remained, in fact if not in name, dependencies of the British Empire. The situation required American Presidents to take strong measures to avoid war. Washington sacrificed his popularity by accepting Jay's Treaty. The resentment against England subsided, but it never disappeared. It lay as a cancer on the pride of Americans. Thomas Jefferson declared the treaty a "monument of folly." He believed "acquiescence under insult" was "not the way to escape war." Although Jefferson was correct, war did not come for another 20 years, until a time when the new nation had become better prepared.

The Louisiana Purchase

The successful conclusion of the War of Independence removed all legal barriers to migration from the Atlantic seaboard into the area west of the Appalachians. Pioneers moved into the Ohio River area in the Northwest and into the Tennessee River area in the South, establishing settlements throughout the future states of Kentucky, Ohio, Tennessee, Illinois, and Indiana. This aggravated the old problem of getting produce to market from this Midwest region. Farmers had two avenues available to them. On flat boats and barges they could float their produce down the Mississippi River to the port of New Orleans. As an alternative, they could pack it over the mountains to Eastern markets. The all-water route cost less. The English, however, never controlled the port of New Orleans. First settled and claimed by the French, it had passed back and forth between the French and Spanish. The foreign Governor in New Orleans could at his will close the port to trade coming down the river, confiscating cargo and barge. He detained barge owners in prison, or, at the least, harassed them with legal red tape before releasing them to make their way back home as best they could.

Western settlers naturally opposed this foreign control over their access to markets through New Orleans. They continually implored their congressmen to remedy the situation. They did more. At times they threatened an uprising against the Spanish hold on both New Orleans and Mexico (Texas). Rumors circulated that Aaron Burr, Vice President under Jefferson, journeyed down the Ohio and the Mississippi Rivers recruiting a military force for just such an invasion of Spanish territory. His trials for treason based on these reports came to naught, but they did destroy any possible future career in public service he may have considered. Nothing concrete ever came of these schemes, but the friction caused President Jefferson to take official action. In 1803 he sent special envoys to Paris to determine the truth about reports concerning the transfer of Louisiana from Spain to France.

Jefferson authorized these envoys, if they discovered such to be the case, to offer France up to $10 million for the port of New Orleans. Jefferson believed the United States could not long maintain peace between their countries unless Western farmers gained assured water access to markets.

Napoleon Bonaparte, at that time first consul and soon to become Emperor of France, met the Americans with a surprise offer. Would they be interested in purchasing the entire territory of Louisiana? No one actually knew how much land this involved. Most of the area had never been seen by white men. There existed no definition of either the western or northern boundaries; only later treaties with England and Spain would determine them. Furthermore, Napoleon's treaty with Spain specifically forbade him to sell this territory to any other power. The United States was thus contemplating an illegal $20-million purchase of a pig-in-a-poke.

No doubt Napoleon expected to retake this same territory as soon as he had successfully conquered Europe; he evidently considered the United States the best guardian and the easiest power from which to retake the land when he wanted it back. History wrote another script. By the time the European powers had disposed of Napoleon in 1815, the power of France had been destroyed, England and the United States had settled their differences, and the United States was preparing to negotiate with Spain for the transfer of Florida and the Oregon northwest. The purchase of Louisiana became secure.

The Louisiana Purchase in 1803 can be aptly seen as a side effect of the conflict between France and England. Shortly after his acquisition of Louisiana, Napoleon became obliged to put down a slave revolt in the French islands in the Caribbean. He sent a select force of experienced troops under the command of his brother-in-law, General LeClerc, one of his best subordinates. The effort failed. Napoleon sent more men, with similarly disastrous results. Not armies, but the climate and yellow fever, a disease common to the region, defeated the French forces. In view of these obstacles to holding possessions in the Caribbean, Napoleon reconsidered his chances of keeping Louisiana during his war with Britain. The

United States could cause him considerable embarrassment if it joined England in war against him and attacked New Orleans. He well understood how untenable his position could become without a strong military presence in the area. Napoleon decided to rid himself of the problem before circumstances forced him to. He cut his losses and made an asset of this perplexing problem. He sold Louisiana to the United States. In his upcoming war against England, he could make good use of the money he would receive from the sale. (Interestingly, in order to pay for this purchase, the United States obtained the money from English banks. So in part, Englishmen financed Bonaparte to make war against them.)

Americans had mixed reactions to this proposal. The purchase delighted Westerners. Control of both the east and the west banks of the Mississippi River assured them of water access to markets in Europe, the West Indies, and the Eastern seaboard. Eastern merchants and manufacturers disapproved. They saw no need to enlarge the territory of the nation. More land meant more people, and "everyone knew that a democracy could function only among closely knit people of a small nation." More land in the West meant more states, and Easterners could see their control of Congress slipping away.

Jefferson looked into the future and visualized the American continent under one nation with freedom of trade and travel for everyone. He viewed the purchase of Louisiana as an important next move toward that goal. Even before the purchase of the Louisiana territory, Jefferson had prepared to send an exploratory expedition into the region. He had for months been instructing his personal secretary, Meriwether Lewis, to lead this journey. Jefferson had also prepared to seek approval from Spain, the publicly acknowledged owner of this land. The knowledge that France had acquired Louisiana, and the subsequent purchase of the entire claim hastened these plans into execution. Lewis obtained the help of William Clark, brother of George Rogers Clark of Revolutionary fame; and they spent two years traveling from St. Louis to the Pacific Ocean and back, following the Missouri River to the mountains and the Snake River on to the Pacific Ocean.

As had Columbus's 1492 crossing of the Atlantic Ocean, the Lewis and Clark Expedition served to dispel fear of the unknown. Soon thereafter, an expedition led by Zebulon Pike followed the Arkansas River to the mountains. Trappers and adventurers spread throughout the vast expanse of the West. Settlers followed. By 1821 the nation included 24 states and 3 organized territories. The northern Great Plains (to become Kansas, Nebraska, and the Dakotas) remained at that time an unorganized territory.

The War of Independence Concluded (War of 1812)

When Napoleon and England resumed warfare in May of 1803, the European pot boiled over again. Britain tried to stop American ships from carrying food and stores to France. France tried to stop trade between England and the United States. The Louisiana Purchase had essentially removed France from the North American continent, France having retained only two small islands off Newfoundland. By that sale France gave up its major claims in America. With little reason for conflict between France and the United States, the two countries have never begun hostilities with one another. Consequently, during the Napoleonic Wars when the participants seized U.S. ships on the high seas, the American people looked on England as the villain, not France. The old resentment against the terms of Jay's Treaty resurfaced. The public raised an outcry for war with England.

President Jefferson kept the peace during his second term, but James Madison, his successor, finally succumbed to the pressure of the hawks. Public opinion favored war. In June 1812 the United States declared war on Great Britain. Called the War of 1812, it was in reality the concluding phase of the War of Independence. That war finally released American trade from the Navigation Acts. The British withdrew into the territory of Canada, north of the border established in the treaty of 1783. The American Navy earned the respect of the Europeans, and the United States took its place among the nations of the Western world as a fully sovereign State.

Many have declared the War of 1812 a useless fight. They base this claim on two facts: (1) The Treaty of Ghent, December 24, 1814, which terminated hostilities, left territorial boundaries between England and the United States much as they existed at the onset of war; and (2) President Madison signed the declaration of war two days after Parliament rescinded the Orders-in-Council, which, by perpetuating the concepts of the old Navigation Acts, had caused much of the friction between England and the United States.

No doubt the two nations could have negotiated a peaceful resolution to their differences in 1812. These questions, however, arise: Without the defeat of the British naval forces on Lakes Erie and Champlain, and without the defeat of British land forces in the Battle of New Orleans, would the United States have moved into the same aura of respect among the powers of Europe? England offered capitulation in 1812 because she needed the trade with the United States in her war with Napoleon. Once Britain had dealt with Napoleon, what assurance would the young nation have had that England would continue to observe the terms of any new treaty? American successes in the late months of that war not only concluded the War of Independence, it established the position of the United States as a world power.

The War of 1812 brought another war hero to the presidency, General Andrew Jackson. The character of Andrew Jackson left a permanent stamp on the operation of American government.

Most engagements of that war the antagonists fought on water. The major land battle, the Battle of New Orleans, occurred in January 1815, about two weeks after the signing of the Treaty of Ghent. In defense of New Orleans, American forces under General Andrew Jackson completely humiliated the pride of the British army under the command of General Pakenham. English casualties, in the thousands, exceeded half their force, a force greater than that under Jackson's command. Americans suffered less than 100 casualties; they held their ground, requiring the British to retreat from the field. That battle did not alter the immediate outcome of the war and certainly had no impact on the terms of the treaty. However, following so closely on the success of the American naval forces at Plattsburg, it made an immense impression on Western nations. Thereafter, they considered the new nation a power to be reckoned with. U.S. citizens could hold up their heads in any company.

War for the young nation in 1812 can readily be considered necessary. To be free, men must always be ready to fight. Sometimes they must come to blows simply because the opposition will not back off until defeated in a scrap. A truism in relations between individuals, it states a truth about relations between nations, because nations have no existence apart from the mortal flesh and blood of their citizens. That little war did succeed in one prominent way; after the Battle of New Orleans, U.S. citizens fought no other battles on American soil against a foreign power until Japan attacked the U.S. fleet in Pearl Harbor on December 7, 1941; and an American President invited that attack. (See Chapter 15.)

A Comment on the Need for Intelligence Gathering

In the interval between the War of Independence and the War of 1812, the United States was on trial. Its very existence as a sovereign nation stood at risk. Any one of the European powers, by attacking in force, could possibly have caused the Colonies (1) to rejoin the British Empire or (2) to abandon their union and become easy pickings for opportunists, which would have created a diversity of national interests in North America similar to what exists today in Central America and the Caribbean. Foreign relations was perhaps the major concern of Presidents Washington, Adams, Jefferson, and Madison, and remains today a primary province of that office. These early Presidents succeeded, and the events of their efforts are instructive.

When dealing with any foreign country, national leaders must know the thinking of the leaders in other governments. Intelligence-gathering is essential. A case in point is the significant loss to the new nation in the clumsy handling of negotiations that led to Jay's Treaty. Before negotiations began, a greater familiarity with European conditions in 1793 might have better informed American leaders on the importance the English attached to American neutrality. Good intelligence work might have discovered the intensity of this anxiety among the ministers of King George's court. Good intelligence work might have determined Napoleon's mood leading into negotiations for the purchase of Louisiana. Advance appraisal of all possibilities prepares the negotiator with educated guesses about the weaknesses of the other side and with insight into his own less obvious strengths. Good intelligence-gathering requires a certain amount of cloak-and-dagger work. The other fellow does not reveal his own weaknesses; he guards that information carefully.

Today's voters need to recognize these realities involved in foreign affairs. Contemporary, public review damages negotiations because it discloses too much information to other parties. Citizens and their representatives in government must of necessity stay removed from negotiations between nations.

The framers of the Constitution expressed this point well when they empowered the president, with the advice and consent of the Senate, to conduct all intergovernmental relations. The people must select their best agents and leave them alone to do what they can. The only permissible review of their actions must come after the fact. Self-interest demands the secrecy that recent actions of Congress and the news media choose to destroy.

Laissez Faire and the Industrial Revolution

In the 17th century, European monarchs fell to revolutions because they resisted the will of the people.Thanks to the proliferation of books flowing from the new printing press, an educated middle class had risen among the populace. Only ignorant masses tolerate rigid, unchanging strangulation of thought and action. These revolts included action to pull away from the dictation of the church. Protestantism became an alternative to Catholicism. Individuals wanted freedom to choose their occupation and where they worked, to interpret the Bible for themselves, to be free of others dictating the details of their lives. Revolution sought individual liberty. The American War of Independence was but a small part of a greater revolution. To put a name to this movement, French writers referred to a government policy of "laissez faire, laissez-passer" — to be free from government restrictions in order to live, worship, work, and move about at will.

Before proceeding, we should recognize the government restrictions that people wanted laid aside:

1. An organization of craftsmen, the guild, determined who could become an apprentice, how many could engage in that craft, and where each could work. The government enforced these exclusionary rules of guilds. (Compare guilds to 20th-century labor unions and to the existing system of licensing journeymen and professionals.)

2. Governments enforced limits on competition. Guild members considered it unfair for a more efficient businessman or craftsman to produce better or cheaper goods and undersell competitors. The police power of the State protected high prices. (Compare present American policies of anti-competition in foreign trade, of antitrust, of regulated government-sponsored monopoly, and of government-controlled farm prices.)

3. Workers opposed machines because they replaced labor. Government forbade their use. (Advance this concept to its logical limit and man should be denied a point to his spear or a sharpened edge to his ax because it improves the efficiency of labor.)

4. The masses and those in authority opposed accumulation of wealth in the hands of individuals. Authorities discouraged

saving; they confiscated wealth. (Compare this to present-day measures of wealth redistribution through taxation.)

5. All governments pursued a policy of restricting and controlling the activities of entrepreneurs, a policy considered to be in the best interest of a nation's well-being.

The early economists — of whom Adam Smith, *Wealth of Nation* (*ca.* 1770) was the English spokesman — taught the doctrines of the free market, capitalism, and laissez faire. They sought to expose the error of beliefs in restriction. And history shows that the Industrial Revolution prospered coincidentally with the acceptance of their teachings. In brief, laissez faire means a government policy toward industry and commerce of protection for private property and contract, as opposed to government intervention and central planning.

Today, many individuals have tried to discredit laissez faire without knowing what it really means. Textbooks and literature often include statements such as the following by Robert Cushman:

> *The Great Depression of the 1930's revealed that the laissez-faire economic theory which underlay most judicial thinking was unable to prevent economic disaster.* (Cushman 1982. 88)

Writers condemn laissez faire with no discussion, as though, of course, everybody knows the evils inherent in it. In truth, abandoning laissez faire caused and prolonged the Great Depression. Some economists, notably the Austrian Ludwig von Mises, spoke out ahead of that event, trying to get governments to stop their foolhardy race into economic disaster. Even so, many historians have condemned offhand this policy of freedom.

Laissez faire means government protection for contract and private property; it lets the consumer make and execute his own plans; it lets producers supply what consumers want to buy; it lets the worker choose where, for whom, and at what form of labor he works; it does not force producers, labor, and consumers to comply with terms of central planning. It does not mean government protection for monopoly or government intervention in the form of subsidies, embargoes, import restrictions, protective tariffs, and regulations on labor, consumers, or producers. The science of economics deals fundamentally with understanding how the free market operates and how government intervention upsets the efficient functioning of industry and commerce.

Present-day confusion about the meaning of laissez faire rests on a distorted interpretation of the record of the 19th century. During those years the U.S. government consistently enacted legislation that favored particular interests. Congress and the courts had in fact favored business and financial interests since the days of Alexander Hamilton. Restrictions forbade free entry into business. The government sponsored a monopoly in banking and inflation of the money supply. High tariffs protected domestic manufacturers from foreign competition, causing consumers to pay higher prices. Courts issued injunctions that forbade labor to organize for cooperative bargaining with employers. Although the influence of laissez faire enabled Americans to embrace the Industrial Revolution and advance their standard of living more rapidly than in other countries, the government philosophy of the 19th century did not operate completely in accord with those principles of freedom. The 20th-century condemnation of laissez faire more correctly applies to government restrictions that prevented the full operation of this philosophy of freedom.

One cannot point to a particular time and say that at this moment conditions of life changed. Previous happenings influence subsequent events. Even the voyage of Christopher Columbus in 1492 resulted from earlier events. One can say, however, that after a given time certain things could develop. In this sense only, can we say that after the English parliamentary elections of 1780, Englishmen and Americans in the Colonies became free to exploit the concepts of their imagination. In this sense, the year 1780 marks the beginning of the Industrial Revolution among English-speaking people. In that election Britons replaced King George's henchmen with individuals opposed to reconquering the American Colonies. In that election the people essentially stripped their king of power. Begun over 500 years earlier, the English Revolution finally established a functional government that was responsive to the people. They no longer had to adhere to the old ways of doing things. If a person wanted to change his way of working, he no longer had to get permission.

Freedom from the government restrictions meant freedom to change. Change opens the way to improvement. Freedom to change means opportunity for people to control their own destiny. Change is the adversary of government-protected vested interests. Today, crusaders for the rights of the common man do not resist change. Change is resisted by the established institutions that have adjusted to the rules and regulations of the past. Change jeopardizes their supremacy. Restrictions favor the existing enterprise. High taxes prevent the newcomer from obtaining capital sufficient to challenge the established order. Without freedom for any and all to change, consumers never learn about the services and products that do not appear because of government-enforced restrictions. Innovation cannot bring to market the new, the imaginative, the departures from the past. Stagnation sets in and leads to economic disintegration. It was no mere happenstance that inventions and use of new methods and new technology blossomed after 1780 in England and the United States. Although in use in the coal mines of England as early as 1702, the steam engine did not come into general use in commerce and industry until the middle years of the next century, when men became free to change.

The use of new technology characterizes the Industrial Revolution. The improved plow increased farming efficiency. Whitney's cotton gin lowered the cost of producing cotton so much that low-cost cloth became available to the general public. Mechanical devices for spinning the thread and weaving the cloth added impetus to this trend. Cotton cloth replaced linens, homespun woolens, and animal skins for clothing. Robert Fulton's steamboat appeared in 1807, and man adapted the steam engine to overland transport on railroads after 1830. As C. W. Crawley points out:

> *Although there was a steamship on the Clyde in 1812 and one on the Seine in 1822, the last great age of wood and sail lasted into the thirties, and ship development reached its perfection, not in size but in design, in the fast clipper. . . . In 1830 there were only thirty-nine steamships . . . registered in the United Kingdom* [of a fleet of 19,907]. (Crawley 1969. 39)

In agriculture, inventions to improve the efficiency of farm labor appeared as follows: 7 in the 17th century, 8 between 1701 and 1750, 30 between 1751 and 1814, and 16 between 1815 and 1848.

Historians reluctantly accept political and economic freedom — political policies of laissez faire — as a necessary ingredient for the Industrial Revolution. Yet in their writings, while pondering the causes of this development, they make statements like the following:

> *Frankland Lewis declared in the House of Commons in 1816,*

[that the cause of advancing industrialization was] *"not because labour was cheaper here than elsewhere, but because our persons and properties were secure — because we had good government . . . and, above all, because we had a vast accumulation of capital, in which no other country could compete with us, and which would not seek employment under laws that yielded a more uncertain production." (Ibid.* 42)

Extension of markets was made possible, particularly, by reduced prices, for the goods of the Industrial Revolution tended to be cheap and plentiful. (Ibid. 43)

Italy's economic ills . . . stemmed . . . from fragmentation. . . . In the eighteenth century, political divisions, trade barriers, poor communications, guild restrictions, small markets, currency differences, and the persistence of privilege had reduced a once great economy almost to subsistence agriculture. (Ibid. 48)

Only one thing is reasonably certain: the turning point. After 1780 the production of industrial goods increased markedly. . . . On the long-term causes of the English industrial revolution, contemporary and nineteenth-century explanation stressed four factors: the change in economic policy from mercantilism to laissez faire, attributed largely to Adam Smith; the expansion of British commerce; the increase in productivity that came from the new machines, and, hence, the engineers and artisans who invented and applied them; the thrift and dedication of the early entrepreneurs who made available the capital and hard work necessary for pioneering new industrial processes. (Ibid. 41-42)

Why did entrepreneurs, capitalists, engineers, and free craftsmen fail to come out of the woodwork, so to speak, until 1780? Were they not there all the while, waiting for a political atmosphere that encouraged free enterprise? The historians give all the evidence and then miss the proper relationship between cause and effect. Their own words admit the truth, but they never quite accept it in their thinking. So they fail to emphasize the fact that the Industrial Revolution became possible only in an atmosphere of (1) political stability, (2) economic and political freedom, and (3) a secure right to private property. If they are to succeed, nations freeing themselves from communism in the 1990s must first adopt a political rule that assures these essentials.

This is a natural reaction of educated man — the Law of Face. Educated people withdraw from the truth that education does not in itself qualify a person to direct his fellowman, that man can thrive in an atmosphere of freedom with no coercive direction by intellectuals, that society rewards thinkers less than doers. Intellectuals rebel against the fact that consumers value knowledge less than they value television, pornography, hamburgers, sex, detective stories, and tales of adventure and romance.

The direction taken by many educators has ignored the will of the people. Consumers want education to aid them in their peaceful societal cooperation. Consequently, any social advancement requires teaching people to think critically. Although many educators accept this objective, evil develops when, after years of application, an educated person finds his ideas and teachings ignored. This thwarts his sense of accomplishment, and he seeks power to force others to see the "truth." As government control tends to gravitate to the educated class, it becomes natural for these thwarted egos to exercise their power to relieve the frustration.

This seems to present a hopeless paradox, and many men have succumbed to hopelessness, truly defeated by this apparent, built-in, self-destroying feature of an educated populace. The events of history reveal what man has done in the past. They show what man will do in the future if he permits the same human traits to control his societal cooperation. (For a final comment, see Chapter 17.)

The principles of human action as delineated by Ludwig von Mises in *Human Action* make it clear that (1) the Industrial Revolution, by necessity, paralleled the growth of freedom with the adoption of the political philosophy of laissez faire and its protection of private property, and that (2) economic development, prosperity, and political freedom will die with the extinction of economic freedom. Mises states:

> *None of the great modern inventions would have been put to use if the mentality of the precapitalistic era had not been thoroughly demolished by the economists. What is commonly called the "industrial revolution" was an offspring of the ideological*

revolution brought about by the doctrines of the economists. (Mises [1949] 1966. 8)

Economic progress and prosperity in the United States persist in spite of government interference, but business enterprise suffers frequent spells of upset because of this intervention.

The United States Organization in 1821		
The Organized Territories	**The Free States**	**The Slave States**
	Connecticut (1783)	Alabama (1819)
Arkansas Territory	Illinois (1818)	Delaware (1783)
Florida Territory	Indiana (1816)	Georgia (1783)
Michigan Territory	Maine (1820)	Kentucky (1792)
	Massachusetts (1783)	Louisiana (1812)
	New Hampshire (1783)	Maryland (1783)
	New Jersey (1783)	Mississippi (1817)
	New York (1783)	Missouri (1821)
	Ohio (1803)	North Carolina (1783)
	Pennsylvania (1783)	South Carolina (1783)
	Rhode Island (1783)	Tennessee (1796)
	Vermont (1791)	Virginia (1783)

This division between "free" and "slave" states preserved an even representation in the Senate between the interests of the North and the South. By treaty with England, the United States established title to the Oregon Territory in 1846. Following the War with Mexico, the nation acquired the Southwest by treaty in 1848. These annexations upset the balance between free and slave states; the nation could no longer ignore the issue of secession. (See Chapter 9.)

Three accomplishments make President Jackson's administration significant to Americans in the 20th century: (1) He restored the power of the presidency, which Congress had usurped during administrations after that of Thomas Jefferson. (2) He demonstrated the political power of disgruntled minorities. . . . (3) He laid the groundwork for the later annexation of Texas and all the Southwest to the Pacific Ocean.

Chapter 6

The Age of Jackson, 1815-1848

The People and the Times

*A*FTER THE FRENCH AND INDIAN WAR, the white population in America regarded Indian disturbances more as a nuisance than a threat to the nation. Most confrontations involved small parties of Indians, perhaps a dozen or two, and a few settlers. A raiding party of one killed John Lincoln, Abraham Lincoln's grandfather, on his Kentucky farm. What history has recorded as Indian wars seldom involved a hostile group exceeding 1,000. William Henry Harrison earned the fame that made him president in a four-hour battle at Tippecanoe Creek against a force of perhaps 500. General "Mad Anthony" Wayne at Fallen Timbers defeated a force of less than 2,000. Andrew Jackson quieted a similar number of Seminoles in Alabama in 1818. The heaviest casualties from one Indian raid numbered at about 500. These are modest numbers compared to the 10,000 Union casualties on December 13, 1862, at Fredericksburg, Virginia, during the War Between the States.

Americans have tended to exaggerate the extent of conflict between white and red men. By the end of the War of Independence, the once strong Confederation of Six Nations numbered less than 5,000. The U.S. population of white men exceeded 12 million when President Jackson moved the eastern Indians to Oklahoma in the 1830s. Less than 60,000 natives began that "Trail of Tears." Of course, those 60,000 considered that event a grim ordeal. John Lincoln's family considered his death at the hands of one Indian a most serious affair too. But to the nation after 1820, Indian problems constituted an annoyance that involved little else than the nation's conscience. Few Americans had contact with the natives beyond the pages of newspapers, books, and magazines.

During the thousands of years they occupied the land, the Indians, so few in number, had not altered the landscape. Trees reclaimed the land as they moved and burned virgin forests to make way for planting their corn. From the grassland of the Great Plains to the Atlantic seaboard spread a great continuous forest interrupted only by rivers and swamps. Someone traveling the Midwest today finds it difficult to imagine the primeval nature of that wilderness. The huge trees — some 150 feet tall with trunks over 10 feet in diameter — nearly shut out the sun for miles at a stretch. Deadfalls on the ground covered with vines created a tangled abatis. Dense thickets choked the spaces where the sun shown through. When young Abe Lincoln's family moved from Kentucky to southern Indiana, Abe and his father Tom had to go ahead at times with axes to clear a trail. Abe later wrote that, "the panther's scream filled night with fear," and "bears preyed on the swine."

From Maine to Georgia, the great majority of white immigrants and their slaves lived on the coastal plain, a narrow strip of land over 1,000 miles long and, for the most part, less than 100 miles wide. Inhabitants of the interior lived along waterways that knifed through the forests.

By 1820 the new government had constructed one road west from the coastal plain, called the National Road or the Cumberland Road. This trail changed from dust to mud as the weather determined. At their worst, most farm roads today are better than the best parts of that one "improved" road into Ohio.

Events in the past did not occur in the abstract, as one might deduce from reading history books. Women and men at that time lived, loved, laughed, and cried just as they do now. The difference between then and now rests in the particulars. In the 1820s mothers bore children and worried about their uncertain future, much as mothers have always done. Those pioneer mothers did not worry about street crime and nuclear war, but about disease, insects, survival in childbirth, keeping warm, and, on the frontier, about Indian raids, wild animals, and leaky roofs. The roof on the one-room log cabin that was home to young Abe Lincoln in Indiana seldom turned the rain completely. Fathers worried about going to prison for debt, success of farm crops, religion and politics, clearing land for their sons, and finding a suitable husband for their daughters. Patterns of life in America did not change much from 1620 to 1820. Most families farmed for their own consumption and sold little produce. George Dangerfield provides this glimpse into the life of the pioneer:

> *The pioneer farmer raised his own wool, cotton, and flax for his . . . clothing, which his women spun and wove and made into garments. . . . His household furniture, his farming utensils, his harness, were all homemade; and his wooden cart, without tires or boxes, and run without tar* [lubrication], *could be heard creaking a mile or more away.*
>
> *The . . . women helped with the planting, the hoeing, and the raking at harvest time; and if there was milking to be done, they did that too.* (Dangerfield 1952. 111)

Planters in the Southern states shipped tobacco and cotton north to Massachusetts, Pennsylvania, and New York; and to Europe, where they bought furniture and clothing. New Englanders built ships and traded with merchants of the Mediterranean, the West Indies, Europe, and England. Philadelphia, Charleston, New York, and Boston, the important ports for this Atlantic trade, were not cities in the modern sense. Within the nation, only five cities could boast a population exceeding 25,000; and the largest of these, New York, had fewer than 124,000 inhabitants. Agriculture remained the mainstay of life, occupying over 90 percent of the families.

Sons lived much as their fathers and their grandfathers had lived before them. Oil from animal fat lighted their homes; wood cooked their food and heated their buildings. Overland transport moved on the backs of horses and mules. Heavy, bulky products moved on ships, barges, flatboats, and in canoes. Roads remained unimproved except to be cleared of trees and boulders. An 1804 Ohio law required stumps over 12 inches high to be removed from all roadways. The larger cities paved only the most important streets. Visitors to the nation's capital, Washington, D.C., found an unpaved Pennsylvania Avenue, and the arteries of the city treated their fine carriages to clinging yellow mud or curtains of fine dust.

Medicine had not become a meaningful science. Doctors knew little more than did the Indian medicine man. Most mothers could do as much for the sick in their family as could a doctor.

The wealthy built their homes of stone and brick, but by far most buildings were framed of wood and sided with clapboards. The better-built homes had wooden floors, but many houses rested directly on the soil with a swept-dirt floor. In December of 1816, when the Lincoln family arrived at their destination in Indiana:

> *The whole family pitched in and threw together a pole shed or "half-faced camp," at the open side a log fire kept burning night and day. In the next weeks of that winter Tom Lincoln (Abe's father), with the help from neighbors and young Abe, now nearly eight, erected a cabin 18 by 20 feet, with a loft.* (Sandburg 1954. 10)

The Lincoln family circumstances were typical for the times in that part of the country. Thomas Lincoln, not poor by pioneer standards, filed for his 160 acres and with cash paid the first quarterly installment as required by law. The farm he sold in Kentucky had over 500 acres, though he sold it at less than market price because of a flawed title. When relatives joined them in Indiana, they too lived for a time in the pole shed that had first sheltered Tom and Nancy Lincoln. A contemporary, William Cobbett, described the trip West:

> *The rugged roads, the dirty hovels, the fire in the woods to sleep by, the pathless ways through the wilderness, the dangerous crossings of the rivers. . . . To boil their pot in the gipsy-fashion* [over an open fire], *to have a mere board to eat on . . .*

to sleep under a shed far inferior to . . . English cowpens. (Dangerfield 1952. 108)

An anonymous woman wrote to President Monroe:

It was on the 6 of May we came here [Barnesville, Ohio]; *we
had no other food for our horses nor cows but what they could
procure in the woods. . . . Your patience sir would not hold out
while I would describe swarms of large flies which inhabit these
uncultivated lands and which sting the cattle. . . . Unsound
corn, sick wheat and mills seven miles off. . . . You will conclude
we did not eat much bread — and neither we did. (Ibid.* 108)

Americans had a saying that cowards never started, and the weak died
along the way.

On their first visit to America, nearly all Europeans remarked about the
absence of homeless street people and beggars so prevalent in the villages
of Europe. Though far from wealthy, all Americans had the essentials of
life: food, clothing, and shelter. In Europe, misguided government action
had created and sustained the destitution and homelessness so common on
the Continent and in Britain. In a society of free men, opportunity and
self-interest keep citizens productive. In 1820, no government-created barriers against work existed in the United States. Any willing worker could
find employment, if not working for others, then for himself. No man
needed a license to practice his trade and pursue his craft. None refused to
employ a person because of his young age or because he would work for
less than some might ask. No one went in want because of misfortune. No
government decrees forbade private charity, and free men shared with their
less fortunate brothers.

Shay and his associates in Massachusetts rebelled against government
confiscation of their farms for unpaid taxes. No matter that they had been
unable to tend their fields for years while they served (often without compensation) in the army during the War of Independence. Shay's Rebellion
arose over injustice at the hands of government. A discriminatory tax
caused the Whiskey Rebellion. These men revolted against the injustice of
government intervention. When government followed the philosophy of
laissez faire, men prospered.

The young nation established an atmosphere of political and economic freedom. As a consequence, from the earliest time its citizens shared in the developments known as the Industrial Revolution. People knew a greater degree of freedom than in any other Western nation, and this relatively greater freedom remained for a longer time. Primarily for this reason, America became a dominant economic power in the Western hemisphere. In the 18th and 19th centuries, visiting Europeans particularly noted this prosperity.

Great Britain emerged from the Napoleonic Wars in 1815 as undisputed master of the seas and the center of world commerce. With less than two percent of the world population, she stood for a century thereafter as the dominant economic power of the Western world. Britain maintained this dominance until she abandoned the policy of laissez faire. The restrictions of the guild philosophy returned in the form of government support for labor unions. Welfare became a function of government. Taxes confiscated the fruits of production to redistribute wealth "according to need." Planned production for the "good of man" replaced production for the "wants of the consumers." Great Britain fell from a world power to an insular, second-rate power in world affairs. Naturally, the most capable Englishmen took their capital and left the country. Opportunity for employment no longer kept pace with the birth rate. Begging and thievery became again the only occupation available to many. When treating the events of the late 20th century (Chapter 16), this study will examine the changes that have caused chronic unemployment, masses of homeless people, and the emergence of marauding bands of young thieves in the United States today.

In America in 1815, this favorable attitude toward government intervention lay in the undisclosed future. Men were free. Life was simple. The needs of the land and the needs of the consumer occupied people's minds and their time. Americans had a restless eagerness to get on with the business of making life more productive. There was work to be done; men were willing to work, and they held no truck with those who would interfere.

Immigrants left one major item behind in Europe, class distinction. As poor became rich, try as they might, they could not build a permanent upper class. The masses not only would not tolerate it, many once-rich became poor and others became rich. An aristocracy developed only in the South, and the evil this created can be seen from examining events of the American Civil War.

Andrew Jackson

Historians have labeled the period of James Monroe's administration "The Era of Good Feelings." By then the Jeffersonian Democrats had adopted just enough principles of the Federalists that there existed, in fact, but one political party. In 1820 Monroe received all but one vote of the electoral college. His only opponent, John Quincy Adams, ran as an independent. The Federalists had no candidate; their party, the party of Hamilton, no longer existed. In the election of 1824, all four presidential candidates claimed allegiance to the same party, the Jeffersonian Democrats. The election of 1824 is interesting in its outcome. Although Andrew Jackson received a substantial plurality in both popular and electoral votes, he did not become president. Since no candidate received a majority of the electoral votes, the House of Representatives, as specified in the Constitution, made the final selection of a President. The House chose Adams.

The results of that election were as follows:

Candidate	Electoral Vote	Popular Vote
Andrew Jackson	99	153,544
John Quincy Adams	84	108,740
William H. Crawford	41	46,618
Henry Clay	37	47,136

As candidates again in 1828, Adams and Jackson each headed his own party. Adams represented the old party, then called the National Republicans, and Jackson represented the new party, the Democrats. Politically, Jackson had everything going for him. He was the hero of New Orleans and of the Seminole campaign in 1818. A popular senator from Tennessee, he had the support of most newly enfranchised voters. He was "one of them" in spite of being a rich plantation owner living in style near Nashville. Jackson received a substantial majority of both popular and electoral votes, vindicating the will of the people defied by the House four years earlier.

Three accomplishments make President Jackson's administration significant to Americans in the 20th century: (1) He restored the power of the presidency, which Congress had usurped during administrations after that of Thomas Jefferson. (2) He demonstrated the political power of disgruntled minorities. As Franklin Roosevelt did later in the 1930s, Jackson sought the support of the forgotten man. (Present power of the Democratic party rests on that demonstration made by Jackson in 1828.) (3) He laid the groundwork for the later annexation of Texas and all the Southwest to the Pacific Ocean. This area, together with the Gadsden Purchase, includes all the territory now known as Utah, Nevada, Arizona, California, New Mexico, and Texas, and parts of Kansas, Colorado, Wyoming, and Oklahoma.

The Louisiana Purchase in 1803 doubled the geographical area of the United States. The annexation of the Republic of Texas in 1845 along with the acquisition from Mexico by treaty in 1848 again doubled the area of the nation. Jackson envisioned the larger United States, as had Jefferson and John Quincy Adams, "from sea to shining sea"; and he acted by sending his personal representative Sam Houston into the heart of the region, the Texas province of Mexico. Always with Jackson's support, even when Congress turned its back on the Texans, Sam Houston led the Texans to become an independent republic and later the 28th state of the Union.

The Strength of the President
Events of the late 20th century illustrate why voters should know something of the nation's need for a strong President, and historical experience since 1789 has supplied many examples. President Jackson saved the union of the states during his administration only to have it lost by the weakness in the men who followed him in that office. Significantly, the people reelected not one of these later Presidents to a second term until another strong-willed President came into office, Abraham Lincoln.

Elected locally, senators and members of the House respond to a sectional constituency. Congressmen from Wisconsin vote for benefits to the dairy industry. California and Louisiana send representatives to Congress who demonstrate a sensitive interest in tidewater oil development. Those from Wyoming closely watch legislation affecting the administration of public lands. Representatives from the corn-producing states along with those from Louisiana, Texas, and Colorado uphold preservation of sugar import quotas. Kansas senators fight to preserve some form of special benefits for wheat farmers. Sectionalism fosters special-interest legislation. It must be countered by a national viewpoint. Americans have only two elected officials in Washington, the President and the Vice President, whose constituency is nationwide. National interest dictates that the President assert dominant leadership.

The Constitution requires advice and consent of the Senate for all treaties with foreign powers, but the day-to-day handling of foreign relations rests with the President. The Constitution wisely separates the powers of legislation, administration, and judicial review, and gives the President a check on acts of Congress through the veto. This separation collapses under a weak President to the detriment of national and individual interests.

Congress will always contain men ambitious to be President, and who accordingly try to exhibit their expertise in the areas that the Constitution reserved for the President. Consequently, a power-grab erupts in Congress whenever a weak person occupies that office. Such a President then finds it difficult to act independently of Congress. As his effectiveness in administration diminishes, the nation experiences adverse results.

George Washington, "the untouchable" throughout most of his administration, never directly faced this power struggle. He did, however, stand firm on the one divisive issue that arose during his presidency, Jay's Treaty of 1894 with England. Jefferson became the first President to encounter congressional efforts to overrun his office. He resisted successfully and so preserved the power of the presidency. Since that time the conflict has never ceased; Congress confronts each new occupant of that office with attempts to usurp his powers.

Popular support strengthens a President in this contest with Congress. John Quincy Adams had the will, the inclination, and the intellectual capacity to be a strong President; but he came off weak because he lacked popular support. Fortunately for the national interest, when the nation needed his strength, it was available. As Secretary of State under James Monroe, John Q. Adams wrote the Monroe Doctrine, which told the world that the United States would resist all foreign imperialism in the two Americas. The same Adams turned international outrage over Jackson's 1818 military offensive in Florida into a peaceful surrender of Spanish claims in that peninsula. The people of the nation wisely supported President Jackson during his two terms following John Quincy Adams. Unfortunately, the nation had no Adams and Jackson team when Russia moved into Cuba during John Kennedy's administration in the 1960s.

In the recent past, the country has seen Richard Nixon hounded out of office by congressional opposition. President Ronald Reagan faced similar efforts. Congress has overpowered all the Presidents after Eisenhower and continues its efforts to set foreign policy, supervise foreign relations, manage the military, and virtually emasculate the presidency. Concurrent congressional oversight of every act of the President and his executive personnel serves the nation poorly, unless, of course, the voters have elected a weak man to the office.

Presidents Nixon and Reagan would have been well served had they answered Congress in a manner characteristic of Andrew Jackson. History records that in response to a decision of the Supreme Court with which he disagreed, President Jackson declared, "It is (Chief Justice) Marshall's decision; now let him enforce it." And Jackson ignored Marshall's court ruling for at least another 12 months. This reference makes no statement of value judgment relative to the merits of President Jackson's action in this affair. It is cited only to illustrate his willingness to assert his own convictions and accept the responsibility. At another time, President Jackson supported the members of Congress when a mob threatened violence during their deliberations. Jackson is said to have reassured the frightened senators by declaring:

> *Gentlemen, I shall be glad to see this federal mob on Capitol Hill. I will fix their heads on the iron palisades around the square to assist your deliberations. The leaders I will hang as high as Haman to deter forever all attempts to control the legislation of the Congress by intimidation and design.* (Schlesinger 1946. 109)

When asked just how seriously Congress should take Jackson's declaration, Senator Thomas Hart Benton of Missouri is said to have replied, "When Old Hickory [Jackson] starts talking about hanging men, other men start looking for rope." (*Ibid.*)

During World War II, President Franklin D. Roosevelt would have been completely dominated by Winston Churchill had he not been strong-willed. And when he went to Yalta, a sick and disabled man, he served his country poorly by reason of his weakness. Confronted by Stalin, he gave away the kitchen, and the United States has been paying the price ever since.

President Harry "Give-Em-Hell" Truman is reported to have said, "If you can't stand the heat, get out of the kitchen." Truman faced difficult decisions as President, and he never vacillated. Right or wrong he met the challenge and dropped the A-bomb on Japan. Only the hindsight of centuries will provide a proper evaluation of decisions President Truman had only months to consider. At the time, the American people thought the nation benefited from his strength of will and personal courage. To say the least, he accepted full responsibility for his actions.

President Jackson encountered intense sectionalism; the South, West, and Northeast each went their separate ways. Only the strength of personal conviction enabled Jackson to solidify these varied interests into a working union. Most notable perhaps was his handling of the threat of secession by South Carolinians in 1832. Jackson supported the Union without wavering and called their bluff. South Carolina backed down. This gave the nation more time to become mature enough to survive the problems of union and civil war. Jackson's immediate successors were not as decisive.

Jackson groomed Sam Houston for his role in Texas and sent him there. A struggle between the United States and Mexico over territorial control of Texas and the Southwest threatened war. Immigrants to that area came from the United States, not from Mexico. These settlers in Mexican-controlled territory north of the Rio Grande held no common bond with the people of Mexico. Jackson took as strong an action as he possibly could short of war, and war did not come until Mexico took the offensive (according to the then-incumbent President, James K. Polk). Many leaders in the United States wanted political control of the entire Southwest, to the Pacific Ocean. Beginning quietly under Jackson, these men accomplished their goal 16 years later, in 1848. Until his death, Jackson worked constantly toward this end even after his departure from high office.

This continual struggle for power between the presidency and Congress sometimes takes unusual turns, but such actions serve the nation well. With weak leadership, the United States will not long endure in the hostile world of reality. A President who cannot face up to his own Congress will not best serve his country when confronted by hostile strength among foreign nations. Reagan would have been no match for Gorbachev had he not been able to meet the small nuisances thrown at him by Congress over arms to Iran and aid to the Contras in Nicaragua. The individual in office as President must have the strength of his convictions and stand by them, or he had better back down and quietly steal away in the night as Nixon did.

The record declares: When choosing among presidential candidates, voters should place high value on the degree of their independent inner strength. The office of President demands a person of that temperament. A President can get advice from the best minds there are, but it remains for him to make the decisions. Andrew Jackson was such a man. The nation will forever be in his debt for the historical example he left.

Jackson and the Bank War (The Business Cycle)

As early as 1818 Andrew Jackson demonstrated his willingness to act independently. When sent by President Monroe to subdue the Indians in Georgia and Alabama, General Jackson faced a choice: he could either stop his mission short of success (because of limitations on his authority) or proceed to a successful conclusion even though his actions might exceed his authority and would likely cause controversy between the United States and Spain and possibly England. He determined his authority by how he understood the object of his mission: to quiet the trouble with the Indians. In pursuing this goal he entered Spanish territory in Florida, seized two important Spanish installations — Pensacola and St. Marks — deposed the Spanish Governor, executed the Indian chiefs, and captured and executed two British subjects who had been supplying war goods to the Indians.

Thanks largely to astute thinking and forceful negotiating by John Quincy Adams, then Secretary of State, this campaign ended in a treaty with Spain wherein Spain ceded to the United States all claims to Florida and defined a boundary between the lands of the Louisiana Purchase and Spanish claims in the Southwest. With Adams's aid, Jackson became a national military hero.

As President, Andrew Jackson contested the established power of the financial interests, embodied primarily in the Bank of the United States and supported by a majority of Congress. Historians label this confrontation during his administration the "Bank War." It developed over renewal of the charter for the second United States Bank. It became a power struggle between financial interests (the beneficiaries of government largesse) and the farmers and laborers (the common man). In the end, Jackson and the common man did dislodge the business and financial interests from some favors flowing from government. Paper money became thoroughly discredited, and the United States, at least for a time, had money based securely on gold. Jackson's bank war with the monied interests caused considerable suffering, evidenced in money panics and unemployment.

Historians do not agree on the causes of business cycles. Since their theories differ, their understanding differs, and their reports of the same historical events contain different facts. This makes interpretation today a difficult task without consulting the original records of that time period. Available literature, however, does state or imply certain facts about which most writers agree.

In all financial crises in the United States, debt grew beyond the abilities of the debtors to service, and banks encouraged that credit expansion. Leading into the panics of 1819, 1831, and 1837, the central bank, the Bank of the United States, fostered credit expansion over a period of months, even years. In time, some events brought further credit expansion to a halt, resulting in financial panic and recession. In 1819, by order from its president, the Bank of the United States stopped renewing all loans. In 1831, that bank's president, Nicholas Biddle, again ordered this action, attempting to blackmail Congress and President Jackson into renewing the bank's charter. In 1837, the sale of public lands came to a virtual standstill following President Jackson's Specie Circular order issued on July 11, 1836, which required purchasers of public lands to make payment in gold or silver.

Characteristically, a prolonged period of speculation in land preceded the financial panics of this period. An expansion of credit financed these speculative binges, and they came to a halt when credit dried up. President Jackson ordered all purchasers of public land to pay in silver or gold because he was concerned about the large volume of bank notes being used in payment. Jackson feared the federal treasury might soon hold little else than these credits of questionable value. Considering the state of affairs at the time, his order virtually assured that much bank credit created by prior land sales would become worthless.

Perhaps the most conspicuous example of speculation preceding a financial crisis was trading in common stock during the 1920s. At that time newsboys and taxi-drivers, as well as financiers, bought stocks with borrowed money to profit by selling at a higher price to a bigger sucker. The collapse of the stock market in October 1929 is possibly the most widely known financial fact of modern history. Not so widely known is the real reason for that event, even though much has been written attempting to explain the Great Depression.

Preceding the panic of 1819, rising prices for most farm products caused a scramble for land. The general prosperity encouraged expansion among manufacturers. Easy credit at the banks fed this boom, and prices for land rose far above previous levels. Then, late in 1818, the directors of the Bank of the United States ordered all their branch banks not to renew any personal mortgages. In addition, the directors ordered the branch banks to present all state bank notes to the issuing banks for immediate payment in gold or silver or in national bank notes. Unable to meet their obligations, state banks closed their doors. Unable to renew their mortgages, manufacturers and farmers lost their property. By the middle of 1819, the Bank of the United States had acquired by foreclosure huge areas of land in the South and West and large numbers of business enterprises in the East. Those who were ruined by foreclosure blamed the bank for their troubles and called it the monster.

This became the first recorded recession for the new nation. It would appear that the new government, through its Bank of the United States, to a large degree encouraged the conditions that led to the collapse. Certainly the Bank's order to call in all loans and paper money triggered an end to the period of easy money. Ludwig von Mises makes it clear that once an easy-money policy begins, it can end only one of two ways: either (1) in a cessation of the easy-money policy, and the above presents an example of how that affects the business of the country; or (2) in an increasing expansion of credit that ultimately causes a complete loss of confidence in the money. The disappearance of money and credit (the crack-up boom) brings business to a standstill and wipes out savings in money forms, a condition worse than the panic described above.

In a message to Congress, President Jackson set forth his reasons for the Specie Circular, which triggered the Panic of 1837:

> *It was perceived that the receipts arising from the sales of the public lands were . . . in effect . . . nothing more than credits in banks. The banks lent out their notes to speculators. They were paid to the receivers [land agents] and immediately returned to the banks, to be lent out again and again, being mere instruments to transfer to speculators the most valuable public lands and pay the Government by a credit on the books of the banks. . . . The spirit of expansion and speculation was not confined to the deposit banks, but pervaded the whole multitude of banks throughout the Union and was giving rise to new institutions to aggravate the evil.*

The especially interesting feature of the panic is that President Jackson set up the very evil that he decried. In his fight with Congress about the composition of the Bank of the United States, Jackson, even against advice from his cabinet and supporters, removed federal funds from the Bank of the United States and deposited them with state banks. State banks had become flooded additionally by new deposits of gold when Congress distributed among all citizens a substantial portion of the gold that had accumulated in the hands of the treasury department.

The directors of the central bank had learned the lesson of sound money in the panic of 1819. State legislators and small Western bankers, however, had not participated in this lesson. Consequently, they used this great influx of hard currency as a basis for issuing an immoderate amount of bank notes and credit, far in excess of their ability to cover in the event of a call. And Jackson's Specie Circular constituted just such a call. The panic of 1837 precipitated a recession that rivaled the one in 1873 and would not be surpassed until the Great Depression of the 1930s. Possibly, had Jackson issued his Specie Circular coincidental with the transfer of federal funds from the central bank to the various state banks, the panic of 1837 might not have occurred.

We must not condemn President Jackson too quickly. In the record of the bank war, no evidence appears that Congress tried to attend to the deficiencies Jackson wanted corrected as a precondition to his approving a renewal of the charter of the Bank of the United States. The following is an excerpt from his message to Congress on vetoing an extension to the charter:

> *A bank of the United States is in many respects convenient for the Government and useful to the people. Entertaining this opinion, and deeply impressed with the belief that some of the powers and privileges possessed by the existing bank are unauthorized by the Constitution, subversive of the rights of the States, and dangerous to the liberties of the people, I felt it my duty at an early period of my Administration to call the attention of Congress to the practicability of organizing an institution combining all its advantages and obviating these objections. I sincerely regret that in the act before me I perceive none of those modifications of the bank charter which are necessary,*

in my opinion, to make it compatible with justice, with sound policy, or with the Constitution of our country.

The present value of the monopoly . . . is $17,000,000, and this the act proposes to sell for three millions. . . . For their benefit (the existing stockholders) does this act exclude the whole American people from competition in the purchase of this monopoly and dispose of it for many millions less than it is worth. This seems the less excusable because some of our citizens not now stockholders petitioned that the door of competition might be opened, and offered to take a charter on terms much more favorable to the Government and country. . . . I cannot perceive the justice . . . of this course. If our government must sell monopolies, it would seem to be its duty to take nothing less than their full value.

Jackson may be criticized for not having the best grasp of economics and particularly the functions of money and banking, but he remained true to his honest dedication to that office and to those people who voted him there. Furthermore, it takes two to create a debt. No one held a gun to the heads of those who borrowed and speculated. Unfortunately, with an end to credit expansion, the shortage of bank credit causes failure among sound businesses as well as among speculators. Also, others defaulted on debts they could have repaid had banks made good on their promises to redeem bank notes in specie.

In regard to the fourth financial panic of the nation, that of 1857, the historian Paul Wellman made this comment:

A money panic . . . August 1857 . . . was the familiar result of over expansion. . . . The times were characterized by extravagance and wild speculations. . . . In nine years more than 21,000 miles of new railroads had been built, much of which was . . . as yet unproductive. Populations did not move into the territories penetrated. At the same time land speculators drew funds far exceeding their investment values. (Wellman 1966. 386)

In Kansas alone, where scarcely one legal title had as yet been granted, there were more acres laid out for cities than were covered by all the cities in the northern and middle states.

> *. . . Lots in "cities," where was scarcely a house, were sold to*
> *the inexperienced and unwary, at prices equaling those in large*
> *cities.* (R. M. Devens, "Our First Century, Great and Memo-
> rable Events," 1876. Quoted by Wellman 1966. 387)
>
> *In August 1857, the Ohio Life Insurance and Trust Company*
> *of Cincinnati . . . failed. The first or second week in September*
> *many banks and business houses began to stop payment in*
> *specie. . . . New York and New England banks held firm into the*
> *month of October, but even these had to succumb at last. . . . All*
> *Northern banks suspended specie payments. . . . commerce and*
> *industry were paralyzed and property values, even in estab-*
> *lished communities, fell from 25 to 75 percent. (Ibid. 1966.*
> 388)

At this point we might think that banks should be regulated to prevent
them from extending the excessive credit that pays for speculation. Just
such reasoning has enabled government to intervene into the operation of
banks and regulate them for the protection of the "innocent depositors and
businessmen." This is a bad trap. If governments had never released some
banks from their contracted obligations — to redeem bank notes in gold,
no bank problem would have arisen. The limits that sound business
practice sets to credit expansion would have worked effectively. Considerations for their own solvency would have forced bankers to be cautious
in issuing bank notes in excess of their gold holding, and in granting credit
based on this fraudulent issue. Those banks that would not have observed
such caution would have gone bankrupt; and the public, warned by their
loss, would have become careful in their choice of banks.

The free market remains the best and most effective control, as Ludwig
von Mises explains:

> *Free banking is the only method available for the prevention of*
> *the dangers inherent in credit expansion. It would, it is true, not*
> *hinder a slow credit expansion, kept within very narrow limits,*
> *on the part of cautious banks which provide the public with all*
> *information required about their financial status. But under*
> *free banking it would have been impossible for credit expansion*
> *with all its inevitable consequences to have developed into a*
> *regular . . . feature of the economic system. Only free banking*

would have rendered the market secure against crises and depressions. (Mises [1949] 1966. 443)

Today even the most bigoted etatists cannot deny that all the alleged evils of free banking count little when compared with the disastrous effects of the tremendous inflations which the privileged and government-controlled banks have brought about. (*Ibid.* 441)

Nonetheless, officials in government have consistently sought to control banking, the money supply, and credit expansion. Such control enables politicians to spend on projects for which the taxpayers are unwilling to be taxed. It also enables them to influence short-term economic cycles, reinforcing their control over elections.

Conquest of Distance

Conquest of distance in transportation and communication accompanied the Industrial Revolution. As long as people remained tied to water for transport, they could not make productive use of the vast land areas lying between navigable waterways. Consequently, until the Englishman George Stephenson, in 1823, adapted James Watt's steam engine to power rail transport, habitable areas existed primarily along navigable rivers, lakes, and oceans. The high cost of overland transport proved prohibitive for farm produce, heavy equipment, and similar items. This economic reality drove Columbus onto the open ocean in 1492. The same reality caused Ohio farmers in the 1780s to convert their grain into whiskey before shipping their harvest to market along the Atlantic seaboard. Plantations in the South cultivated land only a few miles inland from the banks of navigable rivers.

The railroad, which took advantage of the portable steam engine, could not simply be wished into existence. Men had to purchase land for right-of-ways, purchase ties and rails, and build rolling stock — locomotives and cars for grain, cattle, and people. This required a large investment of capital before the first dollar could be earned. The system of voluntary cooperation, capitalism — free-market private enterprise, brought all this together.

In 1830, the United States had 23 miles of railroad track in place. During the next ten years, this mileage increased to 2,808, and by the outbreak of the War Between the States (1861), rail tracks exceeded 31,000 miles. Robert Fulton introduced his steamboat on the Hudson River in 1807; by 1820, some 60 steamboats operated on the Mississippi River and its tributaries. The railroad, along with the steamboat, conquered the barriers of time and cost, which before had prohibited transcontinental shipment of perishables. The railroad with its steam locomotive expanded travel and trade into all parts of the continent. The steamboat opened bidirectional travel on rivers. With advancement in design, steamboats soon became the fast vehicle needed for intra-continental travel and trade.

The conquest of distance accelerated the development of the continent under a stable and free government. All land lying between waterways could then be used by industry and agriculture to produce for sale in the world market. A practical telegraph system was in place by 1845, the telephone by 1878. These improvements in transport and communication created mobility for labor, a condition equally essential for economic development. Without mobility, immigrants who spoke no English stayed isolated from the other citizens, which retarded their Americanization. Geographic mobility fostered individual gains in living standards, aiding assimilation of ethnic groups into a meld that became simply American. Third-generation descendants of German, Dutch, Italian, Chinese, French, and Irish immigrants came to speak a common language and developed a common national heritage.

We should not only know that this happened but should understand why it happened in the United States rather than in Canada, Mexico, or Central and South America. The answer lies in one word: *freedom.* The new nation of 1787 not only assured freedom of self-determination for its citizens, but also enlarged the scope of freedom to include everyone: natives and immigrants, male and female. Freedom translates into opportunity. As men now acknowledge, other large areas of the two Americas offer natural resources — cultivable land, minerals, timber, water, climate — equal to that in the United States. But the governments in these other areas have not protected private property and personal freedom. Other nations denied political and economic freedom either partially — as in Canada — or entirely — as in Mexico. The southern areas had known only the monarchical form of government installed first by their native Indian societies — the Incas, the Mayas, the Aztecs — and later by the Spanish. When each group in turn broke loose from Spain, it installed a dictator or his equivalent. Personal freedom did not enter their institutions. England ruled Canada, and what

European emigrant in the 19th century would choose a government in the Americas ruled by British Parliament in place of the independent and free United States? The choice might now be more open but not then. Consequently, after 1830, immigration to the United States increased substantially, and the convenience of rail transport encouraged people to migrate westward, ever driving the frontier before them.

With sensible leadership, England in the 19th century became the leading world power, industrially and militarily. The British relinquished this position of world dominance early in the 20th century when their leadership passed to men who were willing to sacrifice personal freedom for social goals. In the late 20th century the United States began following the same path. This trend will be more thoroughly examined in Chapter 16.

The Monroe Doctrine

At the end of the 15th century, the monarchs in Spain held the dominant position of power in the Mediterranean, across the Atlantic Ocean, and over the whole of Europe and Coastal Africa. Columbus's voyage of 1492 and the subsequent Spanish conquest of Central and South America brought quantities of precious metals to Spain. Because all Western civilization would exchange labor and goods for gold and silver, the Catholic monarchs commanded more wealth than any other European princes.

Within 100 years this hereditary line of kings and queens had dissipated this remarkable wealth on fruitless small wars with other princely powers of Europe. They used little, if any, to purchase tools and machinery for production. The monarchs commissioned warships, and employed men for military duty. In 1588 the smaller, more maneuverable ships of Queen Elizabeth's navy defeated King Philip's "invincible armada" when a great storm bottled up that armada in a small bay on the French coast. There, the English destroyed that navy the Spanish had built to invade and subdue England, and put an end to Spain's rule of the seas.

Losing control of the seas meant weakened control over foreign colonies. Spain experienced no sudden collapse of its empire, but the stream of silver and gold no longer flowed from the Americas without interruption. When Napoleon's forces invaded early in the 19th century, Spain offered only token resistance, and the king fled into exile.

In spite of the wealth coming from the Americas, in the late 16th century, Spain lost its leadership in the Western world. Paul Kennedy explains why:

*There was a chronic lack of skilled craftsmen . . . and mobility
of labor and flexibility of practice were obstructed by the
guilds. Even the development of agriculture was retarded by the
privileges of the Mesta, the famous guild of sheep owners
whose stock were permitted to graze widely over the kingdom;
with Spain's population growing in the first half of the sixteenth
century, this simply led to an increasing need for imports of
grain. Since the Mesta's payments for these grazing rights went
into the royal treasury, and a revocation of this practice would
have enraged some of the crown's strongest supporters, there
was no prospect of amending the system. . . . the Castilian economy on the whole was also heavily dependent upon imports of
foreign manufactures and upon the services provided by
non-Spaniards. . . . Not surprisingly, Spain['s] . . . trade imbalance . . . could be made good only by the re-export of American
gold and silver. At the center of the Spanish decline, therefore,
was the failure to recognize the importance of preserving the
economic underpinnings of a powerful military machine. Time
and again the wrong measures were adopted. . . . The government directive that the Biscayan shipyards should concentrate
upon large war-ships to the near exclusion of . . . more useful
trading vessels; the sale of monopolies which restricted trade;
the heavy taxes upon wool exports, which made them uncom-
petitive in foreign markets; the internal customs barriers
between the various Spanish kingdoms, which hurt commerce
and drove up prices — these were just some of the ill-consid-
ered decisions which, in the long term, seriously affected
Spain's capacity to carry out the great military role which it
had allocated to itself. . . . Although the decline of Spanish
power did not fully reveal itself until the 1640s, the causes had
existed for decades beforehand.* (Kennedy 1987. 54-55)

Such is the ebb and flow of world power among Western nations. The
United States perhaps revealed the true weakness of Spain's power in the
Americas when Andrew Jackson, with no more than 2,500 soldiers, took
control of Spanish Florida in 1818-1819. In the first 20 years of the 19th
century, Spain lost her possessions in the Americas. Occupied with the
Napoleonic invasions and internal rebellion, Spain could not prevent her

American colonies from gaining independence easily. The final battle for the independence of Mexico was a bloodless coup.

The young republic of the United States needed to take a position relative to these events. These newly independent States were weak, and easy prey for ambitious European and Asian interests. John Quincy Adams, as Secretary of State, wrote the message for President Monroe to deliver to Congress stating the official position of that administration, the Monroe Doctrine. Simply stated, the United States would oppose any attempt on the part of European or Asian powers to colonize in the Americas. In the world of 1820 this carried about as much force as a young pup's yapping in the face of a pack of wolves. But Britain wanted the Americas free of European and Asian interference. She then ruled the oceans, and her leaders considered free sovereign States across the Atlantic as beneficial to English trade as were colonies. Englishmen had learned the benefits of trade with the free United States. They sought to extend this trade to all the Americas. England therefore let the world know that her navy would support the United States in enforcing the Monroe Doctrine. England put teeth into the young pup's bark.

The Monroe Doctrine remained unchallenged until the 1960s, when Russia moved into Cuba under Fidel Castro's cloak. President John F. Kennedy allowed it. Kennedy had his opportunity when Russia installed launch capability for missiles in Cuba. The United States could then have justified entering Cuba to take control. President Kennedy's failure to stand firm on the Monroe Doctrine at that time has resulted in the gradual loss of friendly governments in Central America. Unless the trend is reversed, the United States will lose the friendship of both Central and South America.

Instead of watching local interests, American leadership for the last four decades has actively committed its resources where it has smaller interests — Korea, Vietnam, and the Persian Gulf. Had these same resources been applied in the Caribbean and Central America, the United States would not now be flanked at home by threatening, unfriendly armies. Perhaps this is as it will always be. Through the operation of the Law of Ignorance, human nature gives governments a strange view of foreign relations. The threat immediately at hand is so terrifying that it is ignored, and leaders divert attention to fighting the distant dragon where the consequences of success or failure mean so little.

. . . The attitude the Spanish held toward the Indians is significant. Columbus first expressed it in his report to his benefactors, Ferdinand and Isabel, after his successful voyage in 1492. He observed "how easy it would be to convert these people — and to make them work for us."

Chapter 7

Texas and the Southwest

Spanish Influence South of the Rio Grande

IN THE HISTORY OF THE Americas, the 16th century witnessed the Spanish conquest of the Indians in Mexico, Central, and South America. With their interest focused on silver and gold, the Spanish had little interest in settling the land as did the English the next century. Those who want details can find the story in numerous history texts. These details, however, will offend the senses of a 20th-century American. They tell the story of a superior, organized, well-equipped fighting force overwhelming and nearly annihilating its adversaries. The Spanish had firearms and the Indians did not. It tells of treachery, destruction, and exploitation.

The Spanish had no respect for the natives; to them the Indian was little better than an animal to be subdued.

Because it influences present conditions, the attitude the Spanish held toward the Indians is significant. Columbus first expressed it in his report to his benefactors, Ferdinand and Isabel, after his successful voyage in 1492. He observed "how easy it would be to convert these people — and to make them work for us." His Sovereigns need not send laborers to this land. The natives, enslaved, were "fit to be ordered about and made to work, to sow, and do aught else that may be needed." The Indian appeared to the Catholic Spaniards as an inferior species, more animal than human. He practiced human sacrifice, cannibalism, idolatry, and other sins unacceptable to them. Accustomed to class distinction at home, the intruders easily placed the Indians in a subhuman category, a position only a small step above that of domesticated animals. The immigrants expected the natives to be forever their servants. Once the leadership of the three existing Indian cultures had been destroyed, the Spaniards committed the masses to slavery to work the mines, tend the fields, and do whatever else might serve their masters. The lowliest of the invading Spanish considered himself superior to the best of the Indians. At no point did the Spanish grant the native a voice in government. Since all three cultures of these Indians had been built on an autocracy of priests, Spanish dominance meant little change for the native masses. The great majority of Indians experienced only a change of overlord.

Spanish descendants even now control governments in nearly all countries south of the Rio Grande, and they give little consideration to the plight of the masses, the descendants of native Americans. This remains the cause of mass poverty in all these countries and lies at the heart of revolt. Government, controlled by the elite — the Spanish element, restricts investment by outsiders, which in turn limits opportunity for employment. These elite run a planned economy with a tight rein by government. Revolutionary movements for the last 400 years in Mexico and farther south have stemmed from efforts of the Indian majority to throw off the yoke of Spanish control. Since the people have no history of self-government, each successful rebellion ends in another autocratic regime. Unable to handle democracy, the people immediately accept the leadership of a charismatic general. This was the way of their ancestors; it is the only tradition they know.

This force, at work today south of the United States, keeps Mexican peons poor. It brought Cuba under the control of the Spaniard Castro. It underlies continuous revolution in Central and South America. That force created the conflict of the 1980s between the Contras and the Sandinistas in Nicaragua. The Indian majority in Central and South America remain subject to tyranny at the hands of the Spanish element.

Know the Indian That Spaniards Destroyed

Before shedding too many tears over the fate of the Central-American Indians at the hands of the Spaniards, a person needs to consider the way of life these same natives followed when the Spanish arrived. Holding their position by armed might, the ruling tribes tyrannized all their neighbors.

The Aztecs appeared in Central America in the late 13th century, a barbarian tribe from the north. They lived by warfare and conquest. In their move south, they forcibly took over lands occupied by other Indians. To the last they made perpetual war on all neighboring groups not under their direct control, if for no other reason than to take prisoners to sacrifice to their gods. Without war the Aztecs had no captives to sacrifice, and their gods possessed an insatiable appetite for blood.

The conquistadors under Cortes witnessed the daily rituals. With the victim (conscious and without sedative) stretched out face up on the temple sacrificial table, a priest ripped out the still-beating heart to be offered to the sun god. Even these hardened warriors of Spain became repulsed by the screams of the victims and the smell of rotting flesh. The priests saved choice limbs for their own repast; they tossed the torsos to beasts in the adjoining zoo. One skull rack contained 136,000 human skulls, victims of this religious sacrifice. A Spanish historian records that the number of men sacrificed one year exceeded 50,000. That averages over 136 each day. It is understandable why the Spanish, on seeing such conduct, might feel little compassion toward the natives. The Spaniards erred, though, in generalizing — in believing that all Indians were equally bestial.

The day of the Mayan civilization came and went in the first millennium A.D. Efforts to keep it alive and thriving on the Yucatan peninsula had, by the 16th century, disintegrated into constant civil war that in time would have determined which city-state would put the final blow to their culture. The Spanish merely became the "barbarians."

In South America the Incas had not been the kindliest rulers. By the time the Spanish conquistadors arrived, a majority of the population had been conquered by war and enslaved. Even as the Spaniard Francisco Pizzaro and his men moved toward the Inca capital, the Inca emperor Atahualpa rested from his recent war to destroy his brother, Huascar. Though Huascar and Atahualpa had each been given independent empires by their late father, the forces of greed and envy led to five years of fighting between them until one should destroy the other and become The Inca, the one supreme emperor of all. The Incas had conquered nearly all other tribes along the Andes from Colombia to central Chile. The common man had become enslaved.

Some historians have expressed surprise at how little resistance the Inca warrior offered to Spanish conquest. Yet one may reasonably believe that the common man, the one required to fight and die for The Inca, had nothing to fight for. Life under rule by the Spanish offered the slave little change from his lot under his own emperor.

This must be kept in mind today when considering the threat of conquest in the Western world by the Eastern Bloc. If the West remains strong and intact, they have little to fear from the East. The individuals from the East who must carry the rifles, drive the tanks, and sail the ships do not have much will to fight. Slaves have never made a real fight of it when confronted with free men defending their homes. At the Battle of Marathon in 490 B.C., 10,000 free Greeks defeated a much larger Persian army of conscripts and slaves. The Persians withdrew in defeat, having lost 6,400 men; the Greeks lost only 192.

The free Aztec Indian, on the other hand, presented quite another matter. As described by one Spanish Conquistador, anyone facing Aztec warriors for the first time could be terrified by their screams and ferociousness. The Aztecs killed defeated warriors and the women they could not take as slaves, and burned any plunder they could not carry with them.

Although the Spanish did kill many with the sword and gun and by labor in the quarries and mines, the number of such deaths did not match what came from the silent executioner. The Spaniards brought with them European diseases — particularly smallpox, influenza, and measles — against which the Indians had no natural immunity. As epidemics had for centuries moved across Asia and Europe along the trade routes, epidemics of these diseases covered the New World more completely than did the explorers and conquering armies. History gives no direct information, but we can fairly assume that the mound-builder traders carried diseases up and down the Mississippi and Ohio watersheds. No doubt Spanish explorations north of New Mexico onto the high prairie of the Central Plains introduced these diseases to tribes from Texas to Canada. The Mayas, the Incas, and the Aztecs perhaps were most greatly impacted because they had more intimate contact with the Spaniards. Long before the French and the English began settling North America, the numbers of Indians in that land had been dramatically reduced. By some estimates, in the century after Columbus's 1492 voyage, the native Indian population dropped perhaps as much as 70 percent from a high of 80 to 100 million for North and South America combined. (Braudel [1979] 1981. 36-37)

The War with Mexico, 1846-1848

American leaders in the early 19th century understood the importance of avoiding, in North America, a condition in which there would be many separate States — as has for centuries characterized Europe and presently exists in Latin America. Toward this end, President Andrew Jackson set out to make Mexico a part of the United States and sent his personal envoy Sam Houston into Texas. President Monroe approved and delivered to Congress Adams's statement of the Monroe Doctrine. President Polk took the first opportunity to annex Texas and the Southwest. As a sovereign State independent of Spain at that time, Mexico claimed not only the land now known as Mexico but all of the present states of Texas, Arizona, New Mexico, California, Nevada, and parts of Colorado, Utah, Wyoming, Kansas, and Oklahoma. Mexico controlled what is now the entire Southwestern United States, and did so with a government that changed hands from emperor to emperor at the drop of a hat. This land had been wrested from Spain by war (1821), and many leaders in the United States sought an excuse to take it from Mexico by the same means.

When the government of Mexico encouraged settlement north of the Rio Grande, few of their own citizens moved. All the interest in this wide expanse of prairie came from pioneers moving West from the United States. By the middle 1830s, U.S. emigrants in Texas outnumbered the native Mexicans by nearly four to one, and this discrepancy widened yearly. The extreme divergence in freedom between the United States and dictatorial Mexico bred conditions that would have to be resolved in armed combat. The Americans in Texas declared their freedom from Mexico in 1836, thereby initiating their war of independence.

As chief executive of Mexico, Santa Anna led a force of 4,000 against those Texans that dared affront him. He met his first armed resistance at the old Alamo Mission outside San Antonio. Sam Houston, commanding all Texas forces, ordered Colonel William B. Travis, with his 200 or so men at the Alamo, to fight a delaying action, yielding ground as necessary. But Travis and his men, including such colorful personalities as Jim Bowie and Davy Crockett, remained at the Alamo. So few survived, that we will never know for sure whether these martyrized men realized they had remained for certain death.

There are times in history when an event that seemed rather minor at the moment plays a major role in the lives of those who follow. Before that defense at the Alamo, Texans weakly supported the cause of independence. Sam Houston, their military leader, could find few men to give either time or money to the struggle. The courage and death of those few who defended the Alamo sparked an enthusiasm among American Texans that would not be denied. The cry "Remember the Alamo" brought forth money and volunteers for the army. Within the year the Texans defeated the Mexicans at San Jacinto and captured Santa Anna, who agreed to an independent Texas, ending his claims to this area of Mexico's northernmost province.

Texas immediately sought admission into the United States, but northern opposition in Congress delayed statehood for Texas until 1846. Everyone, even those who favored annexation, understood that the government in Mexico had not recognized Santa Anna's treaty and would very likely go to war with the United States if Texas became part of the Union. Texas did become a state and war did follow, a war that elevated yet another military hero to the presidency, General Zachary Taylor. By 1848, the Mexican forces, led again by Santa Anna, had lost a second time to the Americans. General Winfield Scott led the final campaign that ended Mexican resistance by capturing Mexico City. Santa Anna slipped away during the night when he realized the Americans had prevailed.

The men in the fight, both American and Mexican, served well; but Mexico lost to the better-led Americans. In it figured many young West Point graduates who would be prominent in the War Between the States soon to erupt — William Tecumseh Sherman, James Longstreet, T. J. (Stonewall) Jackson, Jefferson Davis, Robert E. Lee, Ulysses S. Grant.

Between 1833 and 1855, Santa Anna occupied the Mexican presidency 11 times, and was called to lead the military at other times. Yet he lived a full lifetime, dying from the infirmities of age. His claim to fame can only be that of a leader whose self-aggrandizement and corruption were commonplace. Santa Anna demonstrated how those in power could steal from the public treasury and exact bribes from everyone who could pay. He never let the cause of his country interfere with the advancement of his personal fortunes.

In the treaty that ended the War with Mexico, the United States agreed to pay the same amount that earlier had been offered to Mexico for the lands of the Southwest; Texas remained a state in the Union. Fortunately, *for all who lived in that region, the laws of freedom replaced the degradation of corruption.*

President Polk no doubt exceeded the bounds of truth in taking his country into that war. This charge has been levied against nearly every incumbent president who has led the nation into a war. Perhaps it will always be so. Right or wrong, that little war with Mexico gained freedom for millions of people. President Polk's actions separated from Mexico all the land that the American people then wanted. It brought the citizens of that area from anarchy to freedom under government ruled by law. Those who remained under the government of Mexico have suffered a century of violence, with poverty and servitude for the masses.

As a result of this change in political control over the Southwest, free men developed the resources of that land. Had Mexico retained control, none of those resources would now be in use. The Rio Grande valley produces some of the sweetest citrus fruit grown in America, but none of it is on the Mexican side. Lack of freedom, along with an unstable government, has stifled economic development within Mexico's borders. Americans have become the beneficiaries of this territorial expansion in 1848. Try to imagine what conditions would be like in the United States today without the flow of Oklahoma, Texas, and California petroleum. Ask yourself which city you would prefer as home — Mexico City or Dallas, Texas. Take a drive through the Rio Grande valley; travel on both sides of the river. Then decide whether you would prefer to live on the American or Mexican side of that river. The only difference lies in the political system of government, cooperation by hegemony or cooperation by contract. American expansion over the continent has extended the benefits of freedom to all the people living under the government of The United States of America. Never in their history have the Mexicans known real freedom. If Americans do not act to preserve their liberty, we all could be living as those people currently live south of the Rio Grande.

The only difference between whites and blacks in America is the way each are treated by their peers. When men cease referring to each other as black, white, Hispanic, Oriental, or Indian, there will be no difference between Americans from different racial or ethnic origins; and a great human resource will be released to constructive employment.

Chapter 8

Slavery in the United States

The Nature of Slavery

SLAVES CAME TO JAMESTOWN before the Pilgrims landed at Plymouth. In 1619, traders sold 20 African Negroes to tobacco planters of Virginia. By 1860, when Abraham Lincoln became President, the United States had a larger slave population than any other nation in the world.

Slavery is a legal relationship: (1) The owner holds a legal title, as he does for domesticated animals. The slave is a chattel, an item of private property. (2) The legal relationship binds the slave for life, and only an act of the owner can free him. (3) The law, customs, and authority of society recognize and enforce this ownership. (4) This relationship between owner and slave does not evolve from a contract between owner and slave. A person who contracts to work as an indentured servant for a number of years does not become a slave in the sense used here. Neither does the employee who works for wages below his need for subsistence. So-called "economic slavery" is a metaphor, and should be so treated. A slave is a human being involuntarily placed in the status of a beast, a status enforced by law.

No doubt, slavery began as an alternative to complete annihilation of people defeated in battle. It occurred to the victors that some of the conquered could be used to till the land, cut firewood, and build temples and pyramids. Perhaps a young warrior found, among the conquered, a woman who appealed to his tastes. Slavery has existed among humans as far back as recorded history. At the height of the power of Rome, slaves performed most of the menial labor. When the Spanish appeared on the scene, over half the population among the Inca Indians were slaves. Estimates place the number of slaves in Athens during the Golden Age of the Greek civilization (the 5th century B.C.) at about 90,000, nearly 40 percent of the population. The ancients believed that the masses could not properly care for themselves. Consequently, they could embrace slavery as a proper means for the elite to provide for the masses. This social attitude prevails among those today who consider themselves among the elite. It may account for the fact that so many in positions of power see no wrong in government planning for the masses, with its disregard for their freedom.

Historically, men did not restrict enslavement to members of one race or region. All men qualified: black, white, yellow, tan, Asiatic, Arabic, Mediterranean. Enslavement required simply that a person be a loser in battle. Only in the United States did slavery become identified with one race exclusively, the African Negro. Practical considerations — supply, economy, suitability — dictated this condition. Indians and settlers captured the native Indians and sold them for slaves. These people, however, were transported to other continents and to islands in the West Indies as a way to deter escape. On the American continent, escape would have been too easy.

Slavery had proven uneconomical under the feudal system, where slaves became serfs, then free men. In western Europe during the Middle Ages (A.D. 500-1500), the law bound each serf to a specific area of land. He could not leave to work elsewhere. The feudal lord could sell a serf to another lord only as part of a sale of land; the serfs who worked that land went with the land. Legally, they were not slaves, but it was a small distinction. By the 16th century the sheer abundance of serfs had completely destroyed this element of slavery. Land owners willingly permitted their serfs to leave; there were too many laborers for the amount of land. Non-enforcement of the legal tie to the land gave serfs their freedom, though freedom often meant poverty and starvation. To the serf, freedom was a shallow, meaningless change. On migrating to the colonies, these free serfs sought land for themselves; they had no interest in becoming serfs to other landowners if they had a choice. Along the frontier in America they had a choice.

Immigrants brought few slaves with them to the Colonies. By the 17th century, Europeans had become disenchanted with the institution, and some nations had enacted laws making transportation and sale of slaves illegal. Men had begun to view the practice as contrary to the will of God.

The principal forces for slavery in America stemmed from the need for labor to serve a rapidly expanding agricultural system, from the limited supply of workmen, and from the demands placed on laborers by the climate. African Negroes presented the best available source. Cultivating tobacco and cotton, the primary crops, required little training. The climate in Africa, similar to that along the south Atlantic seaboard, hardened Africans to working conditions that Europeans considered intolerable. Plantations needed field hands. Immigrants who left Europe to escape the feudal system and become landowners themselves did not work long for others. These economic and societal conditions dictated that plantation owners purchase Negro slaves as their major source of manpower.

The American Constitution allowed the slave trade to continue until 1809. Thereafter, only slaves born in, or then living in, the states could be legally bought and sold. Due to this restriction, by 1860 cotton planters were paying over $1,000 each for quality slaves.

Although most European countries permitted ownership of slaves, they had outlawed the slave trade. Smugglers purchased Negroes on the west coast of Africa and sold them in the West Indies and in the plantation colonies of America. This supply of Negroes came from intertribal warfare in Africa. Blacks captured blacks and sold them into slavery. As long as the slave trade remained out of the sight of Europeans, it was out of mind. The authorities largely ignored the ban until public opinion finally demanded an end to this trade in human bondage.

Until a large population of free Negroes developed in America, a fugitive Negro slave had no place to hide. In Colonial America, black skin created a strong presumption of slavery. A federal law enacted in 1793 concerning extradition provided for recovery of run-away slaves. A master or his agent might recover a fugitive merely by supplying oral testimony or an affidavit to a local judge, who, without a jury trial, would determine the question of ownership.

That law made kidnapping free Negroes in the North easy and profitable. The South granted a Negro the right to a jury trial in the question of his freedom. As a suspected fugitive in the North, he had no such rights. There is little doubt that some free American Negroes were wrongfully forced into slavery. After all, denied the opportunity of a hearing, how does a person prove he is a free man?

The Sociological Problem

Knowing the facts about slavery is important to Americans today. Much of the current unrest between whites and blacks stems from the Colonial practice of using only Negroes for slaves. There has been insufficient time for blacks to make a full transition from identity as a slave to identity as a freeman. The Emancipation Proclamation of 1863 removed Negroes from slavery in an instant. It takes generations, however, to remove slavery from the mentality of citizens. There yet remains the attitude that white people then developed so universally toward the Negro.

Slavery, confined as it was to the Negro race, caused white Americans to think that Negroes were basically inferior to white men and had been created to serve him. This belief — shared by Spanish immigrants in Mexico farther south toward Indians — is the ignominious crime that must be charged against the institution of slavery. Debased by every means in order to sustain that fiction, all men of color would suffer as long as any of them remained enslaved. Slavery had to disappear before Americans could deal with discrimination.

Had slavery not been abolished by law in the 19th century, the practice would have disappeared with industrialization. In order to gain the type of work that only human beings can perform, the individual must be treated like a human being. As the numbers of free Negroes increased, the opportunity for escape would have increased as well, which would have made it more expensive to keep men in bondage. As a beast of burden, a man is no match for the horse. When the cost of keeping a slave approaches the cost of keeping a horse, the choice favors the horse. Slaves become too costly when machines replace men in the fields. One well-equipped, free laborer can outperform a group of the best field-hand slaves. In time, the comparative cost of using slaves as opposed to employing free men and operating machinery would have abolished slavery.

As stated earlier, the Colonies allowed slavery in order to meet the needs of Southern agriculture. The supply of free labor was inadequate for rapid development of the cultivation of cotton. The introduction of the cotton gin in 1793 made American-grown, short-staple cotton profitable in world markets. A land-rich planter could greatly increase his production of cotton with but a part of one shipload of African Negroes. He bought them and profited by so doing.

The time for stopping slavery in the United States had come and gone in 1787 with the adoption of a new constitution that allowed the importation of slaves for another 20 years. At the expiration of this time — in 1809, Americans owned a breeding stock large enough to supply all the slaves required for continued expansion of the cultivation of cotton. By local reproduction, increase in the Negro slave population outpaced that of the whites. The population mix in the entire South in 1860 approached 40 Negroes for 60 whites; and in the cotton belt, Negroes outnumbered whites. Agricultural development in the South and the expansion of Negro slavery in the United States were two interdependent aspects of one process.

The problems generated by Negro slavery in the United States are sociological. By its very nature, slavery degrades the work performed by slaves. Free men will virtually starve before performing labor that carries the stigma of bondage. It happened in Rome 2,000 years ago. It happened in the 19th century in America. Today in the United States there remains a social stigma attached to employment for domestic service and most forms of menial labor. In 1860 in the South, no white man would work for someone else, doing what he regarded as "nigger" work. In turn, whites considered Negroes as suited only for this kind of labor. This attitude in America condemned the Negro, free or bond, to perform only the most menial tasks. He became an inferior being, not just in the South, but in the North as well. No one accepted Negroes as equal to whites. Whites in general believed that science had proved Negroes were inferior. John C. Calhoun of South Carolina believed this. In 1848 he said:

With us, the two great divisions of society are not the rich and the poor, but white and black; and all the former, the poor as well as the rich, belong to the upper class, and are respected and treated as equals . . . and hence have a position and pride of character of which neither poverty nor misfortune can deprive them. (McPherson 1982. 33)

The Alabama radical William L. Yancey stated it more directly:

The white race is the citizen, and the master race, and the white man is the equal of every other white man. . . . The Negro is the inferior race. (Ibid. 33)

Chief Justice Taney concurred in this opinion. He declared that the Negro had no rights the white man need respect. Even in the North, no candidate for political office could be elected if he endorsed racial equality. Both Congressman George Julian of Indiana and Senator Lyman Trumbull of Illinois publicly declared their opposition to Negroes residing in their states.

Influence on Southern Secession

Racial prejudice influenced most Southern whites to oppose emancipation even though the majority neither owned slaves nor approved of the institution. Whites in the South could not imagine how they might adjust to a society that included Negroes as free men. In most Southern states before 1860, state law required any freed slave to leave the state, and many Northern states forbade free Negroes to settle within their boundaries. As recently as the mid-20th century Herrin, Illinois, and Burlington, Kansas — and no doubt others — forbade a Negro to remain in the city limits after sundown. A group of free Negroes, unable to find a home in existing villages, in 1877 founded their own town — Nicodemus, Kansas. Because of this racial prejudice, many Southern whites who opposed slavery fought for the Confederacy. They could not accept the possibility of living side by side with free Negroes.

Although the morality of slavery was not the great issue, the abolitionists, a small but vociferous minority in the North, based their arguments on morals. They failed to win many converts to their cause, but by their generalized condemnation of all Southerners for Negro slavery, they polarized emotions among the white majority, North and South. Emotional reaction to their provocative literature, sometimes half truths and misrepresentations, contributed strongly toward mass support for the War Between the States. Perhaps the most powerful single abolitionist work was Harriet Beecher Stowe's *Uncle Tom's Cabin.* Paul Wellman summarized the emotional impact:

> *Nothing had ever aroused emotion in America as* Uncle Tom's Cabin *did. It created fury in the North not only against slavery, but against the South itself and the Southern people. So moderate a judge as Abraham Lincoln considered it a contributing cause of the Civil War. When, during that conflict, Mrs. Stowe was introduced to him in the White House, he said, "Is this the little woman who made this big war?"* (Wellman 1966. 337)

Interestingly, the author, Mrs. Stowe, sister to the abolitionist preacher Henry Ward Beecher, knew very little of the life she described. She based her book on the descriptions of isolated and extreme incidents treated as though they were typical.

The slavery institution hindered economic development in the South. It so stigmatized unskilled labor that Southerners could not employ capital in any industry that utilized unskilled free labor. Such labor was for Negro slaves, not for free whites. Southerners could invest their profits from cotton only by buying more land and more slaves to grow more cotton. By 1860, Southern capital invested in slaves exceeded $2 billion, a sum greater than the value of the land these slaves cultivated. When the planter-barons lost their slaves on losing the war, they lost nearly everything. With no funds to pay wages, they could not produce crops to pay the taxes on their land.

The Negro was slave in the South, and the South was slave to the institution cf slavery. And the North offered no help. Northern abolitionists never advocated that the entire country share the social burden and the financial cost of freeing the slaves. Lincoln opposed slavery in principle, but to resolve the problem of free Negroes, he advocated relocating them in Africa. Many, both north and south of the Potomac, shared this attitude. John Randolph, a wealthy Virginia planter, freed all his slaves and shipped them to Africa at a personal cost of over $500,000.

The Solution, If There Is Any

By 1860 all but the oldest Negroes had been born in America. They were not Africans; they simply had black skin. Shipping them to Africa would have been a most inhumane treatment. Freeing them in America was almost as inhumane, considering the racial attitude of whites. To continue their status as slaves would have been inhumane as well. The real problem in 1860 was not slavery but race. Slavery had become so identified with Negro that the world had no place for these four million native-born Americans with black skin.

History records many events stemming from sociological problems that men never really solve. Taking land from one group of people, the Moslem Arabs, and giving it to another group, the followers of Judaism, and calling it Israel, has not solved the sociological problem for the Jews. The Jews are now, and will be for years to come, at war with displaced Moslems. For 300 years Romans persecuted the Christians, thereby creating a problem even greater than that confronting blacks in America. They never solved that problem; it disappeared when pagans and Christians joined forces under Constantine, eliminating the identity of the differences between them.

In 1860, neither continued slavery nor emancipation addressed the real sociological problem of the Negro. Government policy was decided in the course of the War Between the States; leaders in Washington chose emancipation. Emancipation freed Negroes from slavery, but it left the race problem unsolved. That problem remains even now at the approach of the 21st century.

How Americans will solve it remains a guess at best. Historically, governments have used coercion. In 1862, the Emancipation Proclamation by force of arms freed the slaves of the Confederacy. That action confiscated from the Southern aristocracy wealth amounting to $2 billion. Nearly 100 years later the Supreme Court in *Brown v Board of Education of Topeka*, 347 U.S. 483 (1954), reversed the rule set 60 years earlier in *Plessy v Ferguson* (1896) that "separate but equal" satisfied the equal treatment required by the Fourteenth Amendment. This coercive action by government, not favored by most of the people, and followed by numerous "civil rights" statutes from Congress, has caused violence and open conflict between the races. It has failed entirely to address the underlying sociological problem the country brought upon itself by embracing Negro slavery.

The significance of how slavery ended lies in the impact of emancipation, which forced on Negroes a sudden adjustment to a free-labor market. Had economic necessity caused the change, a more gradual pace of adjustment would have allowed them time to prepare for their freedom and increased responsibilities. This statement does not argue for slavery; it simply states reality. Quite possibly, many American Negro slaves of the 19th century would have fared better had they been afforded a more gradual adjustment to change in their legal and social status.

Self-interest decrees that men cooperate with their fellows. Smooth human relations benefit everyone through increased productivity. Toward this end, men need to stop separating individuals into classes by reason of race. Recognizing the dignity of the individual maximizes the benefit of the division of labor through increased cooperation. A person generally performs as his fellowmen expect him to. If his associates expect him to steal, he will be a thief. If his peers treat him as a bum, he will not work. When blacks become accepted as equals, they will govern their conduct in accordance with the customs of the land.

The only difference between whites and blacks in America is the way each are treated by their peers. When men cease referring to each other as black, white, Hispanic, Oriental, or Indian, there will be no difference between Americans from different racial or ethnic origins; and a great human resource will be released to constructive employment. As recipients of welfare, people are an economic drain and a disciplinary problem. Idle hands placed into useful service increase the total product of the economy. Not only do these employed individuals gain self-respect, they contribute to the wealth of the economy. As beneficiaries of the economy, everyone gains from any measure that increases the total product and raises the standard of living.

All the clamor in recent decades about "civil rights" has only increased awareness of the differences. The cause of equal acceptance of all men has been set back many generations. Human dignity has nothing to do with size, ethnic origin, religion, or color of skin. Truly equal rights can flow only from activities directed by rightly understood self-interest. Although it remains difficult to accept this truth in an age so near the time when whites were owners and blacks were chattel, enlightened self-interest directs that people so believe. This requires an understanding of history and a realization of its benefits to all men.

The solution may never come until racial distinction disappears through integrated propagation. Americans would thereby become a mix of Negro and Caucasian. Like the sociological problem that has for centuries dogged the Jews, the problem of ethnic and racial discrimination will remain as long as the minority maintains a distinct identity. Negroes have not come to be treated as equals in the United States; but as all Americans become mulattos, Negroes and Caucasian will disappear as distinct races. English, German, Spanish, Oriental, Italian, Scandinavian, French, and Irish immigrants to the United States have largely lost their identity and become Americans. The War Between the States and Negro slavery ended only six generations ago. It is too soon to expect Negro identity to disappear. Good or bad, this is the way of man; this is history.

In order to know the why of today, we have to understand the past. We need to know and understand the forces influencing the societies of both North and South that culminated in the War Between the States. We need to understand the emotional upheaval which that war generated among its contemporaries. It is proper, therefore, to direct our attention now to that war, that ultimate test of the Union.

. . . President Abraham Lincoln, in 1863 at Gettysburg, declared what only a few Americans then realized, that the nation was fighting for freedom and union: freedom for all — black and white, Catholic and Protestant, immigrant and native-born. . . .

Chapter 9

War Between the States
(The American Civil War, 1848-1865)

Secession

W HEN THE AMERICAN WAR OF INDEPENDENCE created the United States, the new nation included two diverse societies: the industrial North with a labor system based on wages, and the plantation South with its labor system based on slavery. The Constitution adopted in 1789 recognized slavery, but permitted the slave trade for only 20 more years, with slavery itself permitted indefinitely. The Constitution was silent on another pressing issue: the right of a state to secede, that is, to withdraw from the Union it had voluntarily joined. In 1861, when the South perceived that the North was jeopardizing their freedom to extend the slave system to new states joining the Union, 11 Southern states tested their right to secede. The subsequent war resolved both issues: (1) whether the nation was to be a confederation of sovereign states or a union under one indissoluble federal government; and (2) whether this nation, created by a declaration of equal liberty for all men, was to continue with the largest slave population in the world.

A Question of State Sovereignty

Four score and seven years ago our fathers brought forth on this continent a new nation, conceived in liberty, and dedicated to the proposition that all men are created equal.

Now we are engaged in a great civil war, testing whether that nation, or any nation so conceived and so dedicated, can long endure.

With these words President Abraham Lincoln, in 1863 at Gettysburg, declared what only a few Americans then realized, that the nation was fighting for freedom and union: freedom for all — black and white, Catholic and Protestant, immigrant and native-born — and a union that could not be dissolved by any of its parts. A nation born of, by, and for the people, "with liberty and justice for all," could not countenance slavery or secession. Freedom and unity formed the twin foundation stones of the United States of America.

The South, too, fought for freedom as they viewed it. The founders of the Republic and leaders in the South considered the existence of many states — each with substantial power within its borders — a safeguard to liberty. President Franklin D. Roosevelt, when Governor of New York, expressed it well in a radio address to the nation on March 3, 1930:

The whole success of our democracy . . . has been a democracy where through a division of government into units called States the rights and interests of the minority have been respected.

The South wanted freedom from the despotism of the majority exercised by the North. They wanted freedom to continue their way of life, which they considered threatened by the Northern states. In their view, the North had violated protection of their individual freedom as guaranteed in the Constitution. Slavery had existed when they formed the Union. That

Constitution, in essence, guaranteed to the South the institutions they had. When addressing Congress before his state seceded, Georgia's Senator Robert Toombs, emphasized this position:

> *We had our institutions when you sought our alliance. . . . We have not sought to thrust them upon you, nor to interfere with yours. . . . [When it is] demonstrated that the Constitution is powerless for our protection, it will then be not only the right but the duty of the slave-holding states to resume the powers which they have conferred upon this government, and to seek new safeguards for their future security.* (Dowdey 1956. 37)

Warfare between the states had become the only means of settling the question. Was the Union an association of sovereign States, or was the federal government sovereign over all the states? When a state voluntarily joined the Union, did that state entirely relinquish its sovereignty for all time? This question alone marks the difference between the revolt by the 13 British Colonies in 1776 and the secession of 11 American states in 1861. The states, unlike the Colonies, had voluntarily joined a union — either by ratifying the Constitution or by requesting admission by the existing union. Many believed that by a majority vote in convention for that purpose, a state could rescind that action and dissolve its membership in the Union.

As President Lincoln stated at Gettysburg, Americans had engaged in war to determine the answer to that question. Because slavery had become the issue that finally caused men to fight in a test of the right to secede, slavery became part and parcel of that conflagration.

The people had never directly faced the question of state sovereignty with its collateral rights to secede and to nullify an act of Congress. The matter had certainly not just then surfaced. At the Constitutional Convention in Philadelphia (1787), the question of each state's position of influence in the Union caused lengthy debate and nearly broke up the Convention. Small states feared dominance by large states, and Southern states feared dominance by Northern states. Representation in the new government based solely on population satisfied neither faction. The Great Compromise — a two-house legislature — enabled the delegates in Philadelphia to escape their dilemma for the time.

When the Federalists enacted the Alien and Sedition Laws in 1798, some members of the opposition suggested to their leader Thomas Jefferson that they secede. In the Kentucky Resolutions, which he had written, Jefferson had proposed that the states veto these anti-democratic laws. Although he strongly favored the right of states to veto an act of Congress — nullification, Jefferson did not favor secession. In a letter to his cohorts, he stated:

> *It is true that we are completely under the saddle of Massachusetts and Connecticut and that they ride us very hard, cruelly insulting our feelings. . . . The body of our countrymen is substantially republican through every part of the Union . . . but still . . . this is not the natural state.*
>
> *In every free and deliberating society, there must, from the nature of man, be opposite parties and violent dissensions and discords, but, if, on a temporary superiority of the one party, the other is to resort to a scission of the Union, no federal government can ever exist. If to rid ourselves of the present rule of Massachusetts and Connecticut we break the Union, will the evil stop there? Suppose the New England States alone cut off, will our natures be changed? . . . immediately we shall see a Pennsylvania and a Virginia party arise in the residuary confederacy, and the public mind will be distracted with the same party spirit . . . seeing therefore that an association of men that will not quarrel with one another is a thing which never yet existed, from the greatest confederacy of nations to a town meeting or a vestry, seeing that we must have somebody to quarrel with, I had rather keep our New England associates for that purpose than to see our bickerings transferred to others.* (Passos 1957. 357)

Jefferson counseled caution. In recognition of the Law of Disagreement, let states remain united in opposition to the Federalists rather than secede and become divided among themselves. Under Jefferson's leadership, suggestions of secession over the Alien and Sedition Laws came to naught. His reasoning remains today the strongest argument in support of union. There is neither more nor less reason to expect agreement among men because of the size of the group. Once they accept the principle that disagreement justifies scission, cooperation between people will not exist.

Since the very existence of society requires peaceful cooperation, a willingness to resolve differences peaceably within the union best serves the interests of everyone.

A few years later, during Jefferson's administration, the Federalists sought Aaron Burr to lead the New England states to secede. Wise counsel and the lack of a consensus among their brethren in New England prevented secession at that time. The Missouri Compromise in 1820 — which divided the west between slaveholding and non-slaveholding areas along the 36°30' parallel — again postponed a dissolving confrontation. Disagreement over high tariffs caused talk of secession in South Carolina in 1832. Congress agreed then to a compromise that dodged the underlying question of state sovereignty. By compromise again, in 1850 Congress settled similar grievances. It actually satisfied no one.

All peaceful attempts to resolve differences over state sovereignty had brought only temporary expedients. Perhaps war was the only way to settle it. Certainly the 1861-1865 War Between the States did settle it. There remains no doubt today about the possibility of peaceful secession by any part of the Union. Public opinion would condemn such an act as rebellion, and the central government in Washington would quickly end it.

Despotism of the Majority

By its very nature, government is the only agency in society permitted to use force. The people must grant to government the use of force in order to protect society from invasion and to assure that citizens obey the laws. Despotism implies arbitrary, absolute, and oppressive exercise of this coercion. The masses viewed despotism by a dictator or a king as direct opposition to individual freedom. The English, the French, and the American revolutions grew from efforts of the people to escape despotic monarchs. They sought freedom that recognized the dignity of the person, and they chose democracy as the means to achieve that freedom. But despotism is not the province of emperors and kings alone. An intolerant and self-righteous majority, by disregarding the rights of the minority, can be an even more dangerous despot. As Mises warns:

> *The struggle for freedom is ultimately not resistance to autocrats or oligarchs but resistance to the despotism of public opinion. It is not the struggle of the many against the few but of minorities — sometimes of a minority of but one man — against*

the majority. The worst and most dangerous form of absolute
rule is that of an intolerant majority. (Mises [1957] 1985.
66-67)

The rights of U.S. citizens, protected originally by the limitations
placed on government by the Constitution, are now protected solely by the
"Bill of Rights," the first ten Amendments to the Constitution. No majority vote can authorize government encroachment on the rights of individuals. After all, as an alternative to action, men do have the option of
non-action. Seldom is the proposed action mandatory.

Among tribes of the Iroquois Nation, no action would be accepted by
the council until approved unanimously by the members. This rule protected the rights of the individual. It prevented the Iroquois from undertaking all manner of unwise ventures. There being no malcontents, no
abused minority, it assured cooperation by all.

Despotism of the majority can arise within any group when the leaders
proceed without due consideration of the minority. The minority, even
though it is a minority of one, is entitled to its time in the sun. The views
and rights of the minority should never be ignored. This is not a matter of
morality; it is a matter of practical politics. An enthusiastic majority can
defeat its own purposes by forcing a reluctant minority into conduct that it
opposes. The majority needs, or at least expects, support from the minority. How can the majority rightfully expect support from a minority that
has been overrun? Walter Lippman reminds us of this vital feature of
social relations:

> *In making the great experiment of governing people by con-*
> *sent rather than by coercion, it is not sufficient that the party in*
> *power should have a majority. It is just as necessary that the*
> *party in power should never outrage the minority. That means*
> *that it* [the majority] *must listen to the minority and be moved*
> *by criticisms of the minority. . . .*
> *The opposition is indispensable. A good statesman . . . learns*
> *more from his opponents than from his fervent supporters. For*
> *his supporters will push him to disaster unless his opponents*
> *show him where the dangers are.* (Lippman 1939.)

When a minority feels that the majority is overrunning its rights, it has no recourse but revolt. Such was the action of the American colonists in 1776, a minority among the English. Such was the action of the Southern states of the Union. In 1860, Southern leaders perceived themselves a minority with no protection under the Constitution.

The War Between the States was a war for freedom, not freedom for Negroes, but freedom for the individual citizen of a land. People did not fight over slavery. Slavery simply became the issue of the moment about which there could be no compromise. Southerners believed their legal rights were being trampled on by the majority. If the South lost equality of power in the Senate, it would become a regional minority. They could remain in the Union only if the Union allowed slavery in new territories, giving them an opportunity to expand Southern society as new states entered the Union, thereby preserving their equal representation in the Senate.

The differing socioeconomic structures of the two regions created conflicting interests under one government. The South was agricultural, exporting to the North and to the world. A planter-aristocracy could not survive unless slavery experienced no competition from free men. The Republicans, the majority party in the North, favored higher tariffs. Tariffs restrict trade. The Southern aristocracy knew full well that tariffs damaged their regional economy by reducing their competitiveness in foreign markets. It reduced the profitability of slavery, and the South had half its wealth invested in slaves. The South wanted free trade with all countries. The Republican North wanted to use federal tax revenue to finance internal improvements — deepening waterways and harbors and constructing roads, railroads, and canals. These internal improvements connected the new West with the Atlantic seaboard. The South saw no benefit to their economy from this use of tax revenues. Southerners so strongly opposed protective tariffs and internal improvements that in their Confederacy's Constitution (1861) they allowed tariff levies for revenue only and prohibited the use of tax revenues to finance internal improvements. To the people of the South, Republican control in Washington meant the end of protection for their interests.

Before they would ratify it in 1788, Southerners had insisted that the Constitution assure equal representation by states in the Senate. Consequently, as new states entered the Union, it was imperative that half be "slave states," or more to the point, states that had a common interest with the states of the agricultural South, and slavery was the distinctive mark by which each state's interest could be identified. Loss of sectional balance in this body reduced the South to a permanent minority.

When Stephen A. Douglas, the favorite nominee of the Democrats, would not accept slavery in the territories, the South knew they had no opportunity under the Union to protect their position. They realized that public opinion and change was forcing them into a position they could not accept any more than could their representatives to the Constitutional Convention in 1787. Their only hope lay in secession to become an independent nation.

When the forces at work are viewed in this light, it becomes apparent that the South feared despotism of the majority. Washington was interfering with their freedom to the disadvantage of their economy. Slavery was only the symbol. In truth, neither Douglas, Lincoln, nor a majority of Northern representatives in either party advocated freedom for the slaves and equality for the Negroes. Fire-eaters and abolitionists had kept the whipping-boy concept of slavery alive and visible. These extremists represented a small minority, but they used the issue to polarize the partisans in the deeper struggle:

> *What the rest of the nation wanted very much — protection for industry and for industry's markets, expansion of the free-farm system, internal improvements fostered by the central government . . . these the South wanted not at all. But its opposition to these things had to take the form of opposition to any attack on slavery itself.* (Catton 1961. 84)

In human relations, the harder one pushes the more the other resists. The people of the South felt they were being pushed; so they shoved back. When finally they realized they had lost this shoving match, they walked out. When the spoiled rich kid finds he is not getting center attention in the sand-lot football game, he takes his football and goes home. "You play my way, or there will be no game at all." The Southerners had dominated national politics since 1788; they would not accept a minority position in 1860; they left.

Revolt becomes possible whenever government intrudes into the lives of its citizens beyond what they are willing to accept — when they experience despotism. Government intervention always works to the advantage of some and to the disadvantage of others. It enriches some and impoverishes others. Freedom means unhampered control over one's own destiny; it means being free to an extent that does not interfere with the freedom of others; it means limitations on the coercive power of government. Government intervention is special-interest, partisan exercise of power. It restricts the options open to individuals.

Government is always people, not the perfected instrument of God. It is created by men, controlled by men, composed of men, and operated by men. These men who are the government are faulty human beings like everyone else. Government is an imperfect human instrument that has a monopoly on force. When it errs, it carries with its error the power of the sword. If the vote fails to rectify the injury, the people have no recourse but to use the sword.

In 1832, Alexis de Tocqueville expressed concern over the power of the majority in America. He warned:

> *If ever the free institutions of America are destroyed, that event may be attributed to the omnipotence of the majority, which may at some future time urge the minorities to desperation and oblige them to have recourse to physical force. Anarchy will then be the result, but it will have been brought about by despotism.* (Tocqueville 1960. 269)

The people of the South finally realized, in 1861, that they were forced to take up the sword or acquiesce to the control of a government committed to destroying their way of life. They had no choice. Revolt through secession and war was the natural reaction to despotism of the majority. It will always be so.

The Questions

Fighting in the War Between the States began April 12, 1861, at Fort Sumter, Charleston Harbor, South Carolina. It ended effectively four years later with the surrender of Generals Robert E. Lee at Appomattox Court House, Virginia, on April 9, and Joseph E. Johnston at Durham Station, North Carolina, on April 26. During those four years of conflict, out of a population of 31 million, more than one in eight wore a uniform. Casualties exceeded 1 million. More than half a million died, nearly as many Americans as have died in all other wars put together. The South lost over 60 percent of its wealth — destroyed, consumed, or confiscated. Many slaveholding planters became impoverished. War demolished Southern society. Brother fought against brother, and fathers against sons. Emotional wounds of 1865 lingered into the next century.

Why would people of any nation engage in such a costly war and continue it to the point of such devastation? Much has been written explaining the forces that brought this matter to a head. Why 11 states of the South finally asserted their "right" of state sovereignty in 1861 cannot be answered simply. To say that the South finally went to war over slavery ignores the full truth. War resulted from a complex web of forces.

People became so emotionally involved over subsidiary issues that they succumbed to the pressure of warmongers. Society always has men who in disagreement advocate solution by war. In 1861, these men prevailed. Nearly all alike greeted a state of war with relief, relief from tensions building for 80 years. This was a natural relief felt by people who knew that finally there would be a resolution to their differences.

There are times when some people take sides on controversial issues and refuse to budge. Many partisans declared in 1860 — and had been so saying for years before, "We will uphold this position to our dying breath." "Better to die fighting than to live under such oppression." When men of such inflexible nature become leaders, as they did in 1861, war naturally follows.

It would be interesting to read testimonials — some now published — from each of those who died, testimonials expressing their personal dedication to their cause. Soldiers seldom fight with a dedication to death before surrender. If such were so, records of battles would include no prisoners. No man would surrender; he would prefer to die fighting. No battle would see a retreat, much less a rout such as that among the Yankee troops at the first battle of Bull Run (First Manassas). No dedicated "to-the-death" soldier runs from the enemy even in defeat.

The battle cry "Victory or death" is the cry of leaders safely away from the action. Do not be mislead by historians. The soldiers on the firing line rarely embrace the cause of war to the death. There are exceptions, notably the men who fought at the Alamo in 1836, but even among those men seven surrendered. In most wars, such dedication is propaganda. During World War II, even the American officer who declined to surrender during the Battle of the Bulge — "Tell your commander, Nuts!" — fully expected (and rightfully so) a counterattacking relief force to arrive before all died.

War results from disagreement between leaders. The soldiers exposed to death rarely support their leader's cause so absolutely.

There are then two questions: (1) Why did the leaders in America resort to war in 1861? and (2) Why did the people support that war?

The Forces

The factors that brought about schism on a North-South sectional basis can be summarized as follows:

1. The South was captive to an institution (slavery) from which it could not escape.

2. An aristocratic minority held political control in the South. Southerners had no democratic freedom that matched what was common in the North.

3. A wide disparity existed between the two regions in their socioeconomic structure. Southern society remained in a static quasi-feudal system that could not change without destroying the great planter barons.

4. The South opposed the Industrial Revolution that the North eagerly embraced. Southern leaders viewed industrialization as a threat. Personal, democratic freedom fostered dynamic change in the North.

5. The South could see despotism of the majority destroying their way of life. If the Union forbade slavery in states formed from the area ceded by Mexico in 1848, the South would no longer dominate political power in Washington. Unless the South could extend their socioeconomic structure into new territories, the South would become a minority. Southern leaders viewed secession as their only option when they realized they had lost this power struggle.

6. With their hate propaganda, radical minorities — abolitionists in the North and fire-eaters in the South — created substantial sectional hatred among the people.

It becomes apparent that the people could not long work peaceably within the framework of one government. If they could not separate and go their different ways, violence would likely erupt.

The first 60 years of the 19th century brought substantial change to the

Northern states. Men interested in rapid development of the West sought public funds to construct canals and improve roads to connect the seaboard with the interior. Although the central government for the most part stayed indifferent to these "internal improvements," private enterprise and state governments moved into the endeavor with zeal. They built canals and roads connecting the Midwest with the Atlantic seaboard. After 1832, Americans built railroads almost frantically — 30,635 miles of track by 1860, most of it in the North connecting the East with the West. The cost of shipping a bushel of grain from Ohio to New York City dropped from dollars to pennies. The frontier moved west of the Mississippi to the edge of the grasslands of the Great Plains. Eli Whitney demonstrated the efficiency of mass manufacture by using standardized interchangeable parts. Robert Fulton's steamboats moved freight and passengers both upstream and downstream on the Hudson and Mississippi Rivers. New England shipbuilders launched the greatest sailing vessels ever to appear on the oceans, the Yankee Clippers. Farmers began using the steel mold-board plow and McCormick's reaper. Iron ore and coal moved over the Great Lakes to supply newly built steel mills. Productive oil wells were drilled in Pennsylvania. Nowhere in the world did people take to the Industrial Revolution so eagerly as in the Northern states of America.

Meanwhile, the South accepted virtually none of this except Eli Whitney's cotton gin. Just before the war, an Alabama politician declared:

> *"We want no manufactures; we desire no trading, no mechanical or manufacturing classes. As long as we have our rice, our sugar, our tobacco, and our cotton, we can command wealth to purchase all we want."*
>
> *A South Carolina planter rejected the concept of progress as defined in Northern terms of commerce, industry, internal improvements, cities, and reform. The goals of these "noisy, brawling, roistering progressistas," he warned, could be achieved in the South "only by the destruction of the planter class." The popularity of such views posed a powerful obstacle to economic change in the South.* (McPherson 1982. 31)

Only in Virginia had railroad development kept pace with that of her northern neighbors. Short-line units characterized the rest of the South, with frequent gaps of as much as 20 miles between terminals. Besides, they had not been standardized on one track gauge. Rivers remained the principal avenues for transporting freight. Cotton and tobacco composed the bulk of the freight, and planters sent those products to a seaport destined for markets reached by ocean-going ships.

The growing population in the North created cities; but because so many young Southern whites migrated north and west, population in the South increased primarily among Negro slaves. With this migration, nearly three-fourths of the increase in population during the first half of the 19th century occurred outside of the Southern states.

The South in 1861 remained in an 18th-century, quasi-feudal condition. Nearly all new capital investment went into producing agricultural cash crops, and cotton was king. The plantation, virtually self-sufficient, lay at the heart.

There were not really so many of these independent institutions. Less than 12 percent of the white population could be classed as planters, owning 20 slaves or more. But each plantation formed the nucleus around which all other activity centered. On the perimeter of the plantation lived the small, subsistence farmers that annually produced a bale or two of cotton for the cash market. They took their cotton to the plantation to be ginned and baled and sent to market by the planter. The planter milled their grain. He gave them help when they needed it. His schools taught their children. Once a year the planter entertained them and their families with a great barbecue. The planter was the only law, a feudal lord; and the small perimeter farmers were his vassals.

The cities — Charleston, Atlanta, Memphis, Richmond — belonged to the planters; the planters owned them. Each was like a city-state composed of small duchies. There the planters had their homes; there they spent half their time and all the social season. The businesses of the city, factorage and shipping, were operated for them. As in Europe during the Middle Ages, the professionals and artisans served only the aristocratic planters.

Few Southerners received formal education. The aristocracy believed education was unnecessary for the general public, and most states even forbade teaching slaves. Although this ban was not aggressively enforced, less than one percent of the Negroes could read. Too poor to afford schools, most whites educated their children at home or sent them to an elementary school on the plantation. The ruling planter-barons reserved higher education for their own children. Sons of the more wealthy studied in the North and in Europe. Although proportionately fewer youngsters in

the South attended school than in the North, the Southern aristocracy educated a greater percentage of their children in college.

The political system assured a continuation of this quasi-feudal society.
Local political power rested with the Justices of the Peace. The Governor
appointed these officials, and as a group they nominated candidates for
public office. The Justices of the Peace determined who could be Governor, and the Governor in turn determined who could be a Justice of the
Peace. Since none but planter-barons, artisans, and professionals received
an education, city mayors, Justices of the Peace, Governors, and representatives to the state legislature and to Congress came from their ranks.
Democracy held meaning only for the few who belonged to that aristocratic class. Small farmers and poor whites could vote, but aristocrats
determined who would be candidates. Democracy in the South in 1861
more nearly resembled democracy in the former Soviet Union than the
democracy in the North.

The aristocracy controlled the courts and the legislature. This system
maintained control of industrial development and opportunity for newcomers and the poor. Since small landowners gained title to land at the
grace of the nearby planter, planter-lords owned the best land, which protected them against competition from free labor. Free labor could never
cultivate land that was as fertile as the land worked by slaves. Since slave
labor cost more than free labor, profitability of the great plantations
depended on this advantage. The great planters' very way of life depended
on aristocratic control of government.

As in Europe, the lack of freedom in the South impeded economic
development. No such barrier existed in the North. The longer this disparity continued, the greater the differences became. Citizens of the South
who disagreed with these conditions could not change their own lot except
by leaving, and many did. The greater the difference in opportunity
became between North and South, the more emigrants from the South outnumbered immigrants. Nearly one in six Southerners left.

For those who remained, the more rapidly growing Northern population
appeared as a threat to Southern society, and the aristocratic planters
encouraged that fear. Clifford Dowdy elaborates:

> *This . . . majority of Southern whites, largely innocent of
> slave-holding or secessionist tendencies, were drawn in by the
> parochial nature of their society — with its immediacy of love*

> *of their land and respect for the ruling class — and by the all-inclusive nature of the attacks on their society from without. They understood that "Yankee" had come to mean enemy and that Negro slaves might be turned loose among them. But their resentments and fears were played upon . . . for it was the planters who recognized that they were the class who would be destroyed, along with their civilization, if the North gained power over them.* (Dowdey 1956. 8-9)

After touring America in 1832, the French observer Alexis de Tocqueville made this observation about Southerners:

> *If the changes I have described were gradual, so that each generation at least might have time to disappear with the order of things under which it had lived, the danger would be less; but the progress of society in America is . . . almost revolutionary. . . . It must not be imagined, however, that the states that lose their preponderance also lose their population or their riches; no stop is put to their prosperity, and they even go on to increase more rapidly than any kingdom in Europe. But they believe themselves to be impoverished because their wealth does not augment as rapidly as that of their neighbors; and they think that their power is lost because they suddenly come in contact with a power greater than their own. Thus they are more hurt in their . . . passions than in their interests. But this is amply sufficient to endanger the . . . Union. If kings and peoples had only had their true interests in view ever since the beginning of the world, war would scarcely by known among mankind.* (Tocqueville 1960. 402-403)

Thirty years before secession, Tocqueville foresaw the sectional split and the basic forces that created it.

While the planter aristocracy persistently acted to preserve the status quo — a Greek-like aristocratic society of the ancients, the North changed rapidly into an industrialized society that embraced opportunity, freedom, and education for the masses. Such differing societies viewed their needs from government as being at odds with each other. The only way the regions could avoid friction was for one section to adopt a socioeconomic structure more like the other. The South would not budge, and the North viewed the way of the South as archaic.

Southern aristocrats wanted to withdraw from the current of change in the Western world. When the feudal lords of the South could see no alternative, they tried secession as one last effort to avoid industrial change. Had there been no industrial revolution, the South might not have left the Union, at least not then. If true democracy had existed in the South, industrialization might have evolved there as it did in the rest of the free world. But the Industrial Revolution was a reality, and the planter-rulers of the South refused to let it enter their domain.

God's Angry Man, John Brown, may or may not have had the support of the abolitionists. In all probability, he and his sons acted much on their own in attempting to generate a slave uprising. If Brown sought help from the abolitionists, they surely must have encouraged him. Some did give him money and publicly admitted doing so. During the night of October 16, 1859, a small band of abolitionists led by John Brown took control of the unguarded federal armory at Harper's Ferry, Virginia. With the weapons of that armory they intended to arm the slaves and set up in the nearby mountains a camp where runaway slaves could establish a free community for themselves. No slaves appeared, and a contingent of U.S. marines led by Colonel Robert E. Lee soon captured Brown and his followers.

Southern whites lived in constant fear of a Negro uprising. Outnumbered by blacks on their plantations, how secure could they feel? John Brown's raid aggravated that fear. Fire-eaters like William L. Yancey found little difficulty convincing fellow Southerners that Brown's invasion proved that the North wanted to unleash the blacks. This touched a chord with all Southerners. In that brief 36 hours, Brown and his fellow conspirators accomplished what Southern radicals had been unable to do in as many years. He convinced Southern people that the North was the enemy. Then, the Honorable Henry Wise, Governor of Virginia, by failing to commute Brown's sentence from hanging (for treason) to life imprisonment, created a martyr whose memory strengthened the abolitionist cause. Young men rushed to enlist in the militia. Southern planters prepared to replace Northern merchant fleets with their own direct shipping lines to Liverpool. Southern students left Northern universities to return home. The people of the South at last were ready for the message of the radicals.

Southern radical leaders knowingly led their states into secession.

Events leading to secession pivoted around Stephen A. Douglas, the choice of Northerners at the Democratic presidential nominating convention in 1860. Douglas probably could not have forestalled secession, even if he had declined the candidacy when he failed to gain the support of Southern Democrats. William Yancey was determined to draw the South out of the Union, and he finally achieved the position of king-maker among the Southern delegates to that fateful convention. He made an issue of Douglas's stand on slavery in the territories. He worked to get a stalemate at Charleston with but one purpose in mind, as he clearly stated in a letter he made public:

> *No national party can save us; no sectional party can do it. But if we do as our fathers did, . . . we shall fire the Southern heart — instruct the Southern mind — give courage to each other . . .* we can precipitate the Cotton States into a revolution. (Emphasis Dowdey's; Dowdey 1956. 60-61)

Yancey and the radicals who supported him wanted their own sovereign nation. By blocking Douglas's nomination, they virtually guaranteed the election of the Republican candidate, Abraham Lincoln. This could have been to their advantage only as a means of leading the South into secession. The cooler heads of the South did not attend that convention in 1860. Few of these more conservative Southern leaders suspected that Yancey headed a well-organized movement to deadlock the Charleston convention and foment serious thoughts of secession. Perhaps he was not a revolutionary leader, but Yancey certainly greased the rails well enough that less astute men would slide into a position they could not leave.

Secession Meant War
Secession evolved from the fundamental differences between the two sections. But why did secession bring on war between the United States and the new Confederacy? Secession by seven cotton states solved the problem of slavery in the territories. The Southern Confederacy wanted to live in peace and cooperation with the older Union, and their leaders believed they could. Secession immediately removed all problems related to sectional differences in the Union. After these states seceded, Congress admitted Kansas as a free state.

Historians gain little by pondering "what if's." Enlightenment comes from recognizing what did happen and by analyzing its significance. When the election of Abraham Lincoln became official, South Carolina seceded, followed in a matter of weeks by Mississippi, Florida, Alabama, Georgia, Louisiana, and Texas. Delegates from these states met in convention and formed the Confederate States of America. They adopted a constitution, organized a judiciary, formed a legislative body, elected Jefferson Davis of Mississippi as President, and began functioning as a sovereign nation with his inauguration on February 18, 1861. (North Carolina, Arkansas, Virginia, and Tennessee joined the Confederacy after the capture of Fort Sumter.)

Other than making public statements about secession, the incumbent President, James Buchanan, virtually ignored the matter. He neither recognized the new Confederacy nor opposed it with any official action. His term expired in March, and he decided to leave the matter open for his successor to handle.

By the time Lincoln took office in March 1861, he had formed in his mind a clear course of action. He believed his duty as President was to preserve the Union — by armed force if necessary. He acted decisively on the situation at Fort Sumter and in such a manner that the Confederacy would fire the first shot (see below). Lincoln needed the support of public opinion, but loyal unionists were divided on the use of force to preserve the Union. Emotional response to Fort Sumter, however, was immediate. The South had attacked the Union; the Union must fight!

Other Presidents have used their position to get the other side to attack first — Polk in 1846, Roosevelt in 1941. They used the maneuver to solidify public opinion in support of war. A democracy can be more easily led into war if the citizens believe the other nation began the fight. Before that region had been generally recognized as part of the newly annexed state of Texas, President Polk sent a military force into the Rio Grande valley to confront the Mexicans. When the Mexicans attacked, Polk could go to the people with the claim that American blood had been shed on American soil by a foreign power. (See Chapter 15 for President Franklin D. Roosevelt's actions leading the nation into World War II.)

The nation had never settled the issue of secession. As stated earlier, many leaders at the time believed that when a state joined the Union it retained a right to secede. In every case where secession could have resolved an issue, it never surfaced. Debate had centered on the issue at hand and how compromise could be reached (see pages 151-153). In opposing the Alien and Sedition Laws of 1798, Thomas Jefferson had argued against secession on the basis of sound policy; he never mentioned the constitutional right. We can infer that, although he considered the action unwise, he believed the states did have the right to secede. In connection with the compromises of 1820, 1832, and 1850, some parties threatened secession; but no debate occurred.

Only these statements and actions had dealt directly with secession: (1) President Jackson declared in 1832 that, even if South Carolina did secede, he would send a military force to that state to collect the customs and tax levies. (2) President Buchanan told Congress in February 1861 that although the states had no right to secede, the Union had no constitutional right to counter them forcibly. (3) Before his inauguration, Abraham Lincoln vowed that as President he would uphold the laws, collect the taxes, and "hold, occupy, and possess" all property belonging to the Union. He thus implied that he would enforce the laws that the seceding states had claimed no longer applied to their citizens, and that he would use force to take the forts, arsenals, and warehouses that the seceding states had confiscated. By so saying, he artfully dodged the specific issue of using armed force to uphold the Union.

Southern leaders expected Lincoln to back away from this declaration; they did not believe Yankees would support military action. These Southerners fully expected to form their confederacy in peace, and to coexist in peace with the Union from which they had withdrawn. They completely misjudged President Lincoln. They perceived him as weak and indecisive. It surprised them to discover that his quiet demeanor concealed a man with determination and positive ideas about preserving the Union.

In the first decades of the Union under the Constitution, individual political and economic freedom had been important to the citizens. They fought a war and formed a government to preserve this freedom. Jeopardizing freedom had caused the break with England, and this same jeopardy created a schism between the states in 1860. Southerners believed President Lincoln's stand in 1861 challenged that principle, which was the very underlying strength of democracy in the United States. He challenged the freedom that had created the most dynamic society ever known to man. Many believed it inconceivable that the federal government should force persons to remain in the Union when they no longer wanted to do so. Lincoln fully understood this attitude and realized the importance of withholding armed force until the seceding states fired the first shot.

In their first encounter as Presidents, Lincoln outmaneuvered Davis. Lincoln obtained the public support he needed to mobilize the North for war against the South. Southern forces attacked Fort Sumter through no accident, but on direct orders from the Confederate President, Jefferson Davis. Davis sent General P. G. T. Beauregard to Charleston to take charge of military affairs in that region, with instructions to reduce the fort if the federal garrison stationed there would not surrender it peaceably. President Lincoln advised the Governor of South Carolina of his intent to send rations for the troops at Fort Sumter, and requested that this action be peacefully allowed. This forced Beauregard to take military action. If he allowed the garrison to be supplied, the defending Union forces would never surrender without a bloody battle. Lincoln's intended action along with Davis's orders compelled Beauregard to occupy the fort before the rations arrived, which required an assault. Once the Southern military intentionally fired a shot and forcibly captured a fort of the Union, President Lincoln could use the Union military without a declaration of war. At the beginning of hostilities, Lincoln still did not publicly admit that secession was the matter at issue. Consequently, neither Congress nor public opinion needed to address the constitutionality of using armed force to keep states in the union. By armed insurrection, U.S. citizens had captured and occupied territory and installations belonging to the Union. Civil disturbance is an administrative responsibility. Lincoln used armed force to put down civil insurrection.

The entire nation had reacted to the Law of Ignorance. That human trait had prevented people from confronting publicly the possibility of war over secession. They knew in themselves that secession could not be allowed; yet few would openly admit it. Until war over secession became a reality, people could pretend that it would never happen.

Sectional differences caused secession and war, because Southern leaders thought they could make their move and get away with it, and because President Lincoln believed that preservation of the Union justified military action. We may conclude that the leaders entered into war to determine whether any segment of the Union could withdraw and become sovereign. The masses merely responded emotionally to actions taken by their leaders. Even though only a minority in the South supported slavery, nearly all Southerners opposed equality for Negroes. They considered Negroes inferior. Even a majority of Northerners held the same conviction. Consequently, although those Southerners who opposed slavery fought for the

Confederacy, they even more opposed having equality of blacks forced on them. Slavery was their means of racial control. Aided by the antics of John Brown, they had become convinced that the North — the Republican party of Abe Lincoln in particular — sought freedom and equality for Negroes.

The War Between the States was a revolt similar to the American War of Independence from King George III, similar to the revolt by Mexicans for independence from Spain, and similar to the revolt by Texans for independence from Mexico. It differed from these earlier revolts in that the Southern revolutionaries lost their war.

The surprising element was the naiveté of some Southerners in believing that secession would be accepted peacefully by the central government. In all other revolts to break away from a governmental unit, the leaders of the revolt and the citizens concerned had no doubts that success would require armed conflict. Yet strangely enough, many citizens and leaders of the seceding states believed they were exercising a legal right guaranteed by the Constitution, and that the North was entirely wrong in using war to keep them in the Union. When the Union President, Abraham Lincoln, failed to concur, the slavery issue became for the masses a distant second as a cause for fighting. The Southern people saw Union armies trampling on their rights as free men. Once again, as they viewed it, English-speaking people took up arms to preserve their freedom.

The Lessons

That moment in history teaches lessons, both military and social. Consider first, military strategy in total war. To win a war against a cause that the people support, the people's will to fight must be broken. Southern leaders believed they needed simply to repel the invading military forces of the North. Jefferson Davis as President of the Confederacy, when speaking before his Congress on July 20, 1861, declared:

> *This war . . . will last till the enemy shall have withdrawn from . . . [our] borders — till . . . [our] political rights, . . . altars . . . and . . . homes are freed from invasion.* (Catton 1961. 430)

General Robert E. Lee realized that a defensive war strategy would lead to stalemate, a sure loss for the South. But Lee was not in charge; he commanded only the Confederate Army of Northern Virginia. President

Jefferson Davis, a West Point graduate and veteran of the war with Mexico, assumed full military control from the outset and retained it until his army commanders in the field had all surrendered.

The South won a majority of the early battles. These were hollow victories, because Davis's strategy of pursuing a defensive war meant that they had no bearing on the eventual outcome. Defense is often a successful tactic. It is always a losing strategy. Success for the South required destroying the North's will to fight. The Union General William Tecumseh Sherman recognized this truism of total war, and expressed it more clearly than any of his contemporaries. He declared:

> *"We are not only fighting hostile armies, but a hostile people.
> . . . We cannot change the hearts of those people of the South,
> but we can make war so terrible . . .* [and] *make them so sick of
> war that generations would pass away before they would again
> appeal to it."* (McPherson 1982. 460)

Most military commanders since that time learned this fact, as did Lincoln by the time the war entered its third year. Success in total war requires the destruction of the people's will to fight. Unfortunately, not all later civilian commanders became aware of that requirement for success in modern total war. Americans died needlessly in Korea and Vietnam because this lesson from the War Between the States escaped the nation's leaders. That war clearly demonstrated that a strategy of defense leads to stalemate.

The War Between the States demonstrated another military lesson, the importance of logistics. As the war progressed, the Union navy blockade effectively closed seaports the South needed in order to bring in supplies. At the onset of war, the Confederacy lacked manufacturing capacity sufficient to supply its armies. Although the region made great strides in building plants to produce war matériel, the blockade of their principal seaports proved decisive. They could neither ship out their cotton to pay for their purchases nor bring in adequate quantities of badly needed supplies. Southern soldiers fought with inadequate food, often without shoes, and frequently in rags. Their home-manufactured artillery guns never matched the quality of those made in the North and in Europe.

In the 20th century, German commanders tried to wage modern war without the avenues of import for supplies they could not manufacture at home. The sea blockade proved fatal to the German military machine in both World Wars. At the end of World War II, Germany had military jet aircraft superior to anything available to the Allies. Yet the Germans used these planes little because they lacked the fuel to keep them airborne. Both Napoleon and Nazi Germany failed in their assaults on Russia because they could not adequately supply the troops.

The greater lessons to be learned from this American War Between the States, however, are social. In writing the Constitution, the men in Philadelphia in 1787 had tried to protect the few from oppression by the many as well as protect the many from oppression by the few. They had known oppression under the rule of George III, from which they escaped by revolt and war. They were determined that any government of their creation would ensure that no leader could subject the citizens to tyranny.

Only a few voiced concern about protecting the few from the many. Yet James Madison had come to Philadelphia determined to find a way to prevent majorities from violating minority rights. As a student of state governments since 1776, he knew how frequently legislative majorities enacted laws destructive of individual rights. Madison's concern for protecting the minority from the majority resulted in the presidential veto over acts of Congress. The delegates rejected any stronger measure. During ratification, many state conventions insisted on inserting a Bill of Rights into the Constitution in order to assure protection for the individual from despotism arising from any source. But protecting the rights of the few began to erode during the heyday of Hamiltonian Federalism and the John Marshall Supreme Court. The loss of protection against the despotism of the majority became a major factor in precipitating a disastrous war in 1861. Yet few persons at the time learned that lesson, and many do not recognize it today. An even greater rebellion will some day erupt if this ignorance persists. Minorities, when denied, do have a way of replying — through rebellion — as the Southern aristocracy so aptly demonstrated.

That War Between the States illustrated another lesson of social importance: sectional disparity in freedom for the people will create a schism that leads to conflict. All the forces listed earlier that led to secession were symptomatic of that fundamental difference — the lack of individual freedom in the South and its presence in the North. Difference in freedom, although present long before the Revolution of 1776, did not create a meaningful disparity between the two regions until the War of 1812 finally freed the United States from its Colonial status. By 1815, when America finally took its place as an independent nation, the Southern aristocracy had fully gained control in their region. From that point on, freedom in the North bred industrial development. The lack of similar freedom in the South stifled a parallel development there.

Men have everywhere demonstrated their preference for an atmosphere of freedom. As the differences widened between the free North and the feudal South, a greater portion of the increasing population freely chose to settle in the North. At the same time, a qualitative variance increased as those seeking life as an aristocrat moved south, and those seeking greater opportunity moved north.

As always happens in unfree countries, the spread between the rich and the poor widened in the South and precluded the development of a middle class. A middle class is the mark of a free country. It develops out of opportunity. Its presence serves as a checkrein on radicals, and the South very much needed a restraining hand on radicals like Yancey. Unchecked, disparity in freedom finally led to conflict.

This disparity between free peoples and those living under despotism now causes tension in the world between the Eastern and Western Blocs of nations. It caused conflict that erupted into World Wars I and II. In every instance, the region that stifles freedom becomes the aggressor. Despotism cannot tolerate freedom at home or among its neighbors. Only the time of outbreak in hostilities remains in question. In the War Between the States, the following sequence of events determined the timing and triggered the split:

1. Geographical expansion by annexing Texas and cessions from Mexico resulting from the War with Mexico (1846-1848).
2. The Fugitive Slave Law of 1850 and subsequent noncompliance by Northerners.
3. Publication of *Uncle Tom's Cabin* (1851-1852).
4. The Kansas-Nebraska bill passed by Congress in 1854.
5. The Dred Scott decision (1857), wherein the Supreme Court declared the Missouri Compromise of 1820 unconstitutional, reopened the dispute over slavery in the territories.
6. John Brown's raid on Harper's Ferry (1859).
7. William Yancey's success at the 1860 Democratic convention in getting Southern delegates to support a walkout if they

failed to secure a platform plank advocating slavery in the territories.

8. The election of a Republican President, Abraham Lincoln, in 1860.

When their leaders frustrate the will of the people, the will of the people prevails either by the vote or by rebellion. In the 1850s the will of the people became divided along sectional lines. No vote could satisfy both the South and the North. Their interests had become so divided that the vote became powerless to effect reconciliation. But the will of the people must prevail. Either the two factions were to be allowed to separate, or the fundamental law of might would determine which interest would dominate. The North proved to be the stronger, and the will of the people of the North prevailed through armed might. This statement neither condones nor condemns. It merely describes the impact of a truism and explains why.

The results of this schism — the war and reconstruction — still affect American life. The racial problem ceased to be regional and became a concern throughout the Union. The question of state sovereignty — nullification and secession — was decided most emphatically. The South was violently wrenched from its 16th-century feudal system into 20th-century industrialization. A one-party political system developed in the South that was not challenged till the late years of the 20th century.

Insurrection or Revolution?

In 1863, President Lincoln publicly labeled the war as a great civil war. He never recognized the loss of the states. Under his interpretation, the legal governments of those states had been usurped by insurrectionists. The Southern states had been taken over by people acting in a manner adverse to the laws of the Union. Lincoln initiated military action to reinstate lawful government. He was obliged to treat secession as an act of insurrection since the country had never decided what the Constitution directed him to do in response to secession. If the war was truly a police action to put down civil insurrection, the President clearly had authority to use coercion. On the other hand, if the Confederacy of seceded states was a foreign power, the President had no authority to use the army and make war until Congress declared war. Because Lincoln never recognized the Union as dissolved, he acted within his constitutional authority in bringing military action against the Southern insurrectionists without first asking Congress for a declaration of war, and Congress never declared the existence of a state of war.

Now that the guns of that war have been silent for well over a century, men can see the war for what it really was. By secession the Southern states declared their sovereignty. This was regional revolution. The people of the South sought independence from the Union.

Men more commonly think of civil war as an effort to destroy the existing government and supplant it with another. In 1776 the Colonies had no desire to overthrow the British government. The Colonies then fought to assert a right they deemed was theirs under the law of an authority higher than that of George III. In 1861 the Southern Confederacy had no desire to overthrow the government in Washington, and no desire to replace the persons in executive, judicial, and legislative office. The members of the Confederacy went to war in defense of their independence, a right they believed was theirs by an authority higher than the Constitution of the United States. The conflict that Lincoln had labeled a police action against insurrection was, in truth, a war between states. This war can be assigned one of two labels. Because the South lost, "The War of Confederate Independence" is inappropriate. Consequently, President Lincoln's civil war is more correctly labeled "The War Between the States."

The first task of reconstruction was to find surviving Southerners who could overcome the hate generated by war. Lincoln understood that if the Republicans could salvage any political strength in the South, they would need the support of many former Confederates.

Chapter 10

Road to Reunion, 1865-1880
(Reconstruction)

Lincoln's Peace

PRESIDENT LINCOLN WAS A political realist. His interpretation of secession could have come from his understanding of the law, or it could just as easily have been a practical way to justify using the military without asking Congress to declare war. Lincoln interpreted secession as a seizure of territory by insurrectionists. In his view, the government in Washington remained the lawful authority over all the land including the South. The rights of all citizens were protected by that government. Private property, title to real estate, and rules of human relations depended on the laws of the national government. The lawful governments in the South had not broken with the Union. As Lincoln saw it, the organization that called itself The Confederate States of America had unlawfully seized the lands of the South and overthrown their lawful state governments; the Union remained intact; no conflict existed between Washington and the states; the United States had been challenged by some of its citizens. This was civil war, insurrection, rebellion. It was the President's duty to confront such acts with force if necessary. Consistent with this interpretation, both Congress and Lincoln recognized a legal government of Virginia for a time after war commenced. A prewar senator from Tennessee, Andrew Johnson, remained in the Senate until Lincoln appointed him military Governor of that state. (It is noteworthy that 10 of the 11 Confederate states seceded through a special convention called for that very purpose. Only Tennessee seceded through an act of its regularly constituted legislature and approved by its elected Governor.)

Lincoln held consistently to this view until his assassination. It formed the basis of his plan for reconstructing lawful governments as the Union rescued each state from the Confederacy. He approached loyal Unionists in Louisiana, and in 1863 recognized their government organized under his direction. Following Louisiana's example, Tennessee soon formed a loyalist government under Lincoln's plan. But since Congress refused to seat their elected representatives and senators, the status of these state governments remained in limbo and unrecognized when the war ended. Lincoln could not risk an open conflict with Congress during the continuance of hostilities. He had been too occupied preserving popular support for the war.

The substance of Lincoln's plan for reconstruction rested on his insistence that (1) only loyalists would vote and hold office, at least in the beginning. Lincoln had the power to decide when ex-Confederate soldiers and officials would be pardoned and thereby restored to franchise (Article II, Sec. II, Subsec. 1 of the Constitution). Furthermore, (2) officials representing each state were to be elected from natives of that state, not from immigrant Northerners. One can surmise from these two principles that Lincoln foresaw the animosity that would arise among Southerners if Negroes or new settlers from the North participated in their governments. After destroying the Confederacy, President Lincoln did not want to use the force of arms to restore lawful governments in the South. He realized the need for understanding and forgiveness by the North if the South was to accept reunion willingly. On the other hand, he could not countenance reinstating governments composed of the same men who had led the rebellion.

The grievous flaw in Lincoln's proposal lay in the lack of sufficient loyalists to fill all the offices of government. Most Southerners with experience in government had supported secession. They did not qualify as loyalists in organizing a government loyal to the Union.

As President, Andrew Johnson believed in the Lincoln plan. He tried to pursue reconstruction along the lines laid out by his predecessor. When the South faced the problem of having too few experienced loyalists by electing men from the former aristocracy, Johnson was obliged to pardon these men so they could qualify. He had no alternative. Back in session in December 1865, Republican congressmen stiffened their collective backs and refused to go along with the Lincoln plan. From that moment, under the leadership of Representative Thaddeus Stevens, Congress took control of reconstruction.

It is difficult to imagine a different scenario, even if Lincoln had not been assassinated. Given the makeup of Congress, Lincoln would have been severely taxed to bring off reconstruction according to his guidelines. Most likely, the many successes on the battlefield prevented Stevens and his fellow radicals from enlisting public support for their challenge to Lincoln during the last months of the war. Open opposition to a popular president is permissible, however, in times of peace. Even though Andrew Johnson lacked imagination, persuasiveness, flexibility, and tact — qualities strong in Lincoln, he cannot be blamed for the revolt in Congress that brought on radical reconstruction. We will never know how matters might have differed under Lincoln's leadership in the peace.

Reconstruction

Collapse of the Confederacy ended only the armed hostilities. The Union imprisoned Jefferson Davis, the rebel armies disbanded, and the soldiers went home to their families. The Union army assumed control of government for the region. Sectional jealousy and hatred remained in the hearts of the people. One young planter confessed in his diary that if he ever had children, the first principle of their first lesson would be to hate the Yankee. The women, the elderly, and the very young had not been able to work off their frustrations through fighting, as had the rebel soldiers. Years of deprivation and military rule aroused bitterness among these civilians. Unable to fight back, they could only watch and hate the Yankee while he burned their homes, destroyed their crops, slaughtered their cattle and chickens, confiscated their horses, and ran off their pigs. They watched Yankee soldiers strip the furniture from their houses to feed their camp fires. The war took the lives of one in four Southern men between ages 20 and 40. Few Southern families escaped this frightful loss of sons, brothers, fathers, sweethearts, and husbands. Every woman in the South lost one or more of the men in her life. In the grief of these women, hatred for Yankees grew intense and remained to be taught to the yet unborn.

The war created new regional problems that needed attention. What was to be done with four million uneducated, newly freed Negroes? How could the people form governments loyal to the Union? How should those men who fought for, and served in, the insurgent government be punished, if at all?

The first task of reconstruction was to find surviving Southerners who could overcome the hate generated by war. Lincoln understood that if the Republicans could salvage any political strength in the South, they would need the support of many former Confederates. Yet, where could enough of these men be found who were competent to govern? The Negroes comprised over 40 percent of the population in 1860 and had no education. Neither did the poor whites, who composed over 80 percent of the white population. Leadership for the South (and for the Republican Party) could not be found among them.

Much as Lincoln may have realized the importance of forming Southern governments from among loyalists, the supply of qualified individuals was too limited. So Johnson's reconstruction filled public offices with former leaders of the prewar South. Later, under the control of Congress, radical reconstruction filled these offices with educated Negroes and Northerners who migrated south after the war — businessmen, teachers, former officers of the Union army. None others qualified, because Congress accepted only those who had no former connection with the rebel movement.

Without realizing the problem — or refusing to accept it, former Southern leaders and the poor whites equally resented being governed by these carpetbaggers and Negroes. Yet under Johnson reconstruction, wherever local governments had been controlled by the former planters and the professional class, they had been so extremely anti-Negro and anti-Yankee that even their friendly critics labeled them ill-advised, to say the least. A contemporary of the times recorded that sentiment:

> *In the fall of 1865, Gideon Welles, a firm supporter of John-*
> *son's reconstruction program, recorded in his diary. . . . "The*
> *tone of sentiment and action of* [the] *people of the South," he*
> *wrote, "is injudicious and indiscreet in many respects. . . . The*
> *entire South seem to be stupid and vindictive, know not their*
> *friends, and are pursuing just the course which their opponents,*
> *the Radicals, desire. I fear a terrible ordeal awaits them in the*
> *future."* (Stampp 1966. 75-76)

There remained also the race problem. The four million "freedmen," as ex-slaves were called, had no education, no experience with independent responsibility, no homes, no money, and little clothing. What was to be their place in the new order? They could not migrate north; by law many Northern states forbade Negro immigration. The South lay in ruins, the rich farmland overgrown with weeds; much had been intentionally laid waste by Sherman throughout Georgia and the Carolinas, and by Sheridan in the Shenandoah valley. Grant had ordered the land so ravaged that "a crow flying across it [would] have to carry its own rations." Great cities like Jackson, Mobile, Charleston, Richmond, Atlanta, and Savannah lay in ruins, destroyed in the prosecution of the war. The cities, railroads, and factories needed rebuilding. Over this idle land the ex-slaves wandered, some searching to reunite families; many wandered simply because they were free to do so. A large number drifted into the cities, where they were fed and cared for by charitable institutions and the national government through its agency the Freedman's Bureau. In the cities nature took its toll. Crowded together with scant shelter, impure water, inadequate food, and no sanitation, the former slaves succumbed to disease. In many regions during the early years of reconstruction, especially in that area where Sherman's destruction had cleared away crops and livestock, many ex-slaves perished, mostly the very young.

The plantations needed labor, but most planters had no money for wages. In theory, as free men, Negroes could work wherever they chose. In reality, they were tied to the soil because they knew only how to farm. By necessity, Negroes ultimately returned to the farm, as virtual serfs to the planter class. The race problem continued into the mid-20th century with little done to advance Negro assimilation into American society.

Historians and Reconstruction

Due to emotional conflict remaining in both the North and the South, early accounts of that period are suspect. Emotions so warped their thinking that few writers tried seriously to adhere to facts. Many Northerners based their work on hearsay. Only a few of them had observed conditions firsthand, and still fewer produced unbiased reports. News editors tried to influence political affairs through public opinion, and they rarely let truth interfere with their reporting. A majority of Northerners did not know the facts, and the former Southern leaders — who controlled the news media there — devoted their attention to recapturing control of local political institutions. The Southern viewpoint did not appear in print until the next decade.

Contemporary accounts of the period and works by historians for the next six decades were too close to the hatred and racial bigotry to be objective. Typical are these remarks by John W. Burgess, professor of political science and constitutional law and dean of the faculty of political science at Columbia University. In the 1902 preface to his account of reconstruction, he stated:

> *The North is learning every day by valuable experiences that there are vast differences in political capacity between the races, and that it is the white man's mission, his duty and his right, to hold the reins of political power in his own hands for the civilization of the world and the welfare of mankind.*
> (Burgess 1902. viii-ix)

Because ex-slaves were uneducated and observed customs different from those of the white race, they did not fit into the dominant society. This stigmatized all men of color and created a belief in their inferiority. Racial prejudice made it difficult for white writers to give an unbiased interpretation of that time when the nation was first trying to find a place for the freedmen. Since the recent revival of efforts to complete the emancipation of Negroes in America, historians have begun to produce more realistic appraisals of the period. (In particular, see Kenneth Stampp's *The Era of Reconstruction, 1865-1877.*)

What Reconstruction Did Accomplish

Material available today reveals little about what President Lincoln intended to do with freedmen. His plan for reconstructing the South suggests that he would have left the matter in the hands of local governments. The record is clear that Lincoln never intended to free the slaves as part of the war. When he did issue his Emancipation Proclamation, he used it to preserve the Union. By late 1862, reverses in the field had caused Northerners to weaken in their support for the war. Europe showed a growing sympathy for the cause of the South. Lincoln needed a principle, an ideal, to rally Northern support for the war effort and to turn Europe away from the Southern cause. Lincoln had stated earlier that slavery was of little significance to the war, that preserving the Union was the only reason for that costly struggle. He had stated also that if by freeing the slaves he could save the Union, he would do so, and just as surely he would support slavery if that would preserve the Union.

By the end of 1862, Lincoln had decided. He issued his proclamation freeing all slaves in the area controlled by the Confederacy. By so doing he isolated the South from foreign sympathy and support, and at the same time gave Northerners a cause for which to continue the fight. This was smooth politics too. His proclamation freed only the slaves in the South, where it could not be enforced. It did not affect the status of any slave in the area controlled by the Union, where Lincoln would be required to enforce it, or where property of loyal unionists would thereby be confiscated.

From the beginning of his term in office, President Andrew Johnson agreed to treat Negroes as dictated by Southern leaders. Under Johnson, Negroes would have gained status as freedmen, but their social and political status would have remained much as it had been before the war.

By reconstruction, the Republican majority in Congress strove to educate Negroes and establish for them a place in society, with equal legal, political, and social rights. Under their influence, the nation adopted three constitutional amendments dealing with the legal status of the American Negro. The Thirteenth abolished slavery in all states; the Fourteenth granted Negroes citizenship and equal protection under the law; the Fifteenth gave them the vote. But before these changes could become part of the fabric of Southern society, the North grew weary of dealing with Southern reconstruction. The dedicated leaders of the radical movement had died. The majority in the North had become callous to the constant outcry about Southern outrages; and, anyway, they felt they had done enough for the "everlasting 'nigger' . . . [and they wished that all the

Negroes] were in Africa." (Stampp 1966. 15) That same majority did not honestly believe in racial equality. They were content to leave the welfare of Negroes to the people where the freedmen lived.

President Rutherford B. Hayes removed all military personnel from the South, terminating reconstruction "at the point of the bayonet." The year 1877, when Hayes took office and a new Congress convened, saw the end of reconstruction. The former Southern leaders regained control of their local governments.

Perhaps in no other way could the Fourteenth and Fifteenth Amendments have been adopted. Both conflicted with the racial prejudices of a majority of the voters nationwide. Representative Stevens took advantage of Northern vindictiveness to punish the South for their transgressions. While emotions ran high, he and his followers pushed these amendments through Congress, and then required the Southern states to ratify them before they could regain statehood in the Union. In the judgment of historian Kenneth M. Stampp, this achievement alone justified all the wrongs worked on the South during radical reconstruction. As he states:

> *Negroes could no longer be deprived of the right to vote, except by extralegal coercion or by . . . subterfuge. They could not be deprived of equal civil rights, except by deceit. They could not be segregated in public places, except by the spurious argument that this did not in fact deprive them of the equal protection of the laws.*
>
> *Thus Negroes were no longer denied equality by the plain language of the law, as they had been before radical reconstruction, but only by coercion, by subterfuge, by deceit, and by spurious legalisms. . . . When, however, state-imposed discrimination was, in effect, an evasion of the supreme law of the land, the odds, in the long run, were on the side of the Negro.*
>
> *The Fourteenth and Fifteenth Amendments, which could have been adopted only under the conditions of radical reconstruction, make the blunders of that era, tragic though they were, dwindle into insignificance. For if it was worth four years of civil war to save the Union, it was worth a few years of radical reconstruction to give the American Negro the ultimate promise of equal civil rights and political rights.* (Stampp 1966. 214-215)

For the first time, the South accepted the principle of education for the masses including Negroes; all Southern white males obtained suffrage; the rights of women were recognized. Southern states organized their first truly democratic governments.

Reconstruction caused one important side effect not at all desired by the Republican North — a solid Democratic South. Before the war a two-party system had existed there. Although Democrats had dominated, Whigs had presented a respectable opposition. When the war ended, Lincoln endeavored to rebuild a two-party system. At that time, though in the minority and mostly old-time Whigs, many Southern whites opposed the Democrats and secession. The Negroes who did vote sided with the Republicans as the party of their deliverance. The excesses of radical reconstruction under Congress, however, drove nearly all whites into the Democratic Party. When reconstruction ended, the South effectively disenfranchised Negroes by intimidation and other extralegal machinations. This left a one-party system, the solid Democratic South. For nearly a century thereafter, the only meaningful elections in the South were the primaries. In recent years, with the migration of Northerners into the Sunbelt, this pattern has changed. The war did not create the Solid South. The Solid South developed in reaction to a despotism of the majority during the 12 years of radical, Republican reconstruction.

Reunion

Although politicians fostered delay in political reunion, businessmen, writers, and ordinary citizens went about their own affairs accepting a reunited nation. They worked together toward unity as they intermingled and traded commercially with each other. Northern capital moved south to invest where capital was urgently needed. True, antebellum planters resisted the entrance of Northern capital, but those who gained employment from it embraced migration of Northern businessmen — with their capital.

The South had lost over 60 percent of its wealth in the war; only the land remained. Without money and machinery, their land was useless in a wage-labor orientation. Northern money greatly accelerated economic revival. The leaders of the old South swallowed their pride, albeit grudgingly, and accepted this help from their former enemies. As Paul H. Buck explains:

The business brains, capital, and technology of North and South found a community of interest politicians had never known. It seemed as though a vast wall of misunderstanding had fallen, destroying the isolation of the earlier years. (Buck 1938. 184)

Time mended the schism. Young men greeted opportunity, particularly those from the 85 percent who had been the "poor whites" of the prewar plantation system. They eagerly sought reunion, with its opportunity to remain in their homeland and work. Paul H. Buck further elaborates:

If many were bitter over Reconstruction memories, there was in contrast the accomplished fact of Southern restoration to full political rights within the Union to take off the edge of bitterness. If pessimism prevailed in some quarters in regard to race relations, there was also optimism in the observation that the system of free labor was meeting with an unexpectedly high degree of success and that the abolition of slavery had destroyed a provincializing influence.

One thing was still required for the revolution in Southern attitude to be complete. The New must breed a faith and confidence in itself. That faith and confidence was the contribution of young men growing up to manhood in the eighties, young men demanding the right to live a life of action and fulfillment rather than a life of wearing sackcloth amid the ashes of past grandeur. (Ibid. 169)

Had these young men been born 20 years before the war, they would have left the South at their earliest opportunity. After the war, they wanted to stay at home; and they found that they could as the influence of antebellum chivalry disappeared with the death of the older members.

Partisan Politics

Now that we have the power, when do we get the money? Through the ages that question has been asked repeatedly in political circles. Like it or not, the primary ingredient that unites workers into a political party is the expectation of wealth gained from winning an election. In the United States, politicians politely call this patronage. Presidents and Governors appoint persons to public office. State legislators and the national Congress dispense billions of dollars through appropriation bills. With favors paid for out of these money bills, Republican and Democratic Presidents and Governors alike reward the party faithful. Pet projects (distribution of wealth) are approved — perhaps a bridge here, a reservoir there, a major highway improvement, location of a government office (employing many people who will spend their incomes in the locality), appointments to public office (postmasters, judges), special-interest legislation favoring banks, manufacturers, or labor. The list goes on and on. Every state and national party chairman has a detailed list of this patronage to be dispensed when his party takes control. Currently, the amount of wealth involved exceeds a trillion dollars a year. It is small wonder that office seekers raise and spend millions of dollars in elections.

The historical precedent for this spoils system is founded in English practices that predate modern history. The feudal lord who rose to become king did so with the aid of other feudal lords. When he became king — by military success over opposition, he beheaded the opposing leaders, confiscated their property, and distributed their lands among the faithful lesser lords who had helped him gain his position.

As long as man has government, this practice will persist. Reform candidates rise from the crowd when the practice becomes too blatant. "Drive the rascals out" becomes the cry. Reformers take power, and they become more discreet in how they divide the spoils. But the practice goes on under monarchs, republics, and democracies headed by reformers. When the carrot at the end of the stick is large enough, a struggle develops to see who can get it. It becomes a case of winner-take-all. The losers retire to organize for the next round. One thousand years ago (and recently in Russia, Iran, and Romania) the losers lost their heads. Today, at least in the United States, winners do not go to this extreme. They simply revise the tax laws and dispense the appropriations in such a manner as to benefit the party faithful.

The Business Depression of 1873-1879

As governments have always done, Congress in the 1860s financed the war by inflating the money supply and by borrowing. Such credit expansion always artificially stimulates business activity, especially in the hard goods industries — manufacturing, transportation, mining, farming. During the war and for nearly a decade afterward, the nation could not expand industry fast enough, expansion financed largely by credit. But credit expansion cannot go on forever. At some point, new credit must be held to a level that does not exceed new saving. Otherwise, continued credit expansion brings on runaway inflation and complete destruction of the monetary system. The end of credit expansion forces producers to contract their operations, generally rather dramatically. Some credit support for American industry had been coming from Europe, but it disappeared when the shenanigans of the Credit Mobilier were exposed. Credit Mobilier was the construction company organized to build the Union Pacific Railroad from Omaha, Nebraska, to a point in Utah where it would join the Central Pacific, which was being built eastward from the Pacific Coast. Although Credit Mobilier was making a very good profit, many questioned the ethics of its practices. Since some Congressmen owned stock in this corporation, the affair seemed to be soiled with government graft and corruption.

The failure of the Jay Gould-Jim Fisk combine to corner the gold market in the late 1860s additionally cooled European interest in American investments. When Jay Cooke's Northern Pacific Railroad enterprise collapsed in September 1873, panic set in.

These events tarnished President Grant's administration. Gossip implied that he and his cronies profited from these questionable practices. No doubt some did, as also did many members of Congress; but they did so mainly in a manner that has been considered acceptable politics — by patronage and special-interest legislation. Outright illegal conduct was not much greater then than existed before or exists today. The scandals were largely fabrications of the times; newspapermen who opposed the incumbent president used innuendo to aid their cause.

The economy built on credit collapsed with the end of credit expansion as Eastern bankers, aided by President Grant, sought to restore the monetary system to the prewar gold standard. The financial panic of that September ruined countless banks and brokerage houses within a few days. A depression followed that was not equaled until the Great Depression of the 1930s. Unemployment reached a high level; hundreds of banks failed; many farmers lost their land through foreclosures; factories closed, many of which never reopened. Every enterprise using credit suffered. The business climate did not recover until the government quit tampering with the monetary system, which in 1879 was finally restored to the gold standard of 1860.

A gold standard, fully enforced, severely restricts credit expansion and the resultant boom-and-bust phenomenon. Even so, government can widen the limits of credit expansion and increase the money supply (1) by using the central bank to assure that all banks in the country act in unison, (2) by fostering fractional reserve banking, (3) by relieving banks from their contractual obligation to redeem their bank notes and deposits in gold, and (4) by restricting foreign commerce. As a result, credit expansion — followed by certain and necessary contraction — created conditions that led to other panics and business recessions even under a full gold standard, namely those in 1893, 1907, and 1921. None of these approached the severity of the long adjustment period of 1873-1879 until the depression of the 1930s. "The Depression" was ushered in, of course, on the tail of prolonged credit expansion so immense that it forced the United States to abandon the gold standard in 1933. (For a more comprehensive discussion of the economics of the business cycle, see Chapter 14, which deals directly with the Great Depression. It is sufficient here to recognize the events in this postwar period that resulted from partisan politics.)

At one time, Republicans had a clear two-thirds majority in both houses of Congress, which permitted them to ignore opposition in Congress and in the White House. At their hands, the South suffered a humiliation that dwarfed even what arose directly from events of the war. Until reunion became a reality under President Hayes and the Democrats mounted a meaningful opposition in Washington, the South remained in violent turmoil.

. . . The record of industrial development in the United States in the late 1800s includes cases where government used power improperly. . . . The profligate abuses came from government grants of power to act unfairly, not from the operation of entrepreneurs and business employers competing freely in a free market.

Chapter 11

Industrial Development, 1850-1901

People and Their Government

FOR TWO DECADES the War Between the States and postwar reconstruction occupied the attention of most people in the South. Southern homes all felt the loss of life among their young men, the changes required by radical reconstruction, the presence of emancipated Negroes, and the short-age of food and clothing caused by a war fought in their own back yard. That war and reconstruction had been branded in their thoughts. Southern men and women talked of little else than the war and the governmental organizations that were forced on them at the point of Union bayonets. Southern children grew from toddlers to adults in this atmosphere. In 1880 every Southerner over the age of 20 knew about Thaddeus Stevens and Charles Sumner in Congress, about Generals William Tecumseh Sherman and Phil Sheridan, about Nathan Bedford Forrest and the Ku Klux Klan, and about "Beast" Ben Butler. As Paul H. Buck clearly states:

> [In the years that followed the Civil War] *much was said about the need of healing the wounds of strife. Optimists pointed to episodes that seemed to suggest the approach of reconciliation. But actually the years from 1865 to 1880 were dreary years in which there was no peace. The war had ended only on the battlefield. In the minds of men it still persisted. Memories of the past and issues living in the present combined to perpetuate . . . antagonism that victory and defeat had created.* (Buck 1938. 45)

Most Northerners had dismissed the war from their minds by 1867, and those living on the prairie and farther west had hardly known there was a war. People outside the South could not be bothered with the affairs of Negroes and Southern aristocrats. If they discussed politics and government at all, they argued the merits of the just-concluded (1867-1868) purchase from the Russians, that Arctic region called "Alaska." Before the panic of 1873 and the subsequent seven years of depression, they had busied themselves at growing grain, building steel mills, laying railroad tracks, and racing horses at the county fairs or down main street on Saturday night. Politics in Washington entered their minds but once every four years, when they voted for a President. Reconstruction meant much to congressmen, Governors, the party faithful, and those with some special-interest legislation in mind. The majority of the people in the North and West paid little attention to it.

The big news of 1869 was the completion of the Union Pacific-Central Pacific Railroad, which provided continuous rail connection from ocean to ocean: Sacramento, California, to Omaha, Nebraska, to New York City. On May 10 of that year, Western Union Telegraph Company sent a signal nationwide at the very instant when Central Pacific president Leland Stanford drove the last — a gold — spike to connect the two rail lines at Promontory Point near Ogden, Utah. In every Eastern, Central, and Western city, bells rang, whistles blew, and teenagers shouted in celebration.

No matter that the building of that railroad had cost the taxpayers dearly in money and public land. As is generally the case with government subsidies, the taxpayers never realized they had been had by the politicians. People saw the completed project, not the projects that might have been completed if the government had not used the resources where it did.

After the War Between the States, Congress, encouraged by President Grant, deflated the currency to the prewar level. The resulting economic adjustment — the panic of 1873 and six years of depression — touched the lives of the common man, especially indebted farmers. Many Western farmers who lost their homes returned to the East, to their families if they had any. Single men went onto the prairie to become cowboys.

As in all economically depressed periods, unemployed workers and displaced farmers had little to do with causing the slump. Their only sin may have been voting for a politician who supported policies that led to the boom and bust. At such times, even though they do not understand the causes, these men sense that the government caused the problem. Naturally they call for the government to aid them in their troubles. Politicians appeal to this call for help in order to advance their personal ambitions. Their oratory blames the incumbents, right or wrong, and promises prosperity if "you vote for me." Men interested in specific legislation spread the word that prosperity will return when government adopts their proposals.

Senator Henry M. Teller of Colorado, owner of one of the largest silver mines in the West, led the other mine owners in the 1880s to get Congress to support an overvalued price for silver. This legislation enabled Teller and his followers to exchange their silver for gold at an artificially high rate at the expense of American taxpayers. At a 16-to-1 exchange ratio of silver for gold, this enforced bimetallism overvalued silver and repeatedly forced the national government to borrow gold in order to maintain a reserve stock. This interference with the monetary system caused the 1893 money panic and subsequent depression. With only 14 years between periods of economic distress, the man on the street again faced unemployment and depression brought on by government action not of his own doing.

If it were not for wars, taxes, and government-induced changes in the money supply, the majority of citizens could virtually ignore government and what it does. Unfortunately, however, those in the seat of power use war, taxes, and manipulation of the money supply to increase their own fortunes. When matters get out of hand, as they often do, the citizens pay the penalty. Many lose their homes, become exposed to death in war, pay the taxes, and suffer unemployment and lower earnings during depressions.

In the last half of the 19th century, the masses suffered distress from all these forces: two wars, the War Between the States (1861-1865) and the Spanish-American War (1898); high taxes in the form of tariffs; and inflation that caused the panics and depressions of 1857, 1873, and 1893. Many became victims in spite of their own efforts to prevent the problems.

It benefits everyone to understand that such things happen and to prepare for them. We can learn about the views of the congressional and presidential candidates we vote for. One person may not be able to influence the acts of politicians, but he can take precautions to reduce the impact of such events when they do happen. A person becomes an "innocent" victim of the times by ignoring warnings and exposing himself to hazards that are known to follow rapid change. With war or depression appearing in the near future, wisdom dictates avoiding debt.

Unrestricted opportunity to change is fundamental to human freedom. Government barriers to change limit opportunity and stifle progress. Social classes thrive on government restrictions which preserve economic structures that individuals cannot alter. The long period of stagnation known as the Middle Ages was characterized by government barriers to change. Men could not move around or leave the class they were born in. The English and French revolutions were efforts by the masses to remove the shackles that restricted change.

Although freedom cannot exist without opportunity to change, accelerated change induced by government ends up restricting freedom. It creates economic imbalances that in time require periods of adjustment. Economists call these periods "depressions." The forces that drove the country into depression in 1873 and 1893 came out of changes caused by government. By granting free access to land from the public domain, the Homestead Act of 1862 stimulated agriculture before the people needed an increase in foodstuffs. Would-be farmers could acquire acreage free. The result was as predictable then as it is apparent now. Producers did not need to consider one major cost in deciding to increase production: the cost of land. Such circumstances always increase supply beyond demand, and prices fall too low to yield a profit. It happened in agriculture in the 1870s. Encouraged by the immediate profits they realized from farming with free land, farmers bought additional land on credit. The inevitable occurred;

the supply of foodstuffs increased beyond market needs and drove prices down. At the same time, Congress reduced the money supply, which lowered prices even more. It became impossible for many indebted farmers to pay their debts, and they lost their land to foreclosure.

Land came into cultivation too soon because it was free. The force that encouraged farmers to increase production did not come from an increased demand for foodstuffs and its attendant increase in prices. Subsidized by free land, farmers were encouraged to produce more than the market wanted. Change accelerated by government — an increase in the product — caused suffering among the very people the government wanted to help.

Government also aggravated the financial troubles of the railroad industry by accelerating change. In order to please business interests engaged in commerce between the East and the Pacific West, Congress subsidized construction of transcontinental railroads. The Pacific Railroad Acts of 1862 and 1864 authorized the government to give land to companies for constructing such lines, and to lend them money as well. Four Western railroads received land equal to the combined area of Ohio, Illinois, Indiana, Wisconsin, and Michigan. Government loans to these subsidized railroads exceeded $100 million. Nearly all these companies soon went bankrupt because the markets required to support their operation did not exist.

While Congress debated legislation for these land giveaways, private businesses offered to purchase right-of-ways to build railroads into the prairie West. The prices then offered exceeded the prices government and railroads later received in sales to prospective farmers. In other words, private enterprise offered reasonable prices — they did not ask for gratuities; yet Congress turned them down. Such sales would have limited the power of those in government. History has seldom seen politicians and bureaucrats voluntarily relinquish power. The land grants to favored individuals proceeded with predictably disastrous results.

While the government encouraged farmers and railroads to go into debt, it first inflated then deflated the money supply. Greenbacks, the fiat paper money loaned to these interests, reached a low point of value in terms of gold dollars at about 43 cents. Then, in 1873, the government announced that during the next six years it would redeem in gold both greenbacks and all government debt instruments at 100 cents on the dollar.

This intentional deflation of money assured a depression — starting with the money panic of 1873 — and prolonged the adjustment process for six years. Debtors who had borrowed dollars worth 43 cents in gold had to repay them with dollars worth 100 cents. With prices of farm produce falling, indebted farmers quite naturally went broke. Unable to meet the new conditions, railroads indebted to the government on the basis of cheap money also went under. This ill-advised action by government was just one of many that have given "falling prices" a bad name. No one today can countenance even a suggestion of lowering prices, by whatever means. But lower prices resulting from improved efficiency benefit everyone.

Not everybody took this whipsawing without some effort to save themselves. Farmers demanded a return to cheap money. The wage-earners, frequently a debtor class, clamored for cheap money. Silver miners of the mountain West insisted that government support silver at a 16-to-1 ratio with gold. Farmers organized, labor organized, and the silver interests went directly to Congress. Labor and the farmers failed to gain political power, and their organizations disappeared. The silver miners had a partial success in the Sherman Silver Purchase Act of 1890, which required the government each month to purchase 4.5 million ounces of silver and to mint it into silver dollars on a 16-to-1 exchange ratio with gold. The silver miners then took their gold from the sale of silver, bought silver dollars with gold on the open market at a discount, and used silver dollars to pay for material and labor. It was a grand scheme for the owners of silver mines, but for no one else. Such an inconsistent situation could not last. The government soon ran out of gold and had to abandon the support of silver, which brought on the money panic and collapse of 1893.

The masses generally favor taking from the rich and giving to the poor. They see themselves as the recipients of this gratuity. Inflation is a tax on savings and creditors in order to finance gifts to debtors and other favored interests. Most people associate creditors with the rich and debtors with the poor. Consequently, majorities favor inflation. Since government creates the money out of thin air and exchanges it for goods and services, the treasury gains from inflating the money supply. Inflation becomes a means for politicians to spend on projects for which people are not willing to be taxed. Deflation is unpopular with politicians because it drains the treasury. It is unpopular with majorities since it works to the detriment of debtors. As a result, both the masses and the politicians favor inflation as a government policy. ("Inflation" as used here means increasing the money supply. It does not mean rising prices. Inflation always makes prices rise; but as happened in the 1920s, increasing the efficiency of industry can offset this force and thereby conceal the true impact on prices exerted by inflation.)

In the late 20th century, however, the masses are more often creditors, and the wealthy are more likely to be debtors. As workers that rely on retirement programs paid from pension funds, as individual savers in mutual savings and loan associations, as depositors in commercial banks, as purchasers of life insurance, the masses have become creditors because those funds held in trust for them are loaned to other people. The ones doing the borrowing are business enterprises most likely owned by members of the more prosperous class. So public clamor for inflation today is contrary to the public's self-interest.

Of course, neither inflation nor deflation as a government policy can be considered just and equitable. People are more justly served when government remains neutral relative to money. But history evidences constant monetary manipulation by governments. The particulars of the manipulation depend on which group is in office.

In 1873, during the Grant administration, the financiers who had bought greenbacks and government bonds with 43-cent dollars induced Congress to pass laws requiring the federal government to redeem both with gold at 100 cents on the dollar. (Now that we have the power, when do we get the money?) A tug-of-war between inflationists and deflationists brought on the panic of 1893. This struggle has occupied governments throughout recorded history and continues today.

Industrial development only made the problem more complicated. Neither the people nor their elected representatives fully understood the changes that industrialization required of them. Accordingly, examination of the Industrial Revolution is appropriate.

The Industrial Revolution

Imagine a country where all the land has been divided among the people so that every family has 640 acres. If each family produces two offspring to maturity, thereby maintaining a stable population, every new family will also have 640 acres. Suppose, however, that because of improved living conditions the population begins to grow such that each family has three children. After one generation, each family among these heirs will have 426 acres, after two generations 284 acres, and after six generations only 58 acres. From this illustration, it becomes apparent that any social organization based entirely on farming will ultimately reach a point where the population becomes stable. All children who increase the population create excess numbers, and the society would have no place for them.

In 18th-century England, Thomas Robert Malthus stated these two fundamental laws in his essay on population:

> *First . . . food is necessary to existence of man.*
> *Secondly . . . the passion between the sexes is necessary and will remain nearly in its present state. . . . The effects of these two . . . powers must be kept equal.*
> *This implies a strong and constantly operating check on population from the difficulty of subsistence. . . . It appears, therefore, to be decisive against the possible existence of a society, all members of which should live in ease, happiness, and comparative leisure.* (Malthus 1959. 4-6)

Such a state of affairs existed in Europe during the Middle Ages and up to the Industrial Revolution. It remains the situation in China, India, and many other countries. To create conditions that would support increased population, man had to do two things. First, he had to devise means for fewer people to produce a greater supply of food; and second, he had to develop employment for the increasing numbers so they could produce something to exchange with those producing the food.

Mass production of books made knowledge available to everyone that was willing to learn. No longer could government stifle information. This spread of knowledge ushered in a revolution in thought. As men learned, they demanded freedom to use that knowledge. These demands led to political revolution. As men achieved freedom to act, to choose, and to work as they pleased, they applied their imaginations to new methods of doing the old things and to new things to do with the new methods. This freedom in the economic sphere naturally followed freedom of mind and freedom from despotism. Men of Western civilization first obtained freedom in thought, then freedom in government, and finally freedom in labor. It began in the 15th century, reaching a high point at the end of the 19th century.

Economic freedom via the Industrial Revolution manifested itself primarily in the way industry used labor. For thousands of years men worked the soil as self-sufficient farmers. Self-employed craftsmen made products for sale. Their business ventures seldom occupied more than one man or one family. The wage system did not exist. Where people used others in labor, the relationship was that of lord and serf.

Freedom changed the utilization of labor. Entrepreneurs built factories to produce goods for the masses and paid laborers to operate those factories. The earliest factories made cloth, which removed spinning and weaving from the home. They took the wool, the flax, or the cotton and spun the thread and wove the cloth that supplied the needs of every household. Housewives could buy the material they needed for curtains and clothing. Unskilled laborers — male and female, young and old — could perform the simple tasks required to keep these textile mills operating.

Farmers used machines and an improved plow to aid in planting and in harvesting, thereby expanding the output of food per man-hour. The factory system on the farm and in the mills took advantage of the greater efficiency in the division of labor. By using machines, not only did factories enable unskilled workers to make what they otherwise could not, but to make it faster. In factories, the growing population could make something that farmers would exchange for their increased output of food. Population could increase without creating shortages of food.

The energy to perform this feat came first from flowing water that drove large water wheels. Men looked at these mills driven by water and imagined driving these wheels with the steam engine. Mills could then be built wherever the owner needed them — close to a supply of labor, a supply of raw material, a market, or a source of fuel. Using unskilled labor and being flexible as to location, mass production brought low-priced goods within reach of typical people and provided employment for the otherwise unemployable. Surely this was a revolution in the use of labor.

Early in the 19th century, Eli Whitney demonstrated the practicality of manufacturing complicated machines by assembling them from interchangeable parts. He applied this principle to the manufacture of firearms, and so obtained a contract from the government to make rifles for the military. Other men soon built factories and used this concept to manufacture all kinds of products. The late 19th century ushered in the use of the Bessemer process for making better steel at a lower cost. Low-cost, improved steel supplied railroads with a rail that was superior to, and lower in price than, the old iron rail that had been a plague to this mode of transport. Low-cost steel allowed imaginative men to take advantage of all kinds of new inventions. The dynamo for producing electricity supplied a new source of energy that was deliverable to any point. Mass-produced, readily available electricity changed lighting to the electric light bulb; in communication it made possible broad use of the telegraph and telephone.

These changes in industrial operations began slowly in the late 17th century as Englishmen progressed with their political revolution. By the time American colonists completed their political revolution (1815), many of the technologies had become widely known and fully demonstrated. To utilize fully the division of labor in the factory system, Americans needed savings (capital) and laborers, and Europe supplied both to the enterprising Americans.

European governments had been slow to remove the shackles of the feudal-monarchical system. Political freedom never developed in Europe to the same degree it did in the United States in the 19th century, nor has it to this day. Economic progress through specialization of labor moved at a snail's pace in Europe compared to America. As a consequence, wealthy Europeans had limited opportunities for investing their savings, and labor found limited opportunities for employment. Englishmen, Frenchmen, Hollanders, and Germans eagerly invested their savings with American entrepreneurs. American political freedom protected private property and earnings from investments. Invested savings created jobs. Opportunity to work and earn a living in America attracted immigrants by the hundreds of thousands. Political freedom permitted laborers to keep their wages. Taxes on earnings did not begin in the United States until 1913, and tax rates then remained low for 30 years.

By the end of the War Between the States, there were no barriers to industrial expansion throughout the states. The nation had shown an eagerness to occupy the vast Western regions and to build the railroads that would make this all possible. Rich deposits of minerals — gold, silver, copper, zinc, lead, iron, coal — had been discovered along the Great Lakes, in the high plains, in the mountains, and in the Great Western Basin. The world market bid for these products, and Americans went all out to bring them to the willing buyers. Construction of merchant fleets of steamships brought the American continents into the European and Asian industrial markets. By the late 19th century, the Atlantic could be crossed in one week, the Pacific in two. Railroads brought the most remote places in the United States within one week of each other. Petroleum, until the late 19th century used primarily as kerosene for lighting, lubricated the machines in the factories. By the end of the 19th century, processes had been developed and refineries built to supply gasoline and diesel as fuel for the internal-combustion engine. The automobile and the airplane lay just over the horizon.

In the two and one-half centuries after the establishment of Jamestown in Virginia (1607), the English Colonies occupied and settled about 400 million acres. In 1850, nine out of every ten families supported themselves in agriculture. During the succeeding 50 years, the population more than tripled — from 23 million to over 75 million — and settled an additional 420 million acres. By 1900, two-thirds of employed laborers worked for wages in the factory system of the Industrial Revolution.

During those 50 years, in the urban centers people exchanged oil lamps for electric light bulbs. They changed their mode of overland transport from horseback and horse-drawn wagons and carriages to comfortable Pullman sleepers, parlor cars, and diners on the newly built railroads. The time of travel from New York to San Francisco was shortened from 90 days to 5. By 1900, the common man had glass windows in his home, and in northern regions, he heated his house with a coal-fired furnace. Natural gas, where found in quantity, had begun replacing coal. To promote industry, some towns offered natural gas free to all comers. The time for exchanging correspondence with Europe had been reduced from 6 months to 14 days. When urgency justified the cost, messages could be sent by telegraph in a few hours, and between urban homes on the continent individuals could speak with each other over the telephone, though the quality of sound left much to be desired. Although many city streets were dusty when dry and muddy when wet, a few venturesome souls owned electric cars to use around town. In the cities, the electric railway provided an efficient means of mass transit.

The Industrial Revolution changed the way of life for everyone in society. It supplied retail merchants with countless items priced within reach of the working man. It conquered distance in travel and communication. It enriched the common man, bringing amenities that had scarcely been dreamed of at the opening of the 19th century. By the late years of that century, it enabled scientists to work at research, and progress in medicine had so improved health that the average life expectancy rose 20 years, into the 60s.

Like a field removed from the virgin forest, cleared and planted, ready to burst forth with the miracle of a great crop of grain, Western civilization in 1900 was on the verge of bursting forth with the miracles that were to issue from the inventiveness of men's minds. By historians labeled the "Industrial Revolution," this change came about with the adoption of the factory system — which involved efficiency through division of labor, changing technology, and savings invested in machines.

Division of labor thrives only in an atmosphere of freedom. Political stability that protects private property and contract is what fertile soil and water are to crops, forests, and grass. Deny freedom to man, fail to protect his property, and society deprives him of the stimulus that lifted civilization out of the Middle Ages. Freedom and protection of private property are flesh and blood for an advanced standard of living among the multitudes. The narrative of the 20th century tells how the masses, by not properly understanding the consequences, have used their control of government to strangle this economic enterprise. The turning point came in September 1901, when the assassination of President William McKinley catapulted Theodore Roosevelt into the presidency. Riding mass envy of the riches of the industrialists, President Roosevelt attacked both property rights and freedom in economic enterprise.

About Protective Tariffs

In the early decades of the nation, the national government derived nearly all revenue through tariffs, sales taxes on imports. A false notion soon appeared, however, fostered by home industries seeking to create a more profitable atmosphere for themselves. They spread the belief that high tariffs, by restricting imports, would create more factory jobs at home. This notion exists even now more than when the Republicans hiked tariffs considerably following the War Between the States. Called "protective" because the intent was to protect local industry, these high tariffs do nothing but harm.

Government restricts commerce between the United States and other nations in several ways. First, Congress can authorize the executive branch to set trade quotas on specified products or product categories. For many years, the federal government has established very restrictive quotas on the importation of sugar. These restrictions are so severe that the domestic price of raw sugar may be three times that of the world-market price. The difference, as always appears in the instance of quotas, becomes a subsidy paid by American consumers to the sugar producers both domestic and foreign. Quota restrictions do not enrich the government. They levy a surcharge on consumers for the benefit of producers.

A second form of restricting imports denies to specified countries access to local markets. In recent years, Libya has been forbidden to sell petroleum to the United States. Such a prohibition operates only to increase the cost of crude oil in domestic markets. It is impossible to identify the origin of a raw material as universal as oil. In order to circumvent the prohibition, the originating producer need only transfer the product to another agency that may sell it in America. The prohibition benefits no one and penalizes Americans. It does not enrich the government. The alleged purpose is political — to penalize the exporting country.

Although barred by the Constitution from assessing taxes on exports, the government can and does control and, in some cases, prohibit the export of many commodities. Government currently controls to some degree the export of over 40 raw materials. As with all government interference in foreign trade, the net effect increases the cost of the product to all users, including Americans. These restrictions also do not enrich the government.

The most widely used device for restricting foreign trade is the tariff. The Constitution does not forbid Congress to levy a tax on imports. The tariff is a direct tax on products coming into the country. Tariffs do enrich the government. For over 100 years after the adoption of the Constitution, tariffs provided nearly all the revenue for the federal government. In 1861, however, when Republicans took decisive control, Congress increased tariff rates substantially in order to protect local industry. Many tariff rates exceeded 50 percent of the value.

At best, tariffs provide temporary benefits for producers. Because of the monopoly profits resulting from the barrier to foreign competition, producers divert capital and resources away from other endeavors that consumers might otherwise prefer, and channel them into the favored industry. With this increased investment in the protected industry, producers bid against each other for the scarce resources required for that particular production. This causes the prices of these resources to rise, which reduces profits. The monopoly prices supposedly guaranteed by tariffs cease to generate profits for the producers because of the increased costs of materials and equipment. The resulting increase in local competition destroys the perceived benefit of a tariff. Consequently, tariffs give only temporary protection for local producers. It never saves them from competition in the long run. To continue protection for producers' profits, the tariff rate must be regularly increased to offset the increasing costs. This has been the experience in the United States where protective tariffs to benefit local industry have been accepted without question. (See the record in Chapter 15.)

At low rates, the tax does produce revenue for the government. As rates increase, they reach a limit in their ability either to protect producers or to generate revenue for government. Only those foreign producers who have a natural cost advantage to offset the tax can continue to ship into the country. When the rate gets high enough, domestic production increases to such a degree that prices stay below a level profitable to importers. As imports drop, revenue from that tax disappears. The higher prices discourage sales to consumers who prefer to spend their money on other items. Since tariffs benefit local producers for just a short time, they fail both as a means of protecting domestic industry against competition and as a revenue measure.

Tariffs do not increase total production or employment. The tariff-induced expansion locally in the protected industry merely redirects capital and labor away from other, more efficient production. The tariff thereby never increases total production or total employment in the nation. It increases production and employment only in the industry protected by the tax. It correspondingly reduces employment in all industries denied the use of the redirected capital. On the other hand, this redirected capital reduces the productivity of all labor. If the most efficient use of the productive resources lay in the industry protected by the tariff, entrepreneurs would have so invested them without the interference by government.

Consumers pay higher prices and lose other products. The tariff increases, by the amount of the tax, the prices consumers pay. Domestic producers set their prices at the level importers must charge to cover their cost of the item, cost of transport into the country, and cost of the tax levied by the tariff. Because the tariff results in less efficient use of capital throughout industry, consumers pay more for all products no matter where they are manufactured, and all consumers — particularly in the region levying the tax — experience a lower standard of living. Consumers lose because they not only pay a higher price for those products they buy; they also have fewer products to buy because the productive resources have been diverted into the protected industry.

The people see the expansion of industry protected by the tariff; they do not see the plants that fail to appear because the capital was diverted by the tax. The real impact of the levy is never visible; it is seen only in the logic of things. For this reason politicians, with little public opposition, have been able to please special interests by erecting tariff barriers. When the natural site of Industry A is in a region with little or no political influence (a foreign country), and Industry B is located where there is a large constituency (at home), a politician can easily defend his position and support legislation that directs capital into Industry B. In the case of tariffs and other restrictions on foreign trade, however, the redirected capital does not deny Industry A in the foreign country to the benefit of Industry B locally. It denies capital to local industries C and D. The net effect increases consumer prices in all industries — A, B, C, and D. Restrictions on trade reduce efficiency in production worldwide. It redirects capital and production away from the most efficient employment and into the favored industry. Such action countermands the wishes of the consumers, because otherwise the capital would already be so employed, and the redirection would not be necessary. Everyone has lost — producers, government, consumers, and labor. The people suffer through a reduced standard of living.

Wealth Redistribution and Land Reform

Clamor for equality among citizens has become a government policy to redistribute wealth among the "unfortunate" have-nots. This trend among governments of many nations, which is so thoroughly destructive of property rights, justifies our attention. What is the truth here?

Historians label as "land reform" the confiscation of land for distribution to "underprivileged" farmers. When we learn how some of these large land holdings came into being, it is tempting to support land reform. After all, many large domains were put together by men using extralegal, questionable practices. The present owners of these large ranches, however, came into possession through legal means. They are not the ones who perpetrated fraud on the public. In reality, even the original ranchers cannot be held solely responsible. Responsibility for this condition should be placed at the feet of congressmen who passed the enabling legislation and failed to revise the laws when abuses surfaced.

Land reform is merely one small part of the ongoing effort by the multitudes to redistribute all wealth. The Industrial Revolution created opportunity for a person to become very rich during his lifetime by means other than grants of land from governments and kings. The envy of those without riches became focused on those who were most successful in taking advantage of these opportunities. As the masses gained full control of government in the United States, they adopted tax and welfare measures designed to redistribute the wealth of the few.

Wealth is saving; it is the residuum from consuming less than what is produced. It exists in the form of buildings, improved land, individual training and perfected labor skills, tools, machines, technology, food, and a countless number of goods in storage. Money alone is not wealth; it is a claim on wealth. To the individual, money represents wealth because others will exchange wealth for money. The individual considers increased money in hand as increased wealth. Money does have significance to the individual. A greater or lesser quantity in his hands means for him a greater or lesser claim on the wealth that exists in the hands of those who recognize that money. As a claim on wealth, money can be a measure of wealth for the individual, but money cannot buy wealth that does not exist. Money has no value until a person creates wealth by saving. Doubling the total supply of money held by all citizens simply causes a change in prices; it does not affect total wealth. For the same reason, total wealth can double without a change in the money supply. Under such a circumstance, unit prices decline. The vital condition that must exist is the wealth itself, and money exerts no influence on the totality of wealth. If some catastrophe destroys all material wealth, the still-existing money would not buy anything. Money is only a medium by which people exchange wealth.

Private property means control over the use of an item of wealth. Without laws that protect private ownership, private property exists through the owner's ability to appropriate wealth and defend it against all challengers. By cooperation through government, however, men recognize private property and protect ownership from confiscation by local or foreign usurpers.

In the United States since the late 19th century, over 90 percent of all material wealth has been owned by less than 10 percent of the people. The identities of the individuals change, but this proportionate distribution remains fairly constant. That this is true should surprise no one. We have long known how little most people save. Few ever save more than the purchase price of a modest home.

This condition is neither especially good nor evil. In considering the significance of this uneven distribution of wealth, we must consider such things as these:

1. Did this distribution result from free choice, or did it arise from the coercive action of government?
2. What barriers prevent a person from acquiring a larger share of wealth or the income that flows from the use of wealth?
3. Which is more important: (a) the distribution of ownership or (b) the distribution of benefits that come from productive use of wealth?

Meaningful conclusions depend on the implications of these questions. In a few cases, individuals acquired large land holdings as gifts from governments. The King of England granted land in Colonial America to individuals as favors, in settlement of debt, or to encourage colonization. In the area that Spain once controlled, some large land holdings of the present can be traced to a grant from the Spanish monarch. The Dutch made sizable land grants to any person who, at his own expense, brought 50 settlers to the Dutch colony along the Hudson River. Although these grants established considerable wealth in the hands of a few at that time, division among descendants and transfers to others for a variety of reasons have broken up most of these large holdings. Very few personal fortunes today originated from grants of land by kings and governments.

From the time of the earliest settlement, it has been possible in the United States for even the poorest people to amass a large personal fortune before their death. A person works at a job, and the employer pays money wages. This money is a claim on wealth. If someone owns a successful business, he receives a payment that represents profit. How he spends money received for labor and for profit controls entirely who will own the wealth in future years. If he spends all his money on food, clothing, entertainment, automobiles, travel, gasoline, and other items of personality and services, he will accumulate no wealth. On the other hand, if he saves, those savings create new wealth; and he will have accumulated ownership of wealth to that extent. Wealth is transferred by the way savings are handled. Continued saving increases one's ownership of wealth. Savings spent for consumption items transfer ownership of wealth to others.

In a free economy, since wealth accumulation is denied to no one, we may find it difficult to fault the uneven distribution among individuals. Uneven distribution of wealth under freedom results from differences in people's ability and their will to save. There is no way to create a will-to-save equality in everyone or to make everybody equal in ability. If a person believes he should own a greater share of the wealth, nothing in America stands in his way of acquiring it. He just needs to work and save. Those who own wealth accumulated it by desire, work, and dedication to acquisition. There are few exceptions. There is great truth in the saying, "From rags to riches to rags in three generations." It takes nearly as much work and will-to-save in order to keep wealth as it does to get it in the first place.

In the United States only one force hinders anyone from saving and thereby accumulating wealth. That force is government by way of confiscatory taxation and support of barriers to opportunity. Before trying to get the government to confiscate wealth from others on his behalf, the citizen who has difficulty acquiring wealth should examine first the wealth denied him by his government.

The significant importance of wealth lies in the flow of benefits coming from its use. The mere existence of wealth, no matter who owns it, creates a certain standard of living possible among the populace. As savings increase wealth, the standard of living increases for everyone in that society who uses the land, buildings, skills, machines, and the tools that embody that wealth. Food, clothes, and houses become available to the worker at lower prices. Increases in wealth generate increases in the efficiency of labor. Consequently, workers in that society can purchase a greater portion of their needs — food, medical services, comfortable homes, and automobiles — with the proceeds from their labor even though they themselves may own no wealth.

Creating wealth by saving benefits everyone in the society. That wealth builds factories filled with tools and machines, and trains the laborers who work there. The greater productivity generated by this increase in tools, machines, and training increases the per capita output. Each dollar of invested wealth placed at the disposal of labor enhances the productivity per man-hour. The high standard of living in America is due entirely to the efficiency in labor created by the large investment of wealth, including the skills of the labor force. One must not overlook the wealth invested in an educated populace and a trained labor force. All men benefit from the savings of their forefathers, even those who own no wealth.

A true measure of changes in a country's wealth can be made only by examining the living conditions of the working man: the quality of comfort and convenience about his home, the adequacy of his food, the nature and abundance of his accessory comforts, and the number of hours each year he must work in order to obtain these. A survey of the living conditions among ordinary people in the United States today reveals a lifestyle that would have been the envy of kings in 1787. This distribution of the benefits of wealth itself is far more significant than how ownership of that wealth is distributed.

The most significant feature about wealth distribution lies in the change that would follow if government interfered with the natural distribution of ownership. To those who have wealth, possession is the reward they want from saving. Denied the right of ownership and control, they would not save and society would have no wealth. Because most men never save and so never create wealth, the existence of wealth in a society depends on the few who do save. The high standard of living in America is possible because of the savings of the few. If they were denied the benefits they expect to receive from saving, they would lose their incentive to do so. That would eliminate the creation of wealth in the future, and would cause consumption of the wealth presently existing. This pattern would harm everyone. Until more individuals save, we must accept the uneven distribution of such wealth as men do accumulate. The alternative is the loss of all wealth and a return to universal poverty.

The most efficient means to assure equitable redistribution of wealth lies in freedom of opportunity. Under a system that preserves freedom, if a person of wealth uses it in a manner that pleases consumers, he earns profits and retains ownership of his wealth. Continuing such ownership and use serves the people to their advantage. If the owner fails to utilize it in a manner that pleases and serves the public, he suffers losses and becomes dispossessed of his wealth. It passes into the hands of people who do use it in the best interests of consumers. This results from free enterprise, which preserves freedom of opportunity for everyone.

If a person wants the standard of living for the masses to keep rising, rather than support land reform by confiscation and wealth redistribution through taxation, he should support free opportunity for those who are willing to work and save to acquire wealth. In pursuing their own self-interest, these persons use wealth to serve consumers. Government interference forestalls such from happening. To have wealth distributed among those who use it to benefit the masses, people must support the removal of government restrictions on freedom to serve the consumers as they express their wishes through their patronage.

Trusts and Monopolies

By the late 1800s, the public had become upset over the concentration of wealth in the hands of the few. In 1887, Congress established the Interstate Commerce Commission to regulate the railroads. In 1890, Congress passed the Sherman Anti-Trust Act to break up large business ventures controlled by one management. Although these laws stayed on the books, no meaningful enforcement surfaced until Theodore Roosevelt took office as president in 1901. Fear of the unknown had aroused the public. Newspapers and politicians decried the concentration of wealth, claiming such would give rise to monopolies that could charge unduly high prices for their products. That envy and fear describes in a nutshell what drives the criticism of trusts and monopolies.

The facts never substantiated this fear. Historians admit that John D. Rockefeller's Standard Oil Company produced a superior product at a relatively low price. The charge against Rockefeller in 1877 was that he controlled 95 percent of the nation's oil refineries. The fearmongers charged him with "bigness." Standard Oil made profits through the efficiencies of large-scale operation; and as the major owner, Rockefeller became very wealthy. Those who could not compete and dropped by the wayside charged that, without competition, Rockefeller could raise prices. They never charged him with exacting monopoly prices, only that he *might*. The real evil was envy.

A trust is a legal creation. The trusts of the 1890s exchanged Certificates of Trust for shares of stock in operating corporations. These Certificates simply recognized in writing that stockholders had made the exchange, which gave the trust the power to vote those shares, collect the dividends, and pass them on to the rightful owners. The trust constituted merely a legal means for one agency to control the operation of several corporations. The same thing is accomplished today through holding companies. The corporate holding company exchanges its stock for stock of other corporations. The parent corporation thereby becomes the owner and controlling operator of the subsidiary corporations. Trusts and holding companies are legal devices for consolidating the operation of several companies under one management.

Neither trusts nor holding companies involve any inherent evil. Owners of a business venture have more than one means of enlarging their operation. They can grow by winning consumer approval of their products or services, thereby earning profits that are reinvested in the enterprise; or they can increase their capital through the sale of stocks and bonds to investors. With this additional capital the enterprise can expand its core business or purchase other companies.

The trust busters assumed that through mere size one company could gain all the market and become a monopoly. As a monopoly, they assumed, it could raise prices without fear of losing market share to competition. This formed the basis for government action to prevent such a thing from ever happening. The Sherman Anti-Trust Act resulted. Few, if any, trusts and monopolies ever actually realized monopoly prices, but the fearmongers claimed that such might take place. Government action responded to this fear. Instilled in the minds of the public, this fear justified special-interest legislation, giving greater power to bureaucrats. It would not be the first time government enlarged its scope solely to gain more power. To some people, power in government means more than does financial gain.

Such fear-generated thinking is seriously flawed. It takes the approach called "static analysis." Static analysis rules out further changes. It assumes that no one will take counter action in response to changing conditions — that once it is formed, a monopoly can and will exist forever. In truth, such assumptions could be correct only if government prevented others from competing with the monopoly. If government does not protect it, competition causes the monopoly to fail when it increases prices above the levels a competitive market would establish.

The recent experience of the Organization of Petroleum Exporting Countries (OPEC) illustrates the point. Due to price ceilings on domestic crude oil (government barrier to competitive enterprise) in the United States, OPEC became the major producing combine in the world petroleum market in the 1970s. When the United States removed the obstacle to competition with OPEC (the removal of price ceilings), increased production outside OPEC forced world prices down on crude oil to the point commensurate with costs and a free world market. OPEC's ability to charge monopoly prices collapsed.

Laws prohibiting combines, trusts, cartels, and holding companies are unnecessary. Such laws only give bureaucrats power to interfere with a free market. In the long run, this interference disturbs efficient use of scarce resources. The bigness of a business is no evil; neither is monopoly. The evil arises when bigness or monopoly enables that enterprise to charge prices higher than would prevail in a freely competitive market.

The power to do this over any meaningful length of time can exist only by government protection.

Government is the only natural monopoly. Government alone has the power to force on the people the evils so often ascribed to bigness and monopolies. Without government protection, no enterprise can gain and hold monopolistic control on any market. If allowed to, men vote with their feet and leave when conditions become intolerable. Emigration to avoid conditions they did not like made the North American continent a land of Europeans and Asians. Admittedly this is an extreme case, but it remains as an alternative to monopoly exploitation unless, of course, government protects the monopoly by forbidding its citizens to move away. This too has happened in some nations. In the 20th century, autocracies often restrict emigration for this very reason, and presently such restrictions on emigration are being suggested in our Congress.

In the late 1800s, consumers leveled charges of unfair treatment by monopolies, most often against railroads in the prairie West. Farmers and ranchers complained about freight rates charged by the railroad serving their area. At that moment of complaint, these farmers had access to no competing railroad. With prices of farm products falling, the cost of rail freight to Eastern markets consumed an ever larger part of the revenue farmers received from selling their grain and livestock.

Western farmers and ranchers complained that they paid higher rates than their counterparts did in Eastern regions. Some short-haul rates exceeded some long-haul rates. Whether this was unfair "monopolistic" treatment by the "railroad barons" would, under free enterprise, have been decided by market forces. If in truth the railroads profited unduly from monopoly prices, competing operators would have soon built more rail lines into the area. This competition would have brought freight rates down to a level justified by costs.

State and national governments protected railroad monopolies. They did not permit enterprising businessmen to build railroads wherever they might choose. Government required prospective builders to secure a franchise, a bureaucratic permit to build. In plain words, government created and protected the monopolies that farmers complained about. The proper remedy for the situation was not government regulation of freight rates, but removal of government barriers to competitive enterprise. Even so, railroads did not hold farmers and ranchers captive. Other means existed for getting farm produce to market. Boats on the waterways and horse-drawn wagons could carry the grain. Livestock could be driven on foot to alternate shipping points or directly to meat-packers on the Missouri River. These alternatives, however, cost more than transport by rail. Did this condition describe unfair treatment by the railroad?

To prevent government from removing barriers to competition, those enterprises already established raised the specter of "cutthroat" competition. They ridiculed the theories of free-market economists. They convinced the public and legislators that free competition would drive prices below the point at which railroads could make a profit and rail service would thereby deteriorate. The "ins" used government to protect their established position. This was special-interest legislation, and it has been going on since the inception of government. It was a practice in the 17th century that economists had to abolish in order to clear the way for the Industrial Revolution.

Government in the United States protected the railroad monopolies for the benefit of railroad owners and employees until the public gained relief by means of air and highway transport. Government has consistently supported monopolies and monopoly prices in power generation and distribution, transportation, banking and finance, communication, television, radio, and numerous other business activities.

Condemnation should not be aimed at railroad barons as monopoly beasts that unfairly gouged poor farmers. It should be leveled at the voters who kept supporting legislators that perpetuated special-interest legislation. The same charge applies now. Special-interest legislation will continue until voters stop it by electing representatives dedicated to freedom.

A Comment on Historians and This Period

Unfortunately, too little historical literature exists that presents a balanced viewpoint on the great industrial expansion during the last half of the 19th century. Some historians use such phrases as "railroad barons," "profligate exploitation," "grasping motive of personal gain," "ignoring completely the public interest," "lawless arrogance of the industrial magnates," "the railroad octopus," and statements like "the middlemen took a juicy 'cut' from the selling price"; "the . . . farmer was at the mercy of the Harvester trust, the barbed-wire trust, and the fertilizer trust." These expressions arouse an emotional antagonism without aiding understanding. For this reason, people need alternate views in order to achieve a balanced perspective when evaluating the events of this period. The facts are there, but the reader often becomes prejudiced by emotionally charged expressions that warp his perception of them.

In the United States a "public interest" does not exist. There is only the interest of individual citizens. When a writer refers to the public interest, knowingly or in ignorance he separates the interests of the people from that of the government. In an autocratic society the public interest is in the interest of the rulers. In a democracy no public interest exists aside from that of the citizens. If the author believes such does exist, he reveals his belief in dictatorship with himself arrogated to that position. He sets his value judgments ahead of those made by individual citizens. Beware of his conclusions and prejudices.

In a free society, enlightened self-interest is the alternative to dictatorial coercion. When government forbids people to act in their own self-interest, their actions are dictated by government. Every author who decries the exercise of self-interest is a would-be dictator.

Profligate exploitation embodies its own contradiction. No industrialist knowingly wastes any scarce resource. Such conduct would cause for him loss and financial ruin, and he would soon be out of business. Consequently, profligacy cannot exist in free enterprise. It can exist only under the protection of a misguided or corrupt government. Exploitation simply means using a thing for personal gain. As used by these writers, coupled with emotionally charged adjectives, its meaning is intended to portray unfair personal gain. Does a coal-miner act unfairly in extracting ore from the ground to produce steel for the manufacture of automobiles? Does an employer treat labor unfairly when he pays the wages to which the employee has agreed before going to work? Exploitation of voluntary labor is impossible. In the last half of the 19th century, the so-called "exploited" laborers were immigrants coming voluntarily and eagerly to the United States. Some eventually became wealthy industrialists themselves, employing thousands of other workers, immigrants and native-born alike.

Admittedly, the record of industrial development in the United States in the late 1800s includes cases where government used power improperly. In the 1860s, the Republicans gained such a large majority in Congress that they could ignore the opposition. Legislation became law that subsidized particular interest groups. High tariffs, land giveaway to railroaders and farmers, monopoly privilege (especially in banking and finance), direct subsidies, and loans at below-market interest rates — all were involved. When the Democrats regained stronger opposition to the Republicans, some of this ended, but too much continued. The excesses worked against the interests of most farmers and many wage-earners. The profligate abuses came from government grants of power to act unfairly, not from the operation of entrepreneurs and business employers competing freely in a free market.

The better historians charge the evil where it belongs: to politicians who used their positions to further their own interests. That is the story that needs telling. No doubt businessmen profited from the privileges that government would dispense. Just as eagerly, farmers availed themselves of free land given to homesteaders from the public domain. Ranchers took advantage of the land-sale laws that granted special privilege to squatters.

Under the U.S. system of government, freely elected representatives define the rules. If some citizens do not like the way others behave when acting according to those rules, the proper remedy is a rules change by the legislative body. It furthers understanding of history not one whit to employ distorting phrases when writing about the events. If some individual violates the rules (laws), that is fact. Let the facts speak for the color of the times. Historians are unfair to students when they distort facts and criticize people for legal conduct with which those writers disagree.

This fact must be kept in mind when people read about events current or past. All written records become history. Only the time lapse between now and then differs from narrative to narrative. When relating current events, writers for newspapers and magazines and reporters on radio and television become historians. They divide themselves between those presenting fact and those misrepresenting facts to support prejudices. To prevent being misled, a reader must require a writer to separate his facts from his opinions. If he fails in this charge, everything he says is suspect.

Cultures have come and gone throughout history. The fate of the mound builders is no isolated occurrence, nor was the decline of the Mayan culture in Central America. Neither culture could have been destroyed by their enemies had they not first decayed from within.

Chapter 12

Westward Expansion, 1850-1901

Pre-Columbian Indian Culture

IN ORDER TO UNDERSTAND the present status of freedom among the Native American Indians, we must know their culture and something about their history in North America.

Visualize the area of the United States with no roads, no cities, no farm buildings. Gone are all the poles and power lines, telephone lines, and fences. Journey with the Spanish explorer Francisco V. Coronado and his men in the mid-16th century to the top of a prominent hill a short distance east and north of Dodge City in central Kansas. As far as you can see lies a wide expanse of grass unbroken by trees. Great herds of bison and groups of pronghorns, commonly called antelope, graze on the slopes. Moving from the hilltop into any of the valleys, you find trees and bushes along the water course, and the creek runs clear. The floodplain of the river is green in the summer, covered with cottonwood trees, some Western red cedar, and an occasional oak, pecan, or hickory. Low-growing bushes cover the ground. Deer, elk, bobcats, coyotes, bears, cougar, wolves, and a host of small birds and animals make this habitat their home. Traveling east off the prairie, you enter unending forests of maple, hickory, pine, oak, chestnut, cedar, birch, sycamore, hackberry, and pecan as well as many other plant forms. Throughout it all, you meet few human beings and come across little evidence of man's presence.

Although they had numbered many millions before the coming of the white man, the Indians were at that time few because of decimation by diseases brought by Europeans. These primitives also considered other tribes as competitors in the endless struggle to harvest the berries and roots, to hunt the bison and deer, and to bring land into cultivation. As tribal units, they lived under conditions of biological competition.

In spite of the millions of bison and antelope and the hundreds of thousands of deer and smaller game, Indians lacked efficient means of harvesting this food supply. Examine the hunting tools on display in any museum of artifacts from these primitive people. Picture being among herds of wild animals, on foot with only a spear, a stone knife, and a bow-and-arrow set that is accurate to perhaps 30 feet. The arrow weighs less than half that of modern arrows, and the bow delivers barely enough thrust for arrows to penetrate to the vital organs of an animal. The one deadly weapon is the hand-thrown spear. Imagine the difficulty in getting enough meat to feed a family.

Perhaps the most effective hunting method employed by 15th-century Indians was the drive, carried out by the cooperative effort of many hunters. On the prairie, they stampeded bison over a cliff or into a dry wash. Among the stampeding animals, falling on top of each other, many became sufficiently disabled that the hunters could dispose of them with their spears. Many were smothered or crushed by the bodies on top. One successful drive could provide enough food to feed the tribe for many days and enough skins to keep the squaws busy throughout the winter. The men could then retire to the village and occupy themselves in telling tales about hunts past. In one archaeological find, the number of bison skulls approached 200.

In the Eastern forests, the Indians drove deer into an enclosure so confining that the bow and arrow became an effective weapon. Hunters first constructed two palisades of wooden stakes, perhaps eight to nine feet high, forming a great V with a small enclosure at their junction. The hunters would then drive the deer into this trap. Samuel de Champlain, founder of French Canada, witnessed such a drive among the Iroquois in 1615. His records describe one 30-day hunt that captured over 100 deer.

The area north of present-day Mexico — the area principally considered in this book — includes nearly all the climatic conditions found throughout the world. There are near-tropical desert in the Southwest, rain forests and fjords along the Northwest coast, grasslands in the Central Plains, and woodlands ranging from subarctic in Alaska to subtropical in Florida. For this reason, it is impossible to present an in-depth discussion of Indian culture in the area of the United States. They had only one feature in common, a primitive culture. The 15th-century Indian had not advanced beyond the Stone Age. He made his implements of bone, wood, reeds, pottery, and stone. His only metals — gold, copper, and silver — were too soft for making knives, hoes, swords, and spearheads.

Prior to the 16th century, his only domesticated animal had been the dog. He acquired the horse from the Europeans. When he moved, he transported his belongings on his back or lashed them to a travois pulled by his dog. Since he had not developed the wheel, he had no carts to carry person or possessions. When moving any considerable distance, he traveled in a canoe via coastal waterways, streams, rivers, and lakes much as did his counterpart in Europe. In the far North, his dogs pulled sleds over snow and ice.

His society was centered in the tribe, a loose organization of families under the leadership of one strong man or a small council. His economy was based on fishing, hunting, gathering, and limited farming. He cultivated potatoes, corn, beans, tobacco, melons, millet, squash, and peanuts. He made syrup from the sap of the sugar maple tree; and from wild plants he gathered berries, roots, and other edibles. Women wove baskets, dressed animal skins, embroidered costumes with porcupine quills and bits of fur, and fashioned pottery. Men made bows and spears, hunted, fished, and fought with members of neighboring tribes. The differences between tribes in various areas were more a matter of emphasis rather than of kind.

The Pre-Columbian Indians' only contact with other civilizations had been in the far Northeast, and even there it had been limited to isolated forays between a handful of Indians and Norsemen. From the evidence remaining, it appears that the Norsemen developed no lasting colonies in the area, and showed interest only in Iceland, the coastal regions of southern Greenland, and a small part of the northern coast of Newfoundland. By the end of the 14th century, they had disappeared from the region. Their presence exerted no lasting influence on the culture of the natives, and they left no written records of their activities.

The evidence indicates that until 1492, conditions among the North American Indians had changed little for centuries. They had no unity, very little cooperation, no alphabet, and no written language. The most marked variations among them was in their speech. They used more than 200 identifiable dialects, some as different from each other as English and Chinese and Swahili.

Our knowledge of Indian culture in North America comes from writings by Europeans that detail conditions among these primitives at the time of their first meeting. Most written accounts date from the 16th century forward. Knowledge of earlier ages has been constructed from archaeological findings.

In the thousands of years preceding the arrival of the European, American Indians had developed five separate cultures: the Mayas, the Incas, the Aztecs, the Pueblos, and the mound builders. Of these, the Mayas in Central America were the most advanced, but this culture had peaked and was on the decline when the Spaniards arrived. Unfortunately for our knowledge of the Mayan culture, a missionary Spanish priest ordered the destruction of all Mayan records, and the soldier-explorers were all too thorough in their execution of this directive. What is known of Mayan civilization has been reconstructed from archaeological findings and from a translation of journals made by two Mayan families after the Spanish destroyed the records of their priests. These journals record legends and the recollections of old men. They are valuable primarily as a source of clues to assist in interpreting archaeological discoveries. Someday man will discover a way to decode more accurately the Mayan hieroglyphs, and the archaeological artifacts of this long-ago culture will become more meaningful. With the destruction of all existing records and the death of the priests who could interpret their hieroglyphs, the true story of the Mayas became another mystery in man's unknown past.

The Aztecs of Mexico and the Incas in South America had developed a fairly advanced form of social cooperation. These Indian groups dug gold, silver, and copper from mines, and worked these metals into useful shapes; they did not, however, know how to alloy metals.

A culture similar to that of the Mayas, the mound builders, had existed north of the Rio Grande for perhaps ten centuries or more. Their mounds numbered in the thousands along the waterways in the North from western New York to Nebraska, along the Gulf Coast from Florida to eastern Texas, and almost everywhere in between. The variations in their structures suggest that there was no such thing as a civilization of mound builders, but a number of different peoples, stretching over a long period, who built mounds.

About A.D. 500, a new culture began developing along the lower reaches of the river that bears their name. Called Mississippians, this group of mound builders was probably the most advanced Indian group north of Mexico. The city of Cahokia, with over 20,000 inhabitants, was apparently the greatest of their cities, reaching its peak in riches, trade, and influence around A.D. 1100. The merchants traded for goods from regions hundreds of miles away and extended their trade perhaps to the limits of the Mississippi watershed. Their larger mounds rivaled the great pyramid of Egypt, the largest in Cahokia being 100 feet high with a base covering nearly 15 acres. It is but one of some 80 mounds that still remain and can be visited at Cahokia Mounds State Park near East St. Louis, Illinois.

None of the mound builders advanced as far culturally as the Mayas did (they failed to develop a written language), but they came close. In one form or another their societies lasted long enough to be witnessed by Hernando de Soto and other early European explorers. The last remnants, the Natchez of the lower regions of the Mississippi, were virtually wiped out by warfare with the newcomers and by diseases these Europeans brought with them.

At an earlier time, the Pueblos of the Sonora desert area in the Southwest constructed buildings of earthen bricks and maintained a sophisticated system of irrigation for their agriculture. No good record of their culture remains today. The structures still stand, but the inhabitants had gone before Europeans arrived, leaving perhaps in the later part of the 13th century. Since these Indians left the desert in the 13th century and the Aztecs came into Mexico from the north in the 13th century, one wonders whether they could have been the same group.

As with all great cultures that have disappeared, historians wonder what happened to them. What caused their disappearance? Were they destroyed by barbarian tribes? Did their corn crops fail them? Could their culture have succumbed to the stress of internal political troubles?

No culture that survives 1,000 years will fall to raids from nomadic tribes until weakened by disintegration within. The suggestion of political trouble presents the probable cause, because such an explanation is founded on forces generated from the nature of individuals. Similarly, failure of the agriculture would not have been so much a cause of the decline as a symptom of decay in the culture.

Cahokia did not disappear in battle. Had the inhabitants been defeated in combat, their city would most likely have been burned, yet many wood structures remained for early European explorers to see. No sudden event decimated the population; there are no mass graves. Cahokia died over a period of 400 years; some activity remained in the village as late as the 16th century.

Cultures have come and gone throughout history. The fate of the mound builders is no isolated occurrence, nor was the decline of the Mayan culture in Central America. Neither culture could have been destroyed by their enemies had they not first decayed from within. The decline of the Indian cultures no doubt paralleled the experiences of the civilizations in Egypt, Greece, and Rome. From the Greeks and the Romans, we have written accounts of conditions existing throughout the rise and disintegration of their societal structure. We may fairly presume that all cultures experienced similar fates because human nature has not changed for thousands of years. In this respect, people thousands of years hence will no doubt be acting the same way. The as-yet unanswered question remains: Will man ever learn to use his intellect to overcome the influence of those drives in his nature that destroy social cooperation?

Occupation of the High Prairie

Indians acquired horses in the 16th century, thereby gaining mobility equal to that of the bison, their principal food source. Indians could then survive in large numbers on the high plains. By the time the white man's invasion of the Eastern forest forced the native Indians west, they easily moved from the forest out onto the Great Plains. Supplied with guns and horses, Eastern tribes crowded out those in the way. The Iroquois pushed out the Ottawa, the Ojibwa, the Potawatomie, the Winnebago, and others.

Consequently, when white men began settling on the plains after the War Between the States, they found many Indian tribes thriving there, fed and supplied by the great herds of bison.

Until that period in the late 19th century, the final conflict between white and red man had merely been delayed. But on the plains the Indian made his stand. He could not migrate farther west. The hostile environment in the mountains and the high desert basin would not support him. In that desert country between the Pacific West and the Central Rockies, even with horses, Indians could not survive in numbers.

Earlier attempts to organize resistance to the white man had failed. Joseph Brant tried to revive the Seneca and the Six Nations, but he could command too few warriors. The white man's wars had decimated their numbers. General "Mad Anthony" Wayne at the Battle of Fallen Timbers defeated the alliance of tribes under Pontiac. Forces organized by Tecumseh fell before William Henry Harrison's troops at Tippecanoe Creek. Each Indian leader lost his following with the first defeat. Indians followed only successful leaders. They did not organize permanent alliances. It was their way.

On the Great Plains, Indian raids originally sought only to steal the white man's horses. When they finally realized that, with their backs against a wall, they could retreat no farther, they fought for survival. When victorious in battle, they destroyed all the members of the white man's party. They fought to drive him completely from their land. They no longer had a choice. Many red men chose to die fighting rather than submit to white man's rule. This struggle for supremacy on the plains finally ended with the deliberate, virtually complete destruction of the bison herds, thereby starving the Indians into defeat.

Few periods in the history of any country have so captured the romantic attention of people as that time in America when pioneers and ranchers moved onto the prairie, driving the Indians from their last foothold on the continent. That 30-year interval has fascinated not only Americans but Europeans as well. It was the period of the cowboys, the gamblers, the mountain men, the sodbusters, the railroaders, the ranchers, the gunmen, and the miners. To this day, a major body of the fiction material entertaining young and old alike consists of stories about the American West in the last decades of the 19th century. At first it was cowboys, soldiers, farmers, and ranchers against Indians. Then interest shifted to the story of cattle ranchers against the sodbusters; of sheep herders against cattlemen; of

cattle drives to the railheads in Dodge City, Wichita, and Abilene; of gunmen taming the wild towns of the cattle drives; of Wyoming ranchers
grasping land from the public domain through use of the homestead acts;
of gold prospectors invading the sacred lands of the Indians in the Black
Hills; of Custer's Last Stand and Massacre by the Sioux at the Little Big-
horn. These stories are set in that 30-year period. (Those interested in the
details should consult the series of volumes published by Time-Life Books
that cover this period.)

The one feature that characterized this entire era and gives it such fas-
cination is *individualism*. The individual was free in a way that has rarely
been witnessed in recorded history. A great expanse of land lay before the
pioneers, available for the taking. From all parts of the world men came to
the American West, drawn by the promise of opportunity. A few found
riches; many died in the harsh habitat, defeated by cold, drought and
floods, wind, dust, and Indian raids. Those who survived founded family
lines of hard-working, independent-thinking, land-loving individuals who
asked no quarter and gave their support generously to their fellowman. No
one who asked was ever turned away from their doorstep with an empty
stomach.

The existence of a frontier of such vast proportions exerted a great
influence on the cause of individual liberty in America. In the more dense-
ly settled areas, government legislators and bureaucrats alike knew that
disgruntled citizens could vote with their feet by leaving the region of their
authority. This fact alone checked the excesses of government. It was a
constant barrier to unreasonable action by government agents. Those citizens who desired an atmosphere of greater individual liberty could
migrate to the frontier. The disappearance of the frontier dissolved this
quiet restriction on governmental excesses. It was no happenstance that
liberty in America began to disappear along with the final settlement of the
West.

At the approach of the 21st century, the last frontier lies in the forbidding region known as Alaska. That frontier demands a most hardy soul to
choose its climate as a means to escape local despotism. But there are
those individuals, and they are penetrating the inner regions of that land.
Not too many years ago, one such pioneer expressed regret that his Alaska was becoming so crowded. He had observed a neighbor move into his
valley, only 30 miles downstream from the home where he had lived alone
for some 40 years. This incident, however, did not bother him unduly. He

felt he would not have to tolerate such interference too long, since he was then approaching his 90th birthday.

Disposition of the Public Domain

Even before the Colonies gained their independence, eager pioneers pushed into the interior of the continent well ahead of legal controls. Families cleared the land and farmed the soil. Contrary to what sensationalist writers would have us believe, these pioneers experienced little conflict with the natives. Most squatters found a way to live in harmony with their Indian neighbors. When the spirit moved them, they packed up their belongings and moved on, clearing and building and farming and hunting.

Government needed some way to bring legal order to the claims of these squatters. The Northwest Ordinance of 1787 included a system for surveying and platting land of the public domain, a system still in use. Such deviations from this plan that do exist are a matter for lawyers and realtors, of little interest to historians.

Land in Kansas, Nebraska, Wyoming, and most of Colorado is divided by the grid system as follows: one square mile, containing 640 acres, is called a section. A square six miles on a side — 36 sections — is a township, and is located by coordinates of "range" east-west and "township" north-south. Ranges and townships are numbered from a base line, the 6th meridian — longitude 97° 23' 0" W — for ranges and the 40th parallel of latitude for townships. The 36 sections within a township are numbered. Any section of land in this system can be identified by a code like Sec 4, T1N, R6E, this section being section #4 in that township located in the first tier north of the 40th parallel and in the 6th tier of ranges east of the 6th meridian. With the exception of land in the original 13 Colonies, the state of Texas, and small areas of Western lands originally included in the cessions from Mexico, nearly all the land in the United States, including Alaska, is surveyed and identified in accordance with a comparable system.

Pioneers moved West faster than surveyors could accomplish their work, and no legal title could pass until the survey provided means to identify each parcel. To meet this need, Congress passed a land law in 1830 that granted first claim to the individual who occupied the land when the land office received clearance to make sales. In principle this presented no major problem. The land then known to the legislators in Washington was covered with forests that required clearing before the occupant could put it to use. Congress and public opinion agreed that the individual who had improved the land should have first claim on its purchase. This law remained on the books into the time of expansion onto the prairie plains, establishing a permanent legal precedent.

Consequently, the one who occupied land in the public domain, for all practical purposes, owned that land. At the least, no one could legally dispossess him until he had the opportunity to purchase it and had failed to come up with the money. Cattlemen used this legality to acquire large expanses in the West. It was the legality underlying the so-called range wars that form the plot in many Western novels.

Some now advocate selling land in the public domain currently administered by the Bureau of Land Management. Ranchers lease most of it. If and when the government does offer this land for sale, the rancher who holds the lease will have first option to buy it at the price specified in the enacting legislation. Since the government currently sets lease rentals far below market price, it is reasonable to expect the government to offer this land at prices below what it would bring at auction. Public opinion and Congress set the precedent 150 years ago.

As noted earlier, the homestead laws permitted a person to claim, free of charge, 160 acres of the public domain. While a Senator from Tennessee, President Andrew Johnson had made this legislation one of his most pressing goals. His efforts never met success until the Southern states seceded, which left the Republicans in control of Congress. The Homestead Act filled a niche in Republican plans. It was a sop to the common man to offset the giveaway of land to the railroad promoters.

In the eastern and southern regions of the prairie, where rainfall is more plentiful, families could subsist on 160 acres, and many of these plots remain in the hands of descendants of the original homesteaders. In the more arid western areas, however, a quarter section could not support a family. Homesteaders on those high plains never had a chance, and knowledgeable farmers did not make a try. Instead, where the surveyors moved ahead of the pioneers, ranchers used the Homestead law to put together large holdings that could survive profitably. The ranchers had their employees file for a homestead and on that parcel erect the required building. Because the statutes failed to specify a unit of measure for the size of buildings, many 14-by-24 homes were built to measure in inches, not feet. Although smaller than a decent doll house, these buildings met the requirements. The rancher then purchased the homestead from the employee, often for as little as $10. An affidavit proved sufficient to fulfill the requirement that the homesteader improve the land and occupy it for five years. This practice prevailed particularly along the transcontinental railroads; government had been forced to survey ahead of the railroads in order to transfer the alternate sections promised in the land grant.

Imperialism and Manifest Destiny
(The Spanish-American War)

The purchase of Alaska from Russia in 1867-1868 added 375 million acres to the United States, an area equal to nearly one-fifth of the country at that time, an area three times greater than the land given to railroads by the railroad acts of 1862 and 1864. In 80 years, the nation had grown from 13 colonies occupying a narrow band of coastal plain to a united nation larger than all of western Europe. Yet many leaders were not satisfied; they had their eyes on the Caribbean, Mexico, Central America, and the Pacific Ocean. They encouraged revolution in Cuba, in the Hawaiian Islands, and in the Philippines, looking to the day when people of all the world would speak the English language and give allegiance to one country, the United States of America. Such were the imperialistic goals of men in and out of government. This was the American vision of "Manifest Destiny." Temporarily at least these ambitions have been quieted in the 20th century. In the last decade of the 19th century, however, men of influence continually stirred the people to support their dreams for their country.

This pressure for imperialistic expansion erupted in violence in 1898 with a declaration of war against Spain. The warmongers professed only a desire to help Cubans gain their independence from Spain. It was all over by autumn of that year, with a popular and successful invasion of Cuba and the destruction of Spain's Atlantic and Pacific fleets. By the time the fighting ended and all the treaties had been signed, the United States had annexed Guam, the Hawaiian Islands, Puerto Rico, and the Philippines; and an independent Cuba looked to the United States for future aid and comfort.

Today, the significance of that war lies in recognizing the power given the news media by universal education, which created a literate populace. As the wealth of the nation grew, schools multiplied. The aftereffect of the War Between the States increased educational opportunity for all citizens of the South — male and female, black and white. Growing literacy among Americans paralleled the geographical and economic expansion of the nation. As literacy spread, the influence of newspapers increased. People marveled at the amount of news they had at their doorstep each morning. Their evening newspapers told about events of the morning in places halfway around the globe. People read and believed.

In the 1890s, two rivals, William Randolph Hearst with his *Journal* and Joseph Pulitzer with his *World,* competed for circulation supremacy in the New York City market. Pulitzer had gained success with his sensational style, a grand-scale embellishment of the facts. Following Pulitzer's lead, Hearst first honed his skills in this style with his *San Francisco Examiner.* He then left California to purchase the *New York Journal.* He set out to outdo his mentor, Pulitzer, with even more brazen sensationalism. By innuendo, exaggeration, and outright fabrication, these two New York newspapers entertained their gullible readers. Their financial success encouraged imitation by papers throughout the country. These lesser papers copied their style and their stories. Pulitzer's and Hearst's influence on the people of the nation grew as more papers became dependent on them for the amazing stories they discovered.

The efforts of the Cubans to gain independence from Spain furnished glorious material for these New York rivals. As Allan Keller remarked:

> *Both Pulitzer and Hearst saw the rebellion as fodder for their printing presses. With single-minded purpose they moved to change a peasant revolt into an international conflict.* (Keller 1969. 10)

And Bernard A. Weisberger elaborated:

> *The newspapers made Spanish atrocities in Cuba a steady front-page sensation, and as Hearst went, so, inevitably, went Pulitzer. The* Journal *would explain how Spanish troops had resumed "the inhuman practice of beating Cuban prisoners to death," or even drowning them — FEEDING PRISONERS TO SHARKS said the headline. The World, not to be outdone, would run a story that described Cuba as a place with "blood on the road-sides, blood in the fields, blood on the door-steps, blood, blood, blood!"* (Weisberger 1964. 131)

Hearst sent Frederic Remington, a noted illustrator of the American West, to Cuba to create on-the-spot pictures of the war. When Remington wired to Hearst that he found no war and requested his return to New York, Hearst wired back: "You furnish the pictures. I will furnish the war." Hearst portrayed a routine search of a young woman leaving Cuba as a brazen disrobing by three male inspectors. In truth, she was searched by matrons, as she admitted in an interview later in Florida.

Americans became incensed by the "outrageous" treatment the Cubans received at the hands of the "murderous" Spanish. The Spanish government aided the warmongers by sending to Cuba as governor a no-nonsense soldier, General Valeriano Weyler y Nicolau, soon to be labeled by Hearst as "Butcher" Weyler. Hearst then had stories of starvation and torture in political prisons. It mattered not to Hearst and his unsuspecting Americans that the tactics employed by the insurgent Cubans themselves caused the starvation among their fellowmen. Allan Keller comments on these reports:

> *Sensational papers carried stories of Weyler's actions that were either untrue or grossly exaggerated. He was accused of removing women by the score from prison under cover of darkness and shooting them down in cold blood. He was vilified, unjustly defamed, and made into a symbol of Spanish oppression — a symbol that could not help inflaming millions of readers. Journalism as a profession, in too many instances, was degraded beyond belief. When stories without any foundation had Weyler's henchmen throwing Cuban rebels to the sharks, newspaper ethics touched bottom. That another generation would have to witness similar journalistic excesses, such as the charges that German soldiers were cutting the breasts off Belgian nuns, does not reduce the shame of the yellow press in the last half-decade of the nineteenth century.* (Keller 1969. 18)

Both American Presidents Grover Cleveland and William McKinley opposed war. They negotiated, beseeching Spain to grant independence to the Cubans, and in the early months of 1898 McKinley's ministers were on the eve of success. The imperialists, looking toward manifest destiny, would have none of it. Those in government pressing for war included the Assistant Secretary of the Navy, Theodore Roosevelt, son of a wealthy

New York family and soon to become President of the United States as a result of notoriety gained from his part in the upcoming war.

By April, Congress and President McKinley capitulated to the demands of the press-aroused American people. Congress declared that a state of war existed with Spain, and William Randolph Hearst had his war. In that war only a few hundred men died of wounds received in combat. Thousands died and more thousands suffered from malaria, typhoid, yellow fever, dysentery, and other diseases contracted because of inadequate military preparation for large-scale operations on land.

At no time did the truth filter down to the people. Truth became lost in the heat of feelings aroused by the irresponsible sensationalism of Hearst's *Journal* and Pulitzer's *World*.

Some parties might defend such media performance under the guise of freedom of the press. The First Amendment protects the news media from interference by government. Freedom of expression — freedom of speech, freedom of the press, freedom of assembly — is sacrosanct in the United States, and through the years the media have fought in the courts to preserve this liberty. No freedom-loving person can oppose this position. Freedom of expression is one of the most essential freedoms men have. Freedom, however, carries with it responsibility. Unfortunately, many members of the news media are not always so ardent in their support of responsibilities. Instead, they abuse their freedom by propagandizing the people. They consider news reporting a means to influence the public; the truth be damned. Such conduct by both Hearst and Pulitzer was not freedom; it was license. It was outright abuse of freedom, and misled not only their readers, but set a precedent that has misled many people since. Such outrageous behavior under the banner of freedom has helped create among later generations the notion that freedom and responsibility for one's conduct are separate matters. In truth, liberty cannot survive in a society whose citizens disregard the corresponding responsibility. Freedom and responsibility are inseparable.

People need not be so misled. All Americans have equal freedom to disregard media that behave irresponsibly. Public opinion, especially in a democracy, can carry a nation into needless war. Advances in mass education and communication give the news media tremendous influence. In 1898 the newspapers presented guerrilla war in Cuba with a prejudice that favored the Cubans and condemned the Spanish. This was not truth; it was propaganda. In 1988 the media portrayed guerrilla war in Nicaragua in a manner favoring the insurgents and condemning those in the seat of government. Was that truth or propaganda? In 1988 the media portrayed guerrilla war in Afghanistan favoring the natives and condemning the Russians. Was that truth or propaganda? In 1988 the news media portrayed guerrilla war in the Gaza Strip and the West Bank favoring Israel and condemning the Palestinians. Was that truth or propaganda?

Clearly, the Hearst war in 1898 showed that, in order to combat the influence of propaganda, we must exercise a healthy skepticism. The quip "believe half of what you see and nothing you are told by the news media" is more than facetious. We can discover the truth by being cautious and seeking it from more than one source.

Government regulation of the news to ensure truth in the media would merely change the identity of those determining what presentations are responsible and truthful. Government is people, fallible people like everyone else. We seriously question whether placing this responsibility in government hands would help anything, and it would deny to the people freedom of expression, their greatest safeguard of all freedoms. Censorship throttles equally the propagandists and those striving to present the truth. Man must accept the risks of being his own caretaker. The alternative, government regulation, assigns to bureaucrats the responsibility for the content of what a person reads and hears; this is absolute censorship. The free market is man's proper arena for censoring irresponsible news media. We can refuse to patronize those commercial interests that sponsor such abuse. We can ignore the media organizations that propagandize their audience. For now, men remain free to choose.

Society progresses as men realize that cooperation, peaceful coexistence, and specialization of labor greatly increase production and relieve scarcity.

Chapter 13

The Nation Matures, 1901-1918

Philosophy of Government

SOCIAL COOPERATION IS POSSIBLE under but two philosophies of organization: cooperation by contracts and cooperation by command and subordination. No third relationship is conceivable. Individual liberty characterizes contractual cooperation, and serfdom characterizes cooperation by command. In the former, individuals cooperate as equals. No one is master; no one is serf. The people control the conduct of society. By voting they change the laws and who governs. In the latter, the relationship between ruler and ruled is one of commanding and obeying. The ruler decides; he alone has the freedom to act. Only by armed rebellion can the people change the laws and the identity of their rulers.

The first of these is commonly referred to as democracy, the second as dictatorship, communism, socialism, autocracy, aristocracy, or monarchy. For this latter system, this text uses the all-inclusive term *hegemony.* There is no such thing as a socialist democracy. The theory of socialism — everyone producing according to his ability and receiving according to his need — presupposes a central, dictatorial authority. A director determines where, at what task, and to what degree each person works. He controls and distributes the produce of society. No liberty of self-determination can exist in such a society. The director is all-powerful. If a person believes he can change things through the vote, he should examine the history of all nations where a so-called socialist democracy has existed in recent years: the former Soviet Union, the Philippine Islands, Poland, and most nations in South and Central America and in Africa, to name a few. The all-powerful director accepts the results of an election only when they coincide with his desires.

At some time every person must decide which form of social cooperation he will support. He must choose because no one lives beyond the power of social cooperation in some form. The democratic governor exercises only the power given to him by consent of the governed. The director in a hegemonic society rules by force, not by the force of his strength alone but by that of his supporters.

In the long run, no government can exist that contradicts the will of the people. Under democracy, the people peacefully change their leaders by the vote. Under hegemony, they must resort to armed rebellion. Ludwig von Mises makes this pertinent observation:

> *The philosophy that is the characteristic mark of the West and whose consistent elaboration has in the last centuries transformed all social institutions has been called individualism. It maintains that ideas, the good ones as well as the bad, originate in the mind of an individual man. Only a few men are endowed with the capacity to conceive new ideas. But as political ideas can work only if they are accepted by society, it rests with the crowd of those who themselves are unable to develop new ways of thinking to approve or disapprove the innovations of the pioneers. There is no guarantee that these masses of fol-*

lowers and routinists will make wise use of the power vested in them. They may reject the good ideas, those whose adoption would benefit them, and espouse bad ideas that will seriously hurt them. But if they choose what is worse, the fault is not theirs alone. It is no less the fault of the pioneers of the good causes in not having succeeded in bringing forward their thoughts in a more convincing form. The favorable evolution of human affairs depends ultimately on the ability of the human race to beget not only authors but also heralds and disseminators of beneficial ideas. . . .

The dangers inherent in the masses' incompetence are not eliminated by transferring the authority to make ultimate decisions to the dictatorship of one or a few men, however excellent. It is an illusion to expect that despotism will always side with the good causes. It is characteristic of despotism that it tries to curb the endeavors of pioneers to improve the lot of their fellowmen. The foremost aim of despotic government is to prevent any innovations that could endanger its own supremacy. Its very nature pushes it toward extreme conservatism, the tendency to retain what is, no matter how desirable for the welfare of the people a change might be. It is opposed to new ideas and to any spontaneity on the part of the subjects.

In the long run even the most despotic governments with all their brutality and cruelty are no match for ideas. Eventually the ideology that has won the support of the majority will prevail and cut the ground from under the tyrant's feet. The oppressed many will rise in rebellion and overthrow their masters. However, this may be slow to come about, and in the meantime irreparable damage may have been inflicted upon the common weal. In addition a revolution necessarily means a violent disturbance of social cooperation, produces irreconcilable rifts and hatreds among the citizens, and may engender bitterness that even centuries cannot entirely wipe out. The main excellence and worth of what is called constitutional institutions, democracy and government by the people is to be seen in the fact that they make possible peaceful change in the methods and personnel of government. Where there is representative government, no revolutions and civil wars are required to

> *remove an unpopular ruler and his system. If the men in office*
> *and their methods of conducting public affairs no longer please*
> *the majority . . . they are replaced in the next election. . . .*
>
> *In this way the philosophy of individualism . . . inaugurated*
> *an age of freedom and progress toward prosperity.* (Mises
> [1957] 1985. 371-373)

In either event, each member of society must decide which side he will support. Neutrality — by withholding support for either view — makes a decision to support hegemony; because when unopposed, those prevail who are dedicated to using coercion to gain power.

Due to the Laws of Inertia and of Preference, democracy makes change slowly. The caution of age counters the impatience of youth. As a person ages, his impetuous nature, sobered by experience and knowledge, gives way to intelligent caution. Whether good or bad, it is so because of the nature of man. This force under freedom exerts a strong influence on the institutions of his society. It governs the rate of change. If a person supports individual liberty, he accepts this condition and works within its limitations.

Society will always have those who are impatient with this democratic resistance to change. Those who refuse to accept this condition of human nature willingly sacrifice freedom to accelerate the change they consider improvement. They do not tolerate gradual change, the natural way of a democratic society. They mistrust the will of the people to do things "right," that is, "their" way. These men are autocrats; they advocate using the power of government to accelerate social change regardless of the wishes of the people. They regard individual liberty as less important than the benefits they see coming from the new order of things.

This autocratic nature of some individuals surfaces in a variety of ways. Professional educators do not trust the people to manage the public school system through elected school boards. They want a central authority that is removed from the influence of the vote. Such autocratic thinking promoted the Department of Education, a cabinet post of the federal government. Autocrats in seats of power ridicule the free market. Since freedom brings about change slowly, they call attention to the apparent inability of free-market forces to correct some perceived imbalance and claim this demonstrates that the free market does not operate as theoreticians teach. Autocrats support high taxation, because, as 20th-century autocrats express it, the common man does not spend his money wisely. By this they justify government-sponsored social security and medical care, government guarantees for bank and savings-and-loan deposits and for pension funds, and countless other programs financed by taking the individual's money from him in order to spend it "more wisely." Of course, a portion of that money pays the bureaucrats who administer the scheme.

As the 19th century drew to a close, the will of the people began to unite in opposition to individual wealth. The last 40 years of that century, with Eastern financiers in control, had witnessed abuses to which the voters rebelled. They wanted to break this power of business interests. They had suffered depressions and unemployment, inflation and deflation of the currency, and fraudulent use of power. They did not know whether the design of the system or the people administering it were at fault. They sought some means to overcome the recurring cycles of distress. The news media and politicians eager for more power told them that the evil lay in the monopolistic abuse of power by the wealthy. The people suspected that railroads and trusts somehow caused the conditions they found unpleasant.

Yet the abuses they witnessed were caused by the exercise of monopoly power that government had granted and supported by restrictions on the right to engage in business and by high tariffs that caused high prices. The people were fully confused. They failed to realize that in supporting coercion to destroy the wealth of individuals, they supported an assault on individual freedom. Such a state of flux in public opinion offers opportunity for the demagogue, and Theodore Roosevelt was such a man. A Jefferson, Van Buren, or Jackson would have reduced tariffs and eased government restrictions on entering a new business. Roosevelt, on the other hand, was an autocrat. He had little patience with the democratic process. Instead of dismantling government support for business and financial interests, he sought to counter their power with government controls. He obtained the support of the people by bashing the money interests. He played to the mass envy of wealthy people, a feeling that always exists.

Although an impatient autocrat, Roosevelt thought of himself as a reformer, a friend of the people. He failed to realize that by enlarging the scope and strengthening the power of the central government, he was laying the foundation for a monstrous power structure that would one day usurp all individual liberty. Despotism of the late 20th century had its beginning in 1901, when the assassination of President William McKinley elevated Roosevelt to the presidency. It remains to be seen whether public opinion can be led away from this trap baited by the siren song of special-interest legislation that leads ultimately to the complete destruction of democracy.

Theodore Roosevelt, Patrician Demagogue

Since democracy allows change deliberately, autocrats try to accelerate the process. Their virtues do not include patience and tolerance. Nor did Theodore Roosevelt have these virtues. A supreme egoist, he believed no disagreement with his views could be right. Throughout his service in public office he exhibited frustration with the democratic process. In his eyes, the law and the courts operated too slowly; checks and balances in the constitutional organization of government were a hindrance, and the Constitution itself was too rigid.

On inauguration as President, T. R. (as he was often referred to) capitalized on the growing unrest of the people and gave it direction. The legal mechanism was in place in the form of the Sherman Anti-Trust Act. It remained only for a determined President to use this law to break up the largest of private business. Roosevelt picked up his "big stick" and began busting heads. He first attacked the Northern Securities Company, a railroad complex put together by J. P. Morgan, John D. Rockefeller, James J. Hill, and Edward H. Harriman, the very citadel of finance capitalism and corporate business. His most publicized case involved dismantling Rockefeller's Standard Oil Company. Trustbusters measured evil by bigness; yet the only true complaint against Rockefeller's Standard Oil Company was that he sold his products at such a low price that other oil companies could not compete profitably. Rockefeller justified the rebates he received from the railroads on all oil they hauled; his company built and maintained the terminal facilities used by the railroads. The rebates were in truth payments for the use of these facilities.

The people, however, envied bigness and wealth. Roosevelt took advantage of popular animosity and made it his key to reelection and everlasting popularity in the nation. No matter that many large business enterprises held a monopoly by government grant. What conditions at that time actually required was removing governmental restrictions on competition, permitting entry into business by any and all who so desired (including railroading, and banking), and eliminating government subsidies and franchises that favored the few. During the seven years of

Roosevelt's administration and Taft's next four years, the Justice Department brought more than 120 industrial combinations into court to justify their size.

In a free society, consumers can protect their own interests by selecting what and choosing where they buy. Only government can limit this freedom. Government grants of charters and permits restrict consumers by limiting entrance into business. Free of government interference, a business enterprise must cater to the wishes of the consumers as demonstrated by the way they spend; otherwise the business fails and disappears. The wage earner in a free society can equally protect his interest by choosing where he works. Government restricted the freedom of labor in the 1800s by court-ordered injunctions prohibiting labor to organize for cooperative representation before employers.

T. R. envisioned government as the agency of the people in conflict with big business. Had he been a true friend of the people, as he proclaimed, he would have removed restrictions imposed by government. Instead, he acted the part of a true autocrat; he thrust more government onto the people. He interjected the power of his office into disputes between labor and management, advancing the cause of organized labor. At his insistence, Congress passed the 1906 Hepburn Act, which expanded the power of the Interstate Commerce Commission. He even proposed that the federal government require any venture intending to do business in interstate commerce to obtain a permit from a new bureaucracy to be organized for that purpose. This would have additionally limited freedom of choice for the consumers.

A Population in Transition (The Progressive Movement)

Reform has always been the popular cry among those interests not in control of the government. Each reform movement that succeeds in changing the trend in government gets a "handle" for future reference. Reform during Teddy Roosevelt's administration was labeled the *Progressive Movement* or the *Square Deal*. A later Roosevelt, Franklin Delano, would initiate a program that would be called the *New Deal*.

The Progressive Movement allegedly sought to (1) make government more responsive to the people, (2) eliminate the abuses of business interests brought on by industrialization and urbanization, and (3) restore equal opportunity in economic affairs by drawing up new rules of conduct for business. The multitudes have forever sought freedom from favors granted to special interests by government. They do not succeed, however, unless their leaders understand how to achieve these goals. Because politicians masquerading as reformers have generally employed means that enlarge the scope of government, their actions have generally reduced freedom for the citizenry even further. And the Theodore Roosevelt administration did just that.

Lincoln Steffens, in *The Shame of the Cities,* recognized the basic problem: special privilege dispensed by government. Unfortunately, the methods employed by government leaders and "reform" as viewed by most voters took a strange twist. Instead of eliminating government grants of special privilege, government dispensed other special privileges to offset those already existing. Government supported labor in countering the privileges granted to employers. Government created regulatory agencies. Politicians rarely relinquish power; they create new regulatory authority to ride herd on the institutions of their earlier creation.

The reason for this swing away from individual freedom was more fundamental than industrialization and urbanization. By the 20th century, the citizenry of the nation had matured, more nearly reflecting the nature of man in the Old World. Early settlers in the United States had been a hardy, pioneer stock. Independent in their thinking, they were revolutionaries. Above all else they sought freedom of conduct. The harsh conditions of pioneering an unsettled land eliminated those who could not make it on their own. For 250 years this process of specific selection determined the nature of the American people.

The government of the United States reflected the nature of its citizens. During the Constitutional Convention in Philadelphia, no voice asked for government to care for the weak. In 1788 the citizens never questioned that each should care for himself and his own, and they wanted the liberty to do so. They did not shy away from responsibility.

This is not typical of mankind. The Laws of Responsibility and Security say that most people want to be taken care of. They shun responsibility, even for themselves and their own. They want a benefactor to tell them what to do and a protector from the uncertainties of life. President Franklin Roosevelt, playing to this characteristic of man, added two freedoms to those recited in the Bill of Rights. In a 1940 speech promoting passage of the Lend-Lease Act, Roosevelt declared that his administration was dedicated to securing for man four basic freedoms: freedom of speech, freedom of religion, freedom from want, and freedom from fear.

The nature of the American people changed during the 19th century, especially after the War Between the States. Late 19th-century immigrants from Europe were not the independent ones seeking freedom of opportunity; they were refugees from poverty and persecution seeking freedom from want and fear; they were fleeing from responsibility. They had heard that in America everyone could get a job, a high-paying job by Old World standards. These lower-class, peasant types came in great waves after the War Between the States. They changed the mix in the nature of the populace.

Natural propagation created a similar force. Men two or three generations removed from pioneer stock more nearly reflect the natural characteristics of all men. As long as living conditions remained harsh, Darwin's law of natural selection operated to populate America with men and women of an independent nature. The advance in living standards, however, enabled less independent people to multiply. This relentless trend came to a head in America by the first of the 20th century.

The causes were not industrialization and urbanization as such; these were the symptoms of a society in a region with a vanishing frontier. Time alone assures that a secure and settled society will exhibit all the behavioral traits of basic human nature. Americans merely developed the characteristics common among people civilized for hundreds of years. Human nature surfaced in all its variations — good, bad, and indifferent — at the end of the transition. The days of rugged individualism in America ended precisely because a great majority of people will trade freedom for security, that is, until they discover that such a trade plunges them into poverty, and then it is often too late.

The Progressive Movement manifested this undercurrent of transition in the nature of the American people. Adept at sensing the mood of his constituents and an autocrat at heart, Theodore Roosevelt welcomed the trend and made his place in history as a great champion of the people. In this respect, he was a great leader. He led them along the way they wanted to go — down the road to serfdom.

The Dilemma of Civilization

In order to evaluate something as good or bad, there must be a standard. Without a fixed, well-defined standard for comparison, any characterization of a matter as "good" expresses nothing more than personal preference. The one making judgment simply says, "This pleases me."

Science evaluates action on the basis of the accepted theorems of that science. A judgment comments on an act's effectiveness at achieving the desired objective. Ingesting lead arsenate cannot be classified as good or bad until the purpose for such action is known. If the compound is taken to end life, the action taken is good relative to the purpose, though not pleasant.

In evaluating the two patterns of social cooperation, we confront this same reality. Until we decide on our objectives, neither democracy nor hegemony is a superior form of association. Clearly, those trying to form an association that maximizes production and guarantees individual liberty are best served through democratic capitalism, that social organization within which individuals control the invested wealth through private property rights and cooperation by contract. This enables them to make full use of the innovations devised by their imagination. Similarly, hegemony, cooperation by command and obedience, is the better form for those trying to minimize individual responsibility. Should they, however, succeed in creating a hegemonic government, they avoid responsibility by bringing on themselves a condition of general poverty.

Society has persons who want freedom and those who want to minimize responsibility. The problem arises in devising a political institution within which both groups can more nearly achieve their respective goals. Those who try to minimize responsibility need the services of those who will accept the responsibility for everyone. Those who want to maximize individual liberty do not necessarily need those services unless they also value prestige, recognition, and material reward. Without cooperation with others, however, the living conditions of everybody in that society return to biological competition.

In order to maximize the benefits of advancing civilization, each group needs the other, and they must organize their institutions in a way that addresses the needs of both. Those who want to escape responsibility — the sheep — must properly assign their priorities and accept the realities of human nature. In order to entice others to relieve them of their responsibilities, they must grant the recognition and material wealth that are the rewards these leaders demand in return for assuming those responsibilities. The followers cannot have it both ways: equality of economic position and recognition as well as freedom from care, fear, and hunger. At the same time, both groups must not interfere with the rights of the middle class, who want neither wealth, recognition, servitude, nor responsibility for others. They want only the freedom to take care of themselves. A large middle class is the mark of a society in good balance. Theirs is the class that gets squeezed out when a society drifts into despotism. If this middle class is ignored and imposed upon in the struggle between the sheep and the goats, they lead the country into revolt to change the existing order.

Because man is imperfect, his society experiences the constant striving of each class to gain its goals while keeping the behavior of the others in line with reality. The followers at times have had to bring the leaders to task for not discharging their responsibility to those who serve. And leaders at times have had to use force to take the material reward they demand in return for accepting responsibility. Despotism, whether perpetrated by the few (the leaders take from the workers and do not care for them) or by the many (the workers deny wealth and recognition to their leaders), places social cooperation in jeopardy, and if not checked, eliminates the middle class entirely.

Under democracy each member can decide where he wants to fit, and peaceful means lie open for him to seek that place. In deciding, however, he should be aware of the rewards and limitations and accept the conditions. In a society of rulers and ruled — hegemony, individuals are born into their position in the cooperative organization. Each member can move from commander to servant with relative ease, but the reverse movement is often difficult if not impossible. Under hegemony, in order for a person to rise from a follower to a leader, he must use coercion, even violence.

The Progressive Movement marked a change in how the people viewed the services their government should perform. Should government merely enforce peaceful cooperation under defined rules, that is, referee, so to speak? Or should government force leaders to care for the interests of all? The majority of voters clearly wanted their leaders to take a more enlightened role in caring for their welfare. So the movement toward social welfare emerged in the heretofore citadel of unrestricted individual freedom. These questions naturally arise: In return for welfare, did the followers willingly grant wealth and recognition to their leaders for acting in their interest? (During the 20th century, the masses have used political power to confiscate wealth from industrial leaders for distribution among themselves.) Did the leaders in turn properly relieve the workers of their responsibilities for themselves? Did they take proper care of the serving multitudes? Certainly the action of the progressives — to break up trusts and attack personal wealth — violated the interests of the industrial leaders. But, what had those wealth-holders been doing to protect the interests of those who served?

Monetary manipulation by a privileged class — creating the business cycle — proved destructive to the welfare of laborers and farmers. The workers and farmers, a new majority in the 20th century, have retaliated with mass confiscation of wealth for redistribution among themselves. If left unchecked, this infighting between the various interests will destroy all cooperation in a few generations. The emerging most powerful group will appoint a dictator to take charge, and we Americans will see the end to personal freedom in America. The two Presidents Roosevelt each came very close.

Theodore Roosevelt believed that government leaders should be the judges, that "good" trusts should be allowed and "bad" trusts broken up. Theodore Roosevelt and William Howard Taft both attacked big business on the basis of this presumption, but they lacked a proper standard by which to distinguish good from bad. This resulted, quite naturally, in their determination's being largely personal preferences for those in power — those in the Justice Department, political bureaucrats. This constituted government by man, not by law; thus emerged the 20th-century rebirth of this attack on freedom. As the historians Harry J. Carman and Harold C. Syrett state:

> *The Supreme Court was not inclined to consider mere size a violation of the antitrust legislation. Nor were defendants held guilty for past violations of the law if they had abandoned illegal practices before being brought to trial. . . . In general, the Justices appeared willing to accept the elimination of competition if the monopolists refrained from using methods that were blatantly predatory. This view, which came to be known as the "rule of reason," was advanced by Justice White in 1911 in the opinion he wrote for the Standard Oil case; the authors of the Sherman Act, he stated, intended that "the standard of reason [should] . . . be the measure used for the purpose of determining whether in a given case a particular act had or had not brought about the wrong against which the statute provided." The rule of reason . . . set up a subjective standard that per-*

mitted the Court to pursue whatever course it desired. (Carman and Syrett 1952. 366)

Because people are driven by self-interest, it is unrealistic to expect them to act as they should in a complex industrial society until they become aware of this interdependence between leaders and followers. From the beginning of the Republic, financial and business leadership at the helm of government violated its responsibility to the workers. Admittedly, this was partly unintentional, but it happened just the same. Each time the voters wrested control of government from the hands of business interests, their equally ill-informed actions failed to achieve the changes they sought.

In the early years of the American democracy, all interests believed in the principles of social cooperation by contract. After 100 years of imperfect performance, however, people began to lose faith. Their efforts at reform began to support alternate methods. The subsequent 100 years have been the record of this effort. It has incorporated more and more government interference in the daily lives of the citizens. Their objectives have been

1. To remove corruption in business and government;
2. To prevent the recurring boom-bust cycles, or at least to shelter the common man from the problems of depression with its distress for the ones who lose their jobs;
3. To provide some means for the common man to share more generously in the benefits of advances in science, medicine, home conveniences, travel, and general abundance;
4. To protect the security of self and home from abuse by the unruly; and
5. To be free themselves from assaults on person and placid life brought about by recurring wars.

Certainly these are worthy objectives, and just as certainly the American people are farther from attaining them than they were at the close of the 19th century. The failure has stemmed from a lack of understanding about human social behavior. By adopting counterproductive methods, the people have assured their own failure.

Hope, however, rests in a more general acceptance of the truth about human action in society. During the 20th century, the science of economics has developed a model that can guide us toward peaceful coexistence under freedom with material comfort. It remains only for us to grasp this concept and put it to use in society.

Human Action, by Ludwig von Mises, provides this understanding. Altruism will not influence human behavior until people realize that altruism is in their own self-interest. This is a challenge for leaders. It may take generations, perhaps hundreds of years, and may involve decline and rebirth of civilization. Mankind did not learn overnight that cooperation under a free government could produce abundance for the benefit of all.

About Civilization

Advancing civilization may be characterized as the progressive development of a civil order that enables people to achieve their aspirations more easily. Progress can be achieved in a society that (1) fosters a stable government that protects private property and promotes freedom and opportunity, and (2) protects and encourages accumulation of savings, which translates into tools, machines, and adopted technologies that better provide the members of that society with their material needs.

Directors of hegemonic governments stifle innovation and change. They discourage mass education and experimentation. New inventions and improved technologies come from the minds of men who challenge the existing order. Conformity to existing knowledge produces stagnation. The 19th-century explosion of innovations did not happen by accident. Man needed freedom, opportunity, and capital. Advancing civilization in the United States provided all three in that time period. The War Between the States assured a stable government committed to protecting property rights and freedom. The savings in Europe, added to the savings in America, supplied the capital that financed the Industrial Revolution. By 1900, whatever man could imagine would soon be financed, built, and put to use in American industry. This manifested itself in the rapid appearance of new inventions in machinery and methods. The increase in capital investment made labor, on and off the farm, more efficient and productive. The resultant bounty brought the benefits of leisure to an ever-growing segment of the population. It freed thinkers from the necessity of being doers.

Inventions did not cause the change. Inventions do nothing until they are put to work. This requires investment, capital supplied by savings. Although inventions seem just to appear, the ingredient that brings on their appearance is savings used by people free to manage their own affairs.

Only free men can make these changes. Autocrats fear innovation because it challenges orthodoxy. Those indoctrinated under hegemony accept the established order. To make change would defy the very rulers who bestow on them their education and social position.

Development fed on itself; the more the Industrial Revolution progressed, the faster Americans changed their society. Railroads spread a network over the entire continent, providing fast, low-cost overland transport. The automobile, on the scene by 1900, began challenging the railroads for transporting people during the '20s. It needed simply a network of improved roads to serve the locations not accessible by rail. The Wright Brothers demonstrated that powered, heavier-than-air craft could fly; and man approached the eve of flying in space. Electricity and refined crude oil provided the low-cost energy for all these developments. Scientific endeavor prospered; medicine grew from the craft of the mystic to become a meaningful aid to man in prolonging healthful, useful life.

Such developments typify the blossoming of a civilization at its zenith. When society adopts civil institutions that protect contract and property rights and allow freedom to the people, division of labor emerges. Efficiency in labor relieves people from the time-consuming burden of providing food and shelter so characteristic of the life of primitives. Leisure is a product of all advancing civilizations. Only in this atmosphere can the creative genius of thinkers and artists produce the wonders that mark the "golden age" of that civilization. Creativity and artistry do not flourish among ill-housed, ill-clad, hungry men.

In all previous history, as each civilization arrived at its golden age, the seeds of self-destruction had already been sown. At the beginning of the 20th century, Western civilization — then most pronounced in its achievements in America — had reached this stage of flowering, the age that the English historian Arnold Joseph Toynbee has called the beginning of the inevitable decline.

Some analysts have declared that civilization can never develop without freedom and a democratic government, and that a democratic government cannot survive under freedom. So it has happened in the United States. Government under Presidents Theodore Roosevelt, William H. Taft, and Woodrow Wilson turned away from freedom and opportunity. It became directed toward interventionism, which direction, if not reversed, will destroy both democracy in America and — as other nations follow its lead — Western civilization.

This was a very natural development. The law of action and reaction — to every action there is a reaction — decreed that the people would react to repeated cycles of boom and bust, to the excesses of special-interest legislation that favored the capitalists. People wanted a change. Under such circumstances, leaders change either the mood of the people or the direction of government. Otherwise, violent chaos erupts.

The Civilization Cycle

Society progresses as men realize that cooperation, peaceful coexistence, and division of labor greatly increase production and relieve scarcity. Fewer workers are needed to provide the basic necessities of life. More workers can engage in service work, leisure, intellectual and artistic pursuits, and fabricating luxury goods. In time it becomes apparent that the fundamental differences between individuals cause inequality in the distribution of the products of the economy. Some citizens become wealthy, some not so wealthy, and many remain poor. The new poor, however, are better supplied with the necessities of life than when they lived a primitive existence and depended on today's harvest for today's meals.

An absence of great wealth among primitives limits the disparity in wealth to a degree much smaller than in advanced civilizations. Because numbers in a tribe are small, a strong leader can prevent the human traits from destroying cooperation among its members. When no one has great wealth, what does another find to envy in his brethren? With the accumulation of so little wealth, what can cause greed? When all are equally poor, what can make a man feel guilty about his possessions? Compassion is manifested in helping the sick, the weak, and the elderly on a one-on-one basis.

This is not to say that inequality of wealth is evil. Because so few individuals save and because wealth is needed for advancing beyond primitive culture, unequal distribution of wealth becomes a natural condition in the development of civilization. Because of human nature, wealth will not exist unless society permits the savers to retain ownership of the wealth they create. Otherwise, none will save and no wealth will come into existence. As stated earlier, the evil lies in government-supported barriers to opportunity that interfere with wealth redistribution through individual initiative and free enterprise.

Disparity in the amount of wealth owned by each person results naturally from the fundamental differences between individuals. As economic development grows, man creates wealth. Individuals — the ones who save — own this wealth. The greater the total wealth, the more pronounced become the differences in ownership between individuals. This obvious disparity breeds envy, greed, compassion, and guilt, which undermine society itself. Influenced by basic human traits, members of an advanced society press government to be concerned for the poor. Guilt-ridden heirs of successful farmers and merchants wish to do something for the less fortunate. Those not sharing generously in all the good things of life seek to have government redistribute the wealth. To aid the poor, legislatures set price controls on the necessities. They levy taxes on wealth to provide welfare for the needy. Established businessmen press government to enact restrictive legislation "to protect the consumer." In reality, they seek their own protection from competition by energetic newcomers. Skilled craftsmen seek legislation to protect them from an influx of more workers and from technological advances that might make their craft obsolete. Labor unions obtain legislation to assure, to the unions, protection under the shelter of regulation of commerce. A large constituency develops among those with a vested interest in some established order. Efforts to adapt by change through time become stifled by barriers erected by government.

This increase in services and government rules enlarges the number of people employed in government and the extent of intervention into the lives of its citizens. It continuously enlarges the number of nonproductive yet able-bodied workers. Laws forbid children to work. Minimum wage laws deny employment to another group of potential workers. Compassion for the elderly who live longer than they can work overreaches original objectives and starts paying able-bodied senior citizens who consequently withdraw from productive employment. No wonder so many who can work quit and live off these gratuities. At its peak, Rome's population may have been a million. At various times, at least one-third and possibly one-half of them lived on public charity. In addition, we must not overlook the burden of financing through taxation the army of government employees who administer and enforce these endless regulations. This army withdraws another mass of workers from productive labor.

An advanced civilization thus becomes burdened by more and more unproductive members. Those who keep working become too few to maintain the level of production required to sustain the society. Society begins to disintegrate. Workers rebel and evade the law; they go "underground." Farmers whose produce is kept underpriced by faulty legislation either leave the farms to join their city brethren being supported by the system, or they produce only such foods as they require for their own needs. In time, food becomes scarce in the cities. City dwellers leave the city to grow their own food. Division of labor disappears as more and more workers become subsistence farmers. Trade and factory production decline because workers have left their jobs to scrounge for food. The cities become uninhabited. The society reverts to a primitive culture of fishermen, gatherers, hunters, and farmers.

Famine was a constant threat from the dawn of recorded history into the beginning of the period covered by this text. Examine the condition of life in Europe at the time of the formation of colonies in America. Fear of famine persists even now. This latent fear lies at the root of the farm policy of all governments of Western civilization. The policies may be poorly conceived, but they are intended to "keep them down on the farm." Recorded history has shown too many periods when there were not enough farmers, which resulted in insufficient food production. Certainly food production is an admirable goal, but we may just as surely question the appropriateness of the means being used.

This cycle of advance and decline in civilization has happened many times. The process takes many generations. Few people live long enough to see any marked change. In terms of the cycle — hundreds of years from primitive to sophisticated civilization and hundreds of years to revert to primitive — the life of one man is short indeed.

We may ask whether man must forever endure this destiny? Not necessarily. We know how to avoid the collapse or to hasten a rebuilding from decay. It remains only for us to put this knowledge into practice. Time alone will tell whether we will use it to redirect the drives of our nature.

In 1901, Theodore Roosevelt sensed the mood of the voters and redirected the path of government. Taft, his handpicked successor, at first followed this lead. Woodrow Wilson became the next President when President Taft tried to alter this trend during the last two years of his term. Wilson did not actually defeat Taft in the election of 1912. He had the vote-splitting help of Roosevelt and his Bull Moose third party. It made little difference who won that election, Roosevelt or Wilson. Both were committed to interventionism.

Consequently, it becomes appropriate to examine the substance of interventionism in contrast to laissez faire.

Interventionism, Socialism, Capitalism, and Laissez faire

Socialism can take two forms. In the more readily recognized form, practiced in the former Soviet Union, government owns all the means of production — the land, the factories, the tools, the machines — and assigns to members of society where each will work. In the alternate form, which first appeared in Germany, the government retains the outward appearance of freedom by protecting private ownership of property, but dictates to the owners what to produce, how much, and at what price. Government creates bureaucratic agencies to regulate industry and commerce. Interventionism is the name commonly associated with the methods government uses to establish socialism of this German form.

In a society operating under laissez faire, government restricts its use of coercion to the enforcement of rules of just conduct universally applied. Individuals are free to use their knowledge for their own purposes. The government protects private property rights and preserves for individuals the freedom to decide where they will labor. Employer and employee negotiate wages without government interference, and government sees to it that employer and employee do not interfere with the freedom of each other. Industry and commerce remain free to control production to suit the demands of the market as expressed by the consumers' purchasing decisions. The rules of just conduct define boundaries within which each can act freely without interfering with his neighbor to do likewise. Individuals acting alone and in concert (government) are restricted by the same rules.

The difference between socialism — of the Soviet or of the German form — and democratic capitalism (laissez faire) lies not in who owns the productive resources, but in who makes the decisions that determine what products are produced, in what quantity, how designed, and at what price they will be sold. Under socialism, government bureaucrats make these decisions. In a free market, the buying public decides. The consumer votes for or against a product, its design, its price, its quality, each time he makes a purchase.

In America today, consumers no longer control automobile design; law requires automobile manufacturers to build vehicles to specifications set by bureaucratic decree. Autos must be able to sustain a specified crash test, must be equipped with passive restraints, must achieve an arbitrary fuel efficiency, and must burn only a specific fuel. The consumer has a choice only between manufacturers. He can select whatever auto he wants, but only from units that meet the design standards emanating from government. This is not free-market capitalism; this is socialism by intervention. Consumer preferences have no part in decision making about the functional design of automobiles.

Few products on the U.S. market escape some degree of design set by bureaucrats. Some products do not even appear in American markets because they are withheld from consumers by government choice. No medication can be sold in the United States until a bureaucratic committee determines that the product is safe and beneficial to the consumer. Had government in the United States been in control during the 19th and early 20th century to the extent it is now, industry could not have introduced the automobile, the airplane, and the use of natural gas in the home. Had the same degree of bureaucratic interference applied in 1492, Columbus would never have been permitted to sail the Atlantic and discover the Americas. Compare the free and rapid development of the New World to the deliberate, bureaucratic, restricted, government-controlled exploration and development of space. Presently existing building and zoning codes would have prevented the construction of most buildings and residences now in use. The degree of such intervention marks the only difference today between conditions in the United States and in other nations. Private ownership has been retained, but government exercises decision-making control over productive resources.

Citizens of Jamestown, Virginia, in 1610, demonstrated the results of such socialistic management carried to the extreme. No way can the people be better served by such action. The people are limited in their freedom of choice, and the net cost to the consumer increases with every act of intervention. With few brief interludes, this socialist philosophy has guided government leaders in America since President Theodore Roosevelt took office in 1901. Central planning, in opposition to individual consumer planning, is the core characteristic of interventionism, socialism of the German pattern.

Soon after launching intervention, men in power realized that government control of the economy required a much larger share of the national product. Government needed money to pay bureaucrats and to subsidize action for which existing revenues were inadequate. Since revenue from tariff disappears as rates are increased, the government could not enlarge its income from that traditional source. This condition required new taxes, and in 1913 they secured an amendment to the Constitution permitting government to levy taxes directly on wealth, the net income tax. Additionally, the government in 1913 took full control of all banking by creating the Federal Reserve System. Banking had never been free, but the Federal Reserve Act eliminated all remaining independence for banking. The government thereby acquired the engine by which to freely inflate the supply of money, which is an indirect tax on savings. These additional taxes replaced the tariff as government's source of revenue.

The net income tax, followed shortly by the inheritance tax, appealed to the mass envy directed against wealthy industrialists. By graduated rates, these taxes provided benefits for some citizens who paid less than their proportionate share of the cost (free money for the voters). As Al Smith, a 1920s governor of New York, declared, "Tax and Spend and Elect."

Keynesian, statistical, and popular economists do not agree on how inflation and income tax impact the interests of the people. The Austrian School of economics, however, makes it clear that both actions restrict — and can even destroy — the advancement of civilization. When carried to extremes, inflation and the net income tax reduce savings, the source of industrial expansion. Without savings, civilization reverts to the primitive state best observed in the Americas at the time of their discovery by Europeans.

The Will of the People

Both government and business must respond to the wishes of the consumer. Government responds to the vote (or to violent rebellion); business responds to the purchasing decisions of the buyers. Either way, the tastes of the people today fashion the world of tomorrow. If people want any specific condition to appear tomorrow, they need only demand it through the vote, through their purchases, or through violent rebellion. The consequences of this reality are the presently existing subsidies for farmers, pornography in contemporary literature, and interventionism. The people demand these things. When they get them, they may have second thoughts, because their knowledge is not complete. The means people choose do not always achieve the goals they desire, and some are counterproductive.

Since government and business respond to the will of the people, improvement in the institutions of civilization cannot become permanent unless everyone accepts the facts about human nature. Self-interest is the driving force of mankind. It enhances civilization only when we learn that everyone benefits most through cooperation under a system of freedom. Because government action greatly enhances the impact of decisions by a few, government cannot achieve such a goal; it merely aggravates bad situations. Under government planning, the errors of the few bring disintegration of social cooperation because the consequences are so greatly magnified. The world of the 1990s is witnessing this development in the former Soviet Union after only 70 years of government planning and control.

The success or failure of freedom and democracy rests entirely on the knowledge of the voters and the actions of individuals. Congressmen, presidents, and judges, all behave in agreement with the will of the electorate. If the electorate want a welfare state, even though it will self-destruct by its very nature, government will create a welfare state, and the destruction of that culture will follow. The only way to prevent this collapse is to change the will of the people by convincing them that a welfare state is an unachievable chimera.

The destructive actions of governments have always been advanced by well-meaning men acting in innocence of the consequences or by knowledgeable leaders willing to destroy society to benefit themselves. Rarely do conditions elevate to power such a selfish individual as the latter. In recent years, one can think of only one such leader, the Nazi Adolf Hitler. And the will of the free people of the world removed him from his seat of power in one decade, not by the vote, but by armed resistance.

World War I

Voters remain interested in reform while they are distressed by the perceived evil doings of those "rascals." They lose interest as soon as the power of those rascals is subdued. Taft and Roosevelt subdued the rascals in business, at least to the satisfaction of the voters. By 1915, the Progressive Movement had run its course. Exposing corruption in municipal government became the next fad for gossip-hungry readers.

Reform in municipal government, however, became dull when in 1914 the Kaiser and his Teutonic warriors invaded neutral Belgium. The propaganda mills had a new and more exciting grist. Tales of the brutality of German soldiers fascinated the people. Sensational journalism thrives on scandal, gossip, and war. Delighted to have a war, newspaper and magazine publishers dropped long-overworked scandal and gossip. The new fad of the teens became hate propaganda against the Germans. This forced

German immigrants in America and their descendants to change their names, or at the least to Americanize the spelling. Braun became Brown; Wilhelm became William.

Although the majority of Americans had little interest in the affairs of European nations in the first decades of the 20th century, by its involvement in Cuba and the Pacific, the United States had declared itself a participant in world politics. The nation could no longer stand aside when the other world powers went to war. Imperialism and isolation were not compatible. England, Russia, France, Holland, and Germany also had interests in the Pacific. The populace of the United States did not know it, but the imperialistic ambitions of their leaders involved them in all the disputes between other world powers. The nation was forced to align itself with one group or the other in balance-of-power politics — a system that is maintained by pitting one group against another. The division has generally taken the form of cooperation present within the nation, either democracy or hegemony. The hegemonic nations have opposed the democracies and the little nations side with their neighbors.

Woodrow Wilson campaigned for reelection in 1916 on the platform, "I kept America out of war." U.S. partisanship, however, favored England, France, and their allies. The anti-German hate coming from the propaganda mills belied all claims of American neutrality. Germany had no choice but to consider the United States a partner of her enemies. The naval blockade of German ports, coupled with the continued shipments of war supplies from the United States to the Allies forced Germany to unleash her submarines against all shipping not destined for German ports. In 1915, German U-boats sank a passenger liner, the *Lusitania*, with American civilians on board. The next year they sank another liner, the *Sussex*. Newspapers pounced on these acts as "outrageous disregard for lives of neutrals." The media made no mention of the war goods carried in the holds of those same ships.

By the spring of 1917, Wilson capitulated to the inevitable and asked Congress to declare war against Germany and her supporters. The added strength of American soldiers in European trenches tipped the balance against Germany. On November 11, 1918, the combatants signed an armistice.

Woodrow Wilson, the idealist, envisioned a world government to assure continued peace, his League of Nations. In 1919, during the many conferences before the Treaty of Versailles that formally ended World War I, the following story circulated in Paris about a conversation between Wilson and France's Clemenceau; it went essentially as follows:

> **Clemenceau:** *You can never prevent war by no matter what scheme of organization unless we all agree on three fundamental principles. . . . First, to declare and enforce racial equality. . . . Do you accept?*
>
> **Wilson:** *No, . . . The race question is very touchy in the United States, and the Southern and West Coast senators would defeat any treaty containing such a clause.*
>
> **Clemenceau:** *The second thing we must do is to establish freedom of immigration; no country to close her borders to foreigners wishing to come to live there. Do you agree?*
>
> **Wilson:** *No; my country is determined to exclude Orientals absolutely, and Congress is already considering restrictions to European immigration.*
>
> **Clemenceau:** *The third condition of an enduring peace is free trade throughout the world. How about that?*
>
> **Wilson:** *. . . I could never get Congress to agree to a customs union with Europe, Asia, and Africa.*
>
> **Clemenceau:** *Very well, then; the only way to maintain peace is to remain strong and keep our . . . enemies weak.*
> (Morison 1965. 877)

This story sums up the reality about hopes for world peace and Wilson's dream. Domestic politics prevented the United States from accepting that treaty and joining the League of Nations. Another world war, another world government (the United Nations), and the world remains no nearer universal peace. Balance-of-power remains the only functioning deterrent to war.

War will return when one side believes it is strong enough to defeat the other, or when the leaders of one side become desperate and break the peace to prevent internal revolt. The propaganda mills on both sides currently are generating the literature of hate and fear. This sells newspapers and magazines; it keeps people watching the evening news on television; it keeps the citizens united against outsiders. It justifies more and more government intervention into people's lives.

Such propaganda, however, does not enlighten. It poorly serves the peaceful desires of the populace. These media alarmists promote violence, death, and the destruction of social cooperation in order to sell newspapers and attract television audiences. The public welcomes the whole charade because people experience comfort in knowing that they are not alone in their troubles.

Free men fail their heritage by not informing them-
selves. They remain innocent of the events within
government that encroach on their freedom.

Chapter 14

The Great Depression, 1918-1940

The Business Cycle

ONE OUTSTANDING EVENT OF THE 20th century was the business depression of the 1930s. During that depression, worldwide unemployment reached proportions characteristic of Europe in the 17th century. It wiped out nearly all savings invested in financial instruments. The peoples, frightened by events they could not understand, turned in panic to protection by government under the banners of socialism and communism, to charismatic leaders like Adolf Hitler in Germany, Francisco Franco in Spain, and Franklin Roosevelt in the United States. Fascism, socialism, communism, and these charismatic leaders promised the people freedom from their uncertain problems, best expressed by Roosevelt as freedom from want and fear.

A great tidal wave of nationalism washed over the shores of liberty and worldwide cooperation, bringing with it the certainty of conflict, World War II (1939-1945). As a consequence of that war, over 30 million people perished, and millions more died from forces generated by that wave of nationalism. This period of violent change can be best understood when viewed in light of what happens in economic depressions and what forces generate such recurring cycles of distress.

The term *business cycle* refers to periodic swings in the use of labor. Statisticians define a condition they call "unemployment." By first establishing an arbitrary statistical magnitude they call "full employment," they then determine unemployment as the degree to which actual employment fails to match this arbitrary standard. From this determination they say, for example, "In January the unemployment rate was 6.8 percent, a full one percentage point higher than in January a year ago." With this speculation they determine where the nation's business might be in the business cycle.

Statisticians base their concept of full employment on an arbitrary measure they construct for the benefit of politicians. It has little significance to the worker. Whether a person is fully employed or not constitutes a value judgment, and each person determines whether he wants to work more or less. Some can work more than others. Some might be able to work even 120 hours a week, but few would be willing to. Even the slave working under the whip will not exert his full efforts when required to work that much. The value a person places on leisure limits the number of hours he will work; and as he grows more prosperous, he is able to enjoy more leisure.

In a free-market economy, every person can find employment to the extent he desires. There is no reference here to the monetary reward or the hourly rate of pay. It states only what it says; each can find some form of rewarding labor. The exact hourly measure of work per week varies from person to person and month to month according to his rate of pay and his mood at the moment. For these reasons, in terms of the total labor force, there can be no meaningful measure of full employment in the nation. It means only what statisticians assign to it.

In the concept of business cycle, prosperity is the condition where each person can find nearly as much work as he wants. Depression is a state where many cannot find as much as they would like. The cycle is the alternating swing from prosperity to depression and back. At no time does prosperity include every worker; no depression is so severe that no one is working. Statisticians collect their data and, months after the fact, proclaim that on the fifth day of July the economy began to expand, bringing prosperity, lasted for 47 months, and turned down on May 27 in the fourth year of the boom. This is historical data that has no significance to the individual. Each worker knows when he has difficulty finding a job, and each knows when he can get more work than he wants.

The importance of understanding the business cycle lies in understanding the reason for the swing from a general excess of employment opportunities to a general scarcity of them. Only by understanding the causes can we hope to meliorate the consequences of the swings or eliminate the cycle completely.

In the free Western world the cycle is peculiar to the conditions of mass labor working for money wages. The business cycle occurs because of government intervention in the free-market economy and the consequent reactions of free individuals adjusting to this intervention. The cycle can be eliminated either by denying freedom to the people — as in socialist, communist, or otherwise autocratic nations — or by removing government interference with the market. Marxists are correct then in stating that the business cycle is unique to free-market capitalism, but they are wrong in claiming that capitalism itself has this flaw. The flaw is introduced by government interference with individual freedom. The intervention develops because leaders do not agree on how economic forces work in the mass use of money and credit. The masses approve of the intervention because they perhaps understand even less about these matters than do their leaders.

Business cycles appeared with industrialization. The freedom that characterized the Industrial Revolution ushered in conditions that approximated a free-market economy. Until people knew freedom within a more or less free market, there was no general business condition to bust. There can be no bad business where there is no business. With industrialization, a greater portion of the people lived in a money atmosphere. The masses had money, and they began to use banks. Before that time, only international commercial traders used them. Use of banks by the masses enabled bankers to create money and to extend credit based on this fictitious money. Bankers, not government, first created the business cycle. Governments entered the picture only after bankers perfected the mechanics of inflation.

Governments have never permitted freedom in banking. As favored wards of governments, banks have forever operated under special laws with grants of special privileges. Even in the 19th century no government extended laissez-faire principles to include banking. Consequently, forces developing from the conduct of banking can never be attributed to the free-market system itself.

The reason governments never freed banking as they did other businesses comes again from a lack of consensus among economists on the principles of money and banking. They still disagree about the complexities of money and credit, the commodity of banking. Banks deal exclusively with money and credit, and governments grant them the privilege of creating money and credit. Therein lies the heart of the matter. Other businesses use money and extend credit, but only banks can create money and credit out of thin air.

The Austrian school of economic thought, as elaborated by Murray Rothbard, Ludwig von Mises, and others, has developed an analysis of money and credit that I believe is correct. The following discussion is based on theorems elaborated in writings of that school. (See Mises [1934] 1981.) Neither bankers nor government bureaucrats who regulate banks use this information, however. To do so would require them to relinquish power and control, a step they would take very reluctantly.

Credit and Money

Credit is money. Before credit was invented, people used some commodity as a medium of exchange in all transactions other than barter. During the period when gold was universally used as money, gold and claims on gold circulated as money. Most people did not use credit. They did not trust banks, and such skepticism served them well.

To those who use credit and the banking system, credit and money are the same. Credit is a claim on something physical and tangible including commodity money. Money is a claim on the commodity in which it is defined, and that commodity exchanges freely. To businessmen there is no practical difference between bank deposits (bank notes) and deposits with any other financial institution. The difference between specific deposit accounts rests in the credit worthiness of the deposit agency.

Today, men use physical (currency) money as a convenience when making small purchases. They make most payments with checks drawn against their deposit money held by a bank. They conduct most business using credit, which they ultimately settle by transfers of deposit money in the banking system. Entries in computers are fast replacing checks. No matter; for practical purposes, electronic transfers from one bank account to another, checks drawn on banks and other financial institutions, and federal reserve notes are all money. Because they did not understand the above relationship between credit and money, when legislators in 1913 forbade banks to issue bank notes, they placed no corresponding restriction on their authority to create deposit money. Even to this day banks can and do create deposit money, and are in fact the principal agencies of the Federal Reserve System to do so. The Fed encourages or discourages inflation by increasing or decreasing bank reserves, which form the basis for bank-created deposit money.

Governors of the Federal Reserve limit the total amount of this bogus money. Consequently, government through the Fed can stop inflation of the money supply and thereby prevent harmful credit expansion. Without credit expansion based on inflation, there could be no booms needing a corrective phase called "depression." Consequently, government can eliminate the business cycle by refraining from inflation. Business activity would expand as saving increased to support a healthy growth.

The Mystery of Banking

In order to understand money and credit and the business cycle, we must know what bankers do besides hold deposits, grant loans, and pay out on checks drawn by their customers.

Under the gold standard — or any monetary system founded on a commodity, a bank's owners place at the disposal of their business a stock of that commodity — in this case gold. This stock is the bank's "reserve." Gold, either bullion or coin, forms the basis of the bank's operating capital. Gold serves admirably as the basis for money, but it serves poorly as a circulating medium. It is heavy and soft. Gold coins soon wear away when circulated, and their weight is a nuisance in daily use. Due to the high unit value of a small quantity of gold, coins cannot be minted small enough to serve as money for daily transactions. Consequently, people use subsidiary money: they print claims against gold on copper and nickel pieces and on paper. These substitutes freely exchange for gold at the office of the issuing agency. (The United States, in 1933, abandoned all commodities as a basis for money, and the federal government confiscated all gold in the hands of its citizens. The present U.S. dollar is backed not by a commodity, but by U.S. government debt: bonds, notes and bills.)

Banking has always been a privilege granted only to a few. As a favored class, banks have never been obliged to observe the commercial laws that govern businessmen, wage earners, and homemakers; that is, to pay all money contracts when due. During times of panic, governments permit banks to suspend payment in specie. Put plainly, government excuses bankers from their contract to redeem their bank notes with gold. In addition, the sovereign authority in each nation gives one group the exclusive privilege of operating a central bank — a superbank — to handle all the money and credit needs of government and the commercial banks. This central bank conducts little business with individuals; it is a bankers' bank.

Bankers learned that, for daily use, their customers preferred paper notes to gold coins. Since a large quantity of bank notes continually circulated, never returning to the bank for redemption, banks could issue and loan out bank notes (claims on gold) that exceeded the amount of gold they held. Bankers were loaning and earning interest on a fiction they created out of thin air. The interest on these loans that exceeded the gold in reserve was pure profit. Bankers next learned that, as a group, their customers never withdrew all their funds on deposit with the bank. Bankers made loans based on part of these deposits. As long as bank notes circulated in place of gold and as long as depositors as a group never withdrew all their funds, the banker could, with immunity, profit from this questionable practice.

Of course, this was deceit. But it was legal then and it is legal now. Bankers call this practice "fractional reserve" banking. The extent of this deceptive practice during the 1920s can be seen from the figures of that period.

Throughout the '20s, the Federal Reserve System required all banks to maintain reserves against deposits of less than 10 percent on average. Government bonds and federal reserve bank notes qualified as reserves in this calculation; so the measure of total bank reserves included more than just the gold in their vaults. Total federal debt of about $16.6 billion in 1929, federal reserve notes as currency of about $1 billion, and a fund of $3 billion in gold constituted maximum total reserves available to the banking system going into the depression (over $20 billion). But individuals and businesses, particularly insurance companies, held a substantial portion of this fund. As a result, behind the outstanding $72 billion in claims, banks (including the Federal Reserve system) held total reserves of perhaps $15 or so billion, substantially below an honest 100 percent of the outstanding claims.

Obviously, any bank that experienced a "run" — depositors en masse demanding payment in gold for their bank notes and deposits — would soon deplete their funds. Such runs did occur, and the subject banks did go broke. When runs became commonplace — called a "money panic," governments protected not the depositors, but the banks. By legislation, governments suspended payment in specie by all banks, thereby excusing banks from honoring their contracts. Bank notes and deposits could be redeemed by paying out bank notes issued by the central bank. In plain words, bankers could take in their own worthless paper and pay out in exchange worthless paper printed by another, albeit larger, institution.

Until the 1930s and the complete abandonment of the gold standard by all Western countries — as was witnessed in earlier chapters, such bank runs occurred, triggered by various incidents. These money panics ushered in a sudden and sometimes severe drop in business activity. The panic reduced the supply of money in the hands of banks and businessmen simply because it forced bankers to reduce their dishonest issue of bank notes and credit. For a time at least, credit became nearly nonexistent. The evil, of course, was the fractional reserve banking permitted and protected by government and encouraged by the central bank.

Every dollar of currency withdrawn from a bank reduces that bank's reserves by that amount. Each dollar of reserves in 1929 supported about $10 in credit. Consequently, each dollar in currency withdrawn from the banks caused a tenfold reduction in the supply of money and credit. Between 1929 and 1933, depositors withdrew from banks more than $5 billion in currency. This reduction of currency in the banking system could alone have caused a money-and-credit drop of nearly half the amount existing in June 1929. Small wonder that business activity lessened dramatically. Money and credit furnish the means for payment in business transactions. In order for the supply of money and credit to drop to this extent without reducing the physical volume of business and employment, unit prices and wage rates would have had to drop substantially. Yet, in 1929-1933, government and organized labor resisted a reduction in wages. Consequently, business could not profitably reduce prices.

Had free banking been permitted, no banker would have dared expose himself to bankruptcy by issuing "worthless" paper to such an extreme. Consideration for their own solvency would have sufficiently motivated bankers to limit their issue of fiat (bogus) money. Bank customers would have soon learned which bankers operated honestly. In time, only the prudent institutions would have remained. Periodic runs against careless bankers would have constantly eliminated unsound operations. The extensive practice of fractional reserve banking could exist only because of government-encouraged uniform operation of all banks under the protection of the Federal Reserve System.

Cause of the Cycle

Economists do not agree on the underlying reason for the boom-bust cycle or the measures government should adopt to prevent it. For over 50 years, governments of the free West, however, have followed the lead of John Maynard Keynes in his book *The General Theory of Employment, Interest, and Money* (1935). The Great Depression had been with the world for six years before Keynes's book appeared, but it supported the policies of the Roosevelt administration that interventionist politicians and economists alike heartily embraced. (For years before the book appeared, Keynes had been advising the American and British governments on monetary policies. His book merely formalized his earlier advice.) Keynes placed the blessing of his economic theory on government-engineered inflation. Economists supported such intervention because it required government and businessmen to hire economists to advise them on how to function under the scheme.

Inflation, as used herein, means substantial increase in the supply of money. Present-day semantics has made the word synonymous with higher prices. Higher prices are not inflation; they are but a symptom of it. Monetary inflation exerts an upward pressure on prices. During the 1920s, all Western countries pursued a policy of inflation, but most prices did not increase in those nations that remained on the gold standard. Increasing productivity exerted a downward pressure on prices that offset the upward pressure of inflation. Because of this circumstance, the symptom we call inflation — a general increase in prices — never appeared. Consequently, historians of the period conclude that the United States experienced no inflation in the '20s. They thereby rule out inflation as a contributing cause of the boom and subsequent depression.

I reject Keynesianism wherever it disagrees with the economic theory of the Austrian School. Keynes does not convince me as do Ludwig von Mises and Murray Rothbard. (Mises [1949] 1963, or Rothbard [1962] 1970) Mises' *Human Action* appeared only in German until he made an English translation available in 1949. Of course, Keynes' *The General Theory* was published in English. By the time Mises' *Human Action* appeared in English, Keynes had won over nearly all academia in the United States and England. For over five decades, both nations have fashioned their economic policies according to the principles he recommended. To this day Mises is relatively unknown in America, and few economists teach the principles he expounded.

When describing the economy of the real world, Mises and Keynes displayed remarkable agreement, as becomes apparent when their ideas are phrased in the same vocabulary. Both agreed (1) that the market rate of interest is determined by four forces: the supply and demand for credit, time preference, risk, and expectations about monetary inflation. Both agreed also (2) that interest rates influence entrepreneurial action; (3) that once a boom begins, no rate of interest seems too high to discourage speculation; (4) that entrepreneurs make their investment decisions based on rational expectations; (5) that the evil of the boom is malinvestment not overinvestment; (6) that during the boom, wage rates outrun market prices and need adjustment downward in order to reduce unemployment; (7) that the boom ends when the anticipated return from additional investment drops below the market rate of interest. Both agreed (8) that entrepreneurs continue to invest in production as long as the anticipated yield exceeds anticipated market rates of interest. They agreed (9) that uncertainty causes people to hold cash, and the degree of uncertainty determines the size of their cash holding.

They parted ways in making their conclusions because (1) they did not work toward the same goals and (2) they used different methodologies. Mises sought only the truth while Keynes sought to show how government can plan and control the economy so as to avoid the evils he found in the way individuals employ their earnings and savings. Keynes sought a means to achieve social goals as he saw them, thereby exposing himself as an autocrat. Mises believed in individual freedom because his investigations had convinced him that only under freedom can people maximize production to relieve natural scarcity. Keynes did not admit to natural scarcity. He submitted that under his direction productive resources would become so plentiful that capital would receive no rent.

Their conclusions — besides diverging because of their variant goals —
also differed considerably because Keynes employed empirical methodology while Mises used rational methodology. After arriving at what he considered correct principles, Mises analyzed and described the forces at
work in the historical data. I support Mises; as he said, since many forces
are at work in all human action:

> *History cannot teach us any general rule, principle, or law.*
> *There is no means to abstract from a historical experience* a
> posteriori *any theories or theorems concerning human conduct*
> *and policies. The data of history would be nothing but a clum-*
> *sy accumulation of disconnected occurrences, a heap of confu-*
> *sion, if they could not be clarified, arranged, and interpreted by*
> *systematic praxeological knowledge.* (Mises [1949] 1966. 41)

Keynes believed in government control of society. In his view, individuals could not be trusted to invest their savings properly. Accordingly,
government should take their savings from them and make investments for
the good of society. Even though he realized that wage rates went too high
during a boom, he believed it was unjust to lower wages directly. He recommended inflating the money supply so as to reduce real wages by reducing their purchasing power. Because he wanted to achieve certain
social goals, Keynes would not countenance any solution that left matters
in the hands of a free market. He said:

> *The method of increasing the quantity of money in terms of*
> *wage-units by decreasing the wage-unit increases proportion-*
> *ately the burden of debt; whereas the method of producing the*
> *same result by increasing the quantity of money whilst leaving*
> *the wage-unit unchanged has the opposite effect. Having regard*
> *to the excessive burden of many types of debt, it can only be an*
> *inexperienced person who would prefer the former.* (Keynes
> 1964. 268-269)
> *On the whole my preference is for the latter* [allowing wages
> to rise slowly whilst keeping prices stable] . . . *on account . . .*
> *of* [in addition to other considerations] *the social advantages of*
> *gradually diminishing the burden of debt. . . . But no essential*
> *point of principle is involved, and it would lead me beyond the*

scope of my present purpose to develop in detail the arguments
on either side. (Ibid. 271)

Keynes sought means for government to regulate the money supply in order to adjust real wages without changing the nominal wage rate, and to favor the debtor over the creditor. He never attempted to fully determine and explain cause and effect. He simply wanted to develop a case that supported government intervention and inflation as policies of monetary control.

I cannot countenance Keynes's methodology or his social goals. Certainly, since he never really sought the truth, we cannot place his work on the same level as that of Mises. Keynes never fully elaborated a set of economic principles in spite of the title he assigned to his book. The following analysis of the Great Depression is based on the principles set forth by Mises and Rothbard.

The alternating cycles of prosperity followed by a general recession are not, as interventionists preach, the necessary accompaniment of freedom in economic enterprise. The business cycle is a creation of government. Recession is the necessary period of recovery from maladjustments created in the preceding boom. *Credit expansion based on monetary inflation creates the boom.*

In any society, whether capitalist or socialist, only increased saving can create a lasting business expansion. If total saving does not increase, business stagnates. If saving drops, business activity shrinks. This is an economic law. Saving — consuming less than the amount produced — makes it possible for entrepreneurs to divert effort from food production to build tools, machines, and buildings, and to adopt innovations. Continued saving sustains economic activity at a given level. An increase in saving enables society to expand its investment in productive resources and thereby increase the productivity of human labor. This is healthy, and no cyclical ups and downs can occur without sudden, monumental changes in the rate of saving. Since total saving changes gradually, no severe cyclical variations in business activity can appear in an economy not disturbed by some external force.

In a free society, lower interest rates accompany an increase in saving. This is coincidental correlation, not cause-effect relationship. Saving and interest rates react to a common cause: the Law of the Present. Because people prefer consumption now over consumption later, they discount the future. The more they discount the future the less they save, and the greater becomes the spread between present value and value at the end of a time frame, *i.e.*, interest.

Lower interest rates make some ventures profitable that at higher rates are unprofitable or, at best, marginal. Lower interest rates tell the business world that an increase in saving has occurred, saving that enables an expansion in all business enterprises. On seeing this indication of increased savings, eager entrepreneurs embark on activity that had been on hold awaiting just such conditions. This healthy, lasting expansion creates no general malinvestment that needs to be liquidated by a subsequent recession. (For a full explanation, see Rothbard [1962] 1970 or Mises [1949] 1963.)

We must remember that saving is scattered throughout the land; it exists as deposits in banks, in savings and loan institutions, in pension funds, in money market accounts with insurance companies and investment houses; and as purchases of homes, warehouses, and privately held and publicly traded stocks and bonds; an endless list of investments that business calls capital. The total accumulated savings cannot be easily measured, even by the most sophisticated statisticians. The evidence that this cache of saving is increasing or decreasing appears as change in interest rates. Rising interest rates coincide with a drop in saving; falling interest rates with an increase. This is what occurs in a free market. The relationship between savings and interest rates can be distorted, however, by interference with the market.

Many persons lack the patience to let economic forces operate freely. Some seek change, because they envision improved conditions if only people would act as they, the visionary autocrats, would advise. These autocrats strive to influence government to stimulate business. They know that increasing business activity coincides with falling interest rates. They choose to overlook — or are ignorant of — the fact that saving, not money, creates capital and a healthy increase in business. They urge government to inflate the money supply, thereby lowering market interest rates in order to bring on prosperity.

The mechanics government uses to accomplish this goal do not concern our discussion. The relationship to understand is this: market interest rates that are lower than the rate of saving stimulate business to expand on a scale that cannot be sustained. It cannot be sustained because the needed amount of new capital (the creation of saving) does not exist to support the expansion. The artificial boom in business thus created must end, either through runaway inflation or through depression. In all past boom-bust cycles in America, bankers have raised interest rates and stopped credit expansion before runaway inflation destroyed the currency. (Inflation destroyed the Confederate dollar, but this can be considered a natural result of the South's loss in war.)

In summation, an artificial stimulus to business — through credit expansion based on monetary inflation — creates a boom. The lack of savings adequate to sustain the increased volume of production in capital goods eventually asserts itself. Denied the means to continue, many projects close down, principally in primary resources such as mining, steel and aluminum production, farming, new factories, machine tools. Employment in those industries drops, which causes a corresponding decrease in consumer spending. The artificial boom gives way to depression. Depression lasts until the maladjustments created by the boom have been liquidated. Saving must catch up with the expansion that proceeded ahead of saving during the boom. Healthy recovery begins when saving once again creates enough capital to support business expansion.

One circumstance requires emphasis. Interest rates become lower and savings increase when the masses develop greater trust in the value of their money. Savings do not increase because interest rates decline, nor do interest rates decline because savings increase. The two processes respond to a common cause. Interest rates drop and savings increase as the people discount the future less; they have greater trust in government and the stability of the economy. Uncertainty causes the opposite action on both savings and interest rates.

Government can and does create new booms by monetary inflation and by lowering interest rates, thereby encouraging renewed credit expansion. Renewing the artificial boom merely postpones the necessary liquidation of the malinvestments of the prior boom. In time, a depression occurs that government cannot stop, and the economy liquidates all the ills of the past. It takes time, and the ultimate depression becomes more severe because of the postponement. This is what occurred in the 1930s.

The Business Cycle, Credit and Money

In the first two decades of the nation, the National Bank created credit expansion. After a prolonged period of credit expansion fostered by the central bank — Hamilton's Bank of the United States, gold began to flow out of the vaults of American banks. In 1819, to prevent their own insolvency, banks curtailed credit. The president of the Bank of the United States directed all branches not to renew any loans when they came due. This sudden credit contraction, created by such a move, ended the boom that had fed on the expansion. A depression followed.

As described in an earlier chapter, during the Bank War in the 1830s, President Andrew Jackson withdrew federal funds from the central bank and spread them among Western state banks. This windfall of deposits into newly formed banks at a time when Western land was being opened for sale fed a speculation in land that surprised even Jackson. His Specie Circular brought this credit expansion to an end in 1836, which caused a virtual collapse of all credit and severely restricted business for several years.

In both these periods, government protected the banks (not the depositors) by permitting them to remain open while not honoring their obligations to redeem bank notes and deposits in gold. Encouraged by this government-fostered "heads I win, tails you lose" arrangement, banks soon launched another period of credit expansion that ended in a depression beginning in 1857. Greenbacks issued by the government to finance the Civil War fed a new period of inflation and credit expansion that ended in the panic of 1873, a panic triggered by Congress's decision to remove greenbacks from circulation. Another panic began in 1893, followed soon by another in 1901.

In 1913, the federal government entered the picture in a big way with the creation of the Federal Reserve System. Thereafter, according to politicians, the Fed would prevent banks from going under because of runs. Yet, in 1930-1933, nearly one-third of all banks failed, and many more would have failed if government had not closed all banks with the bank holiday of 1933 and virtually placed the taxing authority of the federal government behind bank deposits when the banks reopened. The Federal Reserve succeeded only in compounding the problem, making a great panic out of what might otherwise have been two or three minor ones.

An expansion of credit beyond the increase in saving brings on the unsound boom. Monetary inflation creates that credit expansion. Before 1913 and the Federal Reserve, individual banks created inflation. The government-chartered banks accepted deposits of gold from their customers. Because gold was not the best medium to circulate as money, banks printed bank notes, which were paper claims on gold presumably on deposit in the bank's vaults. These bank notes were IOUs redeemable in gold. Had bankers never printed more bank notes than the value of the gold in their vaults, no inflation would have occurred. But bankers did print bank notes exceeding the value of their gold deposits. By loaning at interest these worthless pieces of paper, banks could be quite profitable. Small wonder that many businessmen wanted to open banks. Government, however, limited the number of banks. This constituted a limited government-fostered monopoly, special-interest legislation that still continues.

If government had allowed the operation of banks by any and all who wanted to enter the business, such freedom would have ended the practice of issuing bogus bank notes. Burned by experience with bankrupt banks, neither the public nor businessmen would have accepted bank notes from any bank that did not demonstrate absolute honesty. Free banking, in this respect, would have put an end to bogus money and credit expansion that exceeded the increase in saving. There would have been no inflation. Without credit expansion based on bogus money, there would have been no major booms requiring adjustment in subsequent recessions.

Instead of government allowing such freedom in banking, the 1913 Federal Reserve Act forbade all agencies, banks and state governments as well, to print money. The Act placed private banks under tight regulation. In effect, government made banks into agencies of the treasury. The instrument for creating inflation became the sole preserve of the federal government. How poorly the scheme worked was demonstrated in the 1930s when the country experienced the most severe deflationary depression of modern times. As is customary among autocrats, those then in government would not admit their own failure. They blamed the depression on insufficient intervention and therefore launched an all-out increase in government control. Liberty and freedom for the other man is not the cherished ideal of self-appointed autocrats.

The Boom of the '20s

The inflation-financed business boom that supplied the allied armies in World War I halted in 1920 with an end to credit expansion. Government followed the policy of freedom and did not intervene in the adjustment in prices and wages. Consequently, the nation's economy quickly liquidated the malinvestments of the boom. Business recovered from the recession in 1921. The depression of 1920-1921 was one of the briefest of any recession in the United States. Those in government who wanted to intervene in the recovery process (conspicuously including Herbert Hoover) had little influence in 1921 on the monetary policies of the administration or the Fed. Keynesian economics had not then infected the minds of those who determined government policy. The truth, as had always been taught by classical economists, still prevailed. Keynes's influence would not enter the scene until the next decade. Government adopted the policy of freedom — of laissez faire, and the economy adjusted quickly.

Increased saving during the 1920s created genuine economic expansion with its attendant improvement in productive efficiency. This increased efficiency exerted a downward pressure on prices. The Fed, however, began in 1922 to offset these forces with inflationary actions that started nearly a seven-year period of credit expansion. While encouraging credit expansion in the '20s, the Federal Reserve Board used price stabilization as a guide to determine the degree of inflation. (This policy guides Fed actions even yet. It is the accepted wisdom of all political leaders. Denying the truth in economic laws, autocrats learn nothing from past experiences.)

The Federal Reserve Board of Governors believed that as long as price indices did not rise materially, the inflation would stimulate business with no harmful side effects. This proved to be incorrect. Without the intervention by the Fed, increased productivity would have lowered prices and raised the living standard for everybody. Inflation, however, assured that only those individuals who experienced higher monetary incomes could enjoy the benefits of increased productivity. Inflation denied those benefits to anyone living on a fixed income. Credit expansion based on inflation not only stimulated the malinvestment of the boom, but it disturbed the impartial free-market allocation of the benefits of an advancing economy. Government intervention always benefits some people at the expense of others, and intentionally so.

The economy experienced a slowdown in expansion from mid-1923 to mid-1924 and again in 1926-1927. Consequently, both in the second half of 1924 and in 1928, the Fed stepped up its inflationary pressures in order to stimulate business. Throughout the period — July 1921 through December 1928, the Fed inflated the money supply at an average annual rate of nearly eight percent. In order to generate the business cycle, increasing money must first flow into the hands of businessmen, and the experience of the '20s fit that requirement. Most new money of that period went into loans to the business community.

In the early years of that decade, the Federal Reserve justified its policy of inflation as a means to accelerate recovery from the 1920-1921 recession, to aid foreign countries (particularly Great Britain), and to aid the farmers. President Harding's Secretary of Commerce, Herbert Hoover, so approved of granting foreign loans in order to aid foreign purchases of American goods that he even considered bad loans beneficial — a cheap way to encourage employment.

By 1924, Benjamin Strong, Governor of the Federal Reserve Bank of New York, and Montagu Norman, head of the Bank of England, had quietly begun coordinating monetary inflation in the United States with the needs of England. Inflation of the U.S. dollar enabled the British to employ inflationary policies in order to maintain high wages without having to face the consequences.

America could not remain in economic isolation when it wanted overseas markets while at the same time closing domestic markets to foreigners by means of high tariffs. Ambition for an overseas empire had drawn America into one great worldwide war, World War I. It drew the country into domestic economic policies that proved disastrous to the people, and it would ultimately draw the nation into the most massive war of destruction the world has yet experienced, World War II.

Artificial stimulation of business sends businessmen into the market looking for additional buildings, machines, and raw materials. Business is said to be increasing its capital spending. Since these items have not been increased by new saving to the extent that new money has appeared, business must bid these resources away from other activities by offering higher prices. As a result, costs of these items increase for all industry, or at least go higher than they would go without credit expansion. The greatest upward pressure is experienced in wages for industrial workers and prices of food, farm produce, steel, copper, aluminum, and all other resources used in production.

Prices of all products, however, do not move at the same rate; some rise faster than others. Under the influence of credit expansion the variance lies in the different forces bidding for the product. Within that group of products used to develop the wholesale price index, wages and prices of land, foods, and farm products actually rose even though the index itself remained fairly steady throughout the 1920s. In the machine tool industry, wage rates rose 12 percent, lumber 19, chemicals 22, and iron and steel 25 percent. The greatest percentage price move occurred in capital goods — prices of common stocks. Quadrupled stock prices, as reflected in *The New York Times* Industrial Average, was the most conspicuous element of the boom, and the severe fall in that index in October 1929 marked the first public awareness that something was wrong with the economy.

Monetary inflation, with its attendant credit expansion, did its work. Production of durable goods, iron, and steel each increased by about 160 percent during the boom, and production of nondurable goods increased by 60 percent. Autocrats and demagogues proclaimed that government had the ability to keep business expanding through a never-ending prosperity, and the people believed them.

Federal Reserve Governor Benjamin Strong died in 1928 before he could witness the damage done by his policy of inflation and credit expansion. His successors changed this policy; they put an end to credit expansion and inflation and ended the boom. By midyear 1929, average weekly hours worked among industrial workers had decreased. Some plants furloughed a portion of their labor force, temporarily, of course; all reductions in employment are temporary at first. Reduced employment becomes more permanent through time. These early signs of a slack in business were then interpreted as seasonal or as mild adjustments caused by a lull in consumer spending.

In October 1929 the stock market collapsed. Common stocks, as measured by *The New York Times* Industrial Average, lost half their value in two and one-half months. Overnight the public became aware that the boom had halted.

The engineer Herbert Hoover held the reigns of power. Consistent with his philosophy of intervention, he marshaled all the power of government to prevent liquidation of the malinvestments of the 1920s. Had he intentionally tried to stop a healthy adjustment of all imbalances that had occurred during the boom, he could not have developed a better prescription.

Hoover's Depression

Herbert Clark Hoover made his fortune in engineering, work that carried him throughout the Western world. He returned to America during World War I to take an active part in government. He was a "forward-looking" politician; he could have been comfortable in either major party. His liberalism was so pronounced that even such democrats as New York

State's Governor Franklin Delano Roosevelt suggested him as a prospective presidential candidate in the middle 1920s.

Hoover was an autocrat. He had tried, unsuccessfully, to influence Presidents Wilson, Harding, and Coolidge to adopt a more active part in supervising the nation's economy. When the business depression appeared, Hoover, as President, did not remain idle. He believed in central government planning. He induced business leaders to cooperate with him to establish order, a planned order defined by himself. He launched an immediate assault on the depression. He called conferences of business leaders on November 18 and again on November 21. He reached all the nation's top industrial leaders and drew them into "the coordination of business and government agencies in concerted action," as Hoover phrased his general aim. He insisted that wages not be reduced, and that industry must accelerate its capital spending. In the winter of 1929-1930, big business obliged the President.

Through his Treasury Secretary, Andrew Mellon, Hoover urged the Federal Reserve to increase credit, and Hoover personally exhorted banks to lower interest rates and make loans freely. In addressing business leaders in December, he proclaimed the nation's good fortune in having the Federal Reserve system, which "would support shaky banks and make capital more abundant." Hoover misunderstood the difference between money and capital. Only saving, not monetary expansion, creates capital. This is the reality that causes malinvestment when credit expands beyond saving.

President Hoover urged all local governments to expand public works. He proposed to Congress an appropriation for increased federal building programs. (Increased public works at a time when capital has already been misallocated to areas that the consumers would not prefer, simply aggravates the problem due to a shortage of saving.) Hoover neglected no area of the nation's business activity. He launched a program of farm subsidies through price supports. As the depression worsened, he supported a moratorium on foreclosure for unpaid debt.

In an address to the American Bankers' Association in October 1930, Hoover summed up the essence of his program:

> *I determined that it was my duty . . . to call upon the business of the country for coordinated . . . action to resist the forces of disintegration. The business community, the bankers, labor, and the government have cooperated in wider spread measures of*

mitigation than have ever been attempted before. Our bankers and the reserve system have carried the country through the credit . . . storm without impairment. Our leading business concerns have sustained wages, have distributed employment, have expedited heavy construction. The Government has expanded public works, assisted in credit to agriculture, and has restricted immigration. These measures have maintained a higher degree of consumption than would otherwise have been the case. They have thus prevented a large measure of unemployment. . . . Our present experience in relief should form the basis of even more amplified plans in the future. (Rothbard [1963] 1983. 217)

Hoover, however, must not be judged too harshly. Many business leaders and economists encouraged every action he proposed. They all sought to ease suffering. The entire nation wanted to limit sacrifice among the people at the base of the economic pyramid. But those in control did not properly understand the forces confronting them. A few men, among them Ludwig von Mises, advocated action that would have enabled a speedy recovery. Throughout the '20s, Mises warned Western nations that inflation-induced credit expansion would bring depression. When depression did in fact develop, he and a few others urged governments to permit prices and wage rates to adjust, as they had done in earlier panics and depressions. They advised that the sooner government removed its interventions in business operation, the sooner business could recover. The advice of those few, however, was lost in the great volume of entreaties for government to do something. Even present-day historians extol Hoover's successor, Roosevelt, as a great leader because he "did something."

When the citizenry chooses to live under the lead of a few, they must be prepared to accept the consequences. In 1929-1940, leaders were poorly informed. They adopted counterproductive actions. Democracy in the United States, however, demonstrated its resiliency. Even in disaster, voters selected leaders who refused to take the route of complete statism, of fascism. Both Hoover and Roosevelt refused to violate the democratic process. Both men did what they believed was right to preserve capitalism — private property and free enterprise. Their failing lay in their innocence of the true forces that operate under laissez faire. Both men chose interventionism in complete ignorance of its results.

Wage rates, especially for workers in durable-goods manufacturing, had risen because of the artificial demand by entrepreneurs flush with low-interest loans. Wages needed to be reduced to a level consistent with productivity and business activity founded on the level of saving. Costs had outrun the level of prices at which the total product could be sold at a profit. This is the maladjustment created by credit expansion based on fiat money. Business expansion based on an increased flow of cheap money raises the prices of capital goods, including labor. When the prices of consumer goods rise enough to cover costs, the greater production of boom conditions shows up in unsold surplus — the condition that Lord Keynes described as insufficient consumer purchasing power. The real cause of the surplus is the misplaced investments generated by the credit expansion. The market is not producing the goods that consumers most urgently want. The market needs to lower the prices of producer goods relative to consumer goods. The faster prices (including wage rates) adjust, the sooner business volume returns and absorbs the available labor.

One of the most fundamental realities in free markets is that freely fluctuating prices balance production and consumption. Freely fluctuating prices assure to consumers all the product they want to buy, and to producers a sale for all they want to sell at that price. A price artificially supported above the free market price creates a surplus of unsold goods. A price maintained below the free market price causes a shortage of the good. A surplus can be eliminated and the high price maintained only by destroying the surplus or removing it from the market. In the case of labor, civilized people do not countenance destroying the surplus (the laborers) to maintain wages above the market-clearing level. Governments, however, use minimum wage rates, enforced school attendance for the young, restriction on child labor, limits on immigration, make-work public projects, government-compensated retirement, unemployment compensation, and other devices to reduce the labor force. These schemes try to keep laborers out of the market in order to support wages above the market-clearing level. Such activity merely takes resources from the employed in order to prevent starvation among those forced into unemployment; it lowers the standard of living for all members of society.

The free market lowers the price to a level at which the entire product can be sold. Under depression conditions, wages need to be reduced to eliminate unemployment. During the Great Depression, about one-fourth of the labor force became unemployed before industry threw in the towel and abandoned Hoover's wage-maintenance program. Industrial leaders, imbued with Hoover's call for patriotic action on wages, lowered wage rates reluctantly. But it became a matter of necessity; their choice was either to reduce wages or close the doors of industry permanently. No business can operate indefinitely while revenue fails to cover the cost of operating. Wages eventually dropped, and workers began returning to work. Industrial leaders chose to try to keep operating, employing workers at some rate rather than not at all.

As the number of unemployed workers increased, as company after company reported losses (many ending operations), as more and more banks closed their doors, as government revenue dropped, Hoover never wavered. He never doubted the correctness of his approach to the growing crisis, even in the face of counsel such as that stated in a 1931 report by Albert H. Wiggin, chairman of the board of the Chase National Bank, quoted, in part, as follows:

> *Past costs of production were forgotten* [in 1921], *and goods were sold for what the market would pay* . . . [but] *we attempted . . . to hold the line firm following the crash of 1929. Wages were not to be reduced, buying by railroads and construction by public utilities were to be increased, prices were to be maintained. . . . The policy has . . . failed. . . . It is bad policy for a government, or for an industry . . . to try to keep prices permanently above the level which the supply and demand situation justifies. . . . We must keep the markets open and prices free. It is not true that high wages make prosperity. Instead, prosperity makes high wages. When wages are kept higher than the market situation justifies, employment and the buying-power of labor fall off. . . . Our depression has been prolonged and not alleviated by delay in making necessary readjustments.* (Rothbard [1963] 1983. 221)

In June 1930, Hoover signed the Hawley-Smoot Tariff Act, which increased rates already so high as to stifle international trade. The tariff is a sales tax levied selectively on items in trade. From the inception of the Union under the Constitution until World War I, the tariff generated nearly all revenue for the federal government. With the ratification of the Sixteenth Amendment (1913), however, the income tax became the main source of federal revenue, and the tariff was transformed into an instrument of intervention.

As with any sales tax, the tariff restricts sales on the goods being taxed. The higher the rate, the greater the restriction. At some level, all trade in that product ceases. This is not conjecture, it is fact, it is logical, it is real. Not only does trade stop in that product, but the producing country generally retaliates with countertariffs, quotas, or outright denial to specific imports from the offending nation.

The Hawley-Smoot Tariff, coming as it did when all nations were experiencing a general recession in business, caused a round of retaliatory measures that nearly brought foreign trade to a halt. Exports from the United States fell from $5.5 billion in 1929 to $1.7 billion in 1932. The depression became worldwide.

The American farmer carried the heaviest burden of this "protectionism." Customarily, farm produce made up the greater portion of American exports. Before Hawley-Smoot, farmers exported from 20 percent (wheat) to 55 percent (cotton) of their product. When foreign trade dropped so drastically, American farming collapsed. Domestic farm prices dropped over 50 percent. Most indebted farmers went bankrupt. Farm mortgage foreclosures became common place. When state governments declared moratoriums on such foreclosures, the burden of bankruptcy shifted to creditors. Rural banks became insolvent, which triggered massive runs on all banks.

As emphasized repeatedly above, the problem generated by credit expansion based on bogus money arises because spending on capital goods outruns saving. In order to recover, the economy needs more savings. "Dissaving" delays recovery, in direct contradiction to Keynes's theories. To offset declining revenues, Hoover raised taxes to balance the budget. He never suggested reduced spending. This tax increase caused a reduction in saving. A tax increase while the economy is attempting to adjust for the malinvestments of a boom not only hampers saving, thereby retarding business recovery, but it also increases revenue very little.

The Revenue Act of 1932 doubled the income tax rate, the sharpest tax increase in American history. Also faced with declining revenue, the states and local governments increased their taxes. The fiscal burden of federal, state, and local governments nearly doubled during the period. These increases in government burden alone would have been difficult for a healthy economy to absorb. In 1932, it was a disaster.

Along with his request in 1932 for an increase in taxes, Hoover presented to Congress a program for more intervention: to create agencies to lend directly to banks, local governments, agricultural lending agencies, and industry (the Reconstruction Finance Corporation and the Home Loan Bank), to increase government aid to the Federal Land Banks, to set up a Public Works Administration, to weaken "destructive competition" in natural-resource use, to make direct loans to states for relief, and to "reform the bankruptcy laws" (*i.e.*, weaken protection for the creditor). (Rothbard [1963] 1983. 253)

In view of these government actions, we should realize that the Great Depression did not arise from economic freedom. The collapse of international trade due to the protectionist barriers imposed worldwide, coupled with increased taxes, literally swept the recession of 1930-1931 into an abyss of chaos. The Great Depression of the 1930s blanketed the free world for a decade.

By the end of 1932, banks were failing on a scale never experienced before or since. In that year 1,453 commercial banks closed, and the first quarter of 1933 witnessed the disappearance of nearly 4,000 more with deposits of over $3 billion.

The Fed had been trying its utmost to expand the money supply and shore up this collapse in banking. It must be understood, however, that although the Fed can absolutely prevent inflation, it can only encourage its appearance and expansion. The Fed can only invite banks to make loans, and citizens to borrow, by lowering the interest rate it charges member banks, by lowering bank reserve requirements, and by increasing bank reserves. It cannot force inflation on a reluctant people. The Fed's ability to stimulate credit by inflation when the citizens choose not to borrow or when bankers choose not to loan, is as futile as pushing rope.

When Hoover exhorted banks to increase loans and expand credit, government no longer controlled inflation. The drivers of the machinery of inflation, the people, were removing their funds from banks. They had begun a great run on all the banks, which is the same as placing the engine of inflation in reverse. This was not on purpose; they knew even less than politicians about the economic consequences of their action. The people had simply lost confidence in the system, and wanted to get their money out of the banks. New bank runs began daily. The amount of currency withdrawn from banks grew from a few hundred million to over $5 billion. Credit vanished.

By early 1933, it became obvious that government had to do something. There were two options: (1) the federal government could do as Roosevelt did — destroy the property rights of bank depositors, confiscate gold, remove the citizens' monetary rights, and put the government in control of a vast engine of inflation; or (2) the government could let the banks fail — as they no doubt would have, had the bank holiday not been declared — exposing the truly insolvent nature of their (fractional reserve) banking system.

The free-market choice would have allowed the banks to fail. The assets of the bankrupt banks would have passed into the hands of their creditors, the depositors, who would thereby have been forced to save. Rapid monetary deflation would have reduced the money supply to an honest backing of 100 percent in gold. The fractional reserve system would have disappeared, and thereafter loans and investments would have been based on people's savings. Inflation and threat of depressions would have ended, and true recovery of business could have begun.

This choice was not even considered. It would have required bankers to relinquish their favored protection by government to profit from loans based on fiction. Free banking would have introduced competition into their protected monopoly. Even suggesting such action would have been ridiculed as impractical. Instead, government pursued the "practical" course of greater inflation and thereby perpetuated the depression for nearly a decade; and people have continued to be exposed to the business cycle.

The details of that depression, well-documented in literature, show what distress unemployment and near panic caused in the financial community. However, those three-out-of-four workers who did stay employed, experienced little change in their standard of living. Even though average hourly earnings had fallen over 20 percent by March 1933, prices had dropped enough that purchasing power remained fairly steady. The depression did little harm to the employed, except for those who had large fixed payments on debt. But it devastated debtors, most businessmen, those who had their savings invested in stocks and bonds, and people who could find no work. Murray Rothbard summarizes:

> *Economic theory demonstrates that only governmental inflation*
> *can generate a boom-and-bust cycle, and that the depression*

*will be prolonged and aggravated by inflationist and other
interventionary measures. In contrast to the myth of laissez
faire, . . . government intervention generated the unsound boom
of the 1920's, and . . . Hoover's new departure aggravated the
Great Depression by massive measures of interference. The
guilt for the Great Depression must, at long last, be lifted from
the shoulders of the free market economy, and placed where it
properly belongs: at the doors of politicians, bureaucrats, and
the mass of "enlightened" economists. And in any other depression, past or future, the story will be the same.* (Rothbard [1963]
1983. 295)

For 60 years, responsibility for the 1930s depression has been laid at the
feet of President Hoover. This is a just accusation, but for all the wrong
reasons. Historians have declared that Hoover's insistence on adhering to
policies of laissez faire caused the severe depression. In truth, had Hoover
actually followed the political course dictated by laissez faire, he might
very well have been reelected in 1932 during a period of prosperity. The
economic effect of Hoover's interventionist policies aggravated the severity of the depression and delayed recovery.

The Roosevelt New Deal

When Franklin Delano Roosevelt became President on March 4, 1933,
the people were in the grip of fear bordering on panic. A planned economy
had failed to halt the deepening of the Great Depression, which had idled
half the productive resources of the free world. Roosevelt had two options.
He could return to a political economic policy of freedom, or he could
continue Hoover's interventionism. Roosevelt had a mandate from the
people; they wanted action; government should "do something." Most historians have applauded Roosevelt for his "brave" action; he certainly did
do something. He launched an assault on free markets that put Hoover to
shame. Some claim that had he tried to return government to a policy of
laissez faire, the nation would have experienced riots or even violent rebellion. Possibly Hoover could have escaped revolution in 1930 by pursuing
the hands-off policies of former years. Any guess about the consequences
if Roosevelt had done so in 1933 is speculation.

President Roosevelt not only followed the lead set by Hoover and state
Governors, he increased the degree and the extent of government inter-

vention. Taking their cue from Nevada's Governor in October 1932, the Governors of 23 states had by March 3, 1933, declared bank holidays, thereby suspending all banking. On the morning of Roosevelt's inauguration — March 4 — most of the other states followed suit. On March 6, by proclamation Roosevelt made the bank holiday nationwide and suspended all transactions in gold. On March 9, Congress confiscated all gold and authorized reopening banks that were in sound conditions. On March 12, F.D.R. went to the people with his first fireside chat. He informed them of the bank holiday and reassured them that federal bank examiners would reopen each bank as their examinations determined that the institution was sound. Within two months, 12,000 banks, holding over 90 percent of bank deposits, had resumed operations. The bank panic ended, but the depression remained.

Roosevelt sought and received from Congress the authority to organize the nation's industries under government planning. The National Industrial Recovery Act (NIRA) authorized the National Recovery Administration (NRA) to have a council of businessmen, labor leaders, and bureaucrats set wages, prices, and general rules for cooperative operation in each industry. This meant government-sponsored industry cartelization for the entire nation. The stated objectives were to raise prices, return labor to full employment, and remove surplus production from the market. This was a rather strange mix of objectives considering the state of the market. If all idle plants and labor were put into production, how could the economy do other than produce new surpluses that could not be sold at these higher prices? Harry Carman and Harold Syrett present a pertinent observation on this program:

> *The inauguration of the National Recovery Administration under General Hugh S. Johnson as Administrator was accompanied by . . . a fervid scramble for privileges among the representatives of virtually every vested-interest group in the United States. . . . but the consumer . . . was left out in the cold. . . . Instead of paving the way for recovery, these regulations often maintained the rigidity that had been one of the principal factors in prolonging the depression.*
>
> *Most businessmen quickly lost their initial enthusiasm for the N.I.R.A. . . .*
>
> *Even more serious than growing business opposition to the*

N.I.R.A. was evidence that the program was failing to achieve its objectives. (Carman and Syrett 1952. 534-535)

Congress also passed the Farm Relief and Inflation Act (the first agriculture adjustment act, AAA). This program sought to do for farmers what the NRA did for industry. Congressional acts soon provided emergency work for the unemployed: the Civilian Conservation Corps (CCC), the Public Works Act run by the Works Progress Administration (WPA), and countless other alphabet programs of lesser notoriety. The administration simultaneously tried to raise prices through gold and silver purchases, by devaluing the dollar, and attempting to renew inflation. As each act of intervention failed, government policy advisors declared that their failure was due to insufficient effort; they recommended more of the same to a greater degree. At no time during the entire decade of the 1930s did Roosevelt — like Hoover before him — doubt that his procedures were the ones government should follow. And it is small wonder, because John Maynard Keynes, in 1935, had published *The General Theory,* which put the blessing of his economic theory on the very policies Roosevelt pursued. Carman and Syrett sum up the net result of these efforts of the Roosevelt New Deal:

The failure of gold purchases to increase prices generally did not prevent the government from undertaking a similar program in silver. . . . This program, however, fell short of both the stated objectives . . . The international results of this silver policy were just the opposite of those intended. . . .

After 1934 the New Deal abandoned its attempts to promote inflation by manipulating the currency and adopted other devices to achieve the same end. In an effort to revive business activity, the Administration continued to employ the powers over bank credit granted by Congress and to increase its loans to private enterprise. While these policies provided the nation's banks with additional funds, they did not succeed in expanding bank credit. . . . In the second half of the thirties, the New Deal also attempted to force up prices through heavy government expenditures. (Carman and Syrett 1952. 528-529)

The developments of 1937-8 seem to indicate that there was a close connection between government fiscal policies and the course of the business cycle during the 1930's; but even if this point is conceded, the fact remains that the Administration was still no closer to a solution of its problem. On the one hand, it was granted by even the most ardent New Dealers that continued deficit financing would eventually produce a runaway inflation and economic chaos worse than depression. On the other hand, a reduction in government expenditures was accompanied by a descent still further into the depths of depression. (Ibid. 532)

In May 1935, the Supreme Court brought relief to the economy by declaring the NIRA and the first AAA unconstitutional. Business began to recover, but Roosevelt and Congress had other plans. To restore government support for organized labor — which was tossed out with the loss of the NIRA, Congress enacted the National Labor Relations Act, more commonly called the Wagner Act, followed soon by the Wages and Hours Act, or Fair Labor Standards Act. New Deal labor policies sought to raise wage rates and support organized labor. Carman and Syrett's observations on this point are interesting:

The New Deal's labor program may have arisen . . . from . . . humanitarian impulses . . . but it was also based on a desire to restore American prosperity and to enhance the strength of the Democratic party. . . . Democratic leaders realized that the industrialization of the United States had created a large . . . labor force that would probably vote in a bloc if it received suitable favors from the party in power. (Ibid. 543)

That the Democrats succeeded in obtaining the support of organized labor has been demonstrated in every election since 1932. Labor-union membership since then has formed the nucleus of Democratic strength among the voters.

As each interventionist scheme failed to revive the economy, the Roosevelt administration adopted stronger measures. The economy would begin to revive, adjusting to each new onslaught, only to be beaten down with a new act of intervention. Because unemployment never dropped below seven million during the entire decade, Roosevelt's advisors claimed government simply had not done enough. And when America entered World War II, bringing "full employment," these interventionists claimed this proved the validity of their methods. They claimed that government finally went far enough along the lines of inflation, make-work, and government spending to revive the nation's business.

That claim is seldom addressed adequately, and these questions remain. Why did the depression last from 1929 until the Japanese attacked Pearl Harbor on December 7, 1941? Why did World War II bring the nation from 12 years of depression back to prosperity?

The Depression Ends

The depression had begun as the unavoidable aftermath of the inflationary boom of the '20s. It started as an attempt by industry to correct for the maladjustment in prices (including wage rates) created by the artificial boom. Prices of raw materials, productive resources (tools, machines, buildings, farm produce, etc.), and labor needed to be lowered with relation to prices for consumer goods. Business expansion had outrun the increase in saving. From the very start, government under the guidance of Hoover and then Roosevelt set out to prevent the very adjustments business needed: lower prices and wages along with increased saving. Government sought to increase prices, to increase expenditures on consumption, and to increase wage rates, all directly counter to what industry needed in order to resume profitable operations. International trade urgently needed trade barriers eliminated: quotas and tariffs. Congress never repealed the 1930 Hawley-Smoot Tariff or modified its terms. For 12 years, government followed precisely the wrong policies.

Conscription for World War II removed over 10 million workers from the labor force by inducting them into the military. This eliminated unemployment, but it alone would not have restored prosperity and profits to business. Government froze prices and wages, and began radically inflating the money supply. In the four years of World War II, government debt increased from $16 billion to over $280 billion. This enforced reduction in all real prices and wage rates finally allowed business to adjust expenses and selling prices to a profitable level and to absorb the oppressive costs of the Hoover-Roosevelt Deals. The absence of consumer goods forced consumers to save, liquidating personal indebtedness.

A government policy in 1945 to reduce spending and to reduce government debt would have set the stage for a long period of prosperity without a need for renewed credit expansion based on bogus money. But fearing that business would collapse with the end of government purchases of war goods, the government continued its inflationary policies and credit expansion. Continued government deficits, with the subsidiary inflation that such action generates, ultimately leads to a crack-up boom: the complete destruction of the monetary system. This may yet appear. History has not yet recorded the end of its story.

We might ask why government could not always bring the nation out of depression in a manner comparable to the action taken to prosecute the war. Such action could succeed, but consider the cost. Because the economy will return to prosperity on its own if permitted to do so, why increase the public debt twentyfold and at the same time destroy a major portion of everything that industry can produce? The people would not countenance such waste. While the nation restores business activity on the basis of such action, the people suffer on a scale they would not tolerate in peace time. During the war, with store shelves empty of consumer goods, the standard of living dropped for everyone. Government rationed meat, sugar, gasoline, and many other consumer products. Even toilet paper was in short supply. Home appliances disappeared from the market. New cars and new tires for the old cars could not be purchased at any price. Shortage of merchandise to sell drove many retail and wholesale merchants to the wall. True, everyone had a job, but in all other respects conditions for most employers and employees were worse than during the depression. To the great majority of the population, the war period demanded a greater sacrifice (even excluding the direct effects of the war itself — loss of liberty and loss of life) than did the 12 years of depression. The people tolerated these conditions because they did not expect the war to continue many years, and they could look forward to spending their money when conditions returned to normal. As acknowledged above, depressions can be eliminated by denying freedom to the people. Under the communist regime, all Russians were employed, and most had an abundance of money. But their standard of living did not reflect conditions we could call prosperous; shoppers found little or no food or other essentials for sale in the shops.

The best government policy is to refrain from creating the artificial boom that brings on the recession. But if a recession is inevitable, a course dictated by laissez faire will minimize the suffering by the people while industry makes the necessary adjustments. To pursue policies matching those of the Roosevelt-Hoover administrations only prolongs the suffering. The laws of economics determine that it must happen again whenever society repeats the errors that brought on and prolonged the Great Depression.

As a government policy, laissez faire has been denied and ridiculed because too few people understand what it means. Because of special-interest legislation by Congress under the control of Eastern financiers and business interests during the 19th century, historians have condemned laissez faire. But special-interest privilege supported by government is interventionism, not laissez faire. Distortion of the truth by historians and the media may be honest misunderstanding, but no good can come from continuing this misunderstanding. Society will repeat its past errors until the truth becomes common knowledge.

The Legacy of Franklin Roosevelt's New Deal
As Governor of New York, on March 2, 1930, Franklin Roosevelt addressed the nation by radio on the subject of States' Rights, that division of power between the state governments and the federal government. Therein he stated:

> *Congress has been given the right to legislate on . . .* [some matters] *but this is not the case in the matter of a great number of other vital problems of government, such as the conduct of public utilities, of banks, of insurance, of business, of agriculture, of education, of social welfare and of a dozen other important features. In these, Washington must not be encouraged to interfere. . . .*
>
> *The whole success of our democracy has not been that it is a democracy wherein the will of a bare majority of the total inhabitants is imposed upon the minority, but that it has been a democracy where through a division of government into units called States the rights and interests of the minority have been respected.*
>
> *The moment a mere numerical superiority by either States or voters . . . proceeds to ignore the needs and desires of the minority, and, for their own selfish purposes or advancements, hamper or oppress that minority, or debar them in any way from equal privileges and equal rights — that moment will mark*

the failure of our constitutional system. (Quoted in Long [1957] 1971. 37-38)

Had Franklin Roosevelt really believed in the principles he stated in that speech, he could have become one of the greatest political leaders of this country. Unfortunately, he was evidently speaking as a typical, unprincipled politician. Three years later, as President, Roosevelt presented to Congress a legislative agenda that violated nearly every taboo he listed in that 1930 address.

In 1935, the Supreme Court began throwing these legislative acts out as usurping powers not granted to the federal government by the Constitution. The two major acts of legislation, the National Industrial Recovery Act and the first Agriculture Adjustment Act, were central to Roosevelt's New Deal. The Court split five to four on these decisions, the majority declaring that these acts were unconstitutional, thereby upholding the interpretation of the Constitution consistent with previous Court decisions.

Justice Owen J. Roberts, one of that majority, in 1944 made this statement supporting the doctrine of *stare decisis*:

> *The evil resulting from overruling earlier considered decisions must be evident . . .* [the result is that] *. . . the law becomes not a chart to govern conduct but a game of chance; instead of settling rights and liabilities it unsettles them. . . . But the more deplorable consequence will inevitably be that the administration of justice will fall into disrepute. Respect for tribunals must fall when the bar and the public come to understand that nothing that has been said in prior adjudication has force in a current controversy. . . . The tendency to disregard precedents in the decisions of cases like the present has become so strong in this court of late as, in my view, to shake confidence in the consistency of decision and leave the courts below on an uncharted sea of doubt and difficulty without any confidence that what was said yesterday will hold good tomorrow. (Mahnich v Southern S. S. Co. 321 U. S. 96. 112-113. 1944)*

In another case that year, Justice Roberts elaborated on this position:

> *The reason for my concern is that the instant decision,*

over-ruling that announced about nine years ago, tends to bring adjudications of this tribunal into the same class as a restricted railroad ticket, good for this day and train only. I have no assurance, in view of current decisions, that the opinion announced today may not shortly be repudiated and over-ruled by justices who deem they have new light on the subject. In the present term the court has overruled three cases. . . . It is regrettable that in an era marked by doubt and confusion, an era whose greatest need is steadfastness of thought and purpose, this court, which has been looked to as exhibiting consistency in adjudication, and a steadiness which would hold the balance even in the face of temporary ebbs and flows of opinion, should now itself become the breeder of fresh doubt and confusion in the public mind as to the stability of our institutions. (Smith v. Allwright. 321 U. S. 649. 669-670. 1944)

Roosevelt, in 1937, was not to be denied his power. He went to Congress with a request that the Supreme Court be increased in numbers, which would have permitted him to appoint to that body men who would uphold his position in spite of the limitations of the Constitution. This attempt to "pack" the Court created substantial opposition in the press, in the minds of the people, and in Congress. The ensuing uproar put a certain end to any such maneuver; Congress did not pass the measure.

Although failing in his direct approach, Roosevelt succeeded in fact. One justice who had voted with the majority — to uphold precedent and support the Constitution as interpreted by earlier decisions of the Court — changed his vote in all later cases that came before the Court. That jurist was Owen J. Roberts, the same man who later (in 1944) so clearly pointed out the evil of just such action. The switch by Justice Roberts turned the 1936 minority into a 1937 majority.

That Roosevelt could so radically alter his conception of the Constitution in four years, and that a Supreme Court justice could abandon his defense of the Constitution (contrary to his inner conviction of sound government) exemplifies the near panic state of mind among officials in Washington during that Great Depression. Consistent failure to revive business had spread confusion among the leaders of all the nations in the West.

Into this atmosphere, John Maynard Keynes of England introduced his strong support for government intervention, with radical inflation of the money supply. This required virtually absolute power in the hands of the central government. With support from Keynes, endorsed by a majority of scholars, Roosevelt became reassured of his position. Thereafter he aggressively sought more and more power for the central government. With Justice Roberts's switch in his vote, the Supreme Court abandoned the doctrine of *stare decisis* in constitutional law. Government by man replaced government by law, and Roosevelt had his way.

The argument advanced to support this usurpation of power claimed the Constitution should be a living document, flexible with changing times and changing conditions. This notion disregards entirely the section in the Constitution itself that provides a means for amending the Constitution as the people perceive a need to change. The Twenty-First Amendment took less than 12 months to become law in 1933. Had the people wanted to abandon States' Rights, this too could have been accomplished long before 1937. The destruction of the Constitution by the Supreme Court's abandonment of *stare decisis* certainly cannot be justified, even under the circumstances existing in the 1930s. Only the leaders lived in near panic; the people had begun to adjust to the real circumstances. Hamilton A. Long concludes:

> *Roosevelt did not submit his program for expansion of Federal power to the people, for approval by amendment of the Constitution, because of the virtual certainty of its defeat — as was widely realized at the time. Instead, the program was forced through the law-making process, through what proved to be a "rubber-stamp" Congress, by ruthless political pressure, under the labels of "Must" legislation and "emergency"; because, it was claimed, the amending process would be "too slow." . . .*
> *Any slowness of the people in approving a proposed amendment is only evidence of their disinclination to agree that it is sound, or needed; this slowness is only proof of their giving the proposal the requisite deliberate consideration, for which usurpation of power by public servants is not a permissible substitute.*
> (Long [1957] 1971. 91)

Because leaders can stampede the masses to accept "emergency" measures in disregard of individual liberty, the Constitution and the doctrine of *stare decisis* must be adhered to. Thomas Jefferson expressed it in his Kentucky Resolutions of 1798:

> *It would be a dangerous delusion were a confidence in the men of our choice to silence our fears for the safety of our rights: that confidence is everywhere the parent of despotism — free government is founded in jealousy, and not in confidence; it is jealousy and not confidence which prescribes limited constitutions, to bind down those whom we are obliged to trust with power: that our Constitution has accordingly fixed the limits to which, and no further, our confidence may go; . . . In questions of power, then, let no more be heard of confidence in man, but bind him down from mischief by the chains of the Constitution.* (*Ibid.* 11)

In his farewell address, President Washington had this to say about government usurping power:

> *If in the opinion of the People, the distribution . . . of the Constitutional powers be in any particular wrong, let it be corrected by an amendment in the way which the Constitution designates. . . . But let there be no change by usurpation; for though this, in one instance, may be the instrument of good, it is the customary weapon by which free governments are destroyed.*

Free men fail their heritage by not informing themselves. They remain innocent of the events within government that encroach on their freedom. At every turn of events that displease them, well-meaning but misguided citizens beseech government to take action. In the cause of "emergency," people relinquish their liberty "for the moment," which becomes permanent with the passage of time and the citizens' neglect. When the masses disavow responsibility for their actions, they encourage demagogues to usurp power. (In Chapter 16, we more thoroughly examine this erosion of liberty.)

Roosevelt's legacy to his country is the further destruction of government by law (discussed earlier in Chapter 9). To restore the Constitution and forestall the growing risk of government by man, Americans need to arm themselves with knowledge, elect individuals who are committed to rule by law, and amend the Constitution to establish procedures that will ensure continued support of such a policy in government.

An ancient adage declares, "For evil to triumph, good men need only do nothing."

Welfare programs such as the United States has instituted in the 20th century dictate that its citizens must continue to fight wars against all outsiders whom they bar from immigration and trade. The only question is when.

Chapter 15

The World at War

Armistice

ON NOVEMBER 11, 1918, Germany and the Allies agreed to suspend fighting. World War I had come to an end, but only for the moment. The Germans were getting the worst of it, and their citizens had tired of war. Fighting had settled nothing. Perhaps the Americans and the English believed that President Wilson's "war to end all wars" had come to an end; but not the French, not the Germans. The French at once built the Maginot Line between their nation and Germany. The Germans countered with their Siegfried Line. These endeavors consumed a large quantity of resources and proved to be of little value when fighting resumed in

1939. During the intervening years, changes in the art of warfare made these fixed emplacements nearly useless. Hitler's Panzer divisions in 1939 flanked the Maginot Line in a sweep through Belgium. When the Allies stormed the Siegfried Line in 1944, the Germans manned the concrete emplacements with children and old men supplied by horse-drawn wagons in the motorized era. Hitler's fighting machine had by then exhausted its means to continue modern war.

As old barriers fell in World War I, the victors created new barriers in the 1919 Treaty of Versailles. The new boundaries for Yugoslavia, Poland, Finland, Estonia, Latvia, Lithuania, and Czechoslovakia removed land from the political entities of Russia, Germany, Austria, and Hungary. That treaty transferred the Alsace-Lorraine district from Germany to France. It demilitarized the Rhineland. Later treaties limited the size of navies and armies that the defeated nations could build. Treaties changed the ownership of African, Pacific, and Asiatic colonies. The Treaty of Versailles and later treaties among world powers merely set the stage for another greater war: World War II. These treaties adopted the position that the division of the world had been settled, that political boundaries were fixed for all time.

Fighting returned with Japan's invasion of Manchuria in 1931, and ended in 1945 with the detonation of atomic bombs over two Japanese cities, Hiroshima and Nagasaki.

The concept that dictated people's actions at the end of World War I dealt more with the symptoms than with the causes of war. Freedom among all humans, with elimination of barriers between people, alone can forestall future wars. Mutual trust and tolerance of each man's individuality perpetuates peace. At the armistice that ended World War I, participants in the treaty conference could envision only the apparent reality as expressed by the French Premier Clemenceau, "to maintain peace, we must stay strong and keep our enemies weak." Even the idealist Woodrow Wilson knew that the barriers then existing in his own nation could not be eliminated, and that the United States and Australia would continue to close their land to unwanted immigrants. The alternative to eliminating barriers is military strength. Armies and navies coupled with the risk of death for many citizens represent the cost of peace in a world of restrictions and barriers. Even then, man can do no more than delay the certainty of another war.

The armistice and subsequent treaties solved none of the differences between nations and added a series of new ones. The allied powers succeeded only in humiliating the people of Germany and loading on them a financial burden in reparation payments for the destruction caused in Europe. The French insisted that the Germans pay for the costs they incurred in the fight. The German economy eventually collapsed under the burden of reparations. In the early 1920s, inflation destroyed the German currency. The scars of that long decade of war and economic chaos remained on the hearts of the German people. They had lost that round, but with renewed strength and under new leadership the people never doubted that they could win the next one. And Adolf Hitler, installed in power in 1933, furnished that leadership.

Treaties, Barriers, and Enforcement

We have summarized below the chronology of events during the first half of the 20th century that established barriers to migration and change:

1898 — The U.S. Navy at Manila harbor, under Commodore George Dewey, destroyed the Spanish fleet and seized the Philippines.

1906 — A treaty ended the Russo-Japanese war in Manchuria.

1908 — In the Root-Tahahira Treaty, the United States and Japan agreed to respect each other's territorial possessions in the Pacific and uphold the Open Door in China.

1915 — Japan presented to China 21 demands that would close trade with China to all nations except Japan. California closed its borders to immigration from Japan.

1919 — The Treaty of Versailles betrayed the German people by ignoring President Woodrow Wilson's Fourteen Points, the basis on which German leaders had agreed to an armistice the previous November. At Versailles, Japan announced her imperialistic desires with demands that German holdings in the Pacific be annexed to the Japanese Empire.

1919 — Because the Senate never approved the Versailles Treaty, by a joint declaration of Congress the United States declared World War I officially terminated.

1922 — The Five Power Naval Treaty limited the Japanese

navy to three-fifths the size of that in the United States and England.

1922 — The Nine Power Treaty again asserted formal recognition of the Open Door Policy in China.

1928 — By the Kellogg-Briand Pact of Paris, 62 nations agreed to refrain from war in international relations. Yet all 62 reserved the right to fight in defense.

1931 — With no foreign interference, Japan invaded Manchuria, in violation of both the Russo-Japanese Treaty of 1906 and the 1919 Treaty of Versailles.

1934 — The Tydings-McDuffie Act terminated the U.S. protectorate over the Philippines and erected tariff barriers and quotas between the two nations, thereby virtually withdrawing from the Filipinos their primary markets for trade.

1934 — Japan began enlarging her navy, scrapping the Naval Treaty of 1922. No nation took military action in opposition.

1935 — Italy invaded Ethiopia — without military opposition from other members of the League of Nations.

1935 — In violation of the Treaty of Versailles, Hitler established universal military training in Germany.

1936 — Also in violation of the Treaty of Versailles, Hitler's army reoccupied the demilitarized Rhineland, again with no opposition from France or England.

1936 — Francisco Franco in Spain led a revolt to overthrow the established government.

1937 — Japan launched an all-out war of conquest on China.

1937 — The Japanese air force attacked and sank the U.S. gunboat *Panay* in China waters. On demand from the American Secretary of State, the Japanese apologized.

1938 — Hitler invaded and seized Austria, with no military reaction from other members of the League of Nations.

1938 — At Munich, in meeting with Hitler and Mussolini, French and English Prime Ministers agreed to Hitler's demands that the Sudetenland of Czechoslovakia be annexed to Germany. As Britain's Prime Minister Sir

Neville Chamberlain announced to his people, "Peace in our time."

1939 — With no military opposition from other nations, Hitler seized all of Czechoslovakia, and Italy invaded Albania.

1939 — Hitler and Stalin signed a nonaggression pact.

1941 — At Japan's military occupation of French Indochina, President Roosevelt in July "froze" all Japanese assets in the United States, and embargoed shipments of gasoline, machine tools, scrap iron, and steel to Japan.

By 1939, Hitler believed that neither England nor France would fight to resist his efforts to take whatever lands he desired in Eastern Europe, and that if they did, his greatly enlarged military forces could readily prevail. On September 1, 1939, Hitler's Panzer divisions rolled across the borders of Poland, and World War II officially began. No longer could the Western world permit the sack of Europe by Hitler's German armies. France and England at Munich had made their last concession; they declared war on Germany in support of treaties guaranteeing Polish independence.

The people of the United States had witnessed all these events and enacted neutrality legislation that forbade shipments of arms and munitions to belligerents, that insisted on cash for sale of war goods sold to foreign nationals, and that prohibited Americans from traveling on ships of belligerent nations. U.S. citizens consistently declared their isolation from events outside the Americas. Like the ostrich they stuck their heads in the sand (The Law of Ignorance).

The League of Nations, created by the Treaty of Versailles, was founded on the principle of force. That treaty defined political boundaries; it forbade Germany to build a military presence; it allowed no members of the League to act independently; it granted to England and the United States a world supremacy that all sovereign nations were obliged to recognize. How could peace be maintained under such terms by any means other than force? Yet the League had no enforcement powers. As observed above, neither England, France, nor the United States used force to contest violations of that or any other treaty until the embarrassment of Hitler's arrogance and contempt for other peoples became too much for the leadership of the democracies.

The United States Builds Barriers Against the World

When the supremacy of the Republican Party became absolute with the secession of the Southern states in 1861, Congress raised tariff rates to levels that restricted trade. The nation also erected immigration barriers against all outsiders. Many of these barriers still stand. Finding and deporting immigrants that have entered this country without permission from Congress remains a major task for federal law enforcement agents. The following chronological list sets out the major actions in these areas:

1907 — President Teddy Roosevelt "negotiated" an agreement with Japan to prevent emigration by Japanese to the United States.

1909 — The Payne-Aldrich Tariff increased both the tariff rates and the number of items so taxed.

1913 — President Wilson's Underwood Tariff increased average rates to 27 percent.

1920 — Three successive laws restricted immigration by Europeans.

1921 — The "Emergency" Tariff Act again raised rates.

1921 — The "Emergency" Quota Act set a rigid quota system on all immigration.

1922 — The Fordney-McCumber Tariff Law increased average rates to 38.5 percent.

1924 — The numbers permitted to enter the country under the quotas were reduced, which further restricted immigration from all nations.

1929 — The National Origins Act made additional reductions in numbers allowed under the quota system.

1930 — By proclamation, President Hoover closed the doors of America against all peoples of all nations.

1930 — The Hawley-Smoot Tariff Act raised rates to an average of 55.3 percent. Retaliation by other countries brought international trade to a near standstill.

Through these restrictive actions, Americans guaranteed that their children would have to fight a war. In spite of the isolationist attitude of the masses, the nation could not avoid participating in the great wars that were bound to come. No nation that controls an area as potentially productive as that of the United States can close its borders to trade and immigration without forcing other nations to war. War becomes their only means of access to the resources of that land. Yet, by adopting an extensive social welfare program, the United States made these barriers mandatory. No nation is sufficiently rich that it can protect its inhabitants from the cradle to the grave and still keep its borders open to all comers. As always, the choice is freedom or war. Welfare programs such as the United States has instituted in the 20th century dictate that its citizens must continue to fight wars against all outsiders whom they bar from immigration and trade. The only question is when. When will another nation become sufficiently desperate or believe its war machine is sufficiently strong to take on the military might of the United States? By erecting the immigration and trade barriers that are necessary to a welfare state, the people of the United States have brought on themselves the need for a large defense budget. America needs a strong military force to defend these positions against the natural desires of the five billion excluded from the resources of North America. These restrictive actions will be paid for with the lives of young American citizens in future wars.

Japan did not want war with the United States in the 1930s. Japan needed colonial (imperial) expansion; but Dutch, French, German, American, and British imperialism had closed opportunities to the Japanese. The United States forced Japan into the Western world in 1853 by sending Commodore Perry, backed by an imposing navy, to negotiate trade agreements with the then-isolationist Japanese. The United States then denied to them equal participation in imperialistic conquest. Indochina, the Philippine Islands, Borneo, New Guinea, Australia, New Zealand, and India had all been grabbed (through military conquest) by Western powers. Leaders in Japan failed to understand why only these nations were privileged to imperialistic conquest. That is a fair question. Of course, the Japanese were not welcome because they could expand only by contesting a Western power. Although China was not part of any foreign empire, Theodore Roosevelt had committed the United States, and secured cooperation from the other Western powers, to preserve the Open Door (independence of China — we do not claim China as a colony, and neither may anyone else).

Western powers forced the Japanese to enter the 20th-century life of the Western world, but denied to them the freedom to participate in carving up the land masses. Westernization, with its attendant improvements in medicine and production efficiency, increased population. Japan, like Germany, had to export excess population or increase foreign trade. Facing barriers to emigration for its people, denied opportunity to expand its territory, and confronted with increasing trade restrictions, Japan's only alternative to war with the Western powers was to accept a declining living standard for its people.

Japan first tried to take China, attacking in 1894, 1905, 1931, and again in 1937. Although the West did not send armies to the aid of China in 1937, the West did ship munitions and food to the armies of Chinese Generalissimo Chiang Kai-shek through Burma. By July 1941, Japan found itself confronted by a dilemma, well-defined by Paul Kennedy, as follows:

> *With the Kwantung (Manchurian) army possessing only half the number of divisions that the Russians had placed in Mongolia and Siberia, and with large forces increasingly bogged down in China, even the more extremist army officers recognized that war against the USSR had to be avoided — at least until the international circumstances were more favorable.*
>
> *But if a northern war would expose Japan's limitations, would not a southern one also, if it ran the risk of bringing in the United States? And would the Roosevelt administration, which so strongly disapproved of the Japanese actions in China, stand idly by while Tokyo helped itself to the Dutch East Indies and Malaya, thereby escaping from American economic pressure? The "moral embargo" upon the export of aeronautical materials in June 1938, the abrogation of the American-Japanese trade treaty in the following year, and, most of all, the British-Dutch-U.S. ban on oil and iron-ore exports following the Japanese takeover of Indochina in July 1941 made it clear that "economic security" could be achieved only at the price of war with the United States. But the United States had nearly twice the population of Japan, and seventeen times the national income, produced five times as much steel, and seven times as much coal, and made eighty times as many motor vehicles each year. Its industrial potential, even in a poor year like 1938, was seven times larger than Japan's; it might in other years be nine or ten times as large. Even granted the high level of Japanese patriotic fervor and the memory of its staggering successes*

against far larger opponents in 1895 (China) and 1905 (Rus-
sia), what it was now planning bordered on the incredible —
and the absurd. Indeed, to such sober strategists as Admiral
Yamamoto, an attack upon a country as powerful as the United
States seemed folly, especially when it became clear that most
of the Japanese army would remain in China; yet not to take on
the United States after July 1941 would leave Japan exposed to
Western economic blackmail, which was also an intolerable
notion. Unable to go back, the Japanese military leaders pre-
pared to plunge forward. (Kennedy 1987. 302-303)

The events at Pearl Harbor on December 7, 1941, reflected the natural reaction of men denied access to areas of the world. Since 1898, trouble had been brewing for control of economic influence in the Pacific.

By its first efforts to expand in Asia — the Sino-Japanese War of 1894-1895, Japan secured the island of Formosa, territory on the Shantung Peninsula, and control of Korea. Japan could not stop with this limited success. In 1906, the Japanese contested Russia for the control of Manchuria, an effort they renewed by an invasion again in 1931 and enlarged to full-scale conquest in 1937. This outreach by the Japanese in 1931 began the second phase of the World at War. It tested the League of Nations. Hitler in Germany watched and learned. Benito Mussolini in Italy also watched and learned. The League of Nations had no power to intervene. The democracies and the USSR declined to take active countermeasures. They all registered official protests, but none made a move to restrain the Japanese by force.

Do not believe that the matter has now been permanently decided. No nation like Japan that is both heavily populated and short of space within its national borders will forever sit idly by and watch backward governments waste such vast territory as China and the USSR control. Japan has been building its economic strength under the military umbrella of America. In time, the industrial strength of Japan will assert itself and demand for its population land space being inefficiently exploited by other Asians. Efforts by Americans to restrict trade with Japan only hasten the day when Japan will again be forced into war to remove barriers.

The Day That Will Live in Infamy

The Japanese launched an air attack on the U.S. military base at Pearl

Harbor, Hawaii, on Sunday morning, December 7, 1941, as President Franklin Roosevelt told Congress, "a date which will live in infamy." With this action, Japan accomplished what Roosevelt had been trying to do for over a year. That attack swept the reluctant, isolationist Americans into World War II. By afternoon of that day, the entire nation felt as one, eager to take on the Axis nations. As Senator Burton K. Wheeler stated, the only thing left to do was "to lick the hell out of them." Congress declared war on Japan the next day. Italy and Germany made their declarations of war on December 11, and the U.S. Congress completed the declarations that same afternoon.

As Sam Houston had his Alamo, as President Polk had his "American blood spilled on American soil by an insurgent foreign power," as President Lincoln had his Fort Sumter, as President Wilson had his sinking of the *Lusitania* and *Sussex*, President Franklin Roosevelt had his Pearl Harbor. In those fleeting 90 minutes, Japan handed the American leadership the catalyst they probably could secure no other way.

No documents have yet appeared that establish beyond doubt that President Roosevelt or any of his high command knew ahead of time the precise time and place this attack would occur. Nonetheless, undisputed facts of record raise a serious question. As was concluded by retired Rear Admiral Robert A. Theobald, U.S. Navy:

> *Our Main Deduction is that President Roosevelt forced Japan to war by unrelenting diplomatic pressure, and enticed that country to initiate hostilities with a surprise attack by holding the Pacific fleet in Hawaiian waters as an invitation to that attack.* (Theobald 1954. 192)
>
> *The recurrent fact of the true Pearl Harbor story has been the repeated withholding of information from Admiral Kimmel and General Short* [the military commanders at Pearl Harbor]. (*Ibid.* 198)

Roosevelt had made no secret of his conviction that the United States should be active in World War II. In March 1941 he sought and received from Congress authority to lend-lease airplanes, ships, and military supplies to England. When Hitler's Nazis attacked the Soviet Union, Roosevelt extended this same aid to the Russians. In July 1941 Roosevelt ordered the Navy to convoy merchant ships carrying military supplies to the Allies across the Atlantic. In November he authorized merchant ships to arm themselves for their own protection against German attack. All these actions violated the neutrality claimed by the United States.

Remembering their experience in World War I, the German high command did not take the bait. They recalled how the sinking of the passenger liners *Sussex* and *Lusitania* had brought American doughboys into the trenches of France in 1918, a move that proved decisively adverse to the German military effort. Germany responded in 1941 with increased U-boat attacks on military targets but none on passenger liners. Consequently, Roosevelt must have realized that his only hope to arouse the American people to war would have to come from Japan. Since Japan had signed the Tripartite agreement with Germany and Italy, any war gesture by Japan against the United States would involve Germany and Italy as well.

In the Pacific, Roosevelt exerted continuous pressure on Japan. The United States supplied the Chinese with financial and material aid in its struggle with the Japanese invasion. In May 1941 Roosevelt stopped shipment of all supplies to Japan from the Philippines. In July he ordered all Japanese assets in the United States frozen and ordered an embargo on shipments to Japan of gasoline, scrap iron, steel, and other critical war matériel. On November 26, 1941, Roosevelt's Secretary of State Cordell Hull virtually terminated the Washington conference with Japanese envoys by submitting to them demands that no Japanese leader could honorably accept.

Roosevelt's embargo and seizure of Japanese assets constituted sufficient provocation. These actions confronted the Japanese with a choice. Either they succumb to United States pressure and agree to all the demands made by the Americans, or they initiate military action against the United States. Since the United States had broken the Japanese diplomatic code, Roosevelt and his chief military officers General George C. Marshall and Admiral Harold R. Stark knew by the first of November 1941 that the Japanese had decided on war.

Throughout November and the first week in December 1941, Japan had special envoys in Washington trying to get the United States to reverse its stance. There can be no doubt that Roosevelt and his high command knew that the United States would not alter its position, and that the Japanese would not capitulate to American demands. By November 26 they all knew that war was imminent, a matter of days.

Considering the circumstances, it seems inconceivable that such a large portion of the Pacific fleet would be bottled up in one harbor at Honolulu. With actual warfare approaching so rapidly, proper precautions would have kept the fleet alert, perhaps at sea and dispersed to some degree. Equally questionable was Roosevelt's withholding of critical information from Army and Navy commanders in Hawaii.

There can be only two possible explanations for such conduct. Either Roosevelt and his high command were flagrantly derelict in their duty, or they purposefully enticed Japan to attack so as to arouse the American public in support of war.

Military leaders must constantly make decisions that they know will cause death to some of the exposed personnel. It would be no obstacle to them to issue an order to concentrate the fleet in Pearl Harbor, knowing that such an order meant death to some of the civilians and soldiers there. That is merely a circumstance of war. As Commander-in-Chief, President Roosevelt could just as readily concur in such a decision. After examining all available evidence, George Morgenstern concludes:

> *No amount of excuses will palliate the conduct of President Roosevelt and his advisers. The offense of which they stand convicted is not failure to discharge their responsibilities, but calculated refusal to do so.*
>
> *They failed — with calculation — to keep the United States out of war and to avoid a clash with Japan. They reckoned with cold detachment the risk of manipulating a delegated enemy into firing the first shot, and they forced 3,000 unsuspecting men at Pearl Harbor to accept that risk. The "warnings" they sent to Hawaii failed — and were so phrased and so handled as to insure failure.*
>
> *Pearl Harbor provided the American war party with the means of escaping dependence on a hesitant Congress in taking a reluctant people into war. Then the very scale of the disaster gave Roosevelt and his advisers the opportunity to distract attention from the policy which had produced the disaster. By cleverly leading the people to regard December 7 as a purely military calamity and by inciting the public to fix the blame for it upon the field commanders, Roosevelt and his administration hoped that the policy of which Pearl Harbor was the*

inevitable product would never be questioned. (Morgenstern 1947. 329)

Winston Churchill, the British Prime Minister throughout that war, evaluated that "calculated refusal" somewhat differently:

The President and his entrusted friends had long realised the grave risks of United States neutrality in the war against Hitler . . . and had writhed under the restraints of a Congress whose House of Representatives had a few months before passed by only a single vote the necessary renewal of compulsory military service, without which their Army would have been almost disbanded in the midst of the world convulsion. Roosevelt, Hull, Stimson, Knox, General Marshall, Admiral Stark, and, as a link between them all, Harry Hopkins, had but one mind. Future generations of Americans and free men in every land will thank God for their vision. (Churchill 1950. 602)

On that day "which will live in infamy," the U.S. military experienced 4,575 casualties of which 3,303 died. When compared to the losses in each battle of the War Between the States, in the first days of the invasion of Europe in 1944, in the Battle of the Bulge in December 1944, and in the battles to take Iwo Jima and Okinawa, this number becomes relatively small. Damage to the fleet included loss of five battleships (two of which were old and obsolete), a minelayer, and three destroyers; damaged but salvageable were three battleships, three destroyers, and a repair ship. Conspicuously, Washington had ordered the only two aircraft carriers in the Pacific fleet to other arenas. As history has shown, the price paid in loss of lives, airplanes, and ships proved to be small in comparison with the accomplishments of this engagement. Perhaps the military high command misjudged the capability of the fleet to defend itself at Pearl Harbor and losses exceeded their prebattle estimates. But no commander can know ahead of time precisely the extent of losses such action will cause. He must appraise the potential gain and send into the action such a force as he believes the situation warrants.

If one truly believes that the United States belonged in World War II, the affair at Pearl Harbor on that December day, tragic as it was to the participants, takes on a different meaning. That action at one instant solidified public opinion behind American participation in war. Within weeks, American industry began producing ships, guns, ammunition, military aircraft, tanks, and trucks; and military bases began training hundreds of thousands of civilians to become the sailors and soldiers who would use these instruments of modern war. As a military action, Pearl Harbor can be seen as a masterful stroke of leadership well executed or a momentous stroke of luck. It is difficult to imagine any other means by which the might of the U.S. democracy could have been as effectively organized in support of the Allies in that war. But, does the end ever justify the means? Do the American people really grant to their president that much power — willingly?

Aftereffects

World War II could not have been avoided because of the mind-set of the leadership in the major world powers. Elected officials in the democracies of the Western world and dictatorial rulers — Franco in Spain, Mussolini in Italy, Hirohito in Japan, Stalin in Russia, and Hitler in Germany — as well as public opinion generated by the news media, pursued goals that could only lead to another war. In spite of their lip service to freedom, all influential leaders acted to reduce individual liberty. A new creed had captured the minds of men, the creed of freedom from responsibility. The Laws of Fear and Ignorance dominated their thoughts. The horrors of World War I, coupled with the insecurity generated by the Great Depression, conditioned the public mind for demagogues; and the world is never short of autocrats. Every moment in history has had demagogues in the wings eager and ready to assume the reins of power. The United States had Franklin Delano Roosevelt, who even renounced his ideology in order to ride into power on the tidal wave of mass hysteria that called for autocratic leadership.

In Germany, Adolf Hitler gave the people what they wanted — his guarantee that they need fear no more. He declared that if they would give him authority and power, he would lead all Germans into fulfilling the Third Reich. Roosevelt told the masses that all they had to fear was fear itself, and he launched a program to free every American from responsibility — freedom from want, freedom from fear. From that day forward Big Brother (government) would take charge. No longer would people need to watch out for their own needs. Government would guarantee cradle-to-grave security — the great social chimera of all ages, the pot at the end of the rainbow, the perennial song of the siren.

As a consequence, Americans now have:

Social security to assure funded retirement for all the elderly.

Medicaid to provide medical treatment for all the poor and Medicare for the elderly.

Government guarantee that no one will lose from depositing money in banks or savings and loans (FDIC) or in pension funds either public or private (PBGC).

FHA (Farmers Home Administration) to grant low-interest loans to everyone who wants to own his home.

Environment Protection Agency (EPA) to guarantee clean water and pure air and no change in the ozone or in the oxygen content of the atmosphere.

Department of Energy to guarantee that Americans will never run short of energy — no more brownouts from shortage of electricity, no more shortages of gasoline, coal, oil, or natural gas.

Department of Education to guarantee to all young Americans a proper education.

Food and Drug Administration to guarantee to all Americans that no food or medication will be sold that has not first been proven safe and effective.

Subsidies to tobacco growers and to dairymen and to producers of wheat and corn and milo and hay, and protection from competition for peanut farmers and sugar producers and automobile manufacturers and steel mills, and on and on.

It is really pointless to go on. All the earth's resources are limited, and the United States is not excepted. Although man might want conditions to be otherwise, scarcity is a condition of life. The only two real problems involved are (1) how man will divide among the many the limited product of his efforts and (2) how he can relieve scarcity for the greatest good for the greatest number.

Man has two ways to address the first of these: (1) He can select from among his numbers one person or a group of persons to determine how much will go to each and to identify the particular individuals who qualify.

This is cooperation through command and obedience — hegemony. Or, (2) He can set forth fundamental rules designed to maximize freedom of conduct for each to produce for himself. This is cooperation by contract — freedom, not freedom from want, not freedom from responsibility, but freedom from the dictates of others, freedom to choose and work and play as the individual prefers.

Choosing hegemony assumes that the form of government exerts no influence on the quantity of goods available for distribution. The experience of the colonists at Jamestown in 1709 demonstrated how foolish such an assumption can be. The assumption of plenty under hegemony has been proven false in countless cases. Examine the 20th-century record of performance in the USSR; examine the experience of Communist China in comparison to that of free China on Taiwan; examine the record of communist East Germany in contrast to that of free West Germany; examine the experience of Western civilization during the last 500 years in comparison to the achievements of the rest of the world; examine the free North in the United States in contrast to the autocratic South before the War Between the States.

Hegemony also assumes the perfection of the individuals chosen to make the decisions. History has demonstrated that the Law of Immorality influences the conduct of those given power. People call this "corruption in public office." It is a dream to believe that when society installs someone in public office he will remain above all influence of prejudice, selfishness, and temptation. Yet Big Brother government can function with benefit to all only if occupants in public office are godlike in character. Ludwig von Mises remarks on this probability:

> *Unfortunately the office-holders and their staffs are not angelic. They learn very soon that their decisions mean for businessmen either considerable losses or — sometimes — considerable gains. Certainly there are also bureaucrats who do not take bribes; but there are others who are anxious to take advantage of any "safe" opportunity of "sharing" with those whom their decisions favor.*
>
> *In many fields of the administration of interventionist measures, favoritism simply cannot be avoided. . . . There is no neutral or objective yardstick available to make the decision free from bias and favoritism.* (Mises [1949] 1963. 735)

Human beings will always be susceptible to the declarations of demagogues. The siren song of freedom from fear, freedom from want — the balm to soothe the anxieties of people who recoil from the Law of Responsibility — will always appeal to the masses who do not realize that responsibility goes hand in hand with freedom from dictation. Unfortunately, the physical law of scarcity cannot be repealed by human law. Scarcity can be relieved only by human labor; and people working in cooperation under a political system of private property, division of labor, and freedom have consistently produced the greatest good for the greatest number. Because of human nature, division of labor assures maximum production to relieve natural scarcity.

When people erect barriers to change — to migration and trade — those restricted by the barriers try to circumvent them. Within a nation, they employ the power of government — special-interest legislation. When sovereign national boundaries interfere, the restricted group resorts to war.

This is not to say that man goes to war to gain relief from rules essential for cooperation. These restrictions — rules of just conduct — are the boundaries necessary for restraining recalcitrant individuals from asocial conduct.

Two Little Wars, Korea and Vietnam

As an unelected President, Harry Truman made the decision to drop atomic bombs on two Japanese cities, thus ending World War II. His contemporaries acclaimed him a hero for this decision. Certainly the military personnel of the Pacific fleet in 1945 rejoiced to be reprieved from the costly task of defeating Japanese forces in their homeland.

Abandoned by his own political party, Harry Truman conducted his own campaign and defeated Thomas Dewey in the presidential election of 1948. Inaugurated in 1949 as a President in his own elected right, Truman had every right to a big ego. He could be independent of the Republicans and the lesser leaders of his own Democratic Party. Truman had the people's support, and their support increased his strength in office.

When North Korea invaded South Korea in 1950, Harry Truman, as the elected leader of the greatest world power, felt no hesitancy. He confidently puffed out his chest and ordered General Douglas MacArthur to move U.S. military forces into Korea to "show them who's boss." President Truman then announced to his people and to all the world that the United States would enforce peace worldwide, even if American conscripted soldiers had to die to do so. He never sought a declaration of war from his own Congress. The resolution adopted by the security council of the United Nations (at Truman's instigation?) justified the move, according to Harry Truman. Truman made the decision. Truman acted. In deciding to send American youth to their death to enforce peace, Truman accepted the division of the world as it stood. He decided that change was not desirable nor to be allowed.

Either in innocence of, or in disregard for, military history or with a too greatly inflated ego, Truman undertook a military action destined to lose through stalemate. The lessons of the 620,000 lives sacrificed in the War Between the States escaped his ken. All admonitions by earlier Presidents, admirals, and army generals — to avoid war on Asian soil if at all possible — went unheeded. And American youth, in the slavery of conscription, went to Asia to die fighting a war that carried little significance to the interests of American citizens. MacArthur believed Truman's directive — to contain the North Koreans — was a hopeless waste of lives and munitions. He proposed either to fight the war to win, which required destruction of the opposing force, or to abandon the fight entirely. Truman ordered a limited defensive war, as Jefferson Davis had done in the 1860s. Truman found it necessary to relieve his commanding General Douglas MacArthur when MacArthur went over his President's head to take his case to the people.

In the end, incoming President Dwight David Eisenhower found a means to withdraw from all military fighting in Korea. He determined that pursuing that war to final victory did not warrant the cost in resources and lives. Eisenhower accepted a permanent stalemate.

In the 1960s, another President, John Fitzgerald Kennedy, ignored the failure of the French military in Vietnam, ignored the lesson of the American Civil War about defensive strategy, ignored Truman's debacle in Korea, and ignored the admonitions against war on Asian soil. Kennedy ordered American men into Vietnam to pursue limited war. Lyndon Baines Johnson, on assuming command at Kennedy's assassination, continued the losing strategy of his predecessor. L.B.J., as candidate, tagged Barry Goldwater, his presidential opponent in 1964, with the "war label"; and the people overwhelmingly supported Johnson. The people did not want military involvement in Vietnam. But L.B.J. as President sent more and more American soldiers for slaughter on the battlefields of a hopeless, defensive, limited war.

How many lives must America sacrifice to hopeless defeat before leaders learn the great military lesson of the War Between the States? How many more lives must be sacrificed before American citizens quit using conscript labor to wage war that has no significance to liberty in the United States? Admittedly, conscription for service in combat is compatible with liberty when liberty is really threatened. The questions, however, are these: How many of the 5.5 billion lives on this earth can the 250 million Americans protect against invasion of their civil liberties? Do the citizens of the United States believe there is no limit to their nation's resources? Can the United States afford to police the peace of the entire world? Are American Presidents within their authority to employ slave labor to enforce peace in Asia, South and Central America, Africa, and Europe?

The importance of studying these two little wars lies in searching for answers to these questions. A free people can remain free only through knowledgeable exercise of the vote. Certainly the events of these two wars in the last half of the 20th century demonstrate further advance of the assault on liberty in America.

Causes of War

The fundamental causes of war are the economic, cultural, political, and religious differences that generate intolerance and restrictions on human freedom. People resort to violence to gain relief from inordinate restrictions imposed forcibly on the free actions of individuals, restrictions that exceed the rules needed for cooperative conduct. Rules of just conduct define the limits within which free men can act without interfering with the freedom of others. There could be no society without some limitations on independent action. Thinking people accept these rules and the forms of government which make sure that recalcitrant individuals obey them. The restrictions people fight about are those barriers that intentionally favor some people to the disadvantage of others.

Scarcity of land and means of survival causes biological competition among all forms of life. By use of reason man rose above this competition and produced a greater supply through cooperation. Man uses government to replace individual brute strength with law and cooperation. Nevertheless, primitive groups and nations still engage in violence to obtain exclusive right to more and more territory for hunting, fishing, gathering, and farming. Civilized man has simply expanded the boundaries of this exclusive territory. As to causes for violent action, there remains little difference between primitive and civilized groups. Peoples differ in language, religious practices, political philosophy, and many customs that affect everyday life. Because of these differences, they define their territories with political boundaries. Because each nationality establishes its own laws and institutions, differences between nations are more common than similarities. When necessary, nations fight to preserve the differences and the boundaries. When violence brought on by these struggles involves more than an occasional incident, history labels it "war."

Primitive men fought to gain exclusive use of land, to take slaves, and to relieve boredom. When times of peace prevailed for any prolonged interval, the primitives planned annual war games to relieve their boredom. These contests, which seldom lasted more than a day or so, enabled young bucks to demonstrate their bravery and their ability in the art of combat. Most of these affairs carried no real danger to the participants. Counting coup, by which individual warriors gained recognition, constituted no more than touching the opponent without being struck or touched in return. In some of these games, however, the threat to participants was rather more serious. Captives became meat for the feast that always followed. After the feast, each tribe retired to its village until boredom dictated that they arrange another day of war games. By success in hunting and war games, young males gained the acclaim demanded by the Law of Recognition.

White colonists came to America to acquire land where they could live free from political and religious oppression. They took the land from the inhabitants, an action common among primitives for thousands of years. Primitive tribes shuffled control over areas as the relative strength of the tribes varied. Had the Indians raised no barriers to this action, there would have been no serious wars between them and the immigrants from Europe. The natives seriously objected when they finally realized that the white man would in time take all the land. Only then did they employ their skills at war in wholesale slaughter. The contest between natives and whites had become a matter of survival. It was war for the exclusive control over basic needs of existence — for the use of nature's resources, land and water. The barriers of cultural differences forced the Indian to total war.

Wars between political entities are begun by leaders ambitious to gain the wealth, position, and power that free men do not willingly give them. The Law of Greed drives them to extremes, and they use the Law of Fear to marshal support by the people. In the fourth century B.C., Alexander the Great sought to conquer and rule the Western world, and he nearly succeeded. At the beginning of the Christian era, the Caesars of Rome sought wealth that came with plunder and taxation on more men over larger areas of land. The Vikings of the north country raided and plundered the Atlantic coastal regions of Europe after the decline of Rome. Philip II of Spain used riches from the New World to finance his military efforts to expand his Habsburg Empire. In the early 1800s Napoleon dreamed of being Emperor over all of Europe. By the 19th century, successful overseas conquest enabled Englishmen to boast that the sun never set on the British Empire.

These aggressive wars held little gain for the warriors. They received only wages for their part. The plunder and recognition benefited the ambitious leaders. Such leaders formed their armies from slaves and mercenaries. Free men do not willingly place life at risk for the benefit of other persons' ambitions. Of course, the armies of the countries being overrun included free men. Young and old fought for their homes, and in some cases for their lives and the lives of their families. Although free men seldom begin a war, history has shown exceptions — when leaders have been able to mislead their people into supporting a war of aggression. Such was the case in 1846 when American armies at President Polk's orders invaded Mexico to force the sale of the Southwest region. Lincoln began military action against the seceding states in 1861 with an army of volunteers. Theodore Roosevelt and William Randolph Hearst whipped up enthusiasm for the little war with Spain in 1898. Nonetheless, when wars begun by free men have dragged on through years, the people have deserted the cause. This then forced the leaders to employ "slaves" to conclude the action — what other name can we call a man forced into combat under the laws of conscription after the people have deserted the fight?

War has been the instrument of empire building, and through rebellion has often caused the breakup of those same empires. In all cases, however, mass support for war could be aroused only through fear of restrictions imposed on one group by a stronger one. Without fear of barriers to freedom, men do not continue war long enough to cause a serious threat to man or the wealth of nations.

Wars within one political entity begin when ambitious men seek to oust those in power. These leaders enroll the support of the masses through fear that the ones in power will impose some harsh treatment on them.

Eighteenth-century colonists in America supported the War of Independence because they feared losing their freedom. In 1836, Sam Houston led the Texans to independence from Mexico by confronting the masses with General Santa Anna's massacre of prisoners taken near San Antonio. In 1860, William Yancey and his cronies obtained general support for the Southern cause through fear that the North would free the Negroes. In all these affairs a good case can be made that the feared danger was more fiction than reality, and many citizens at that time disagreed with their leaders on that very matter.

Within a society that limits individual freedom and controls the action of its citizens in all areas of their lives, no avenue for releasing tension and friction remains. The central authority regulates all the activities of its citizens, leaving little autonomy to the individual. The natural resentments, unrest, and aggressiveness that such regulation creates must be focused upon some external enemy, toward some outside threat, in order to prevent internal revolt. As a consequence, authoritarian government creates ideological friction between the various sovereign nations. The autocratic group most often becomes an aggressor.

In a society that allows local autonomy and individual freedom, the members can express their resentments and work off their frustrations within their organization without violent action. Change through peaceful means remains open to those in disagreement with the order of things. If it were not for strong, aggressive leadership, no war of consequence would develop among free people.

It becomes apparent that internal rebellion and wars between autonomous entities develop from the frustrations and friction brought on by governmental barriers to change — barriers to the free movement of person, ideas, and capital. Intolerance creates barriers — laws limiting migration and trade, laws setting tariffs, laws mandating a particular religion or a particular language, laws protecting some established interest group, laws seeking to prevent change, laws banning free expression and exchange of ideas. These laws create future wars. When laws secure life and liberty, and when man and his property can freely move about the world, political boundaries lose their significance. Man has no reason to resort to violent action.

We must understand that, beyond the rules of just conduct necessary for cooperation, every act to restrict human conduct supports the cause of future violence. Those who support restrictions on immigration must be prepared to go to war to enforce them. Those who vote for tariffs and trade restrictions increase the probability that their children will have to fight because of that vote. Ignorance and intolerance erect the barriers that require war to destroy. The Law of Greed generates intolerance among leaders. Leadership exploits the Law of Fear to bring the masses to a mental state prepared for war. War is the product of leadership in an atmosphere of barriers to freedom. War will continue as long as barriers to freedom remain.

Liberalism and National Imperialism

Near universal acceptance of the philosophy of 18th-century liberalism subdued the cause of war among Western nations in the 19th century. "Liberalism" here means what it did before the 20th-century semantic revolution in America; it is a political philosophy based on belief in the autonomy of the individual: his freedom from arbitrary authority in all spheres of life, and government under law by consent of the governed. By the same token, national imperialism, embraced by leaders at the end of the 19th century, built new barriers that brought on the great wars of the 20th century.

Eighteenth-century liberalism developed from the realization that an economic order based on the private ownership of the means of production eliminates opposition between the interests of all the people. That is so because each person's pursuit of rightly understood self-interest enables him to attain the greatest possible degree of whatever he most values.

In his essays (*ca.* 1690), John Locke perhaps first published in English the political philosophy that expresses this principle. He was supported by Adam Smith in his *Wealth of Nations* (1776). Locke and Smith influenced the statesmen who wrote the American Constitution at Philadelphia in 1787. Locke's influence is particularly evident in the passages that recognize the sovereignty of the people, dignity of the individual, separation of executive and legislative functions, freedom of speech, thought, and religion, right to private property, and rule by law. In his treatise on government, Locke defined freedom for man under government as having a fixed, well-defined rule to live by, not "subject to the inconstant, uncertain, unknown arbitrary will of another man."

Liberals advocated free trade between nations, free movement of people and capital within and beyond political boundaries, removal of government interference with industry and commerce. Liberalism supported belief in freedom. "Government governs best that governs least." Liberal society recognized the dignity of the individual, that all political power rests with the people. Man creates government to serve his common needs: to protect private property by cooperation under law rather than by brute strength, to restrain recalcitrants, and to assure maximum freedom consistent with cooperation. Under liberalism the citizens are the government. The general welfare — the greatest good for the greatest number — has no identity separate from the welfare of each citizen.

National imperialism gives government an existence separate from the people. General welfare becomes government welfare. The citizen serves the nation. Imperialism is the philosophy of autocrats, the very political system that liberalism sought to replace. Ludwig von Mises makes this distinction:

> *The idea of liberalism starts with the freedom of the individual; it rejects all rule of some persons over others; it knows no master peoples and no subject peoples, just as within the nation itself it distinguishes between no masters and no serfs. For fully developed imperialism, the individual no longer has value. He is valuable to it only as a member of the whole, as a soldier of an army. For the liberal, the number of fellow members of his nationality is no unduly important matter. It is otherwise for imperialism. It strives for the numerical greatness of the nation. To make conquests and hold them, one must have the upper hand militarily, and military importance always depends on the number of combatants at one's disposal. Attaining and maintaining a large population thus becomes a special goal of policy.* (Mises 1983. 78-79)

Liberalism ignores boundaries, removes restrictions, promotes freedom. Imperialism erects barriers along the boundaries of the nation. International friction develops from policies of imperialism. Liberalism promotes peace.

The 18th-century liberalism embraced in the United States and Europe accounted for the long period of peace in the Western world during the 19th century. Mass war returned to Western civilization when political institutions rejected the teachings of the 18th-century liberals and adopted national imperialism in its place. Perhaps not alone among the nations, the

United States under Theodore Roosevelt, Herbert Hoover, and Franklin Roosevelt certainly participated broadly in this movement toward national imperialism. Immigration laws, by 1930, had completely shut the doors of America to all outsiders; tariff rates had risen to a point that nearly eliminated international trade; governments had established restrictions on the freedom of the individual. Conditions created by such action in America and Europe became the fertile ground for international war. From one war to the next only the specifics varied.

Harmony of the Rightly Understood Interests

Recognizing the harmony of interests among men generates the politics of freedom. Liberals succeeded in educating only a few to the correct understanding of this doctrine. Imperialism, the doctrine of brute selfishness, operates in direct opposition to the general interest of all. Allan Bloom says it well:

> *Self-interest is hostile to the common good, but enlightened self-interest is not. And this is the best key to the meaning of enlightenment. . . .*
>
> *Americans are Lockeans: recognizing that work is necessary (no longing for a nonexistent Eden), and will produce well-being; following their natural inclinations moderately, not because they possess the virtue of moderation but because their passions are balanced and they recognize the reasonableness of that; respecting the rights of others so that theirs will be respected; obeying the law because they made it in their own interest.* (Bloom 1987. 167)

Even when an individual makes a gift to another, he acts from self-interest. The giver derives pleasure in seeing the other in possession of the gift. During his lifetime Andrew Carnegie, one of the wealthiest men in the nation, gave away nearly all his riches. This was philanthropic, but he acted from self-interest. He wanted to see his wealth put to that particular use. Philanthropy in this instance satisfied his selfish desires. The person who refrains from killing his most ardent enemy acts from self-interest. Perhaps he prefers to retain a clear conscience by not submitting to murderous emotions. Perhaps he views the risk of detection and punishment too great a price to pay for the desire to harm one of his fellows. Perhaps he is motivated by a desire to obey what he believes is the will of God. No matter what his thoughts, he behaved from consideration for his own self-interest as he understood it.

Nature does not generate plenty as in a Garden of Eden. The natural state of life is conflict. Each individual competes with all other members of its species. The means of subsistence are scarce, and life is not guaranteed for all. Only the strong will live. The conflicts never end. The source of the conflict lies in the reality that in nature each individual's portion reduces what is available to others. This biological competition can be viewed daily in the wild. Primitive man lives under conditions of biological competition.

The harmony of all men's rightly understood self-interest asserts itself because civilized man realizes that cooperation under the division of labor greatly enlarges the total supply. The greater production achieved through specialization provides the lowliest individual a greater bounty than he can have under biological competition. When man learned that competition between groups to produce more and better goods led to an increased supply of all goods, a common interest appeared to all humans. Competition to outdo one another in production to satisfy the consumer replaced biological competition. This realization makes for harmony among mankind as a whole. Because every person essentially desires the same things — bread, shoes, clothes, houses, the economies of large-scale production bring these items to him at lower cost. The desire for bread by one person does not lessen the availability of bread for others. Bread costs something because nature does not provide an unlimited supply of wheat, but the mass demand for bread does not increase the cost to the individual; on the contrary, it makes it cheaper.

To achieve the benefits of the division of labor, people must cooperate freely under the direction of consumers. This is cooperation in a free-market economy. No other system of social organization can gain for everyone the benefits equal to that available through voluntary cooperation. Under the market economy each individual determines his actions out of rightly understood self-interest, and his conduct produces a greater harvest for himself and his fellowman as well.(For an in-depth discussion of this doctrine, see Mises (1949) 1963, 673.) Brute selfishness is different from the self-interest referred to in this work. Brute selfishness ignores knowledge; it is primitive reaction to biological competition.

Barriers and restrictions that generate violence are created by men acting in innocence of reality or in defiance of the consequences. Envy of another man's riches has caused much mischief in this manner. Action prompted by this envy overlooks the fact that the circumstances that made such accumulation of wealth possible are the same circumstances that furnish the individual himself with a greater supply of this world's goods. Laws that erect barriers to individual wealth operate to the detriment of all, poor and rich alike. They help prepare the stage for wars.

World Peace

In *A Study of History,* Arnold Toynbee declares that in all prior civilizations the universal state (peace) has arrived only after one power has conquered all competing powers. Peace arrives by virtue of one force ruling all peoples. This may have been the case through time; but in all prior experiences, civilization itself disappeared and war returned.

Rule by force can never prevail over time. If there is no outside force to contest the rulers, then internal (civil) war will erupt. In a struggle against insurrection, the latest technology — one that may be effective against threat from without — may be useless. Rulers cannot use the A-bomb to subdue rioters; it is overkill and destroys the peaceful natives along with the insurgents. Yet constant internal fighting destroys cooperation and society itself.

The only unifying force that will bring world peace is an ideology. Toynbee would turn to religion for the source of this ideology. He sees all mankind living happily in peace when conditions "liberate Western souls for fulfilling the true end of man by glorifying God and enjoying Him once again." (Toynbee 1957. 349)

The intolerance exhibited by contemporary religious groups would belie the expectation that an ideology for peaceful coexistence could come from that source. Religions in fact forestall universal acceptance of one ideology. The most terrible wars of all history have been those prompted by religious differences.

A peace-bringing, unifying ideology can more likely come from universal acceptance of the doctrine of the harmony of the rightly understood interests of all members of a free society. Society needs leaders, needs a middle class, and needs the great majority who simply want to work and enjoy the fruits of their labor. Rightly understood self-interest requires each individual to recognize his dependence on the other members of society. Those who are dissatisfied with their lot must be free to try to alter it.

Mobility between the classes and geographically over the globe cannot be restricted by any arbitrary ruling force.

Peace will come when all peoples accept this one ideology and remove all barriers to mobility and change. Nations can exist and will do so, but the power of one nation cannot be used to exert coercive force on any other, either accelerative or restrictive. Rulers of nations and their citizens must realize that it advances their own self-interest to cooperate with all other nations. Each nation must first remove all barriers and restrictions, and establish internal peace consistent with this ideology. "Social justice" and "economic equality" can never be goals to be coerced by man within nations or between nations. Coercion in pursuit of such goals destroys all productive cooperation. (See Chapter 16.)

For their own self-interest, leaders must recognize and serve the needs of the proletariat, or they will cease to lead. American leadership is trying to win support from the external proletariat in the Third World; yet they are failing to serve the internal proletariat of their own country. Their efforts are vain. As Toynbee states, in such a situation both "the internal and the external proletariat secede from that civilization and form the foundations for a new civilization." (*Ibid.* 358)

If there is no territory to which they can retire, they become the barbarians, overthrow the established order and its leaders, and bring about the decay of that civilization.

Since the end of World War II, it has not been the events themselves so much as the operation of the federal bureaucracy that has affected the course of liberty in America. . . . Erosion of freedom in America no longer proceeds slowly. The assault on liberty progresses at a pace that can destroy all freedom in another generation.

Chapter 16

Assault on Liberty, 1946-1998

Civil Service and Bureaucracy

𝒯HROUGHOUT THE HISTORY of the American republic, one interesting item keeps reappearing. Voters elect candidates who promise "change." Having become disillusioned with the performance of those in office, citizens try to change the direction of their government. In instance after instance, the elected candidates fail to accomplish the change the citizens desire. This is probably because neither the voters nor the elected officials know precisely what the public wants or how to achieve it. By the advantage of hindsight, historians eventually record the true feelings of the citizens, and put together a clear record of the efforts of the officials. From this it becomes startlingly apparent how little people learn from history. The record of the past reveals all man's past mistakes; yet new generations continuously repeat these same mistakes. Yes, truly, we learn from history how little we learn from history.

About the end of the 19th century, the corruption that newspapers exposed among government employees brought a call for reform. Change at that time took the form of a "civil service system." The people had become disgusted with the conduct of many political hacks appointed to office by the incoming administration. It mattered little which political party was the culprit. The spoils system had to go. Civil service was the solution adopted.

Civil service meant that before a prospect was hired, he had to demonstrate his capacity by passing tests designed to evaluate the skills and knowledge suited to the position he wanted. Once employed, he was protected from removal by a change in administration. Newly elected officials could not replace him with someone preferred by the new president, governor, or city mayor. The great acclaim this concept received from the news media and the people assured that civil service would thereafter be sacrosanct. No future administration in government could alter it or destroy it. The public took to it more readily than ducklings take to water.

At the time Americans adopted civil service, the government employed fewer than one-half million persons. From this beginning has grown a class of professional bureaucrats now numbering over four million. Once employed, the individual civil servant cannot be fired — literally. Incompetence, inattention to duties, incompatibility with fellow workers, or downright "uncivil" conduct does not justify removing a civil service employee from his job.

When Congress decides that government should perform some function, it creates a new agency to carry out its wishes. Congress not only charges this new agency with the administration, but also with writing the details of that administration. These details are official regulations, and are as much a part of the law of the land as is the enabling legislation. They inform the public how to comply with the new law and define the specifics of administration for agency members. If Congress included such details in the basic legislation, it is doubtful that a majority of congressmen would approve. Such is the fact of present-day politics. A majority of Congress can be secured only in striving for some desirable end. The specifics for achieving that end must be left to the administrative agency created for the purpose. The result is a bureaucracy of permanent members who are virtually beyond the control of the people, because, once created, the agency cannot be controlled. Its members have tenure far exceeding the consensus of Congress.

This permanent bureaucracy remained relatively small until the 1930s when, under the Roosevelt administration, the federal government began trying to be all things to all people. Since 1933, the size of this professional government has mushroomed. It is such a large component of the functioning government that today elected officials and appointed chief operating officers can exert little influence over the agents they are appointed to direct. Each agency is now virtually beyond the control of the people as exercised by the vote.

At the end of the 20th century, bureaucratic strangulation is the big problem with American government and the greatest threat to freedom. The permanent government bureaucracy has developed a life of its own. Some critics claim the only way elected officials can regain control is to cease appropriating funds for any agency the populace opposes.

Voters in 1992 elected Bill Clinton to the presidency because he promised them change. In 1976 they elected Jimmy Carter to the same office for the same reason. In the off-year election of 1994, voters again expressed their desire for change by altering the composition of both houses of Congress, and changing control of most state legislatures and offices of Governor. It is apparent that the people want change. But what change? This time, however, by switching control of both the state governments and Congress to a different political party — the Republicans, the voters have assigned a mandate to a body with sufficient power to be effective. Time will tell whether elective officials can regain control of the professional bureaucracy and effect change.

Since the end of World War II, it has not been the events themselves so much as the operation of the federal bureaucracy that has affected the course of liberty in America. So it is more appropriate to examine these threats to liberty than to examine the events of history *per se*.

The Problem Confronting Labor and the Farmers

When those delegates gathered in Pennsylvania that summer in 1787, not one of them believed in government of and by the people. In their view democracy posed a threat to good government. They feared a majority as much as they feared a despotic monarch. Accordingly, they wrote a document that structured a government with limited powers. They tried their best to create a constitutional democracy within which the rights of the individual would be safe from tyranny by a despotic tyrant or a despotic majority. The Constitution created a government in which all power comes from the people, one in which the people grant to government only the recited powers and reserve all others to themselves or their state governments.

The constitutional democracy they created remains perhaps the best form of government yet devised. Even though it was not absolutely democratic (for servants, slaves, women, and free men without property could not vote), it was devised to protect the rights of the individual against usurpation of power by a majority or a tyrant. Until man can improve on this concept, it behooves citizens to recover and preserve the limitations of power originally written into the Constitution. Under this democratic republic, government receives its powers by grant from the people; and the people are protected from their government by the limitations to those powers, all as delineated in the contract of origin.

For a century and a quarter the people supported the concept of limited powers for both the majority and the executive. The Industrial Revolution created a new class of people, the wage-earning laborer. With expansion of the franchise, the new wage-earning class together with the farmers became the majority. No longer did the financiers and industrialists control government. Farmers and laborers had experienced problems brought on by government controlled by others. They began to question the nature of the system.

Although the fundamental cause of distress had not changed, political ideology among the citizens made a major shift. The people discarded belief in limited government. In its place, they installed Big Brother government. Currently, every small ill that reaches public awareness brings forth cries for government action. With Supreme Court approval (interpretation of the power to regulate interstate commerce), government can now determine the size of an individual's garden and dictate what he may plant. Government can direct the detailed conduct of employee and employer. Government can set wages and prices. Government can design the products that industry produces and dictate their distribution. No act of government lies beyond the power of regulators, unless the individual can prove that his personal rights as set forth in the Bill of Rights are being infringed. And the Supreme Court has demonstrated that it can and will enlarge or reduce the scope of these rights.

Under the Racketeer Influenced and Corrupt Organization law (RICO), government can charge an individual with a crime and immediately attach his property so as to deny to him the ability to employ counsel of his choice to represent him in court. Fostered by the popular War on Drugs, on the pretext of searching for drugs government agents can enter private property and seize whatever items they choose. They have seized commercial fishing boats, yachts, automobiles, guns, buildings, cash, and countless other items of private property on this pretext. The law does not require that the individual even be charged with a crime. And the government agency making the confiscation becomes the sole owner of the items taken. Seldom can the injured citizen regain possession of his property. This has happened in numerous cases, and continues to this moment. One rancher in Montana was killed trying to defend his home when government agents broke in during the early morning hours.

Admittedly government seldom exercises these powers to their fullest, but freedom does not exist for people living under free conditions "allowed" by the generosity of government agents. People know liberty only when they are protected by enforcement of the law — law that limits the power of government.

The evil that so disturbed farmers and wage-earning workers and has even brought industry to the government trough, has been the business cycle, a creature of government manipulation of credit and the money supply. Every money panic and depression has arisen from misuse of government power over money and credit. The ones who suffer most are those who borrow money on a long-term payment schedule. Debtors seem to ignore the reality of the contract they so assume. A debt is a money contract. The debtor must repay that debt in money, not in purchasing power. Farmers who borrow money and spend it at prices prevailing when wheat sells at $3 become devastated when they must repay that debt with wheat selling at $1.50. Similarly, the wage-earner who borrows when he is earning $500 a week is destroyed when his weekly earnings drop to $300. This has happened in every money panic and depression since the beginning of the Republic.

The problem arises through misuse of long-term debt. It matters not that inflation favors the existing debtor. No course of inflation runs in a straight line. Over the short term — and even during long-term inflation

— prices of farm produce and weekly earnings of labor drop during the deflationary recession that government creates. The wise man recognizes that a debt must be repaid in money, and that the purchasing power of money can change dramatically over time. He recognizes that earnings fluctuate with changes in the value of money. Debt of a size that must be repaid over a long time frame or from earning power that can change dramatically, incurs the risk of complete financial disaster. Such is the disaster that marks the real farm problem and the problem confronting the new class that developed out of the Industrial Revolution — the wage earner.

Before the Industrial Revolution, debt was little used outside of commerce among capitalists. These operators protected themselves by dealing in money based on gold or other scarce commodities. They could not be whipsawed by governments because governments had little influence on money and credit. The common man, the farmer, needed little money. He owned his land and produced from it everything he and his family required. With an annual cash income of $100, he could buy what he did not produce. Because governments performed only minimal services, taxes on property remained small, which required little money. People in agrarian societies did not need to understand much about money, banking, and credit.

The Industrial Revolution, however, brought laborers and farmers into the world of finance. Today, farmers produce for the cash market, and wage-earners live entirely in a money-and-credit environment. And these individuals know very little about fiat money and government control over supply. In the 1930s, government undercut all citizens. The Depression, caused by misguided inflation, ruined everyone, debtors and creditors alike. Labor earnings dropped, farm prices fell; and with the bankruptcy of the national government in 1933, Roosevelt's New Deal outlawed the use of gold as money. Thereafter, even the informed person became powerless to protect his finances against government manipulation of money and credit.

In spite of these facts, few people today recognize the truth. They still trust government to protect them from the evils of debt and depressions. Yet government is the very agency that causes violent swings in the value of money and the availability of credit. Government brings on depressions. Government is the wolf, not the shepherd. Until people become aware that misuse of credit is as disastrous to a person's financial health as cocaine is to bodily health, depressions will wipe out debtors as surely as floods destroy crops.

Autocrats in control of governments attempt to control this phenomenon by using inflation. They reason that if they control the supply of money so as to prevent fluctuations in prices, debtors will not be injured. This idea sounds great. In practice it fails. Read the editorials in current periodicals that deal with business and economics. None agree on precisely the correct amount by which the money supply should be expanded or contracted. Not only that, various political interest groups want more or less inflation as they see their own particular position. The committee charged with operating the system faces this combined political pressure and disagreement among special interests. They must also deal with disputes among themselves as to the precise amount money and credit should be altered. In severe panics such as occurred in 1933, government even loses control completely. The task lies beyond the capability of any human being. There are too many variables, too many conflicting forces, too many unknowns. In the final analysis, such attempts to stabilize prices end either in a deflationary debacle — such as the world experienced during 1929 to 1939 — or in a complete inflationary crack-up boom such as Germany witnessed in the 1920s and occurred in the American South in the 1860s. Runaway inflation, with complete destruction of the money, causes a collapse of business and commerce. That creates conditions far worse than the country experienced in the 1930s.

About Social Justice

Since the beginning of the 20th century, pressure groups have justified nearly every government encroachment on liberty as action to achieve social justice. The confiscation of gold in 1933 and the default on debt during the expansion of the money supply in the 1920s are even today justified as acts to prevent social injustice. But these apologists do not define precisely what they mean by social justice. So we must examine the actions and consequences themselves to discover what they were seeking.

In writing about F.D.R.'s New Deal, Supreme Court Justice Robert H. Jackson defended the government's action to invalidate debt contracts to be repaid in dollars of a specified gold content. He wrote:

> *On June 5, 1933, the Congress passed a joint resolution which declared such gold payment contracts to be against public pol-*

icy and void, and made them dischargeable dollar for dollar in
any legal tender currency, which of course meant the devalued
dollar. By this simple act all the explosive injustices lurking in
the private gold standard were swept away and gold-clause
creditors were placed in the same position as others in the
hardships of the deflation. (Jackson 1941. 100)

Congress and President Roosevelt considered this action necessary because throughout the 1920s monetary inflation had devalued the dollar. Government had issued $25 billion face value of gold-backed bonds, but held less than $5 billion worth of gold in the treasury. Inflation had so devalued the dollar that people would no longer sell gold for dollars at the official rate of $20 an ounce. Had the gold-clause in commercial and government debt been left intact, the devaluation of the dollar by monetary inflation would have increased the size of the debt in dollar terms. Government had two options: either (1) compound the fraudulent acts of the 1920s by defaulting on gold-backed bonds and confiscating all gold holdings, or (2) admit publicly that the U.S. government was insolvent. Roosevelt and the New Deal Congress chose the former.

Roosevelt's New Deal confiscated from all citizens their gold holdings. Government declared ownership of gold illegal — except, of course, for foreigners, who lay beyond the reach of the United States government. Congress then changed the official dollar/gold exchange ratio, increasing the dollar price of gold to $35 per ounce, thereby reducing the purchasing power of dollar savings.

In this case, wholesale repudiation of debt and confiscation of savings became social justice. Government punished the thrifty, the wise, the cautious. As Jackson stated, all gold-clause creditors were placed under the same hardships of the deflation. We may assume that social justice meant confiscation of property, particularly from those most eagerly trying to avoid the losses generated by unwise and fraudulent government actions. No demonstration of the Law of Envy is more blatant than this.

The net income tax authorized by the Sixteenth Amendment (ratified in 1913) became confiscation of virtually all individual earnings in the top bracket, which was taxed at a 94-percent rate in the 1940s. When the state income tax was added to this, some persons had virtually nothing left of their earnings. Top rates on inheritance became very nearly as confiscatory, and many members of Congress openly admitted they would prefer a rate of 100 percent. To them, social justice meant denying inheritance to any and all. When confiscating wealth from the individual, politicians generally employ the shield of "social justice."

Today, Americans gain no security by owning wealth when the multitudes know about it. Security for the individual lies exclusively in his training, skills, knowledge, and good sense to keep his material wealth concealed from his neighbor (government) and in a liquid form that he can quickly move beyond the reach of government. As a persecuted minority in Europe and Asia for centuries, the Jews learned this lesson. Consequently, many became diamond merchants. One small bag of diamonds, easily concealed, can represent a sizable fortune, and throughout the world diamonds are nearly as acceptable as gold as a medium of exchange. Currently, each year sees a larger number of wealthy Americans leave the country, revoking their U.S. citizenship to avoid confiscation of their wealth by U.S. tax laws. Under stress, today's "law" protects only the powerful. Protection of private property under government by man is a chimera.

Friedrich A. Hayek made this observation about social justice:

> The appeal to "social justice" has nevertheless by now become the most widely used and most effective argument in political discussion. Almost every claim for government action on behalf of particular groups is advanced in its name, and if it can be made to appear that a certain measure is demanded by "social justice", opposition to it will rapidly weaken. . . . In consequence, there are today probably no political movements or politicians who do not readily appeal to "social justice" in support of the particular measures which they advocate. (Hayek 1976. 65)
>
> Even though until recently one would have vainly sought in the extensive literature for an intelligible definition of the term, there still seems to exist little doubt, either among ordinary people or among the learned, that the expression has a definite and well understood sense.
>
> But the near-universal acceptance of a belief does not prove that it is valid or even meaningful any more than the general belief in witches or ghosts proved the validity of these concepts. What we have to deal with in the case of "social justice" is sim-

ply a quasi-religious superstition of the kind which we should respectfully leave in peace so long as it merely makes those happy who hold it, but which we must fight when it becomes the pretext of coercing other men. And the prevailing belief in "social justice" is at present probably the gravest threat to most other values of a free civilization. (Ibid. 66-67)

Like most attempts to pursue an unattainable goal, the striving for it will also produce highly undesirable consequences, and in particular lead to the destruction of the indispensable environment in which the traditional moral values alone can flourish, namely personal freedom. (Ibid. 67)

Social justice throughout the 20th century in America has meant taking from those who save — from the thrifty, from the hard-working — and giving to the spendthrift and indigent. Such social justice, left unchecked, will destroy civilization as surely as the ocean tides rise and fall. The great power of Rome collapsed precisely for this reason.

About Prohibitions

For 300 years (1600-1900), immigrants came to the United States to find individual freedom. Nowhere else in the world could an individual exercise free control over his labor, earnings, spending, thoughts, religion, speech — his very life. In America, the only restriction was the universal law of social cooperation: Do nothing that infringes on the freedom of others to do likewise.

The English philosopher John Stuart Mill, when writing *On Liberty* in 1859, stated:

The sole end for which mankind are warranted, individually or collectively, in interfering with the liberty of action of any of their number, is self-protection. That the only purpose for which power can be rightfully exercised over any member of a civilised community, against his will, is to prevent harm to others. . . . The only part of the conduct of any one, for which he is amenable to society, is that which concerns others. In the part which merely concerns himself, his independence is, of right, absolute. Over himself, over his own body and mind, the individual is sovereign.

As recognized by Mill, the history of man illustrates the constant violation of this dictum both by individuals as individuals and by individuals acting in cooperation through their institutions. In the first decade of the 20th century, Americans abandoned this philosophy of freedom and began imposing prohibitions on personal conduct that involved only the persons themselves.

The problem that arises in applying the principle to specific action is illustrated by issues like the following: Is legal suppression of prostitution based on moral teachings by philosophers or on the harm brought to society by the spread of venereal disease? If venereal disease is the primary consideration, would not medical prevention and care be a more appropriate means of addressing the problem? Do supporters of legalized abortion believe the unborn infant is not yet human? Or are opponents correct in their claim that abortion is tantamount to murder? And when does the taking of life constitute murder? When does it become a duty, a merciful act? Does legal prohibition of alcohol, heroin, marijuana, cocaine, or opium infringe on individual liberty as defined by Mill? Or does the user of these substances restrict the freedom of other members of society? Likewise, can one justify legal opposition to gambling on the grounds of Mill's stated principle? Is morality the reason for these prohibitions against conduct over which Mills declared man's independence to be absolute? The conflict exemplified by these questions constitutes the fundamental issue underlying a major part of criminal law in the late 20th century.

Throughout history mankind has differentiated prostitutes from others of society. Female prostitutes have been at times exalted as high priestesses or condemned as criminals. In the United States few places have allowed this practice as legal conduct. Legislating against prostitution has never stopped the practice. Consumers want the service, and suppliers consider the financial reward sufficient to risk arrest and conviction. Today, society only loosely enforces the laws, yet the laws remain.

Colonials consumed wine, ale, rum, brandy, and whiskey in quantities greater than late 20th-century society accepts. In 1919 the Eighteenth Amendment forbade all manufacture and sale of alcohol for use as a beverage. This was Prohibition, the hallmark of the 1920s. Prohibition generated bootlegging, gang wars, street killings, and Chicago's Al Capone. Capone personified the successful criminal. His income has been estimated at more than one-half billion current dollars a year. The reform movement in the late 19th century generated this prohibition on individual liberty.

Prohibiting the sale of alcohol proved to be a catastrophe. Consumers wanted to drink alcohol, and a criminal element arose to supply it. The sale itself being illegal, suppliers never refrained from violating all other laws in pursuit of the trade. Profits from illegal sale of alcohol paid for bribes to law enforcement officials. In Chicago's St. Valentine's Day massacre, Al Capone's gangsters executed seven members of his competitor's operation. These criminals resorted even to murder — mass murder in this incident. Gang-style killings became commonplace.

This was the roaring '20s, the period when men voted dry and drank wet. In spite of the Eighteenth Amendment, bootleggers delivered liquor to the customer's door. Speakeasies flourished. There was no law against drinking, and Americans as a whole were not prohibitionists. They bought the illegal product, thereby supporting both corruption in law enforcement and open street warfare among the mobsters who defied the laws in order to bring liquor to their customers.

The extent of this illegal conduct never abated through law enforcement. Only repeal of Prohibition in 1933 put an end to it. Since taking that logical step, Americans have dealt with alcoholism as a sickness, and have offered treatment to the victims. Before this could take place, however, government had to bring the problem out of a forbidden area and give it legal status.

The same could be done today with other, presently illegal drugs. But as long as commerce in a product that consumers want remains illegal, society cannot work toward dealing with the associated problems. The experience of the roaring '20s could be a lesson for the present.

As the beneficiary of Prohibition, organized crime perfected its existence in the 1920s. By the time Prohibition ended, organized crime had taken control of illegal gambling and prostitution; and, when sale of narcotics became illegal, they entered that field. The current street wars by gangs of drug distributors has replaced the street killings among bootleggers of the 1920s.

Americans have never been willing to devote the resources necessary to enforce any law that great numbers of people do not voluntarily obey. Society has generally resolved the issue by resorting to the principle and the practical. Society either (1) endures illegal activity and the abuse to the innocents that occurs; or (2) refrains from prohibiting the action, and the people tolerate as legal a conduct they otherwise condemn. In all laws that prohibit a personal conduct, the real question is not whether the conduct is right or wrong morally but whether the great majority of society will obey the prohibitionary laws. The repeal of Prohibition did not make a statement of universal approval on drinking alcohol. Repeal simply recognized that such a large number of citizens wanted to drink alcohol that society would not grant government enough resources to enforce Prohibition. Meanwhile, innocent people suffered more from illegal bootleggers than they did from legal drinkers. Society decided the matter not on the morality of drinking, but on the practical judgment about which action protected the greatest number of innocents. It became apparent that prohibiting the sale of alcohol provoked conduct among criminals that harmed others more than did legalizing it.

By similar reasoning, in the late 20th century Americans have begun lifting legal prohibitions against gambling. On the same grounds, society is now debating the question of legalized narcotics. The current "War on Drugs" will not stop the sale and use of drugs. It may, however, arouse public awareness of the real issue and develop a sound legal position based on intelligent discussion.

Perhaps Mill's statement about liberty should be expanded to include the following concepts: In the gray area between pure principle and its application to specific conduct, the defense of liberty should be measured in comparatives. The question is which prohibition protects the greater number of people, prohibiting the conduct or prohibiting government from enacting unenforceable laws regarding it. Does not society produce the greatest good for the greatest number when it tolerates the greatest liberty for its members?

The history of prior efforts at legal prohibitions, particularly those relating to alcohol in the 1920s, helps us evaluate the current "War on Drugs." Is the drug problem a problem about drugs or a problem about undue legal restrictions on liberty? We can ask the same questions about prohibitions on gambling and prostitution, conducts that are concerns of personal morality more than concerns of government.

An intolerant person wants to prohibit for others conduct he himself avoids because of his own self-imposed morality (the Law of Intolerance). (For those interested in a comprehensive examination into drives within man that involve this subject, see Friedrich A. Hayek's three-volume set *Law, Legislation, and Liberty*.)

America's experience in the 1920s with Prohibition illustrates another danger to liberty. The mere frivolity of the subject of the Eighteenth Amendment — a prohibition of the manufacture and sale of alcohol — set a precedent that has reappeared in recent years. The serious advocacy of such minor matters as the Equal Rights Amendment and Balanced Budget Amendment should be a warning.

The Constitution can be effective only as long as it states universal principles. For the people to attempt specific legislation by amending the Constitution spells potential disaster. In no way can the Constitution adequately deal with the legislative flexibility required for Congress to meet the financial needs of the nation, and determine how these funds are to be raised. Specific taxing and appropriation measures are matters proper for the legislative body, subject only to presidential veto. Most certainly the people cannot through the Constitution properly regulate everyday conduct of individual citizens with regard to social relations between genders. Furthermore, before the law, females have equal rights with males without disturbing the Constitution. Finally, it is questionable to what extent even the Legislature should be dealing with such matters.

People have been wise not to involve the Constitution in the specifics of day-to-day operation in government. This precedent, now at rest, is best left sleeping. Even the most imaginative among us cannot conceive the risks to social cooperation should this precedent of frivolity be awakened and loosed among the citizenry.

Judicial Imperialism

Where there is no rule by law, there can be no liberty. As we saw in earlier pages, rule by man has been rapidly replacing rule by law in the United States. The final breakdown of rule by law began early in the 20th century when leaders adopted the philosophy that government should care for the weak and the poor, which began the great experiment in "social reform." The concept of social reform struggled for universal acceptance until 1937, when a majority of the Supreme Court began supporting legislation that conflicted with established constitutional law developed during the previous 150 years of the Republic. Since that time, with legal precedent meaning little to court decisions, the law is whatever any temporary five-justice Supreme Court majority declares it to be.

This situation underlies the intense interest exhibited by senators at every confirmation hearing on presidential appointments to the federal judiciary. Senators make the appointee's political ideology, more than his legal expertise, the primary consideration. Solely on the basis of Bork's ideology the Senate rejected President Reagan's September 1987 appointment of Robert Bork to the Supreme Court. Bork failed to support the neoliberal philosophy of recent courts; he did not embrace the belief that the Court should advance social goals in adjudicating cases; he rejected the notion that judges should rewrite the laws; he supported "original understanding" of the Constitution; he favored rule by law in preference to rule by man.

The final usurpation of power by judges developed during the last half of the 20th century. The ultimate point of departure can be identified with the Supreme Court ruling in *Brown v Board of Education* (1954). The Earl Warren Court in that decision upset the long-standing interpretation of the Fourteenth Amendment, *i.e.*, that by providing separate but equal facilities, though racially segregated, government satisfied the requirement for equality under the law. For over half a century "separate but equal" met the requirements of the Constitution. The same social objective could have been attained without destroying the doctrine of *stare decisis* (legal precedent). The mass support for *Brown v Board of Education* stems from a condition determined by the trial court, that the separate facilities were not equal. The Supreme Court could have upheld precedent by deciding in favor of the plaintiff on this basis. Thereafter, Negroes could have entered otherwise segregated facilities unless truly equal facilities were furnished. But this was not what either the plaintiff or the Court wanted. They wanted "separate but equal" reversed. It matters not whether the change ordered by the Supreme Court was good or bad; it upset completely the concept of rule by law. With that and other decisions that ignored precedent, the Warren Court sent a message to the lower courts. Judges could thereafter ignore the doctrine of *stare decisis*; they could adopt social justice as the deciding criteria for adjudicating future cases.

If the people wanted a different rule of law, they would certainly have had ample time to make the change. The previous interpretation of the Fourteenth Amendment had stood for nearly six decades. The people not only did not want to change, they met enforcement of the new judicial ruling with open and sometimes violent opposition. In 1957, President Eisenhower sent federal troops to Little Rock, Arkansas, to force Governor Orval Faubus to comply with the new judicial law.

Thus began an era wherein judges went beyond ruling on the law. They began ordering the Executive branch to positive behavior — like busing to achieve racial balance in the public schools. In 1987, Missouri federal judge Russell G. Clark ordered the Kansas City school board to double property taxes in order to pay for desegregation changes he had earlier ordered them to make. On April 18, 1990, the U.S. Supreme Court declared the tax increase levied by Judge Clark to be invalid because of faulty mechanics, but the Court upheld his right both to order the school district to levy the tax and to bar Missouri officers from enforcing the state constitution and statutes that prohibited these taxes. (*Missouri, et al v Kalima Jenkins, et al.* [1990] 58 LW 4480)

Under such judicial imperialism, judges now write the laws and direct the execution of their edicts. They have become legislator, executive, judge, and jury. No matter that the objectives these judges seek may be good and are supported by many of the citizens. The evil lies in the usurpation of power by public officials whom the electorate cannot remove from office by the vote because federal judges hold office for life.

Freed from the shackles of the Constitution, legislation, and prior court rulings, judges have arrogated to themselves power to enact the social reforms pressure groups have failed to gain by the legislative process. Judges have gone far beyond tyranny of the majority; some judges would decide how wealth will be distributed. An example is the Pennzoil-Texaco fiasco in a Texas court (1988). A state court in that civil case, involving a broken contract, awarded to Pennzoil a payment from Texaco that far exceeded the total asset value of the Pennzoil Company. It was many times larger than the alleged contract's potential value to Pennzoil. The judge in that case let the jury verdict stand. It required a lengthy appeal to a higher court before the parties could agree to a more reasonable settlement. In addition to forced busing to achieve racial balance in the schools, judges have limited capital punishment, ended school prayer, forced on states the rule of "one man one vote" in contradiction to terms prescribed in their own state constitutions, and legalized abortion on demand. Legislative acts by elected public officials have not directed any of these social changes.

Government either by an unrestrained majority or by judicial imperialism is rule by man rather than rule by law. Until 1937 the restraint on tyranny by the majority had been the Constitution as interpreted by the nine members of the Supreme Court. When President Roosevelt, in 1937, proposed to eliminate this restraint on the power of the people acting through their elected representatives, Justice Owen Roberts switched his support, and government by law became a thing of the past. The will of the majority prevailed. Since that time, neither Congress, the President, nor the imperial judiciary is restrained by law. Individual freedom for Americans now exists only by default. The professional bureaucrats in Washington can dictate to any individual much as did the Politburo in Communist Russia. The difference rests solely in the degree to which government bureaucrats exercise their power.

We may agree that none, some, or all these changes were desirable; but the consequence has been a breakdown of both constitutional and common law. Many court cases are no longer controlled by the Constitution or legal precedent. Today's lawsuits are often not guided by the framework of common law — the recognized rules observed for centuries because people believed them to be just, though not codified by legislation, but enforced by custom, judges, and public opinion. Confusion remains as the only certainty today.

The Tort Liability Crisis

Perhaps the most conspicuous casualty of this loss of rule by law has been the so-called tort crisis: awards stemming from suits over loss through alleged injury in some event. The common law for centuries required the injured party to show that the defendant caused his injury by intent or neglect. The injured party could not collect if he had himself contributed to the loss by his own actions, or if he had voluntarily assumed the obvious and known risk. Additionally, the plaintiff had to file his suit within a prescribed time frame. Under common law, contracts formed voluntarily between parties served to prevent later tort action if either of the parties suffered a loss. When decisions did favor the plaintiff (the injured), common law limited damage awards to compensation for the actual loss (out-of-pocket costs, such as the expense of repairing the damaged property).

Since the 1960s, judges have increasingly ignored mutually agreed-to risk (contract) as a bar to compensation in tort cases. They have allowed awards as compensation for pain and suffering, mental anguish, and loss of consortium (a spouse's company). Likewise, they have allowed payments to punish the defendant (punitive damages). At the same time, judges no longer require the suit to show that the defendant either carelessly or intentionally disregarded the rights of the plaintiff. In medical malpractice torts, the plaintiff simply needs to prove that the medical defendant participated in treatment. In cases involving injury from use of a product, the plaintiff needs only to show that the defendant could have been the one who made the product involved in the incident. The need to demonstrate negligence or intent on the part of the defendant has been thrown out the window. Additionally, no time limitation prevents filing a claim. A 30-year-old individual can bring suit for malpractice against the physician who attended his birth. Juries need not consider intervening changes in medical knowledge or in accepted practice. As this is being written, the Supreme Court has before it a case wherein the plaintiff is seeking $2 million in recompense for damage he claims to have suffered from a drug administered to his grandmother during her pregnancy. He claims it altered his genetic makeup to his detriment. The drug was removed from the market over 20 years ago. How far can judicial reality stray from a predictable rule of law? Just to consider such a claim is to open a Pandora's Box of imaginative improbabilities.

Tort cases forced the Manville Company into bankruptcy for supplying asbestos to the world for years before anyone even suspected that such action could possibly present a hazard. Neither passing time, lack of intent, nor absence of negligence presented a barrier to this destruction of Manville. Evidence now coming to light indicates that asbestos was not in truth the culprit in many of those injury cases. No matter. The Manville Company has been destroyed by unrestrained tort liability.

Plaintiffs can now bring suit for compensation for injuries they merely fear may occur in future years. As the basis for seeking compensation, judges now accept mental anguish over fear that there may possibly be suffering caused by some future incident — such as a burnout at a nuclear power plant or chemicals leaking from an old or yet-to-be constructed waste disposal site. All these grounds for a tort action conflict with long-established common law, and are a legal reality peculiar to the United States. English courts continue to follow the law that, from Colonial times, formed the basis for the U.S. legal system.

Court destruction of contract denies to consumers the freedom to make deliberate choices. Without the freedom to choose, a person is denied the ability to protect himself. He cannot look out for his own safety.

Contract, informed or otherwise, cannot be the engine of safe-

ty unless it is binding for better and for worse. . . . If the informed consumer is not free to make foolish choices on his own, he can never be free to make wise, lifesaving ones either. (Huber 1988. 212)

Without freedom to make choices enforced at law by contract, man is no longer free

to plan in advance, to make commitments, and to arrange deals on terms mutually agreeable to the parties involved. Modern tort law abrogates our freedom to cooperate. . . . Applied as it has been in recent years, open-ended tort law serves only as an engine of social destruction. (Ibid. 221)

Uncontrolled tort law has caused prices of services and merchandise to increase in order to cover jury awards, and has also reduced the availability of those items most severely affected. Already, many doctors have withdrawn from obstetrics. Of those remaining in practice, some are paying insurance premiums that consume a major portion of their fees. Unless this condition changes, mothers-to-be will have to leave the country to obtain the benefits of modern medicine. Medical assistance in child birth will cease to be available in America at any price. Nurses have left their chosen field because liability insurance premiums now consume such a large portion of their compensation. Already, developers of new, beneficial drugs withhold them from the market for fear of the unpredictable, high costs of tort liability. Manufacturers have withdrawn vaccines from the market, and some foreign manufacturers no longer sell in the United States. The manufacturer of a new oral medication proved safe for abortion and in general use in Europe, refuses to sell the product in the United States out of concern about the high cost and unpredictable incidence of tort liability. Manufacturers have withdrawn most contraceptives from the market to avoid tort liability. This action has forced women to search for alternate means to avoid pregnancy. They have turned to government (the taxpayers) to finance the cost of tort liability so manufacturers will again supply their needs. This situation will spread to all areas that plaintiffs can attack in the tort lottery. The unknown risks of tort liability have stifled innovation. The United States now lags behind its earlier achievements in the new, the novel, the improved. Lawyers use improved products as additional evidence that the earlier product was inferior and consequently at fault for injury, real or imagined.

Faultless conduct no longer protects a defendant from being outrageously assessed to pay "damages" to an ambitious litigant. A jury ordered New York City to pay $650,000 to a man who threw himself in front of a moving subway train. The plaintiff claimed the subway driver should have stopped more quickly. The sky is the limit. A California jury awarded $54 million to the parents of a brain-damaged child. Invested at five percent, the earnings from that sum would forever support, in style, both child and parents.

The tort crisis has become a lottery with no requirement to make an investment. One recipient of a jury's generosity compared his experience to being on a TV game show with a much larger prize. The jury award against Ford Motor Company exceeded $100 million when a following vehicle rammed the rear end of a Pinto stalled on a freeway exit. Today, to seek an award by the court, a person need only suffer some injury, real or imagined, from receiving medical service or from use (or abuse) of a product manufactured by a company with "deep pockets." When judges replaced the doctrine of *stare decisis* with "social justice" as the basis for the new common tort law, lawyers and juries looked for a pool of wealth to tap. They found that wealth in the hands of governments, insurance companies, and large business entities. Judges ignored contract and responsibility. Social justice decreed only that the injured be paid. In order to pay the lawyers and claimants, insurance companies increased premiums, business increased prices, and governments increased taxes. As in all matters of cost, the consumers foot the bill. The net effect transfers wealth from the many to the few.

Interestingly, the destruction of law in tort liability masqueraded under justice for the consumer, as protection for the multitudes who need a keeper. Peter Huber explains:

> *The inventors of the new tort, of all people, should have been the least surprised by the mounting randomness and incoherence of jury outcomes. A central tenet of their faith was that the consumer is unqualified to make intelligent choices about safety for himself. That, after all, was why disclaimers of liability were no longer enforced, why contract had been buried deep in the earth with the stake of tort driven through its heart. Private*

choice, in short, was to be replaced by public prescription.
Whose public prescription? Not that of the pharmacologists at
the FDA, or toxicologists at the EPA, or mechanical engineers
at the FAA, but of the juror, pulled off the voter lists at random,
solemnly sworn to his duty, and instantly educated in a contest
of courtroom experts. . . . The member of the public judged
incompetent to make wise choices in the market place for him-
self was now being called upon to make wise choices in the jury
box for others. It was a theory of the idiot/genius, incapable of
dealing with the objects that lay within his own experience, but
infinitely capable of errorless flash judgment when it came to
the experience of others. (Huber 1988. 50-51)

As legislatures currently enact laws to end this tort lottery, judges
declare such acts unconstitutional. They claim the acts limit the freedom of the jury and by so doing deny due process to the plaintiff, a
protection guaranteed by the Constitution. How might these same judges
interpret a Constitutional amendment designed to accomplish the same
goal? Would not the new amendment conflict with the older Fourteenth
Amendment? Destruction of common law loosed a terrible, destabiliz-
ing force within the legal system. We have yet to see the mischief it will
cause.

Despotism (Rule by Man)

Erosion of freedom in America no longer proceeds slowly. The assault
on liberty progresses at a pace that can destroy all freedom in another generation. Congress, the entrenched bureaucracy, and the judiciary all contribute. The only safeguard for individuals rests now in the remaining
decentralization of this power. Destruction of the Constitution and usurpation of power by the imperial judiciary have nearly destroyed rule by law.
Americans find themselves living under rule by man, the tyranny that
Greeks discarded in the 7th century B.C. under their ruler Draco. Legislatures, Congress, the Executive bureaucracy, and judges know few restrictions other than their personal whims, and the final tribunal — the federal
Supreme Court — is under no restraint by Constitution, precedent, or
legislation. A verdict by five unelected public officials remains our only
safeguard against tyranny by a majority or any of these self-appointed care-
takers of the good of man, but no law now restrains the action of judges.

The question is not whether one approves or disapproves of the decision, say, in *Brown v Board of Education*. The question is whether the benefit (real or imagined) from such a ruling was worth destroying the meaning of both a written Constitution and rule by law. There can be no doubt that this action — ignoring as it did legal precedent and followed soon by a series of such "reversals"— finally destroyed the reluctance of judges to deviate from prior law. Social justice, as each judge perceived it, replaced rule by law.

Injustice has always existed. No one today can defend all existing social institutions and laws. Perfect justice will never exist among institutions of imperfect people. They may always seek to achieve justice, but in the process the ends never justify the means. Abandoning rule by law through judicial imperialism cannot justify the injustice worked on blacks in America. Have they gained justice through this act? What a sacrifice. As a consequence, all Americans suffer from the loss of liberty. It remains for future generations to restore liberty through the ballot. The alternative is violent rebellion.

The judgment of man through more than 2,000 years approved rule by law. Rebellions and revolutions have sought to achieve such rule. Liberty exists only with its attainment. Yet, in the short span of one century, the people of America have relinquished this liberty without a struggle. Most probably, they did so without even knowing it. There are some legal scholars who believe the abandonment of law has proceeded so far that no legal means remain for the people to regain it. Certainly an attempt to reestablish the doctrine of *stare decisis* could be confusing, due to the many conflicting rulings now set forth by the Supreme Court. Robert Bork would return to the doctrine of "original understanding," but this could also lead to subjective jurisprudence and still not establish a predictable rule of law. Perhaps the solution can be achieved by a series of Constitutional amendments promulgated by a convention assembled for that purpose, as provided for in Article V of the Constitution. This problem remains a challenge for imaginative minds of free citizens.

Return of Government Restrictions
(The Attack on Wealth and Freely Changing Prices)
The Industrial Revolution developed as governments adopted the philosophy of laissez faire. In the 20th century, guided by social justice, governments adopted anew those restrictions discarded in the 18th century,

the restrictions that kept Western civilization in the Middle Ages for 1,000 years. As set forth below and in an earlier chapter, those restrictions were as follows:

1. An organization of craftsmen — the guild — decided who could become apprentices, determined how many could engage in that craft, and assigned where each could work. The government enforced these exclusionary rules.

2. Governments restricted competition. Guild members considered it unfair for a more efficient businessman or craftsman to produce better or cheaper goods and to undersell competitors. The police power of the State protected high prices.

3. Workers opposed machines as evil because they replaced labor. Government forbade their use.

4. The masses and those in authority opposed accumulation of wealth in the hands of individuals. Authorities discouraged saving; they confiscated wealth. Government to this extent discouraged private property.

5. All governments pursued a policy to restrict and control the activities of entrepreneurs, a policy considered to be in the best interests of the nation's well-being.

Governments under the control of special interests have more and more reestablished those restrictions that marked the Middle Ages. Labor unions foster higher wages than the market-clearing level, and restrict a person's entry into those fields where labor has organized. No one can freely enter a trade today. Under the ruse of "consumer protection," lawyers, doctors, engineers, plumbers, electricians, and other trades control entry into their field through licensing restrictions. Members of each trade set the requirements for obtaining a license in their own respective fields. Governments control price and restrict quantities on nearly all imports. Through the use of confiscatory taxes, government limits wealth accumulation. The Law of Envy overrides the fact that the standard of living among the citizens depends entirely on the amount of capital invested in their country. The greater the per capita investment, the more productive labor becomes, and the higher the living standard becomes for all the citizens. Confiscation of personal wealth, coupled with little protection for private property, has condemned the citizens of China to perpetual poverty. Similar action today lowers living standards to the same level wherever they are adopted.

The two restrictions most damaging to American citizens are those against wealth accumulation and those against freely fluctuating prices. Without wealth, no matter who owns it, everyone lives as the Indians did before the immigration of the Europeans and as Europeans did during the Middle Ages. Without freely fluctuating prices, wealth moves out of production into consumption, and new savings leave the country. The current living standard in the United States requires both wealth and flexibility in prices.

Prices guide the consumer in spending for food, clothing, shelter, and all the other items on the market. Nearly everyone is familiar with this function of price. What most men do not see is how price determines supply. Prices do more than allocate spending on consumption; they direct the investment of capital into producing what consumers want most. Prices guide production by farmers, miners, coopers, smithies, millers, weavers, etc. The auto industry makes more small cars than large luxury ones, because more buyers purchase the compacts. They cost less. The price the company must charge for the better products in order to cover costs restricts the market for them. If luxury cars could be sold at the same price as compacts, few people would buy the small units, and compacts would disappear from the market.

With every price increase some buyers decide to spend their money on other products, and some producers decide to make other items. If market demand for peanuts bids up the price considerably above cost of production, farmers plant more peanuts and less other crops. If the market for apples diminishes, prices fall as producers sell their inventory before it spoils. Each successive reduction in price drives some producers out, because they can no longer cover their costs of production. Soon, the market price settles where all remaining producers can sell their entire output at a profit. The total volume sold will have decreased from what it was before the price drop, and consumers will be paying less for the apples they purchase.

It follows that if an agency (government) enforces a price above what clears the market, there will be buyers who quit buying and sellers who cannot dispose of their entire stock. A price is said to "clear the market" when all sellers who are willing to accept that price can sell their entire stock, and all buyers who are willing to pay that price can buy all they want. If the higher price continues to hold, other sellers shift into the production of that item, which increases the supply even more. On the other side of the price coin, if government decrees a maximum price below the market-clearing level, more buyers enter the market at the lower price, and some sellers withdraw. The first case — that of coerced minimum prices — creates a market surplus. The second case — that of enforced maximum prices — creates a market shortage. There is no such thing as an absolute surplus or an absolute shortage. Surpluses and shortages exist only with reference to a particular price.

When the U.S. government enforced a maximum price on crude oil after World War II, producers sold their available supplies and reduced exploration for future production. By the early 1970s, an acute shortage of oil appeared in the United States. This shortage created the cartel of the Organization of Petroleum Exporting Countries (OPEC), and gave it the power to exact monopoly prices. The shortage persisted until the United States removed price controls, which enabled domestic oil producers to sell their production at the free market price. The subsequent increase in domestic oil production created by new drilling soon changed a shortage into a glut. Price determines supply. A freely fluctuating price assures a supply sufficient to satisfy the demand.

Since social reform began in the early 20th century, government has established a minimum wage on labor. Each successive increase in that wage has caused some employers to withdraw from the market, which reduces the demand for workers at that rate. This does not say that those thrown out of work are not worth the higher minimum wage. It does say that there are fewer opportunities; because as labor costs increase, the selling price of the product must rise and sales decline. With lower unit sales, the employer needs fewer workers. The net result nationwide is reduced employment with every increase in the minimum wage. The same is true for every cost levied on business by government mandate. All cost increases reduce employment. The ones who suffer are those least qualified for employment: the young, the illiterate, the slow learner, and the disabled. Then, because these "disadvantaged" individuals cannot find work, the government enacts mandates that require industry to employ them at the same pay as experienced and competent workers. In this way, government tries to conceal from the public the harm done originally by their ill-chosen policies. Every time government interferes with business and burdens the operation with costs of any form, it reduces employment.

In 1933, when a surplus of hogs appeared at the existing market price, F.D.R.'s New Deal paid hog producers to slaughter their sows in order to reduce the supply of pork. Since the slaughter of workers to reduce the supply of labor is not possible, an ever-increasing number of unskilled (mostly young) would-be wage earners remain permanently unemployed because of a minimum wage set and enforced by government.

Currently in New York City and a few other locations, maximum price controls restrain property owners from setting their rents at a level that returns to them a profit. As a result, owners do not maintain the buildings, and potential builders refrain from constructing new apartments and houses. At these levels of rent that do not cover costs, a shortage of housing has appeared. Because government forbids human organs to be sold at any price (they must be free), the demand far exceeds the supply. At a price, any price, supply would increase and more nearly satisfy this demand. But the supply will never increase until government sets the market price free, thereby encouraging more individuals to sell their organs to be delivered when they die. With a supply inadequate to meet the demand, an alternate form of rationing must exist to allocate the limited supply. Without price to determine who will receive the product, government must step in and do the rationing. Bureaucrats supplant the price system to determine which individuals will receive the scarce organs.

Prices set at fixed levels always restrict supply or demand and create a shortage or a surplus. Only freely fluctuating prices can maintain a balance.

Rigid prices restrict people's freedom of choice. We can see the extreme in every government-controlled market. Empty shelves greet consumers where maximum prices exist; wasting supplies confront markets where minimum prices exist. Enforced minimum prices on wheat have at times generated piles of unused grain over much of the high prairie. Enforced minimum prices on dairy products has forced government to buy a large portion of production so as to conceal from the public the unnecessarily high prices they pay for their milk, cheese, and butter. Minimum wages have created hordes of unemployed vagrants in the cities of America. As in Europe before the Industrial Revolution, thievery, a life in the military, or starvation becomes the lot for thousands of young Americans. It is small wonder that many have turned to dealing drugs as a means of livelihood.

Enforced minimum prices ultimately require government to buy the surplus and destroy it or to ration production. For years government has rationed the production of peanuts in order to prevent a surplus at the government-enforced minimum price. Comparably, government-enforced maximum prices ultimately require government to ration the limited supply. Both cases limit investment, thereby reducing the total supply to consumers. The living standard drops below what would exist in a market with freely fluctuating prices.

In the long run everyone loses. The trend toward more and more government control ultimately destroys all production, all saving, all investment, and brings back conditions existing 500 years ago. Conditions in 16th-century Europe will again become reality in the Western world. China, India, the USSR, and the countries of South and Central America and of Africa reached that level of primitive subsistence during the last part of the 20th century. To join them, nations of Europe and North America need only to continue pursuing current social goals and restrictions on freedom enforced by the power of government.

So far, Americans are still free to choose, either freedom under law or tyranny by popular vote.

About the Optimum

Not too long ago, the English demographer Thomas Malthus and the English naturalist Charles Darwin (not in cooperation) startled the world with some observations about life forms and why the species on this planet are as they are and appear in the quantities they do.

In 1798, Malthus observed that each species has controls that limit its numbers — predation, disease, available food and space, and the quality of the habitat. He observed also that each species increases in numbers until it reaches the limit that the habitat can support. If one control does not work with adequate results, then another will. The highest healthy population that the habitat will support is called the "optimum." Since the habitat will not support unlimited numbers, if the population of any species exceeds the optimum, early death along with reduced reproduction reestablishes the optimum.

This process of control does not operate in a smooth manner. A plot of total numbers does not show a straight line, or even a slightly wavy line at the optimum. There are drastic swings from top to bottom. As nature for a time produces weather conducive to lush vegetation, the holding capacity of the habitat grows. Then some natural occurrence — drought, flood, fire, avalanche, earthquake — reduces the holding capacity exactly at the time when the numbers of predators have increased due to greater numbers of the quarry. A very substantial decrease in numbers results. If this does not occur soon enough, disease reaches epidemic proportions and brings the same result.

Darwin's work, published in 1859, observed that the seed of each life form enters this world in a live-or-die struggle. By the generous bounty of the natural order, the number of seeds is in the multimillions, and no two seeds produce exactly identical results. Even though the differences between individual specimens may not be easily seen, the differences are there. In larger species, such as the oak tree among plants and man among mammals, marked differences can be seen without a microscope. Those particular seeds germinate and flourish that produce the specific form best adapted to their habitat. The healthiest specimens in turn produce the most seeds. Consequently, the specific type that becomes most numerous is the type best suited to that habitat.

These statements are not theories, but statements of natural laws: the Law of the Optimum and the Law of Natural Selection.

Habitat for all life forms includes food and water, space (shelter), disease, and predation. In the case of man, one more element applies: association. The form and complexity of human association greatly influence his control over available food and water, his utilization of space for shelter, and his control of predation and disease. For this reason, there is no way to determine that a specific number of human beings is an optimum number for this space. A change in social institutions might make possible a tenfold increase in his numbers, or it might cause the existing numbers to exceed the optimum.

During the winter of 1609-1610, the population in the Virginia Colony at Jamestown dropped from over 500 to less than 100 primarily because of starvation. In spite of the organic fertility of the habitat, the social institutions were not in place to support even 100 Englishmen at that time in that habitat. Today in Ethiopia, Zimbabwe, Cuba, and many other countries, a change in their social institutions has brought on famine and epidemics. In China, India, and Mexico the numbers have often exceeded the optimum for hundreds of years, and conditions will not change until the people in these regions change their social institutions. The government in China controls numbers by law that permits families to have only one child.

Famine and epidemics have been common throughout the world from the beginning of recorded history. In the Americas when the Spaniards arrived, the number of Indians was below the optimum. The appearance of the Spanish changed this condition because the Indians lacked social institutions capable of dealing with the new diseases brought from Europe. Only within Western civilization has man altered his social institutions in such a manner as to enable numbers to increase without challenging the optimum. Even so, demographers today regularly publish horror stories about the threat of overpopulation. They do not exclude the United States. If the American people fail to preserve their present heritage of freedom with protection of private property, these demographic predictions for the United States will become reality.

In all nations where government protects private property and individual freedom, an insufficiency of food and the necessities of life have disappeared completely. If this freedom were worldwide, man would probably never approach the optimum. World population could increase perhaps tenfold and there would still be room for more. The theoretical limit would never be reached because of two drives in human nature: (1) The Law of Self-Interest would impel men to practice birth control to such a degree that births would never outrun deaths to an extent that could cause population to exceed the optimum. (2) The Law of Inquisitiveness would stimulate the minds of free men to invent new ways to produce more and more.

The external physical limits to man's ability to produce are determined by the limits to the sun's energy and the water supply. Already man has demonstrated that food can be produced on land mass constructed in vertical layers. This opens a frontier for agriculture in the mass of land under the earth's surface. With piped-in energy from the sun and with water piped in from the sea, man can make layers on layers of productive farm land. Water, after all, is never consumed; it is simply used and recycled. What is the limit to the energy of the sun?

It will take millions of years before man will approach the theoretical optimum if he learns to live in peace with his neighbor and allows individual freedom to expand to the limits established by natural laws. Long before then, voluntary birth control will hold numbers below the optimum.

Under present social conditions, however, the 5.5 billion human beings press the optimum. For man to avoid the optimum, he must continue improving his social institutions directed toward an ever-increasing production; otherwise, the species will face a dramatic fall in numbers.

Increased production through advances in technological innovation, knowledge, and improved political institutions (capitalism) has enabled man to increase numbers while remaining below the optimum. If Western civilization disintegrates, it will begin with a decay in man's social institutions. The number of people will then decrease dramatically through the action of natural controls — exposure, predation, famine, and disease.

These remarks indicate no value judgment on whether emphasizing material goals is good or bad. Most humans, however, have demonstrated that they prefer conditions that make it easier for them to attain the goals they value most highly. When people spend less time and effort on providing food and shelter, they have more time and energy for pursuing the ideal things in life. We should keep this in mind when forming value judgments about "materialism" in modern civilization. Starving masses do not produce scientists, philosophers, and artists.

The Significance of Knowledge

Ideology creates society among men and provides the source of power over them. Without the unifying influence of an ideology, there can be no cooperation. Society is the product of cooperation, and so the product of ideas. Ideas create the power that gives birth to a society, a culture, a civilization.

Society has no existence outside the lives of its members. To ascribe human traits to a society that are counter to the ideology of its members is an error in method. To understand the social institutions, it is necessary to look at the ideas of the individuals. The forces that cause individuals to act are the forces that move the ebb and flow of society.

In the long run, human governments always reflects the ideas of the people. When those handling the affairs of government are not in tune with the ideologies of the majority, change will bring them into agreement. Either the people will change their ideology, or those in government will adopt the concepts of the masses. If neither changes, the people will replace those in government with others who will change the ways of government. The outcome is the same whether the government is hegemonic or democratic. The difference exists in the means — violent rebellion or peaceful balloting.

If all the people of the world really want freedom, they will construct such a state of affairs in the course of time. The continuing struggle, however, between those who desire freedom above all else and those who desire equality in economic circumstance above all else will first need to be resolved. Until that is resolved and one ideology finally prevails among the masses, mankind will experience conflict and wide swings between barbarism and advanced civilization.

Equality before the law is the only equality man can have under freedom. Freedom encompasses this condition. Economic equality as an ideology, however, conflicts with freedom as an ideology, and generates conflict. This opposition exists because of the inborn differences between individuals, differences that will always exist, as Darwin has pointed out.

Most men have not accepted this truism, but it must be agreed to before any real progress toward universal cooperation and peace can be made. Man must realize that only under a system of cooperation and peace are all men — geniuses, dynamos of industry, intellectuals, and the working masses — best provided with the things in life they value most. For this system to succeed, they must permit the differences among individuals to operate freely.

Additionally, those who seek material wealth and recognition must realize that they cannot achieve or retain these positions without the aid of the masses. They must, therefore, share with the multitudes by accepting responsibility for their security and welfare. This does not mean material charity. It means preserving a system of government that maximizes freedom and refrains from legislation that favors some at the expense of others. It means that those in power cannot use that power for self-interest to the harm of others. It means preserving rules of cooperation that are impartial in their operation, rules of just conduct that seek no particular ends by specific means. (This study is not designed to discover the specifics, but to uncover general principles. The field of political philosophy is a complex and as-yet relatively untouched discipline.)

Motivation that prompts people to allow their leaders wealth and recognition and to allow leaders to care for the people can come only from the rightly understood self-interest, not from coercion by government. Cooperation precludes the existence of any government-mandated right to welfare or any form of government-guaranteed employment. Observing this dictum concerns more than altruism and morality. It concerns laws of social cooperation (praxeology). Disregard for the laws of praxeology leads to the disintegration of civilization.

This statement makes no value judgment about morality. Morality as taught by theologians and philosophers certainly influences the actions of great numbers of people. Unfortunately, the Law of Immorality influences great numbers also. Appealing to morality alone will not create worldwide social cooperation. To influence the actions of the masses, we must appeal both to morality and to knowledge. The prime mover of human action is the Law of Self as influenced by rightly understood self-interest. At man's present level of development, reason and knowledge have proven to be necessary forces to create cooperation among individuals.

The great swings in the ideologies of the multitudes cause cycles in civilization between sophistication and barbarism. Of course, men seldom achieve the goals they seek, but this is due to their innocence. They select the wrong means; or as in the case of the conflicting ideologies of freedom and economic equality, they choose ends that cannot both be achieved together. Again, the cause is lack of correct understanding. Even the best-educated of men often miscalculate the consequences of their actions.

At any given time, it is difficult to get a consensus among leaders. This lack of agreement stems from the laws of human nature. The Law of Disagreement dictates that variations in experience and knowledge cause different responses. If men are ever to achieve consensus, they will reach it through a higher degree of understanding and wisdom, supported by a common experience.

Possibly, however, with each rebound from barbarism, men can agree on more and come closer to a consensus. Because he is curious, man will always be a seeker. The Law of Inquisitiveness influences his efforts in this direction. As long as the period of barbarism does not destroy the record of his past, each succeeding civilization will have the knowledge possessed by its predecessor from which to build anew. Our present knowledge is limited by the lack of a good record of earlier civilizations. Only about the Greco-Roman civilization do we have a fairly comprehensive record. Something is known about Egyptian and Oriental civilizations, but we know virtually nothing about human efforts in North and South America before the 15th century A.D. The accumulated knowledge we do have, however, covers a span of some 5,000 years. If we can extend the continuity of knowledge for another 5,000 years, we just may establish a society of peaceful, free men on this earth.

Men are free to choose; but if they choose to follow the principles of equality, security, and constancy instead of freedom, responsibility, and opportunity, individual liberty will disappear from their society.

Chapter 17

Free to Choose

Rules of Just Conduct
*L*IBERTY IS NOT ABSOLUTE. The free individual is at liberty to act only within a framework of rules of just conduct universally applied. Each person is responsible for his own actions. Absolute freedom is license, not liberty. The tabloid newspapers popularized by Hearst and Pulitzer at the end of the 19th century were not exercising "freedom of the press." These publications did not let truth interfere with the stories they distributed among a gullible public. This was literary licentiousness, a blatant disregard for the responsibility that accompanies freedom.

Friedrich A. Hayek explains universal rules of just conduct:

> *These rules of conduct have . . . not developed as the recognized conditions for the achievement of a known purpose, but have evolved because the groups who practiced them were more successful and displaced others. They were rules which, given the kind of environment in which man lived, secured that a greater number of the groups or individuals practicing them would survive.* (Hayek 1973. 18)

Hayek further clarifies his subject with these remarks:

> *The understanding that "good fences make good neighbors," that is, that men can use their own knowledge in the pursuit of their own ends without colliding with each other only if clear boundaries can be drawn between their respective domains of free action, is the basis on which all known civilization has grown. . . . Law, liberty, and property are an inseparable trinity. There can be no law in the sense of universal rules of conduct which does not determine boundaries of the domains of freedom by laying down rules that enable each to ascertain where he is free to act.* (Hayek 1973. 107)

A universal rule restricts one person no more than another. Such rule is more naturally negative than positive. It does not tell people how to act; it defines the behaviors that no member of society is allowed to do — fraud, theft, murder, for example. In contrast, legislation bestowing benefits to a special group — subsidies to farmers, price controls on certain products, mandates requiring specific citizens to perform specific tasks — goes beyond the scope of universal rules of just conduct. It is enacted to favor identifiable citizens to achieve identifiable ends. Government is attempting to favor some at the expense of the rest. This is special-interest legislation.

Legislation of this sort is government intervention, which restricts freedom unnecessarily, to the detriment of all members of that society, even those it is intended to favor. This is true because intervention lowers the general living standard for everyone. The people it is intended to benefit are merely harmed less. If carried too far, intervention completely destroys social cooperation, and all members are reduced to equality at the primitive subsistence level.

Contract and Private Property

We discussed earlier how courts have destroyed the meaning of contract in liability cases arising through some tort action at court. If courts destroy contract in one area of social behavior, contract will disappear entirely. Once it has been demonstrated that contract should not be recognized in one area, it is a small step for lawyers to destroy the meaning and influence of contract in all areas. Without contract, private property can no longer exist by any means other than brute strength. Without contract and private property, social cooperation disappears and division of labor along with it.

At the same time, government attacks private property rights in many other ways — confiscation through inordinately high marginal tax rates on income, estates, and gifts; regulation of maximum prices; dictation of design of products; mandated use of property; restrictions on the ones a seller may accept as a buyer (export restrictions).

A universal rule applied equally to all does not violate the rights of private property. Government invasion of property rights, however, does unduly interfere with freedom when it is designed with particular individuals in mind and seeks to achieve identifiable benefits for them. The current trend in legislation — masquerading as protecting the handicapped, the aged, the young, ethnic minorities — intentionally favors specific groups of individuals.

Such legislative acts do not limit their influence to setting "good fences" between neighbors. They grant to one group the right to trespass on the rights of others. The evil lies not so much in the excessive cost of conformity — though this alone is a considerable mark against it. The evil lies in the negative influence it exerts on social cooperation. Special-interest legislation discourages cooperation and creates animosity.

Legislation that grants privilege to a few generally originates from a desire to "protect the masses as consumers." In other words, the intended result is to relieve the citizens from responsibility for their own conduct. On the very face of it, such action eliminates freedom. Freedom and responsibility are the two sides of the same coin. A man relieved of responsibility for his own conduct is no longer free. He becomes an automaton behaving within extreme limits. Anyone who is not free to express his personal preferences is not free to act in accordance with them. He cannot be both at liberty and at the same time free from responsibility.

The Special Case of Land

Treatment of land as private property is a special case. The way it is used in one location affects many people well beyond that location. Cultivating, harvesting, grazing, erecting structures, and disposing of waste influences the way that land will handle rainfall and wind. Improper agricultural practices in the 1930s created the "dust bowl." Topsoil from the prairie blew as far away as the Ozark hills in Missouri and Arkansas. Travelers caught in a dust storm could not see the ground. Dust blown by the prairie winds stripped automobiles of their paint. Drifts of dust covered highways so deep that autos could not move, and drifts sometimes buried fences completely.

In the 20th century, the U.S. Army Corps of Engineers has channelized rivers and drained swamps. The resulting increase in the speed of runoff has caused floods hundreds of miles downstream. The government's answer has been to build dams to create flood-control lakes. Cities have discharged human sewage into rivers that provided drinking water for people miles downstream. No one's conduct in land use is ever isolated from another's.

The Indians in North America did not recognize private ownership of land. They considered themselves merely custodians of the land while they occupied a particular area. Civilized people of the 20th century cannot take such an extreme legal position toward real estate. But they can formulate rules of just conduct that prevent landowners from destroying the land by agricultural methods that erode the soil and pollute the water and air.

This does not mean that people should be denied the use of land or that private ownership of land should not be allowed. It means that everybody has a stake in land usage. Everyone breathes the air and drinks the water. Those who use the land are entitled to rules of just conduct that protect the interests of everybody else. Within the framework of those rules, landowners know the limits to how they can use their land.

The question might be asked: Does freedom give an industry the right to discharge pollutants into the rivers, the air, or underground water? Few would sanction such action. It would be unwarranted privilege granted to a select few. Protecting the rights of all citizens to clean air and water is clearly a proper function of government. The simple rule that recognizes pollution as contrary to the rights of all citizens is sufficient. Enforcing such a restriction should be no different than enforcing restrictions against theft, fraud, and murder. But legislation that requires certain individuals to take specific action violates the freedom of all.

Recognizing reality, however, limits government attempts to rectify former neglect and abuse of this principle. Twentieth-century Americans have not adequately addressed the impact of population growth and industrialization on land, water, and air. Most problems have been virtually ignored for over a century. Governments have, however, been stirred to action by those willing to push the panic button, and much poorly conceived legislation has been enacted. To require immediate and full enforcement of the principle of clean air and clean water would create chaos. Legislation declaring the intent to enforce such controls 25 or 50 years hence, however, would allow people enough time to bring their activities into compliance without completely disrupting society. Such legislation could also forbid new construction and new agricultural activity that pollute air and water.

No one can provide specific solutions to all the situations now present. We do have air pollution, water pollution, land erosion, and increasing threat of floods. The best solutions may not yet be apparent. The conditions have not been sufficiently studied to suggest any comprehensive plan of action. I am presenting my perception of the questions and making this observation: Society in the United States has recently reacted in panic proportions. I might even suggest that government has overreacted to the realization that the old questions have not been addressed. Creating a bureaucracy to determine the risks and define an immediate solution (the Environmental Protection Agency) raises more problems than it solves.

For over a century, Americans have allowed some individuals to ignore the problem. To try all at once to correct for all mismanagement of the past neither resolves any situation nor treats fairly those who have acted in good faith within the framework of our legal structure.

First, we need to identify each condition that could put civilization at risk. We can then establish the degree of that risk. While some are making efforts to understand the problem, others can be developing the technology to solve it and to arrange an orderly timetable for change. We cause only chaos if we attempt to change in a decade those conditions that we spent over a century creating. Yet if we fail to attend to the situation, cooperation in society will disappear, and we are condemned to losing the advanced civilization that now exists.

The Challenge

On completing a survey of this study, we might ask, "What can we do to help restore freedom in America?"

Government is controlled by the will of the people. Today's intrusive government is the politicians' answer to the wants of the citizens. The people demand that government redistribute wealth, that government assure its citizens safe foods, effective drugs, clean water, unpolluted air, freedom from want, freedom from fear, full medical services to everyone regardless of cost, a guaranteed income for life, and so forth. The challenge is to change the will of the people. To change the ways of government, we must change the wants of its citizens. The people must become informed. This is a matter of educating the masses to a correct understanding of freedom; it means showing them that continued efforts to cure all problems through government leads to serfdom. Over 50 years ago, Friedrich A. Hayek wrote a little book that everyone should read, *The Road to Serfdom*. The message in that book is even more appropriate today than when first published.

The heralds of liberty need tools, a forum, and organization. The first requirement, then, is to create a body of literature — this book being one small part — that tells the story of freedom and its perilous state in the United States. Whether we like it or not, however, visual and audio materials will reach a far wider audience than will the printed word. Books and pamphlets may contain the information; but to reach the greatest numbers, it must be presented in more popular forms. These are the tools that have not yet appeared in abundance — documentary programs for television, audio cassettes, video tapes, compact discs for the multimedia computer, computer files for distribution via bulletin boards and the internet. These are the tools needed to present the case for freedom. These items need our attention. Therein lies the opportunity for entrepreneurs. With the cost exceeding the capability of most individuals, their production becomes a task for organizations of cooperating individuals.

To make the most efficient use of these tools, the freedom movement needs a forum. Presently that forum is provided mainly by television, radio, and the printed word. A new means of mass communication is developing, called *cyberspace*. It is the new information highway. The instruments of this new development are the computer and the fax machine connected to telephone, radio, and satellite. In order to access these means of mass communication, the agencies for freedom need to pool their resources in talents and finances. For an adequate forum from which to disseminate the information contained in the tools, freedom needs access to television and radio broadcast stations, newspapers, magazines, book publishers, audio and video production studios, and computer network bulletin boards.

Some individuals might think that schools should provide a forum for reaching the young. The present public school monopoly, however, is not ideologically receptive to the concept of freedom. Perhaps, if and when the people realize that freedom should be taught in the schools, the citizens will take appropriate action to do so. Meanwhile, the public school monopoly is dedicated to keeping the people ignorant. Ignorance is the agency of control for those in power. Knowledge is the only offsetting key to preserve freedom. Until the people regain control of their schools, public schools will continue to be operated in a manner that assures continued ignorance of the masses. Intentional or accidental, it is happening. Before the schools can become available as a forum for spreading the concept of freedom, the people must break loose from federal and state regulation and financing of the schools. The public school system must relinquish its monopoly and break free of its socialistic bias.

Today, numerous organizations and individuals print material and distribute it to interested parties. This mass of information will never reach the multitudes as long as it remains in its printed form. To reach the greater numbers, it needs to be reformatted into media that the masses will see and hear. This can be expedited through organizing to develop a united, cooperative effort. The organizing effort should include as many as possible of the presently existing agencies that are working in the defense of freedom — agencies such as the Cato Institute, the Freedom Foundation, the Ludwig von Mises Institute, the Reason Foundation, Hillsdale College, and the Blankenship Foundation for the History of Liberty. Surely there are many other similar organizations now operating independently. The effectiveness of these groups would be magnified if they formed a steering committee or clearing house to provide information and assistance for those seeking to help in the cause.

The preservation of freedom is a task of salesmanship. Selling is like telling a story to a continuous parade of people. By the time you have told your story once, the persons listening have changed. It is time to start anew and repeat the story. Life is that way. Every year produces a new group of minds that need to be informed with the truth. The task is never completed. To assure continuity of this endeavor, a means must be developed to provide effort that is not dependent on any one person or small group of individuals. To accomplish this, we create organizations.

Perhaps one of the existing agencies could invite each of the other existing organizations to send a delegate to a two- or three-day meeting to discuss ways they might all help one another. Hillsdale College in Hillsdale, Michigan, and the Blankenship Foundation for the History of Freedom at the University of Oklahoma, for example, are centrally located and have the physical facilities. Those attending that meeting might create a coordinating agency that could expand the effectiveness of all participants. Certainly a count of supporters would be a step forward by determining their combined strength in numbers. From their supporters, enthusiastic leaders could be enlisted to seek public office. A platform of goals could be addressed. Cooperation along with division of tasks could enhance present efforts, and should increase greatly the effectiveness of all concerned. The individual agencies now in existence need not lose their autonomy by such cooperative effort, any more than the individual loses his independence by cooperating with his neighbor, the act that forms peaceful society.

We can take a cue from history and learn from the teachings of praxeology. Cooperation through division of labor will produce a greater harvest. As our forebears formed the Union in 1789, present citizens can form a cooperative society designed to preserve freedom in that union. The price of freedom is eternal vigilance. The key to freedom is knowledge of the truth. Through cooperation man seeking freedom can find and preserve it.

What Can We as Individuals Do?

We can offer our money and volunteer our labor to help those agencies that best pursue the goals we consider most important. We can join — or create — local political activist groups that work for the preservation of freedom. We can recommend readings to our friends and relatives. Certainly we can take active interest in local political activities in the school district, in the city, the county, and the state where we reside. Candidates for public office can be sought who believe in principle and freedom. Most importantly, we can become informed, not only by reading the literature on freedom, but informed about the beliefs of individuals in positions of political influence. To vote correctly, the voter must be informed not only about issues, but about candidates.

The problem is not, how we can help, but how we can properly allocate our limited time and means to help most effectively. The cause will require much more wisdom than one mind can provide. The more minds active in this endeavor, the greater the development of avenues for effective action, and the greater the number of ideas on what, where, how, and when to proceed.

The task is to create awareness of truth in the minds of as many persons as possible. The people must know that their interests are best served by social institutions that adhere to the principles of liberty. As the numbers of converts grow, our political influence will grow correspondingly. The proper candidates for public office will appear when it becomes evident that organizations exist to support them and others of like ideology.

The first task is to develop the numbers of people who are prepared to support the movement for restoring freedom. From numbers will come ideas. The particulars of what to do and when to do it will emerge from our discussions with others of like ideology. AND, we must have faith that the time will come when the people will realize that the political scene not only should be, but can be changed.

Perhaps that change will come with the holding of another Constitutional Convention. From such a convention, appropriate amendments to the Constitution can be forthcoming. The delegates can determine how best to amend the Constitution to assure freedom for the people over centuries to come. Surely the experience of the past 500 years has provided a tremendous store of knowledge that can be employed by our contemporaries.

Freedom is a condition of the relationship between a citizen and his government. Spread the truth. Big Government is the wolf, not the shepherd. And explain *why.* The Law of Self-Interest directs politicians to act as the people demand; they want to be reelected. The same law encourages bureaucrats to keep enlarging the scope of government. They benefit personally from bigger budgets and more government activity. Both politicians and bureaucrats will act contrary to the good of society when they see their self-interest at risk. The people must learn to ask less and less from their government, and vote for politicians who will legislate accordingly.

Urge the institutions you support with money to unite in a national movement. The key today is consolidation for a united effort. Lincoln declared, "United we stand; divided we fall." That applies to the cause of freedom. Freedom lovers, unite under one banner, and stand up to be counted.

Men are free to choose; but if they choose to follow the principles of equality, security, and constancy instead of freedom, responsibility, and opportunity, individual liberty will disappear from their society. If they continually fail to learn from the past, they will not merely remain innocent and ignorant; they will choose action that in time will destroy social cooperation and return civilization to the primitive stages experienced for ages upon ages.

Bibliography

Andrews, Charles McLean. 1904. *The American Nation: A History*. Vol. 5. *Colonial Self-Government 1652-1689*. New York: Harper & Brothers, Publishers.

Andrist, Ralph K., ed. 1969. *The American Heritage History of the Confident Years*. New York: American Heritage Publishing Co., Inc.

Anzovin, Steven, and Janet Podell, eds. 1988. *The U.S. Constitution and the Supreme Court*. The Reference Shelf, Vol. 60. No. 1. New York: The H. W. Wilson Co.

Ashley, Maurice. 1961. *Great Britain to 1688*. Ann Arbor: The University of Michigan Press.

Bailey, Thomas A. 1961. *The American Pageant: A History of the Republic,* 2nd ed. Boston: D. C. Heath and Co.

Baity, Elizabeth Chesley. 1951. *Americans Before Columbus*. New York: The Viking Press.

Bassett, John Spencer. 1906. *The Federalist System 1789-1801.* New York: Harper & Brothers, Publishers.

Beard, Charles A. 1943. *The Republic: Conversations on Fundamentals.* New York: The Viking Press.

Bloom, Allan. 1987. *The Closing of the American Mind.* New York: Simon and Schuster.

Blow, Michael, ed. 1967. *The American Heritage History of the Thirteen Colonies.* New York: American Heritage Publishing Co., Inc.

Bork, Robert H. 1990. *The Tempting of America: The Political Seduction of the Law.* New York: The Macmillan Co., Inc.

Bowen, Catherine Drinker. 1966. *Miracle at Philadelphia: The Story of the Constitutional Convention May to September 1787.* Boston: Little, Brown, and Co.

Bowers, Claude G. 1929. *The Tragic Era: The Revolution After Lincoln.* New York: Blue Ribbon Books.

Bradford, William. (1909) 1920. *Bradford's History of the Plymouth Settlement, 1608-1650.* Rendered into modern English by Harold Paget. New York: E. P. Dutton & Co.

Braudel, Fernand. (1979) 1981. *Civilization and Capitalism — 15th-18th Century.* Vol. 1. *The Structures of Everyday Life.* Trans. from the French, rev. by Sian Reynolds. New York: Harper & Row, Publishers.

Buck, Paul H. 1938. *The Road to Reunion, 1865-1900.* Boston: Little, Brown & Co.

Burgess, John W. 1902. *Reconstruction and the Constitution 1866-1876,* New York, Chicago: Charles Scribner's Sons.

Carman, Harry J., and Harold C. Syrett. 1952. *A History of the American People.* Vol. 2. *Since 1865.* New York: Alfred A. Knopf.

Catton, Bruce. 1961. *The Centennial History of the Civil War.* Vol. 1. *The Coming Fury.* Garden City, New York: Doubleday & Co., Inc.

Churchill, Winston S. 1957. *A History of the English-Speaking Peoples,* Vol. 3. *The Age of Revolution.* New York: Dodd, Mead & Co.

_____. 1950. *The Second World War: The Grand Alliance.* Boston: Houghton Mifflin Co.

Claiborne, Robert, and the Editors of Time-Life Books. 1973. *The First Americans.* New York: Time-Life Books, Inc.

Corwin, Edward S. 1958. *The Constitution and What It Means Today.* Princeton: Princeton University Press.

Crawley, C. W., ed. (1965) 1969. *The New Cambridge Modern History.* Vol. 9. *War and Peace in an Age of Upheaval, 1793-1830.* Cambridge: At the University Press.

Cumberland, Charles C. 1968. *Mexico: The Struggle for Modernity.* New York: Oxford University Press.

Cushman, Robert F. 1982. *Leading Constitutional Decisions.* 16th ed. Englewood Cliffs, New Jersey: Prentice-Hall, Inc.

Dangerfield, George. 1952. *The Era of Good Feelings.* New York: Harcourt, Brace, and Co.

Daniels, Jonathan. 1970. *Ordeal of Ambition: Jefferson, Hamilton, Burr.* Garden City, New York: Doubleday & Co., Inc.

Dowdey, Clifford. 1956. *The Land They Fought For: The Story of the South as the Confederacy 1832-1865.* Garden City, New York: Doubleday & Co., Inc.

Dulles, Foster Rhea. 1959. *The United States Since 1865.* Ann Arbor: The University of Michigan Press.

Durant, Will, and Ariel Durant. 1968. *The Lessons of History.* New York: Simon & Schuster.

Eisenhower, Dwight D. 1948. *Crusade in Europe.* Garden City, New York: Doubleday & Co., Inc.

Freeman, Douglas Southall. 1945. *Lee's Lieutenants: A Study in Command.* 3 vols. New York: Charles Scribner's Sons.

Friendly, Fred W., and Martha J. H. Elliott. 1984. The *Constitution: That Delicate Balance.* New York: Random House, Inc.

Galbraith, John Kenneth. (1954) 1988. *The Great Crash 1929.* Boston: Houghton Mifflin Co.

Greene, Evarts Boutell. 1905. *The American Nation: A History.* Vol. 6. *Provincial America, 1690-1740.* New York: Harper & Brothers, Publishers.

Hayek, Friedrich A. 1944. *The Road to Serfdom.* Chicago: The University of Chicago Press.

_____. 1973. *Law, Legislation and Liberty.* Vol. 1. *Rules And Order.* Chicago: The University of Chicago Press.

_____. 1976. *Law, Legislation and Liberty.* Vol. 2. *The Mirage of Social Justice.* Chicago: The University of Chicago Press.

_____. 1979. *Law, Legislation and Liberty.* Vol. 3. *The Political Order of a Free People.* Chicago: The University of Chicago Press.

Henderson, Nevile. 1940. *Failure of a Mission.* New York: G. P. Putnam's Sons.

Hill, Christopher. 1972. *The World Turned Upside Down: Radical Ideas During the English Revolution.* New York: The Viking Press.

Hordern, Nicholas. 1971. *Aldus Encyclopedia of Discovery and Exploration.* Vol. 4. *God, Gold and Glory.* London: Aldus Books, Ltd.

Huber, Peter W. 1988. *Liability: The Legal Revolution and Its Consequences.* New York: Basic Books, Inc.

Jackson, Robert H. 1941. *The Struggle for Judicial Supremacy: A Study of a Crisis in American Power Politics.* New York: Random House, Inc.

Josephson, Matthew. 1938. *The Politicos, 1865-1896.* New York: Harcourt, Brace, and Co.

Keats, John. 1973. *Eminent Domain: The Louisiana Purchase and the Making of America.* New York: Charterhouse.

Keller, Allan. 1969. *The Spanish-American War: A Compact History.* New York: Hawthorn Books, Inc.

Kennedy, Paul. 1987. *The Rise and Fall of the Great Powers: Economic Change and Military Conflict from 1500 to 2000.* New York: Random House.

Keynes, John Maynard. (1935) 1964. *The General Theory of Employment, Interest, and Money.* New York: Harcourt Brace Jovanovich, Publishers.

Lancaster, Bruce. 1955. *From Lexington to Liberty: The Story of the American Revolution.* Garden City, New York: Doubleday & Co., Inc.

Lippman, Walter. August 1939. "The Indispensable Opposition." *The Atlantic Monthly.* Atlantic Monthly Co.

Long, Hamilton Abert. (1957) 1971. *The Constitution Betrayed.* Philadelphia: Your Heritage Books, Inc.

McClellan, Grant S., ed. 1976. *The Right to Privacy.* The Reference Shelf. Vol. 48. No. 1. New York: The H. W. Wilson Co.

McPherson, James M. 1982. *Ordeal by Fire: The Civil War and Reconstruction.* New York: Alfred A. Knopf.

McReynolds, Edwin C. 1957. *The Seminoles.* Norman, Oklahoma: University of Oklahoma Press.

Malthus, Thomas Robert. 1959. *Population: The First Essay.* Ann Arbor: The University of Michigan Press.

Mexico. 1985. By the Editors of Time-Life Books. Amsterdam: Time-Life Books, Inc.

Meyer, Michael C., and William L. Sherman. 1979. *The Course of Mexican History.* New York: Oxford University Press.

Mill, John Stuart. 1859. *On Liberty.* Vol. 43. *Great Books of the Western World.* Chicago: Encyclopaedia Britannica, Inc., 1952.

Mises, Ludwig von. (1949) 1966. *Human Action: A Treatise on Economics,* 3rd rev. ed. Chicago: Henry Regnery Co.

_____. 1983. *Nation, State, and Economy.* Trans. by Leland B. Yeager. New York: New York University Press.

_____. (1934) 1981. *The Theory of Money and Credit.* Trans. by H. E. Batson. Indianapolis: Liberty Classics.

_____. (1957) 1985. *Theory and History: An Interpretation of Social and Economic Evolution.* Washington, D.C.: The Ludwig von Mises Institute.

Morgenstern, George. 1947. *Pearl Harbor: The Story of the Secret War.* New York: The Devin-Adair Co.

Morison, Samuel Eliot. 1965. *The Oxford History of the American People.* New York: Oxford University Press.

_____. 1971. *The European Discovery of America: The Northern Voyages A.D. 500-1600.* New York: Oxford University Press.

_____, 1974. *The European Discovery of America: The Southern Voyages A.D. 1492-1616.* New York: Oxford University Press.

Mumford, Lewis. 1944. *The Condition of Man.* New York: Harcourt, Brace, and Co.

Passos, John Dos. 1957. *The Men Who Made the Nation.* Garden City, New York: Doubleday & Co., Inc.

Rosenstiel, Annette. 1983. *Red & White: Indian Views of the White Man, 1492-1982.* New York: Universe Books.

Rothbard, Murray. (1962) 1970. *Man, Economy, and State: A Treatise on Economic Principles.* One-volume ed. Los Angeles: Nash Publishing.

———. (1963) 1983. *America's Great Depression.* 4th ed. New York: Richardson & Snyder.

Rubin, Louis D., Jr. 1977. *Virginia: A Bicentennial History.* New York: W. W. Norton & Co., Inc.

Sandburg, Carl. 1954. *Life of Lincoln.* New York: Harcourt, Brace, and Co.

Schlesinger, Arthur M., Jr. 1945. *The Age of Jackson.* New York: Book Find Club.

Sexton, John, and Nat Brandt. 1986. *How Free Are We? What the Constitution Says We Can and Cannot Do.* New York: M. Evans and Co., Inc.

Smellie, K. B. 1962. *Great Britain Since 1688.* Ann Arbor: The University of Michigan Press.

Stampp, Kenneth M. 1966. *The Era of Reconstruction, 1865-1877.* New York: Alfred A. Knopf.

Stephenson, George M. 1939. *American History Since 1865.* New York: Harper & Brothers, Publishers.

Sundquist, James L. 1986. *Constitutional Reform and Effective Government.* Washington, D. C.: The Brookings Institution.

Theobald, Robert A. 1954. *The Final Secret of Pearl Harbor: The Washington Contribution to the Japanese Attack.* New York: The Devin-Adair Co.

Tocqueville, Alexis de. 1960. *Democracy in America.* Vol. 1. Earlier trans. rev. by Phillips Bradley. New York: Alfred A. Knopf.

Toynbee, Arnold J. 1957. *A Study of History.* Abridgment of Vols. VII-X by D. C. Somervell. New York: Oxford University Press.

Trevelyan, George Otto. (1899) 1964. *The American Revolution.* Condensed one-volume ed. Ed. by Richard B. Morris. New York: David McKay Co., Inc.

Trevor-Roper, H. R. (1956) 1968. *The Crisis of the Seventeenth Century: Religion, the Reformation and Social Change.* New York: Harper & Row, Publishers.

Tytler, Alexander Fraser. *The Decline and Fall of the Athenian Republic.*

Underhill, Ruth Murray. 1953. *Red Man's America: A History of Indians in the United States.* Chicago: The University of Chicago Press.

Wallace, Anthony F. C. 1970. *The Death and Rebirth of the Seneca.* New York: Alfred A. Knopf.

Weisberger, Bernard A. and the Editors of LIFE. 1964. *The LIFE History of the United States.* Vol. 8 *1890-1901: Reaching for Empire.* New York: Time, Inc.

Wellman, Paul I. 1966. *The House Divides: The Age of Jackson and Lincoln, from the War of 1812 to the Civil War.* Garden City, N.Y.: Doubleday & Co., Inc.

White, Leonard D. 1951. *The Jeffersonians: A Study in Administrative History, 1801-1829.* New York: The Macmillan Co.
Williams, T. Harry. 1952. *Lincoln and His Generals.* New York: Alfred A. Knopf.

⤜⧉⤛

Permissions have been granted by the publishers to use passages from the following works:

Fernand Braudel. 1979, 1981. *Civilization and Capitalism — 15th-18th Century,* Vol. 1. New York: Harper & Row Publishers.
Alan Bloom. 1987. *The Closing of the American Mind.* New York: Simon and Schuster.
Bruce Catton. 1961. *The Centennial History of the Civil War. The Coming Fury.* New York: Doubleday & Co., Inc.
Edward S. Corwin. 1958. *The Constitution and What It Means Today.* New Jersey: Princeton University Press.`
Robert F. Cushman. 1982. *Leading Constitutional Decisions.* New Jersey: Prentice-Hall, Inc.
Clifford Dowdey. 1956. *The Land They Fought For: The Story of the South as the Confederacy 1832-1865.* New York: Doubleday & Co., Inc.
F.A. Hayek. 1973, 1976. *Law, Legislation and Liberty.* Chicago: The University of Chicago Press.
Christopher Hill. 1972. *The World Turned Upside Down: Radical Ideas During the English Revolution.* New York: Viking Press.
Robert H. Jackson. 1941. *The Struggle for Judicial Supremacy: A Study of a Crisis in American Power Politics.* New York: Random House, Inc.
Paul Kennedy. 1987. *The Rise and Fall of the Great Powers: Economic Change and Military Conflict from 1500 to 2000.* New York: Random House.
James M. McPherson. 1982. *Ordeal by Fire: The Civil War and Reconstruction.* New York: Alfred A. Knopf.
Ludwig von Mises. 1957, 1985. *Theory and History: An Interpretation of Social and Economic Evolution.* Washington, D.C.: The Ludwig von Mises Institute.
John Dos Passos. 1957. *The Men Who Made the Nation.* New York: Doubleday & Co., Inc.
Annette Rosenstiel. 1983. *Red & White: Indian Views of the White Man.* New York: Universe Books.
Kenneth M. Stamp. 1965. *The Era of Reconstruction.* New York: Alfred A. Knopf.
Alexis de Tocqueville. 1973. *Democracy in America.* New York: Alfred A. Knopf.
Anthony F.C. Wallace. 1970. *The Death and Rebirth of the Seneca.* New York: Alfred A. Knopf.
Paul I. Wellman. *The House Divides: The Age of Jackson and Lincoln, from the War of 1812 to the Civil War.* 1966. New York: Doubleday & Co., Inc.

Index